10 99

D0008250

AMERICAN WARS AND HEROES
Revolutionary War through Vietnam

Adapted from
American Military History
Office of the Chief of Military History
United States Army

General Editor
Maurice Matloff

Editor
Stanley M. Ulanoff
Colonel, AUS (Ret)

ARCO PUBLISHING, INC.
NEW YORK

Published 1985 by Arco Publishing, Inc.
215 Park Avenue South, New York, NY 10003

Adapted from
American Military History
Office of the Chief of Military History
United States Army
Maurice Matloff, General Editor

Stanley M. Ulanoff, Editor

Contributing Editors:
Robert W. Coakley
Benjamin F. Cooling, III
Joseph R. Friedman
Vincent P. Jones
Charles V. P. von Luttichau
Morris J. MacGregor, Jr.
Charles B. MacDonald
Lida Mayo
B. C. Mossman
Charles F. Romanus

Maps by Maj. James P. Holly and B. C. Mossman

Dust Jacket Art by H. Charles McBarron

All rights reserved. No part of this book may be
reproduced, by any means, without permission in
writing from the publisher, except by a reviewer
who wishes to quote brief excerpts in connection
with a review in a magazine or newspaper.

Library of Congress Cataloging in Publication Data
Main entry under title:

American wars and heroes.

1. United States—History, Military.   I. Matloff,
Maurice, 1915–   .   II. Ulanoff, Stanley M.
E181.A45   1984   973   84-14592
ISBN 0-668-06315-7

Printed in the United States of America

Contents

1. The American Revolution: First Phase   1

2. The Winning of Independence, 1777–1783   31

3. The War of 1812, 1812–1815   62

4. The Mexican War, 1846–1848   88

5. The Civil War, 1861   105

6. The Civil War, 1862   130

7. The Civil War, 1863   157

8. The Civil War, 1864–1865   183

9. The Spanish American War, 1898   202

10. World War I: The U.S. Army Overseas   220

11. World War II: The Defensive Phase   244

12. World War II: The War Against Germany and Italy   267

13. World War II: The War Against Japan   293

14. The Korean War, 1950–1953   323

15. The U.S. Army in Vietnam   350

CHAPTER 1

The American Revolution: First Phase

The American Revolution came about, fundamentally, because by 1763 the English-speaking communities on the far side of the Atlantic had matured to an extent that their interests and goals were distinct from those of the ruling classes in the mother country. British statesmen failed to understand or adjust to the situation. Ironically enough, British victory in the Seven Years' War set the stage for the revolt, for it freed the colonists from the need for British protection against a French threat on their frontiers and gave free play to the forces working for separation. *(Maps 1 and 2)*

In 1763 the British Government, reasonably from its point of view, moved to tighten the system of imperial control and to force the colonists to contribute to imperial defense, proposing to station 10,000 soldiers along the American frontiers and to have the Americans pay part of the bill. This imperial defense plan touched off the long controversy about Parliament's right to tax that started with the Stamp and Sugar Acts and ended in December 1773, when a group of Bostonians unceremoniously dumped a cargo of British tea into the city harbor in protest against the latest reminder of the British effort to tax. In this 10-year controversy the several British ministries failed to act either firmly enough to enforce British regulations or wisely enough to develop a more viable form of imperial union, which the colonial leaders, at least until 1776, insisted that they sought. In response to the Boston Tea Party, the king and his ministers blindly pushed through Parliament a series of measures collectively known in America as the Intolerable Acts, closing the port of Boston, placing Massachusetts under the military rule of Maj. Gen. Sir Thomas Gage, and otherwise infringing on what the colonists deemed to be their rights and interests.

Since 1763 the colonial leaders, in holding that only their own popular assemblies, not the British Parliament, had a right to levy taxes on Americans, had raised the specter of an arbitrary British Government collecting taxes in America to support red-coated Regulars who might be used not to protect the frontiers but to suppress American liberties. Placing Massachusetts under military rule gave that specter some substance and led directly to armed revolt.

The Outbreak

The First Continental Congress meeting at Philadelphia on September 5, 1774, addressed respectful petitions to Parliament and king but also adopted nonimportation and nonexportation agreements in an effort to coerce the British Government into repealing the offending measures. To enforce these agreements, committees were formed in almost every county, town, and city throughout the colonies, and in each colony these committees soon became the effective local authorities, the base of a pyramid of revolutionary organizations with revolutionary assemblies, congresses, or conventions, and committees of safety at the top. This loosely knit combination of *de facto* governments superseded the constituted authorities and established firm control over the whole country before the British were in any position to oppose them. The *de facto* governments took over control of the militia, and out of it began to shape forces that, if the necessity arose, might oppose the British in the field.

In Massachusetts, the seat of the crisis, the Provincial Congress, eyeing Gage's force in Boston, directed the officers in each town to enlist a third of their militia in minutemen organizations to be ready to act at a moment's warning, and began to collect ammunition and other military stores. It established a major depot for these stores at Concord, about twenty miles northwest of Boston.

General Gage learned of the collection of military stores at Concord and determined to send a force of Redcoats to destroy them. His preparations were made with the utmost secrecy. Yet so alert and ubiquitous were the patriot eyes in Boston that when the picked British force of 700 men set out on the night of April 18, 1775, two messengers, Paul Revere and William Dawes, preceded them to spread the alarm throughout the countryside. At dawn on the 19th of April when the British arrived at Lexington, the halfway point to Concord, they found a body of militia drawn up on the village green. Some nervous finger—whether of British Regular or American militiaman is unknown to this day—pressed a trigger. The impatient British Regulars, apparently without any clear orders from their commanding officer, fired a volley, then charged with the bayonet. The militiamen dispersed, leaving eight dead and ten wounded on the ground. The British column went on to Concord, destroyed such of the military stores as the Americans had been unable to remove, and set out on their return journey.

By this time, the alarm had spread far and wide, and both ordinary militia and minutemen had assembled along the British route. From behind walls, rocks, and trees, and from houses they poured their fire into the columns of Redcoats, while the frustrated Regulars found few targets for their accustomed

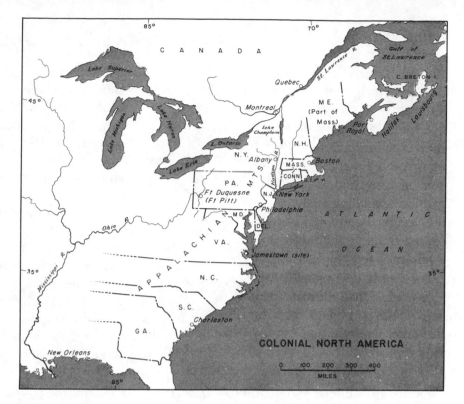

MAP 1

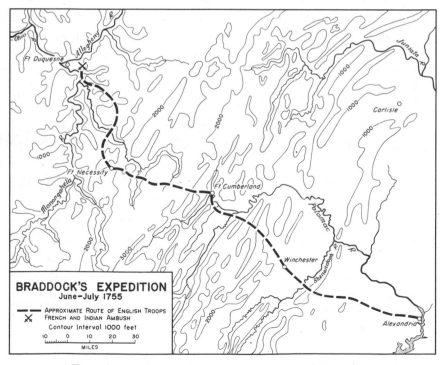

MAP 2   French and Indian War (Seven Years' War)

volleys or bayonet charges. Only the arrival of reinforcements sent by Gage enabled the British column to get back to the safety of Boston. At day's end the British counted 273 casualties out of a total of 1,800 men engaged; American casualties numbered 95 men, including the toll at Lexington. What happened was hardly a tribute to the marksmanship of New England farmers—it has been estimated 75,000 shots poured from their muskets that day—but it did testify to a stern determination of the people of Massachusetts to resist any attempt by the British to impose their will by armed force.

The spark lit in Massachusetts soon spread throughout the rest of the colonies. Whatever really may have happened in that misty dawn on Lexington Green, the news that speedy couriers, riding horses to exhaustion, carried through the colonies from New Hampshire to Georgia was of a savage, unprovoked British attack and of farmers rising in the night to protect their lives, their families, and their property. Lexington, like Fort Sumter and Pearl Harbor, furnished an emotional impulse that led all true patriots to gird themselves for battle. From the other New England colonies, militia poured in to join the Massachusetts men and together they soon formed a ring around Boston. Other militia forces under Ethan Allen of Vermont and Benedict Arnold of Connecticut seized the British forts at Ticonderoga and Crown Point, strategic positions on the route between New York and Canada. These posts yielded valuable artillery and other military stores. The Second Continental Congress, which assembled in Philadelphia on May 10, 1775, found itself forced to turn from embargoes and petitions to the problems of organizing, directing, and supplying a military effort.

Before Congress could assume control, the New England forces assembled near Boston fought another battle on their own, the bloodiest single engagement of the entire Revolution. After Lexington and Concord, at the suggestion of Massachusetts, the New England colonies moved to replace the militia gathered before Boston with volunteer forces, constituting what may be loosely called a New England army. Each state raised and administered its own force and appointed a commander for it. Discipline was lax and there was no single chain of command. Though Artemas Ward, the Massachusetts commander, exercised over-all control by informal agreement, it was only because the other commanders chose to co-operate with him, and decisions were made in council. While by mid-June most of the men gathered were volunteers, militia units continued to come and go. The volunteers in the Connecticut service were enlisted until December 10, 1775, those from the other New England states until the end of the year. The men were dressed for the most part in homespun clothes and armed with muskets of varied types; powder and ball were short and only the barest few had bayonets.

Late in May Gage received limited reinforcements from England, bringing his total force to 6,500 rank and file. With the reinforcements came three major generals of reputation—Sir William Howe, Sir Henry Clinton, and Sir John Burgoyne—men destined to play major roles in England's loss of its American colonies. The newcomers all considered that Gage needed more elbowroom and proposed to fortify Dorchester Heights, a dominant position south of Boston previously neglected by both sides. News of the intended move leaked to the Americans, who immediately countered by dispatching a force onto the Charlestown peninsula, where other heights, Bunker Hill and Breed's Hill, overlooked Boston from the north. (*Map 3*) The original intent was to fortify Bunker Hill, the eminence nearest the narrow neck of land connecting the peninsula with the mainland, but the working party sent out on the night of June 16, 1775, decided instead to move closer in and construct works on Breed's Hill—a tactical blunder, for these exposed works could much more easily be cut off by a British landing on the neck in their rear.

The British scorned such a tactic, evidently in the mistaken assumption that the assembled "rabble in arms" would disintegrate in the face of an attack by disciplined British Regulars. On the afternoon of the 17th, Gage sent some 2,200 of his men under Sir William Howe directly against the American positions, by this time manned by perhaps an equal force. Twice the British advanced on the front and flanks of the redoubt on Breed's Hill, and twice the Americans, holding their fire until the compact British lines were at close range, decimated the ranks of the advancing regiments and forced them to fall back and re-form. With reinforcements, Howe carried the hill on the third try but largely because the Americans had run short of ammunition and had no bayonets. The American retreat from Breed's Hill was, for inexperienced volunteers and militia, an orderly one and Howe's depleted regiments were unable to prevent the Americans' escape. British casualties for the day totaled a staggering 1,054, or almost half the force engaged, as opposed to American losses of about 440.

The Battle of Bunker Hill (for it was Bunker that gave its name to a battle actually fought on Breed's Hill) has been aptly characterized as a "tale of great blunders heroically redeemed." The American command structure violated the principle of unity of command from the start, and in moving onto Breed's Hill the patriots exposed an important part of their force in an indefensible position, violating the principles of concentration of force, mass, and maneuver. Gage and Howe, for their parts, sacrificed all the advantages the American blunders gave

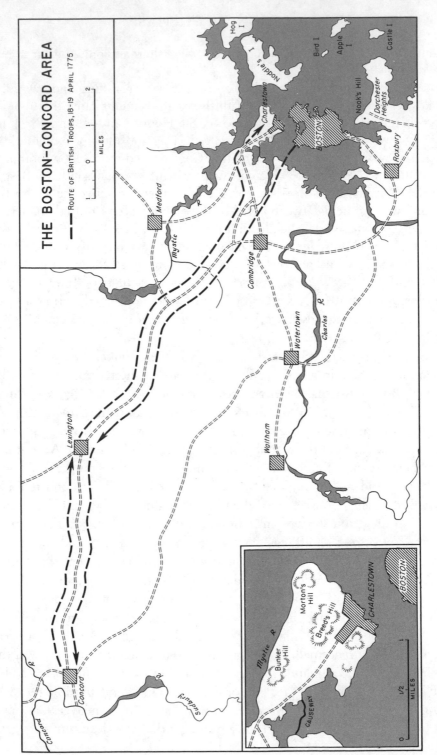

THE BOSTON-CONCORD AREA

——— ROUTE OF BRITISH TROOPS, 18-19 APRIL 1775

MILES

2   1   0   1   2

Concord

Sudbury R.

Lexington

Concord R.

Waltham

Watertown

Charles R.

Medford

Mystic R.

Cambridge

Charlestown

Noddle's I.

Hog I.

Bird I.

Apple I.

Castle I.

BOSTON

Nook's Hill

Dorchester Heights

Roxbury

Mystic R.

Bunker Hill

Morton's Hill

Breed's Hill

CHARLESTOWN

BOSTON

CAUSEWAY

MILES

0   1/2   1

MAP 3

them, violating the principles of maneuver and surprise by undertaking a suicidal attack on a fortified position.

Bunker Hill was a Pyrrhic victory, its strategic effect practically nil since the
two armies remained in virtually the same position they had held before. Its
consequences, nevertheless, cannot be ignored. A force of farmers and townsmen, fresh from their fields and shops, with hardly a semblance of orthodox
military organization, had met and fought on equal terms with a professional
British Army. On the British this astonishing feat had a sobering effect, for it
taught them that American resistance was not to be easily overcome; never again
would British commanders lightly attempt such an assault on Americans in
fortified positions. On the Americans, the effect was hardly sobering, and in the
long run was perhaps not salutary. Bunker Hill, along with Lexington and Concord, went far to create the American tradition that the citizen soldier when
aroused is more than a match for the trained professional, a tradition that was to
be reflected in American military policy for generations afterward.

Formation of the Continental Army

The response of George III and his ministers to the events at Lexington,
Concord, and Bunker Hill was a determined effort to subdue the rebellious
colonists by force. It took time to mount this effort, and after Bunker Hill the
Americans enjoyed a respite lasting almost a year. During most of this period
the Second Continental Congress, though forced by events in New England to
take on itself the leadership of an armed revolt, proceeded hesitantly, still seeking
a formula for reconciliation that would preserve American rights. Military
preparations were designed for a short struggle, to endure no longer than the
end of the year 1776. Nevertheless the Americans took advantage of the respite
to create a national army, to consolidate their hold on the governmental machinery throughout the thirteen colonies, to invade Canada, and finally to force
the British to evacuate Boston.

The creation of a Continental Army was in the long run perhaps their most
significant achievement. Some time before Bunker Hill the Massachusetts Provincial Congress, aware of the necessity of enlisting the support of all the colonies
in the struggle against the British, appealed to the Continental Congress to adopt
the New England army. Although there is no formal record of the action, Congress evidently did vote to adopt it on June 14, 1775—the accepted birthday of the
U.S. Army. On the same day it voted to raise ten companies of riflemen—the
first soldiers to be enlisted directly in the Continental service—in Pennsylvania,
Maryland, and Virginia, to march north to join the army before Boston.

The next day, June 15, Congress chose George Washington, a Virginian, to be Commander in Chief. The choice was made for geographical and political as much as for military reasons. The New Englanders felt that in order to enlist the support of the southern colonies, a southerner should be chosen for the post of command. Washington's military experience was perhaps greater than that of any other southerner, and he came from the largest and most important of the southern colonies. His impressive appearance, quiet and confident manner, and good work in the military committees of Congress had impressed all.

The choice proved fortunate. Washington himself recognized, when he accepted the command, that he lacked the requisite experience and knowledge in handling large bodies of men. His whole military experience had been in frontier warfare during the French and Indian War. But experience as a political leader in his native Virginia and in directing the business affairs of his large plantation at Mount Vernon also stood him in good stead. He brought to the task traits of character and abilities as a leader that in the end more than compensated for his lack of professional military experience. Among these qualities were a determination and a steadfastness of purpose rooted in an unshakable conviction of the righteousness of the American cause, a scrupulous sense of honor and duty, and a dignity that inspired respect and confidence in those around him. Conscious of his own defects, he was always willing to profit by experience. From the trials and tribulations of eight years of war he was to learn the essentials of strategy, tactics, and military organization.

Congress also appointed four major generals and eight brigadiers to serve under Washington, set up a series of staff offices closely resembling those in the British Army, prescribed a pay scale and standard ration, and adopted Articles of War to govern the military establishment. The same mixture of geographical, political, and military considerations governed the choice of Washington's subordinates. Two-thirds of them came from New England, in recognition of the fact that the existing army was a New England army. Three others—Charles Lee, Horatio Gates, and Richard Montgomery—were chosen because of their experience in the British Army. Lee, in particular, who had come from England to the colonies in 1773, was in 1775 deemed the foremost military expert in America, and he was for a time to be Washington's first assistant.

The army of which Washington formally took command on July 3, 1775, he described as "a mixed multitude of people . . . under very little discipline, order or government." Out of this "mixed multitude," Washington set out to create an army shaped in large part in the British image. Basing his observations on his experience with British Regulars during the French and Indian War, he wrote: "Discipline is the soul of an army. It makes small numbers formidable;

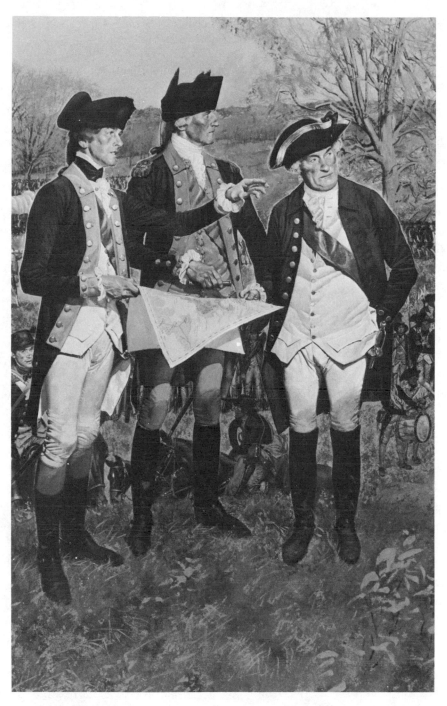

GENERAL WASHINGTON (*center*) WITH MAJ. GEN. ARTEMAS WARD (*right*) and an aide (*left*) visiting the field, July 1775.

procures success to the weak and esteem to all." Employing Gates, his experienced adjutant general, to prepare regulations and orders, the Commander in Chief set out to inculcate discipline. A strenuous effort was made to halt the random comings and goings of officers and men and to institute regular roll calls and strength returns. Suspicious of the "leveling" tendencies of the New Englanders, Washington made the distinction between officers and enlisted men more rigid. Various punishments were introduced—lash, pillory, wooden horse, and drumming out of camp—and courts-martial sat almost constantly.

While establishing discipline in the existing army, Washington had at the same time to form a new one enlisted directly in the Continental service. Out of conferences with a Congressional committee that visited camp in September 1775 emerged a plan for such an army, composed of 26 regiments of infantry of 728 men each, plus one regiment of riflemen and one of artillery, 20,372 men in all, to be uniformly paid, supplied, and administered by the Continental Congress and enlisted to the end of the year 1776. Except for the short term of enlistment, it was an excellent plan on paper, but Washington soon found he could not carry it out. Both officers and men resisted a reorganization that cut across the lines of the locally organized units in which they were accustomed to serve. The men saw as their first obligation their families and farms at home, and they were reluctant to re-enlist for another year's service. On December 10, despite pressures and patriotic appeals, most of the Connecticut men went home and militia from New Hampshire and Massachusetts had to be brought in to fill their places in the line. Others, who had jeered and hooted when the Connecticut men left, also went home when their enlistment expired only three weeks later. On January 1, 1776, when the army became "Continental in every respect," Washington found that he had only slightly more than 8,000 enlistments instead of the 20,000 planned. Returns in early March showed only a thousand or so more. "I have often thought how much happier I would have been," wrote a sorely tried commander, "if, instead of accepting a command under such circumstances, I had taken up musket on my shoulder and entered the ranks, or, if I could have justified the measure to posterity and my own conscience, had retired to the back country and lived in a Wigwam."

With enlistments falling short, the only recourse was to continue to use short-term militia to fill the gaps in the lines. A Continental Army had been formed, but it fell far short of the goals Washington and Congress had set for it. This army was enlisted for but a year and the whole troublesome process would have to be repeated at the end of 1776. The short term of enlistment was, of course, a cardinal error, but in 1775 everyone, including Washington, anticipated only a short campaign.

, While organizing and disciplining his army, Washington had also to maintain the siege of Boston and overcome his deficiencies in supply. In these efforts he was more successful. Congress and the individual colonies sponsored voyages to the West Indies, where the French and Dutch had conveniently exported quantities of war materials. Washington put some of his troops on board ship and with an improvised navy succeeded in capturing numerous British supply ships. He sent Col. Henry Knox, later to be his Chief of Artillery, to Ticonderoga, and Knox in the winter of 1775–76 brought some fifty pieces of captured cannon to Cambridge over poor or nonexistent roads in icebound New York and New England. By March 1776, despite deficiencies in the number of Continentals, Washington was ready to close in on Boston.

The Invasion of Canada and the Fall of Boston

The major military operations of 1775 and early 1776 were not around Boston but in far-distant Canada, which the Americans tried to add as a fourteenth colony. Canada seemed a tempting and vulnerable target. To take it would eliminate a British base at the head of the familiar invasion route along the lake and river chain connecting the St. Lawrence with the Hudson. Congress, getting no response to an appeal to the Canadians to join in its cause, in late June 1775 instructed Maj. Gen. Philip Schuyler of New York to take possession of Canada if "practicable" and "not disagreeable to the Canadians."

Schuyler managed to get together a force of about 2,000 men from New York and Connecticut, thus forming the nucleus of what was to become known as the Northern Army. In September 1775 Brig. Gen. Richard Montgomery set out with this small army from Ticonderoga with the objective of taking Montreal. To form a second prong to the invasion, Washington detached a force of 1,100 under Col. Benedict Arnold, including a contingent of riflemen under Capt. Daniel Morgan of Virginia, to proceed up the Kennebec River, across the wilds of Maine, and down the Chaudière to join with Montgomery before Quebec. (Map 4)

Montgomery, advancing along the route via Lake George, Lake Champlain, and the Richelieu River, was seriously delayed by the British fort at St. Johns but managed to capture Montreal on November 13. Arnold meanwhile had arrived opposite Quebec on November 8, after one of the most rugged marches in history. One part of his force had turned back and others were lost by

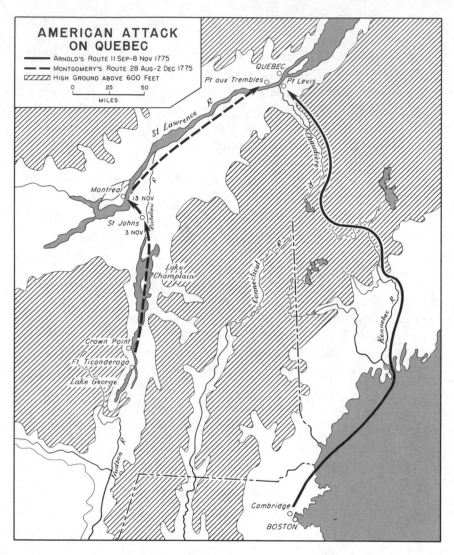

AMERICAN ATTACK ON QUEBEC

ARNOLD'S ROUTE 11 SEP-8 NOV 1775
MONTGOMERY'S ROUTE 28 AUG-2 DEC 1775
HIGH GROUND ABOVE 600 FEET

0   25   50
MILES

MAP 4

starvation, sickness, drowning, and desertion. Only 600 men crossed the St. Lawrence on November 13, and in imitation of Wolfe scaled the cliffs and encamped on the Plains of Abraham. It was a magnificent feat, but the force was too small to prevail even against the scattered Canadian militia and British Regulars who, unlike Montcalm, shut themselves up in the city and refused battle in the open. Arnold's men were finally forced to withdraw to Point aux Trembles, where they were joined by Montgomery with all the men he could spare from the defense of Montreal—a total of 300. Nowhere did the Canadians show much inclination to rally to the American cause; the French *habitants* remained indifferent, and the small British population gave its loyalty to the governor general. With the enlistments of about half their men expiring by the new year, Arnold and Montgomery undertook a desperate assault on the city during the night of December 30 in the middle of a raging blizzard. The Americans were outnumbered by the defenders, and the attack was a failure. Montgomery was killed and Arnold wounded.

The wounded Arnold, undaunted, continued to keep up the appearance of a siege with the scattered remnants of his force while he waited for reinforcements. The reinforcements came—Continental regiments raised in New York, New Jersey, and Pennsylvania—but they came in driblets and there were never enough to build a force capable of again taking the offensive, though a total of 8,000 men were eventually committed to the Canadian campaign. Smallpox and other diseases took their toll and never did the supply line bring in adequate food, clothing, or ammunition. Meanwhile, the British received reinforcements and in June 1776 struck back against a disintegrating American army that retreated before them almost without a fight. By mid-July the Americans were back at Ticonderoga where they had started less than a year earlier, and the initiative on the northern front passed to the British.

While the effort to conquer Canada was moving toward its dismal end, Washington finally took the initiative at Boston. On March 4, 1776, he moved onto Dorchester Heights and emplaced his newly acquired artillery in position to menace the city; a few days later he fortified Nook's Hill, standing still closer in. On March 17 the British moved out. It would be presumptuous to say that their exit was solely a consequence of American pressure. Sir William Howe, who succeeded Gage in command, had concluded long since that Boston was a poor strategic base and intended to stay only until the transports arrived to take his army to Halifax in Nova Scotia to regroup and await reinforcements. Nevertheless, Washington's maneuvers hastened his departure, and the reoccupation of Boston was an important psychological victory for the Americans, balancing the disappointments of the Canadian campaign. The stores of cannon and ammunition the British were forced to leave behind were a welcome addition indeed to the meager American arsenal.

The New Nation

The Declaration of Independence on July 4, 1776, established a new nation and transformed a limited revolt to secure rights within the British empire into a far-reaching one, aimed at complete independence from British control. Since the king and his ministers had determined to restore British rule, the Americans now faced a long, hard struggle for independence requiring a sustained national effort such as they had not expected in 1775.

The new nation was still a weak confederation of thirteen independent states. Such national feeling as existed was a new phenomenon growing out of common opposition to British measures. Colonial tradition, divided loyalties, the nature of the economy, and the spirit of a revolt born in opposition to the use of military force to suppress popular liberties, all worked against the creation of any new strong central authority capable of mobilizing resources effectively for the long struggle that lay ahead.

The thirteen states proclaiming their independence in 1776 possessed a total population of about two and a half million people, but not all the males of military age were part of the military potential. About 20 percent were Negro slaves who except under special circumstances were not eligible for service, though Negroes did serve in the Revolution and not in segregated units. Perhaps one-third of the "politically active" Americans remained loyal to the British Government. As in any society there were also the apathetic and indifferent who swayed with the tide. The genuine patriots still provided a far larger potential of military manpower than the British could possibly transport and supply across the Atlantic, but most of the men of military age were farmers who married young and immediately started large families. Whatever their patriotic sentiments, few were ready to undertake long terms of military service, fearing that if they did their farms and families at home would suffer. Accustomed to the tradition of short-term militia service under local commanders, they infinitely preferred it to long-term service in the Continental Army.

The economy of the thirteen new states was neither self-sufficient nor truly national. The states were essentially a collection of separate agricultural communities, accustomed to exchanging their agricultural surplus for British manufactured goods and West Indian products. Manufacturing was still in its infancy and America produced few of the essentials of military supply. Despite diligent efforts to promote domestic production during the war years, the Continental Army had to rely primarily on captures and imports from Europe and the West Indies, run through a British blockade, for much of its military hardware and even for clothing. While the country produced foodstuffs in ample quantity, transport from one area to another was difficult. The normal avenues of commerce ran up and down the rivers, not overland; roads running north and south were few and inadequate. There was always a shortage of wagons, boats, and other means of transportation. Under these circumstances, it was far easier to support local militia for a few days or weeks than any sizable and continuously operating national army in the field.

The governmental machinery created after the Declaration was characterized by decentralization and executive weakness. The thirteen new "free and independent states" transformed their existing *de facto* revolutionary governments into legal state governments by adopting constitutions. Almost invariably, these constitutions vested most of the powers of government in the state legislatures, successors to the popular assemblies of the colonial period, and severely restricted the executive authority of the governors. At the national level, the same general distrust of strong authority was apparent, and the existing Continental Congress essentially a gathering of delegates chosen by the state legislatures and without either express powers of its own or an executive to carry out its enactments, was continued as the only central governing body. Articles of Confederation stipulating the terms of union and granting Congress specific but limited powers were drawn up shortly after the Declaration, but jealousies among the states prevented ratification until 1781. In the interim, Congress exercised most of the powers granted it under the Articles, but they did not include either the right to levy taxes or the power to raise military forces directly under its auspices. Congress could only determine the Confederation's need for troops and money to wage war and set quotas for the states to meet in proportion to their population and wealth. It had no means of insuring that the states met their quotas, and indeed they seldom did.

The decentralized structure provided no adequate means of financing the war. The state legislatures, possessing the power to tax that Congress lacked, hesitated to use it extensively in the face of popular opposition to taxation, and were normally embarrassed to meet even their own expenses. Congress very early took unto itself the power to issue paper money and to negotiate domestic and foreign loans, but it shared these powers with the states, which also printed paper money in profusion and borrowed both at home and abroad to the extent they could. The paper money was a useful expedient in the early part of the war; indeed the Revolution could not have been carried on without it. But successive issues by Congress and the states led to first gradual and then galloping inflation, leaving the phrase "not worth a Continental" as a permanent legacy to the American language. The process of depreciation and the exhaustion of credit gradually robbed both the states and Congress of the power to pay troops, buy supplies, and otherwise meet the multitudinous expenses of war.

Evolution of the Continental Army

Under these circumstances it is not surprising that Washington never got the kind of army, molded in the British image, that he desired. The experience before Boston in 1775 was repeated many times, as local militia had to be called in continually to give the American Army a numerical superiority in the field. The Continental Army, nevertheless, became the center of American resistance, and its commander, Washington, the symbol of the patriot cause. The extent to which militia could be expected to rally to that cause was very largely determined by the Continental Army's success or failure in the field.

Though the militia belonged to the states, the Continental Army was a creation of the Continental Congress. Congress prescribed its size and composition, chose its generals, and governed the system for its administration and supply. Suspicious on principle of a standing army and acutely aware of historic examples of seizure of political power by military leaders, its members kept a watchful eye on the Army's commanders and insisted they defer to civilian authority. Washington countered these suspicions by constantly deferring to Congressional wishes, and he was rewarded by the assiduity with which Congress usually adopted his recommendations.

Lacking an executive, Congress had to rely on committees and boards to carry out its policies—unwieldy devices at best and centers of conflicting interest and discord at worst. In June 1776 it set up a Board of War and Ordnance, consisting of five of its members, the lineal ancestor of the War Department. In 1777 Congress changed the composition of the board, directing that it henceforth be made up of persons outside Congress who could devote full time to their military duties. Neither of these devices really worked well, and Congress continually handled administrative matters by action of the entire membership or by appointment of special committees to go to camp. In 1781 the board was replaced by a single Secretary at War.

Under the Articles of Confederation the states were responsible for raising troops for the Continental Army, for organizing and equipping them, and for appointing officers through the rank of colonel. State authorities called out militia sometimes at the request of Congress and sometimes on their own initiative. When they joined the main army, militia normally shared in its supplies and equipment. The states, however, maintained an interest in supplying and administering the troops of their own "lines" as well as their militia, and the Continental agents had continually to enlist state assistance in their own efforts. Lines of authority crisscrossed at every turn.

It was an inefficient military system for an organized national effort. Washington could never depend on having enough trained men or supplies. He continually inveighed against sending militia to fight his battles and by early 1776 had concluded that he needed an army enlisted for the duration of the war. Congress did not, as has often been charged, ignore his wishes. In October 1776 it voted a new establishment, superseding the plan developed for the army before Boston in 1775 and haphazard arrangements made in the interim for raising Continental regiments in various states. This establishment was to contain 88 battalions of infantry, or about 60,000 men, enlisted to serve three years or "during the present war," with each state assigned a quota in proportion to its population under the system set up in the Articles. After the disastrous retreat across New Jersey in December 1776, Congress went further and authorized an additional 22 battalions to be recruited by Washington's officers directly into the Continental service. These 110 battalions remained the authorized strength of the Continental Army until 1781, when Congress cut it to 59.

Neither the 88 battalions, nor the 110, nor even the 59 ever existed except on paper. The Continental Army never had as many as 30,000 men at any one time, and very rarely was Washington able to muster as many as 15,000 effectives in the field. The states were simply unable to meet their quotas. By the winter of 1777–78, the effort to enlist men for three years or the duration collapsed, and the following spring, with the sanction of Washington, Congress reverted to a system of one-year enlistments and recommended to the states that they institute a system of drafting men from the militia for one year's service. This first American wartime draft was applied irregularly in the various states and succeeded no better than had earlier methods in filling the Continental ranks. Bounties, instituted by both the states and the Congress very early in the war and progressively increased one step behind the pace of inflation, also produced only temporary and irregular results.

The coin did have another side. In reality the shortage of arms and ammunition and of facilities for producing them limited the number of men who could be kept continuously in the field as effectively as did the failure of enlistment drives. The militia system enabled many able-bodied males to perform part-time military service and still remain most of the time in the labor force that kept the economy going. It is doubtful whether the American economy could have sustained such an army as Washington and Congress proposed in 1776, even had there been a central administration with adequate power. As it was, the small Continental Army that did remain in the field intermittently suffered extreme hardship and near starvation. On the other hand, American ability to raise local armies in any threatened region helped to balance the strategic mobility that the British Fleet gave to the British Army. Although militia generally did not perform well in regular warfare, when highly motivated and ably led, they could fight well on terrain suited to their capabilities. Given the conditions under which the Revolution was fought, the American military system was more effective than its critics have recognized, though it failed to provide adequately for a sustained military effort over a period of years.

Perhaps Washington's greatest achievement was simply in maintaining the Continental Army continuously in the field. Despite its many vicissitudes, that army did take shape during the war as the first distinctively American military organization, neither quite a replica of the professional British Army on which it was modeled nor yet the type of national army raised by conscription that was to appear in France after the Revolution of 1789.

The Continental Army operated in three main territorial divisions or departments—the main army under Washington largely in the Middle States, the Northern Army in northern New York, and the Southern Army in the Carolinas and Georgia. Although Washington was Commander in Chief of the whole, the commanders of the Northern and Southern Armies still operated with a considerable measure of independence. Congress, rather than Washington, named their commanders and communicated directly with them. Of the two "separate armies," the Northern Army was by far the most important until 1777 and the Southern Army existed largely on paper; by 1780 the situation was reversed as the British transferred their main effort to the southern states.

The Continental Army was composed mainly of infantry and artillery, with very little cavalry. The basic unit of infantry organization was the regiment or battalion composed of eight companies. Organization above this level was highly flexible. A brigade was usually formed of several regiments and was commanded by a brigadier general; a division consisted of a similar grouping of several brigades commanded by a major general. Artillery was organized into a brigade of four regiments under a Chief of Artillery, Brig. Gen. Henry Knox, but the various companies were distributed among the infantry battalions. There was a small corps of engineers and an even smaller contingent of artificers, who handled the servicing and repair of ordnance.

Washington was provided with a staff generally corresponding to that of the British Army. The most important staff officer was the Quartermaster General, responsible not only for transportation and delivery of supplies but also for arranging the camp, regulating marches, and establishing the order of battle of the army. There were also an Adjutant General, a Judge Advocate

General, a Paymaster General, a Commissary General of Musters, a Commissary General of Provisions, a Clothier General, a Chief Surgeon, and a Chief Engineer. Each of the separate armies also usually had staff officers in these positions, designated as deputies to those of the main army.

All these staff officers had primarily administrative and supply functions. The modern concept of a general staff that acts as a sort of collective brain for the commander had no real counterpart in the eighteenth century. For advice on strategy and operations, Washington relied on a Council of War made up of his principal subordinate commanders, and, conforming to his original instructions from Congress, he usually consulted the council before making major decisions.

Both organization and staff work suffered from the ills that afflicted the whole military system. Regiments were constantly understrength, were organized differently by the various states, and employed varying systems of drill, discipline, and training. In the promotion of officers in the state lines, Continental commanders shared authority with the states, and the confused system gave rise to all sorts of rivalries, jealousies, and resentment, leading to frequent resignations. Staff officers were generally inexperienced, and few had the patience and perseverance to overcome the obstacles posed by divided authority, inadequate means, and poor transportation and communication facilities. The supply and support services of the Continental Army never really functioned efficiently, and with the depreciation in the currency they came close to collapse.

The British Problem

Whatever the American weaknesses, the British Government faced no easy task when it undertook to subdue the revolt by military force. Even though England possessed the central administration, stable financial system, and well-organized Army and Navy that the Americans so sorely lacked, the whole establishment was ill-prepared in 1775 for the struggle in America. A large burden of debt incurred in the wars of the preceding century had forced crippling economies on both Army and Navy. British administrative and supply systems, though far superior to anything the Americans could improvise, were also characterized by division and confusion of authority, and there was much corruption in high places.

To suppress the revolt, Britain had first to raise the necessary forces, then transport and sustain them over 3,000 miles of ocean, and finally use them effectively to regain control of a vast and sparsely populated territory. Recruiting men for an eighteenth century army was most difficult. The British Government had no power to compel service except in the militia in defense of the homeland, and service in the British Army overseas was immensely unpopular. To meet Sir William Howe's request for 50,000 men to conduct the campaign in 1776, the ministry resorted to hiring mercenaries from the small German states, particularly Hesse-Cassell (hence Hessians). These German states were to contribute almost 30,000 men to the British service during the war—complete organizations with their own officers up to the rank of major general and schooled in the system of Frederick the Great. Howe did not get his 50,000 men but by midsummer 1776 his force had passed 30,000 British and Hessians, and additional reinforcements were sent to Canada during the year. Maintaining a force of this size proved to be virtually impossible. The attrition rate in America from battle losses, sickness, disease, and desertion was tremendously high. English jails and poorhouses were drained of able-bodied men, bounties were paid, patriotic appeals were launched throughout England, Scotland, and Ireland, and all the ancient methods of impressment were tried, but the British were never able to recruit enough men to meet the needs of their commanders in America.

Providing adequate support for this army over a long ocean supply line was equally difficult. Even for food and forage, the British Army had to rely primarily on sea lines of supply. Transports were in short supply, the hardships of the 2- to 4-month voyage terrible, and the loss of men and supplies to natural causes heavy. Moreover, though the Americans could muster no navy capable of contesting British control of the seas, their privateers and the ships of their infant navy posed a constant threat to unprotected troop and supply transports. British commanders repeatedly had to delay their operations, awaiting the arrival of men and supplies from England.

Once in America, British armies could find no strategic center or centers whose capture would bring victory. Flat, open country where warfare could be carried on in European style was not common; and woods, hills, and swamps suited to the operations of militia and irregulars were plentiful. A British Army that could win victories in the field over the Continentals had great difficulty in making those victories meaningful. American armies seemed to possess miraculous powers of recuperation, while a British force, once depleted or surrendered, took a tremendous effort to replace.

As long as they controlled the seas, the British could land and establish bases at nearly any point on the long American coast line. The many navigable rivers dotting the coast also provided water avenues of invasion well into the interior. But to crush the revolt the British Army had to cut loose from coastal bases and rivers. When it did so its logistical problems multiplied and its lines of communications became vulnerable to constant harassment. British armies almost inevitably came to grief every time they moved very far from the areas where they could be nurtured by supply ships from the homeland. These difficulties, a British colonel asserted in 1777, had "absolutely prevented us this whole war from going fifteen miles from a navigable river."

The British could not, in any case, ever hope to muster enough strength to occupy with their own troops the vast territory they sought to restore to British rule. Their only real hope of meaningful victory was to use American loyalists as an instrument for controlling the country, as one British general put it, to help "the good Americans to subdue the bad." There were many obstacles to making effective use of the Tories. Patriot organization, weak at the center, was strong at the grass roots, in the local communities throughout America, whereas the Tories were neither well organized nor energetically led. The patriots seized the machinery of local government in most communities at the outset, held it until the British Army appeared in their midst, and then normally regained it after the British departed. Strong local control enabled the patriots to root out the more ardent Tories at the very outset, and by making an example of them to sway the apathetic and indifferent. British commanders were usually disappointed in the number of Tories who flocked to their standards and even more upset by the alacrity with which many of them switched their allegiance when the British Army moved out. They found the Tories a demanding, discordant, and puzzling lot, and they made no really earnest effort to enlist them in British forces until late in the war. By 1781 they had with their armies some 8,000 "provincial rank and file"; perhaps 50,000 in all served the British in some military capacity during the war.

On the frontiers the British could also expect support from the Indian tribes who almost inevitably drifted into the orbit of whatever power controlled Canada. But support of the Indians was a two-edged sword, for nothing could raise frontier enthusiasm for battle like the threat of an Indian attack.

Finally, the British had to fight the war with one eye on their ancient enemies in Europe. France, thirsting for revenge for defeat in the Seven Years' War, stood ready to aid the American cause if for no other purpose than to weaken British power, and by virtue of a Family Compact could almost certainly carry Spain along in any war with England. France and Spain could at the very least provide badly needed money and supplies to sustain the American effort and force the British to divert their forces from the contest in America. At most the combined Franco-Spanish fleet might well prove a match for the British Fleet and neutralize that essential control of the seas needed by the British to carry on the American war.

Of Strategy

The story of the American Revolution can hardly be told in terms of long-term strategy and its success or failure. Neither side ever had any really consistent plan for the conduct of the war. The British, who retained the strategic initiative most of the time, failed to use it to great advantage. They were highly uncertain about their objective; plans were laid from year to year and seldom co-ordinated even for a single year. Blame for this uncertain approach falls in almost equal part on the administration in England and the commanders in America. If King George III, Lord North, his Prime Minister, and Lord George Germain, Secretary of State for the American Department—the three British officials mainly responsible for the conduct of the war—never provided the timely guidance that might have been expected of them, their inability to do so came about in part because the commanders in the field never furnished accurate enough predictions of what to expect and differed so much among themselves as to the proper course to pursue. In assessing blame in this fashion, one must keep in mind the difficulties of logistics and communications under which the British labored, for these difficulties made it virtually impossible to co-ordinate plans over great distances or to assemble men and materials in time to pursue one logical and consistent plan.

American strategy was primarily defensive and consequently had to be shaped largely in terms of countering British moves. Uncertainties as to the supply of both men and materials acted on the American side even more effectively to thwart the development of a consistent plan for winning the war. Yet Washington was never so baffled by the conditions of the war or uncertain of his objective as were the various British commanders. After some early blunders, he soon learned both his own and the enemy's strengths and weaknesses and did his best to exploit them. Though unable to develop a consistent plan, he did try to develop a consistent line of action. He sought to maintain his principal striking force in a central position blocking any British advance into the interior; to be neither too bold nor too timid in seeking battle for limited objectives; to avoid the destruction of his army at all costs; and to find some means of concentrating a sufficient force to strike a decisive offensive blow whenever the British overreached themselves. He showed a better appreciation than the British commanders of the advantages in mobility their Navy gave them, and after 1778, when the French entered the war, he clearly saw that the decisive blow he desired could be struck only by a combined effort of the Continental Army and the French Fleet.

The British Offensive in 1776

If the British ever had a single strategic objective in the war, it was the Hudson River–Lake Champlain line. By taking and holding this line the British believed they could separate New England, considered to be the principal center of the rebellion, from the more malleable colonies to the southward. Howe proposed to make this the main objective of his campaign in 1776 by landing at New York, securing a base of operations there, and then pushing north. He wanted to concentrate the entire British force in America in New York, but the British Government diverted part of it to Canada in early 1776 to repel the American invasion, laying the groundwork for the divided command that was so to plague British operations afterward.

After the evacuation of Boston, Howe stayed at Halifax from March until June, awaiting the arrival of supplies and reinforcements. While he tarried, the British Government ordered another diversion in the south, aimed at encouraging the numerous loyalists who, according to the royal governors watching from their havens on board British warships, were waiting only for the appearance of a British force to rise and overthrow rebel rule. Unfortunately for the British, the naval squadron sent from England under Admiral Sir Peter Parker was delayed and did not arrive off the American coast until late in May. By this time all hopes of effective co-operation with the Tories had been dashed. Loyalist contingents had been completely defeated and dispersed in Virginia, North Carolina, and South Carolina. Parker, undeterred by these developments, determined to attack Charleston, the largest city in the south. There South Carolina militia and newly raised Continentals had prepared and manned defenses under the guidance of Maj. Gen. Charles Lee, whom Washington had dispatched south to assist them. The South Carolinians, contrary to Lee's advice, centered their defenses in Fort Moultrie, a palmetto log fort constructed on Sullivan's Island, commanding the approach to the harbor. It was an unwise decision, somewhat comparable to that at Bunker Hill, but fortunately for the defenders the British had to mount an un-co-ordinated attack in haste. Clinton's troops were landed on nearby Long Island, but on the day the Navy attacked, June 28, the water proved too deep for them to wade across to Sullivan's Island as expected. The British Army consequently sat idly by while the gunners in Fort Moultrie devastated the British warships. Sir Peter Parker suffered the ultimate indignity when his pants were set afire.

The battered British Fleet hastily embarked the British soldiers and sailed northward to join Howe, for it was already behind schedule. For three years following the fiasco at Charleston the British were to leave the south unmolested and the Tories there, who were undoubtedly numerous, without succor.

Howe was meanwhile beset by other delays in the arrival of transports from England, and his attack did not get under way until late August—leaving insufficient time before the advent of winter to carry through the planned advance along the Hudson–Lake Champlain line. He therefore started his invasion of New York with only the limited objective of gaining a foothold for the campaign the following year.

The British commander had, when his force was all assembled, an army of about 32,000 men; it was supported by a powerful fleet under the command of his brother, Admiral Richard Howe. To oppose him Washington had brought most of his army down from Boston, and Congress exerted its utmost efforts to reinforce him by raising Continental regiments in the surrounding states and issuing a general call for the militia. Washington was able to muster a paper strength of roughly 28,500 men, but only about 19,000 were present and fit for duty. As Christopher Ward remarks, "The larger part of them were raw recruits, undisciplined and inexperienced in warfare, and militia, never to be assuredly relied upon."

Washington and Congress made the same decision the South Carolinians had made at Charleston—to defend their territory in the most forward positions—and this time they paid the price for their mistake. The geography of the area gave the side possessing naval supremacy an almost insuperable advantage. The city of New York stood on Manhattan Island, surrounded by the Hudson, Harlem, and East Rivers. (*Map 5*) There was only one connecting link with the mainland, Kingsbridge across the Harlem River at the northern tip of Manhattan. Across the East River on Long Island, Brooklyn Heights stood in a position dominating the southern tip of Manhattan. With the naval forces at their disposal, the Howes could land troops on either Long Island or Manhattan proper and send warships up either the East or Hudson Rivers a considerable distance.

Washington decided he must defend Brooklyn Heights on Long Island if he was to defend Manhattan; he therefore divided his army between the two places—a violation of the principle of mass and the first step toward disaster. For all practical purposes command on Long Island was also divided. Maj. Gen. Nathanael Greene, to whom Washington first entrusted the command, came down with malaria and was replaced by Maj. Gen. John Sullivan. Not completely satisfied with this arrangement, at the last moment Washington placed Maj. Gen. Israel Putnam over Sullivan, but Putnam hardly had time to become acquainted with the situation before the British struck. The forces on Long

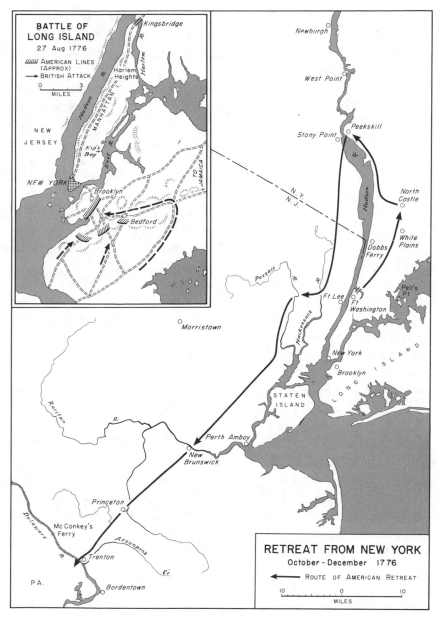

MAP 5

Island, numbering about 10,000, were disposed in fortifications on Brooklyn Heights and in forward positions back of a line of thickly wooded hills that ran across the southern end of the island. Sullivan was in command on the left of the forward line, Brig. Gen. William Alexander (Lord Stirling) on the right. Four roads ran through the hills toward the American positions. (*inset, Map 5*) Unfortunately Sullivan, in violation of the principle of security, left the Jamaica-Bedford road unguarded.

Howe was consequently able to teach the Americans lessons in maneuver and surprise. On August 22 he landed a force of 20,000 on the southwestern tip of Long Island and, in a surprise attack up the Jamaica-Bedford road against the American left flank, crumpled the entire American position. Stirling's valiant fight on the right went for naught, and inexperienced American troops fled in terror before the British and Hessian bayonets, falling back to the fortifications on Brooklyn Heights. It seems clear that had Howe pushed his advantage immediately he could have carried the heights and destroyed half the American Army then and there. Instead he halted at nightfall and began to dig trenches, signaling an intent to take the heights by "regular approaches" in traditional eighteenth century fashion. Washington managed to evacuate his forces across the East River on the night of August 29. According to one theory, wind and weather stopped the British warships from entering the river to prevent the escape; according to another, the Americans had placed impediments in the river that effectively barred their entry. In any case, it was a narrow escape, made possible by the skill, bravery, and perseverance of Col. John Glover's Marblehead Regiment, Massachusetts fishermen who manned the boats.

Washington had two weeks to prepare his defenses on Manhattan before Howe struck again, landing a force at Kip's Bay above the city of New York (now about 34th Street) on September 15. Raw Connecticut militia posted at this point broke and ran "as if the Devil was in them," defying even the efforts of a raging Washington to halt them. Howe once again had an opportunity to split the American Army in two and destroy half, but again he delayed midway across the island to wait until his entire force had landed. General Putnam was able to bring the troops stationed in the city up the west side of Manhattan to join their compatriots in new fortifications on Harlem Heights. There the Americans held out for another month, and even won a skirmish, but this position was also basically untenable.

In mid-October Howe landed again in Washington's rear at Pell's Point. The American commander then finally evacuated the Manhattan trap via Kingsbridge and took up a new position at White Plains, leaving about 6,000 men behind to man two forts, Fort Washington and Fort Lee, on opposite sides of the Hudson. Howe launched a probing attack on the American position at White Plains and was repulsed, but Washington, sensing his inability to meet the British in battle on equal terms, moved away to the north toward the New

York highlands. Again he was outmaneuvered. Howe quickly moved to Dobbs Ferry on the Hudson between Washington's army and the Hudson River forts. On the advice of General Greene (now recovered from his bout with malaria), Washington decided to defend the forts. At the same time he again split his army, moving across the Hudson and into New Jersey with 5,000 men and leaving General Lee and Maj. Gen. William Heath with about 8,000 between them to guard the passes through the New York highlands at Peekskill and North Castle. On November 16 Howe turned against Fort Washington and with the support of British warships on the Hudson stormed it successfully, capturing 3,000 American troops and large quantities of valuable munitions. Greene then hastily evacuated Fort Lee and by the end of November Washington, with mere remnants of his army, was in full retreat across New Jersey with Lord Charles Cornwallis, detached by Howe, pursuing him rapidly from river to river.

While Washington was suffering these disastrous defeats, the army that had been gathered was slowly melting away. Militia left by whole companies and desertion among the Continentals was rife. When Washington finally crossed the Delaware into Pennsylvania in early December, he could muster barely 2,000 men, the hard core of his Continental forces. The 8,000 men in the New York highlands also dwindled away. Even more appalling, most enlistments expired with the end of the year 1776 and a new army would have to be raised for the following year.

Yet neither the unreliability of the militia nor the short period of enlistment fully explained the debacle that had befallen the Continental Army. Washington's generalship was also faulty. Criticism of the Commander in Chief, even among his official family, mounted, centering particularly on his decision to hold Fort Washington. General Lee, the ex-British colonel, ordered by Washington to bring his forces down from New York to join him behind the Delaware, delayed, believing that he might himself salvage the American cause by making incursions into New Jersey. He wrote Horatio Gates, ". . . *entre nous,* a certain great man is most damnably deficient. . . ."

There was only one bright spot in the picture in the autumn of 1776. While Howe was routing Washington around New York City, other British forces under Sir Guy Carleton were attempting to follow up the advantage they had gained in repulsing the attack on Canada earlier in the year. Carleton rather leisurely built a flotilla of boats to carry British forces down Lake Champlain and Lake George, intending at least to reduce the fort at Ticonderoga before winter set in. Benedict Arnold countered by throwing together a much weaker flotilla of American boats with which he contested the British passage. Arnold lost this naval action on the lakes, but he so delayed Carleton's advance that the British commander reached Ticonderoga too late in the year to consider undertaking a siege. He returned his army to winter quarters in Canada, leaving the British with no advance base from which to launch the next year's campaign.

Although its consequences were to be far reaching, this limited victory did little to dispel the gloom that fell on the patriots after Washington's defeats in New York. The British, aware that Continental enlistments expired at the end of the year, had high hopes that the American Army would simply fade away and the rebellion collapse. Howe halted Cornwallis' pursuit of Washington and sent Clinton with a detachment of troops under naval escort to seize Newport, Rhode Island. He then dispersed his troops in winter quarters, establishing a line of posts in New Jersey at Perth Amboy, New Brunswick, Princeton, Trenton, and Bordentown, and retired himself to New York. Howe had gained the object of the 1776 campaign, a strong foothold, and possibly, as he thought at the time, a great deal more.

Trenton and Princeton

While Howe rested comfortably in New York, Washington desperately sought to reconcentrate his forces and redeem the defeat in New York. General Lee had the misfortune to fall into British hands on December 12, and his 2,000 remaining men then made haste to join Washington. Eight decimated regiments were also pulled from the Northern Army, and with some Pennsylvania militia Washington was able to assemble a force totaling about 7,000 by the last week of December 1776. If he was to use this force, he would have to do so before the enlistments expired on December 31. With great boldness, Washington formulated a plan to strike by surprise at the Hessian garrisons at Trenton and Bordentown on Christmas night, when the troops might be expected to relax their guard for holiday revelry. A Continental force of 2,400 men under Washington's personal command was to cross the Delaware at McConkey's Ferry above Trenton and then proceed in two columns by different routes, converging on the opposite ends of the main street of Trenton in the early morning of December 26. (*Map 6*) A second force, mainly militia, under Col. John Cadwalader was to cross below near Bordentown to attack the Hessian garrison there; a third, also militia, under Brig. Gen. James Ewing, was to cross directly opposite Trenton to block the Hessian route of escape across Assunpink Creek.

Christmas night was cold, windy, and snowy and the Delaware River was filled with blocks of ice. Neither Cadwalader nor Ewing was able to fulfill his part of the plan. Driven on by Washington's indomitable will, the main force did cross as planned and the two columns, commanded respectively by Greene and Sullivan, converged on Trenton at eight o'clock in the morning of December 26,

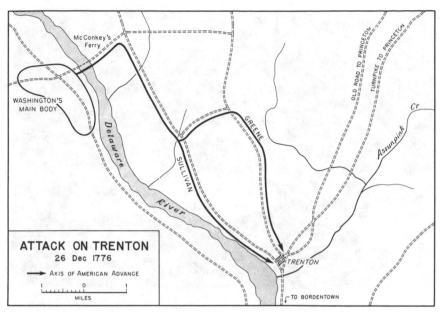

MAP 6

taking the Hessians completely by surprise. A New England private noted in his diary for the 26th: "This morning at 4 a clock we set off with our Field pieces and Marched 8 miles to Trenton whare we ware attacked by a Number of Hushing and we Toock 1000 of them besides killed some. Then we marched back and got to the River at Night and got over all the Hushing." This rather undramatic description of a very dramatic event was not far wrong, except in attributing the attack to the "Hushings." The Hessians surrendered after a fight lasting only an hour and a half. Forty were killed and the prisoner count was 918. Only 400 escaped to Bordentown, and these only because Ewing was not in place to block their escape. The Americans lost only 4 dead and 4 wounded.

Encouraged by this success, Washington determined to make another foray. By an impassioned appeal to the patriotism of the men, supplemented by an offer of a $10 bounty in hard money, he was able to persuade at least part of his old army to remain for six more weeks. With a force of around 5,000 Washington again crossed the Delaware on the night of December 30–31. By this time Cornwallis had hastily gathered together the scattered British garrisons in New Jersey, and took up a position confronting Washington at Trenton on January 2, 1777. Convinced that he had the Americans in a trap, he put off battle until the next day because of the exhausted state of his troops. In the night Washington slipped away, leaving campfires burning brightly to deceive the British. The

ALEXANDER HAMILTON'S ARTILLERY AT TRENTON, *with a 6-pounder brass field gun in the foreground.*

next morning he struck another surprise blow at Princeton, inflicting heavy losses on two British regiments just leaving the town to join Cornwallis. Washington then went into winter quarters in the hills around Morristown, New Jersey. Cornwallis did not pursue. The British had had enough of winter warfare, and Howe drew in his outposts in New Jersey to New Brunswick and Perth Amboy.

Trenton and Princeton not only offset the worst effects of the disastrous defeats in New York but also restored Washington's prestige as a commander with friend and foe alike. In the execution of the two strokes east of the Delaware, Washington had applied the principles of offensive, surprise, and maneuver with great success and finally achieved stature as a military commander. If these victories did not assure him that he could recruit such an army as Congress had voted, they did at least guarantee that he would be able to field a force the following year. Sir William Howe found that, despite his smashing rout of the Americans in New York, he was left with little more than that city, a foothold in New Jersey, and the port of Newport in Rhode Island.

CHAPTER 2

The Winning of Independence
1777–1783

The year 1777 was most critical for the British. The issue, very plainly, was whether they could score such success in putting down the American revolt that the French would not dare enter the war openly to aid the American rebels. Yet it was in this critical year that British plans were most confused and British operations most disjointed. The British campaign of 1777 provides one of the most striking object lessons in military history of the dangers of divided command.

The Campaign of 1777

With secure bases at New York and Newport, Howe had a chance to get the early start that had been denied him the previous year. His first plan, advanced on November 30, 1776, was probably the most comprehensive put forward by any British commander during the war. He proposed to maintain a small force of about 8,000 to contain Washington in New Jersey and 7,000 to garrison New York, while sending one column of 10,000 from Newport into New England and another column of 10,000 from New York up the Hudson to form a junction with a British force moving down from Canada. On the assumption that these moves would be successful by autumn, he would next capture Philadelphia, the rebel capital, and then make the southern provinces the "objects of the winter." For this plan, Howe requested 35,000 men, 15,000 more effective troops than he had left at the end of the 1776 campaign. Sir George Germain, the American Secretary, could promise him only 8,000. Even before receiving this news, but evidently influenced by Trenton and Princeton, Howe changed his plan and proposed to devote his main effort in 1777 to taking Philadelphia. On March 3, 1777, Germain informed Howe that the Philadelphia plan was approved, but that there might be only 5,500 reinforcements. At the same time Germain and the king urged a "warm diversion" against New England.

Meanwhile, Sir John Burgoyne, who had succeeded in obtaining the separate military command in Canada, submitted his plan calling for an advance southward to "a junction with Howe." Germain and the king also approved this plan on March 29, though aware of Howe's intention to go to Philadelphia. They seem to have expected either that Howe would be able to form his junction by the "warm diversion," or else that he would take Philadelphia quickly and then turn north to aid Burgoyne. In any case, Germain approved two separate and un-co-ordinated plans, and Howe and Burgoyne went their separate ways, doing nothing to remedy the situation. Howe's Philadelphia plan did provide for leaving enough force in New York for what its commander, General Clinton, called "a damn'd starved offensive," but Clinton's orders were vague. Quite possibly Burgoyne knew before he left England for. Canada that Howe was going to Philadelphia, but ambitious "Gentleman Johnny" was determined to make a reputation in the American war, and evidently believed he could succeed alone. Even when he learned certainly on August 3, 1777, that he could not expect Howe's co-operation, he persisted in his design. As Howe thought Pennsylvania was filled with royalists, Burgoyne cherished the illusion that legions of Tories in New York and western New England were simply awaiting the appearance of the king's troops to rally to the colors.

Again in 1777 the late arrival of Howe's reinforcements and stores ships gave Washington time that he sorely needed. Men to form the new Continental Army came in slowly and not until June did the Americans have a force of 8,000. On the northern line the defenses were even more thinly manned. Supplies for troops in the field were also short, but the arrival of the first three ships bearing secret aid from France vastly improved the situation. They were evidence of the covert support of the French Government; a mission sent by Congress to France was meanwhile working diligently to enlist open aid and to embroil France in a war with England. The French Foreign Minister, the Comte de Vergennes, had already decided to take that risk when and if the American rebels demonstrated their serious purpose and ability to fulfill it by some signal victory in the field.

With the first foreign material aid in 1777, the influx of foreign officers into the American Army began. These officers were no unmixed blessing. Most were adventurers in search of fortune or of reputation with little facility for adjusting themselves to American conditions. Few were willing to accept any but the highest ranks. Nevertheless, they brought with them professional military knowledge and competence that the Continental Army sorely needed. When the misfits were culled out, this knowledge and competence were used

to considerable advantage. Louis DuPortail, a Frenchman, and Thaddeus Kos-
ciuszko, a Pole, did much to advance the art of engineering in the Continental
Army; Casimir Pulaski, another Pole, organized its first genuine cavalry contingent; Johann de Kalb and Friedrich Wilhelm von Steuben, both Germans,
and the Marquis de Lafayette, an influential French nobleman who financed
his own way, were all to make valuable contributions as trainers and leaders.
On the Continental Army of 1777, however, these foreign volunteers had little
effect and it remained much as it had been before, a relatively untrained body
of inexperienced enlistees.

When Howe finally began to stir in June 1777, Washington posted his
army at Middlebrook, New Jersey, in a position either to bar Howe's overland
route to Philadelphia or to move rapidly up the Hudson to oppose an advance
northward. Washington confidently expected Howe to move northward to
form a junction with Burgoyne, but decided he must stay in front of the main
British Army wherever it went. Following the principle of economy of force,
he disposed a small part of his army under General Putnam in fortifications
guarding the approaches up the Hudson, and at a critical moment detached a
small force to aid Schuyler against Burgoyne. The bulk of his army he kept
in front of Howe in an effort to defend Philadelphia. Forts were built along the
Delaware River and other steps taken to block the approach to the Continental
capital by sea.

In the effort to defend Philadelphia Washington again failed, but hardly
so ignominiously as he had the year before in New York. After maneuvering
in New Jersey for upward of two months, Howe in August put most of his
army on board ship and sailed down the coast and up the Chesapeake Bay to
Head of Elk (a small town at the head of the Elk River) in Maryland, putting
himself even further away from Burgoyne. (*Map 7*) Though surprised by
Howe's movement, Washington rapidly shifted his own force south and took
up a position at Chad's Ford on Brandywine Creek, blocking the approach to
Philadelphia. There on September 11, 1777, Howe executed a flanking movement not dissimilar to that employed on Long Island and again defeated
Washington. The American commander had disposed his army in two main
parts, one directly opposite Chad's Ford under his personal command and the
other under General Sullivan guarding the right flank upstream. While Lt. Gen.
Wilhelm von Knyphausen's Hessian troops demonstrated opposite the ford, a
larger force under Lord Cornwallis marched upstream, crossed the Brandywine,
and moved to take Sullivan from the rear. Washington lacked good cavalry
reconnaissance, and did not get positive information on Cornwallis' movement
until the eleventh hour. Sullivan was in the process of changing front when

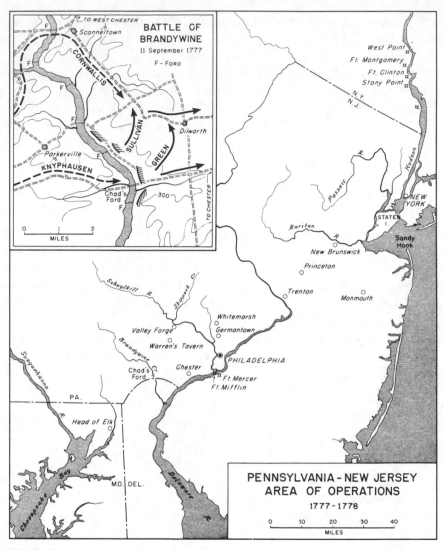

MAP 7

the British struck and his men retreated in confusion. Washington was able to salvage the situation by dispatching General Greene with two brigades to fight a valiant rear-guard action, but the move weakened his front opposite Kynphausen and his forces also had to fall back. Nevertheless, the trap was averted and the Continental Army retired in good order to Chester.

Howe followed with a series of maneuvers comparable to those he had executed in New York, and was able to enter Philadelphia with a minimum of fighting on September 26. A combined attack of British Army and Navy forces shortly afterward reduced the forts on the Delaware and opened the river as a British supply line.

On entering Philadelphia, Howe dispersed his forces, stationing 9,000 men at Germantown north of the city, 3,000 in New Jersey, and the rest in Philadelphia. As Howe had repeated his performance in New York, Washington sought to repeat Trenton by a surprise attack on Germantown. The plan was much like that used at Trenton but involved far more complicated movements by much larger bodies of troops. Four columns—two of Continentals under Sullivan and Greene and two of militia—moving at night over different roads were to converge on Germantown simultaneously at dawn on October 4. (*Map 8*) The plan violated the principle of simplicity, for such a maneuver was

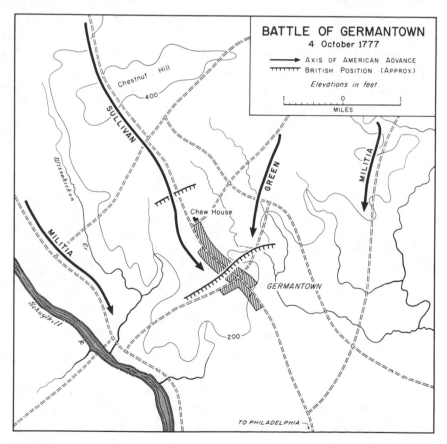

MAP 8

difficult even for well-trained professionals to execute. The two columns of
Continentals arrived at different times and fired on each other in an early morning fog. The two militia columns never arrived at all. British fire from a stone
house, the Chew Mansion, held up the advance while American generals
argued whether they could leave a fortress in their rear. The British, though
surprised, had better discipline and cohesion and were able to re-form and send
fresh troops into the fray. The Americans retreated about 9:00 a.m., leaving
Howe's troops in command of the field.

After Germantown Howe once again concentrated his army and moved
to confront Washington at Whitemarsh, but finally withdrew to winter quarters
in Philadelphia without giving battle. Washington chose the site for his own
winter quarters at a place called Valley Forge, twenty miles northwest of the
city. Howe had gained his objective but it proved of no lasting value to him.
Congress fled west to York, Pennsylvania. No swarms of loyalists rallied to the
British standards. And Howe had left Burgoyne to lose a whole British army
in the north.

Burgoyne set out from Canada in June, his object to reach Albany by fall.
(Map 9) His force was divided into two parts. The first and largest part—7,200
British and Hessian Regulars and 650 Tories, Canadians, and Indians, under
his personal command—was to take the route down Lake Champlain to Ticonderoga and thence via Lake George to the Hudson. The second—700 Regulars
and 1,000 Tories and Indian braves under Col. Barry St. Leger—was to move
via Lake Ontario to Oswego and thence down the Mohawk Valley to join Burgoyne before Albany. In his preparations, Burgoyne evidently forgot the lesson
the British had learned in the French and Indian War, that in the wilderness
troops had to be prepared to travel light and fight like Indians. He carried 138
pieces of artillery and a heavy load of officers' personal baggage. Numerous
ladies of high and low estate accompanied the expedition. When he started
down the lakes, Burgoyne did not have enough horses and wagons to transport
his artillery and baggage once he had to leave the water and move overland.

At first Burgoyne's American opposition was very weak—only about 2,500
Continentals at Ticonderoga and about 450 at old Fort Stanwix, the sole American bulwark in the Mohawk Valley. Dissension among the Americans was rife,
the New Englanders refusing to support Schuyler, the aristocratic New Yorker
who commanded the Northern Army, and openly intriguing to replace him
with their own favorite, Maj. Gen. Horatio Gates. Ticonderoga fell to Burgoyne
on June 27 all too easily. American forces dispersed and Burgoyne pursued the
remnants down to Skenesborough. Once that far along, he decided to continue
overland to the Hudson instead of returning to Ticonderoga to float his force

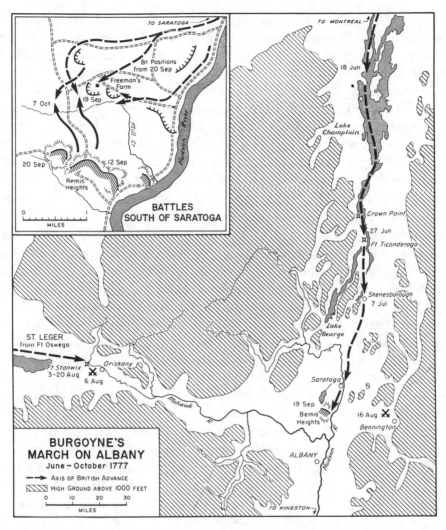

MAP 9

down Lake George, though much of his impedimenta still had to be carried by boat down the lake.

The overland line of advance was already a nightmare, running along wilderness trails, through marshes, and across wide ravines and creeks that had been swollen by abnormally heavy rains. Schuyler adopted the tactic of making it even worse by destroying bridges, cutting trees in Burgoyne's path, and digging trenches to let the waters of swamps onto drier ground. The British were able to move at a rate of little more than a mile a day and took until July 29 to reach Fort Edward on the Hudson. By that time Burgoyne was desperately short of horses, wagons, and oxen. Yet Schuyler, with a unstable force of 4,500 men discouraged by continual retreats, was in no position to give battle.

Washington did what he could to strengthen the Northern Army at this juncture. He first dispatched Maj. Gen. Benedict Arnold, his most aggressive field commander, and Maj. Gen. Benjamin Lincoln, a Massachusetts man noted for his influence with the New England militia. On August 16 he detached Col. Daniel Morgan with 500 riflemen from the main army in Pennsylvania and ordered them along with 750 men from Putnam's force in the New York highlands to join Schuyler. The riflemen were calculated to furnish an antidote for Burgoyne's Indians who, despite his efforts to restrain them, were terrorizing the countryside.

It was the rising militia, rather than Washington, who were to provide the Northern Army with its main reinforcements. Nothing worked more to produce this result than Burgoyne's employment of Indians. The murder and scalping of a beautiful white woman, Jane McCrea, dramatized the Indian threat as nothing else probably could have done. New England militiamen now began to rally to the cause, though they still refused to co-operate with Schuyler. New Hampshire commissioned John Stark, a disgruntled ex-colonel in the Continental Army and a veteran of Bunker Hill and Trenton, as a brigadier general in the state service (a rank denied him by Congress), and Stark quickly recruited 2,000 men. Refusing Schuyler's request that he join the main army, Stark took up a position at Bennington in southern Vermont to guard the New England frontier. On August 11 Burgoyne detached a force of 650 men under Hessian Col. Friedrich Baum to forage for cattle, horses, and transport in the very area Stark was occupying. At Bennington on August 16 Stark nearly annihilated Baum's force, and reinforcements sent by Burgoyne arrived on the field just in time to be soundly thrashed in turn. Burgoyne not only failed to secure his much-needed supplies and transport but also lost about a tenth of his command.

Meanwhile, St. Leger with his Tories and Indians had appeared before Fort Stanwix on August 2. The garrison, fearing massacre by the Indians, determined to hold out to the bitter end. On August 4, the Tryon County militia under Brig. Gen. Nicholas Herkimer set out to relieve the fort but were ambushed by the Indians in a wooded ravine near Oriskany. The militia, under the direction of a mortally wounded Herkimer, scattered in the woods and fought a bloody afternoon's battle in a summer thunderstorm. Both sides suffered heavy losses, and though the militia were unable to relieve Stanwix the losses discouraged St. Leger's Indians, who were already restless in the static siege operation at Stanwix.

Despite his own weak position, when Schuyler learned of the plight of the Stanwix garrison, he courageously detached Benedict Arnold with 950 Continentals to march to its relief. Arnold devised a ruse that took full advantage of the dissatisfaction and natural superstition of the Indians. Employing a half-wit Dutchman, his clothes shot full of holes, and a friendly Oneida Indian as his messengers, Arnold spread the rumor that the Continentals were approaching "as numerous as the leaves on the trees." The Indians, who had special respect for any madman, departed in haste, scalping not a few of their Tory allies as they went, and St. Leger was forced to abandon the siege.

Bennington and Stanwix were serious blows to Burgoyne. By early September he knew he could expect help from neither Howe nor St. Leger. Disillusioned about the Tories, he wrote Germain: "The great bulk of the country is undoubtedly with Congress in principle and zeal; and their measures are executed with a secrecy and dispatch that are not to be equalled. Wherever the King's forces point, militia in the amount of three or four thousand assemble in twenty-four hours; they bring with them their subsistence, etc., and the alarm over, they return to their farms. . . ." Nevertheless, gambler that he was, Burgoyne crossed the Hudson to the west side during September 13 and 14, signaling his intention to get to Albany or lose his army. While his supply problem daily became worse, his Indians, with a natural instinct for sensing approaching disaster, drifted off into the forests, leaving him with little means of gaining intelligence of the American dispositions.

The American forces were meanwhile gathering strength. Congress finally deferred to New England sentiment on August 19 and replaced Schuyler with Gates. Gates was more the beneficiary than the cause of the improved situation, but his appointment helped morale and encouraged the New England militia. Washington's emissary, General Lincoln, also did his part. Gates understood Burgoyne's plight perfectly and adapted his tactics to take full advantage of it. He advanced his forces four miles northward and took up a position, surveyed and prepared by the Polish engineer, Kosciusko, on Bemis Heights, a few miles below Saratoga. Against this position Burgoyne launched his attack on September 19 and was repulsed with heavy losses. In the battle, usually known as Freeman's Farm, Arnold persuaded Gates to let him go forward to counter the British attack, and Colonel Morgan's riflemen, in a wooded terrain well suited to the use of their specialized weapon, took a heavy toll of British officers and men.

After Freeman's Farm, the lines remained stable for three weeks. Burgoyne had heard that Clinton, with the force Howe had left in New York, had started north to relieve him. Clinton, in fact, stormed Forts Clinton and Montgomery on the Hudson on October 6, but, exercising that innate caution characteristic of all his actions, he refused to gamble for high stakes. He simply sent an advance guard on to Kingston and he himself returned to New York.

Burgoyne was left to his fate. Gates strengthened his entrenchments and calmly awaited the attack he was sure Burgoyne would have to make. Militia reinforcements increased his forces to around 10,000 by October 7. Meanwhile Burgoyne's position grew more desperate. Food was running out; the meadows were grazed bare by the animals; and every day more men slipped into the forest, deserting the lost cause. With little intelligence of American strength or dispositions, on October 7 he sent out a "reconnaissance in force" to feel out the American positions. On learning that the British were approaching, Gates sent out a contingent including Morgan's riflemen to meet them, and a second battle developed, usually known as Bemis Heights. The British suffered severe losses, five times those of the Americans, and were driven back to their fortified positions. Arnold, who had been at odds with Gates and was confined to his tent, broke out, rushed into the fray, and again distinguished himself before he was wounded in leading an attack on Breymann's Redoubt.

Two days after the battle, Burgoyne withdrew to a position in the vicinity of Saratoga. Militia soon worked around to his rear and cut his supply lines. His position hopeless, Burgoyne finally capitulated on October 17 at Saratoga. The total prisoner count was nearly 6,000 and great quantities of military stores fell into American hands. The victory at Saratoga brought the Americans out well ahead in the campaign of 1777 despite the loss of Philadelphia. What had been at stake soon became obvious. In February 1778 France negotiated a treaty of alliance with the American states, tantamount to a declaration of war against England.

Valley Forge

The name of Valley Forge has come to stand, and rightly so, as a patriotic symbol of suffering, courage, and perserverance. The hard core of 6,000 Continentals who stayed with Washington during that bitter winter of 1777–78 indeed suffered much. Some men had no shoes, no pants, no blankets. Weeks passed when there was no meat and men were reduced to boiling their shoes and eating them. The wintry winds penetrated the tattered tents that were at first the only shelter.

The symbolism of Valley Forge should not be allowed to obscure the fact that the suffering was largely unnecessary. While the soldiers shivered and went hungry, food rotted and clothing lay unused in depots throughout the country. True, access to Valley Forge was difficult, but little determined effort was made to get supplies into the area. The supply and transport system broke down. In mid-1777, both the Quartermaster and Commissary Generals resigned along with numerous subordinate officials in both departments, mostly merchants who found private trade more lucrative. Congress, in refuge at York, Pennsylvania, and split into factions, found it difficult to find replacements. If there was not, as most historians now believe, an organized cabal seeking to replace Washington with Gates, there were many, both in and out of the Army, who were dissatisfied with the Commander in Chief, and much intrigue went on. Gates was made president of the new Board of War set up in 1777, and at least two of its members were enemies of Washington. In the administrative chaos at the height of the Valley Forge crisis, there was no functioning Quartermaster General at all.

Washington weathered the storm and the Continental Army was to emerge from Valley Forge a more effective force than before. With his advice, Congress instituted reforms in the Quartermaster and Commissary Departments that temporarily restored the effectiveness of both agencies. Washington's ablest subordinate, General Greene, reluctantly accepted the post of Quartermaster General. The Continental Army itself gained a new professional competence from the training given by the Prussian, Friedrich Wilhelm von Steuben.

Steuben appeared at Valley Forge in February 1778 arrayed in such martial splendor that one private thought he had seen Mars, the god of war, himself. He represented himself as a baron, a title he had acquired in the service of a small German state, and as a former lieutenant general on the staff of Frederick the Great, though in reality he had been only a captain. The fraud was harmless, for Steuben had a broad knowledge of military affairs and his remarkable sense of the dramatic was combined with the common touch a true Prussian baron might well have lacked.

Washington had long sensed the need for uniform training and organization, and after a short trial he secured the appointment of Steuben as Inspector General in charge of a training program. Steuben carried out the program during the late winter and early spring of 1778, teaching the Continental Army a simplified but effective version of the drill formations and movements of European armies, proper care of equipment, and the use of the bayonet, a weapon in which British superiority had previously been marked. He attempted to consolidate the understrength regiments and companies and organized light

STEUBEN TRAINING AMERICAN FORCES AT VALLEY FORGE

infantry companies as the elite force of the Army. He constantly sought to impress upon the officers their responsibility for taking care of the men. Steuben never lost sight of the difference between the American citizen soldier and the European professional. He early noted that American soldiers had to be told why they did things before they would do them well, and he applied this philosophy in his training program. His trenchant good humor and vigorous profanity, almost the only English he knew, delighted the Continental soldiers and made the rigorous drill more palatable. After Valley Forge, Continentals would fight on equal terms with British Regulars in the open field.

First Fruits of the French Alliance

While the Continental Army was undergoing its ordeal and transformation at Valley Forge, Howe dallied in Philadelphia, forfeiting whatever remaining chance he had to win a decisive victory before the effects of the French alliance were felt. He had had his fill of the American war and the king accepted his resignation from command, appointing General Clinton as his successor. As Washington prepared to sally forth from Valley Forge, the British Army and the Philadelphia Tories said goodbye to their old commander in one of the most lavish celebrations ever held in America, the *Mischianza,* a veritable Belshazzar's feast. The handwriting on the wall appeared in the form of orders, already in Clinton's hands, to evacuate the American capital. With the French in the war, England had to look to the safety of the long ocean supply line to America and to the protection of its possessions in other parts of the world. Clinton's orders were to detach 5,000 men to the West Indies and 3,000 to Florida, and to return the rest of his army to New York by sea.

As Clinton prepared to depart Philadelphia, Washington had high hopes that the war might be won in 1778 by a co-operative effort between his army and the French Fleet. The Comte d'Estaing with a French naval squadron of eleven ships of the line and transports carrying 4,000 troops left France in May to sail for the American coast. D'Estaing's fleet was considerably more powerful than any Admiral Howe could immediately concentrate in American waters. For a brief period in 1778 the strategic initiative passed from British hands, and Washington hoped to make full use of it.

Clinton had already decided, before he learned of the threat from d'Estaing, to move his army overland to New York prior to making any detachments, largely because he could find no place for 3,000 horses on the transports. On June 18, 1778, he set out with about 10,000 men. Washington, who by that time had gathered about 12,000, immediately occupied Philadelphia and then took up the pursuit of Clinton, undecided as to whether he should risk an attack on the British column while it was on the march. His Council of War was divided, though none of his generals advised a "general action." The boldest, Brig. Gen. Anthony Wayne, and the young major general, the Marquis de Lafayette, urged a "partial attack" to strike at a portion of the British Army while it was strung out on the road; the most cautious, General Lee, who had been exchanged and had rejoined the army at Valley Forge, advised only guerrilla action to harass the British columns. On June 26 Washington decided to take a bold approach, though he issued no orders indicating an intention to bring on a "general action." He sent forward an advance guard composed of almost half his army to strike at the British rear when Clinton moved out of Monmouth Court House on the morning of June 27. Lee, the cautious, claimed the command from Lafayette, the bold, when he learned the detachment would be so large.

In the early morning, Lee advanced over rough ground that had not been reconnoitered and made contact with the British rear, but Clinton reacted quickly and maneuvered to envelop the American right flank. Lee, feeling that his force was in an untenable position, began a retreat that became quite confused. Washington rode up amidst the confusion and, exceedingly irate to find the advance guard in retreat, exchanged harsh words with Lee. He then assumed direction of what had to be a defense against a British counterattack. The battle that followed, involving the bulk of both armies, lasted until nightfall on a hot, sultry day with both sides holding their own. For the first time the Americans fought well with the bayonet as well as with the musket and rifle, and their battlefield behavior generally reflected the Valley Forge training. Nevertheless, Washington failed to strike a telling blow at the British Army, for Clinton slipped away in the night and in a few days completed the retreat to New York. Lee demanded and got a court-martial at which he was judged, perhaps unjustly, guilty of disobedience of orders, poor conduct of the retreat, and disrespect for the Commander in Chief. As a consequence he retired from the Army, though the controversy over his actions at Monmouth was to go on for years.

Washington, meanwhile, sought his victory in co-operation with the French Fleet. D'Estaing arrived off the coast on July 8 and the two commanders at first agreed on a combined land and sea attack on New York, but d'Estaing feared he would be unable to get his deep-draft ships across the bar that extended from Staten Island to Sandy Hook, in order to get at Howe's inferior fleet. They then decided to transfer the attack to the other and weaker British stronghold at Newport, Rhode Island—a city standing on an island with difficult approaches. A plan was agreed on whereby the French Fleet would force the passage on the west side of the island and an American force under General Sullivan would cross over and mount an assault from the east. The whole scheme soon went awry. The French Fleet arrived off Newport on July 29 and successfully forced the passage; Sullivan began crossing on the east on August 8 and d'Estaing began to disembark his troops. Unfortunately at this juncture Admiral Howe appeared with a reinforced British Fleet, forcing d'Estaing to re-embark his troops and put out to sea to meet Howe. As the two fleets maneuvered for advantage, a great gale scattered both on August 12. The British returned to New York to refit, and the French Fleet to Boston, whence d'Estaing decided he must move on to tasks he considered more pressing in the West Indies. Sullivan was left to extricate his forces from an untenable position as best he could, and the first experiment in Franco-American co-operation came to a disappointing end with recriminations on both sides.

The fiasco at Newport ended any hopes for an early victory over the British as a result of the French alliance. By the next year, as the French were forced to devote their major attention to the West Indies, the British regained the initiative on the mainland, and the war entered a new phase.

The New Conditions of the War

After France entered the war in 1778, it rapidly took on the dimensions of a major European as well as an American conflict. In 1779 Spain declared war against England, and in the following year Holland followed suit. The necessity of fighting European enemies in the West Indies and other areas and of standing guard at home against invasion weakened the British effort against the American rebels. Yet the Americans were unable to take full advantage of Britain's embarrassments, for their own effort suffered more and more from war weariness, lack of strong direction, and inadequate finance. Moreover, the interests of European states fighting Britain did not necessarily coincide with American interests. Spain and Holland did not ally themselves with the American states at all, and even France found it expedient to devote its major effort to the West Indies. Finally, the entry of ancient enemies into the fray spurred the British to intensify their effort and evoked some, if not enough, of that characteristic tenacity that has produced victory for England in so many wars. Despite their many new commitments, the British were able to maintain in America an army that was usually superior in numbers to the dwindling Continental Army, though never strong enough to undertake offensives again on the scale of those of 1776 and 1777.

Monmouth was the last general engagement in the north between Washington's and Clinton's armies. In 1779 the situation there became a stalemate and remained so until the end of the war. Washington set up a defense system around New York with its center at West Point, and Clinton made no attempt to attack his main defense line. The British commander did, in late spring 1779, attempt to draw Washington into the open by descending in force on unfinished American outpost fortifications at Verplanck's Point and Stony Point, but Washington refused to take the bait. When Clinton withdrew his main force to New York, the American commander retaliated by sending Maj. Gen. Anthony Wayne on July 15, 1779, with an elite corps of light infantry, on a stealthy night attack on Stony Point, a successful action more notable for demonstrating the proficiency with which the Americans now used the bayonet than for any important strategic gains. Wayne was unable to take Verplanck's, and Clinton rapidly retook Stony Point. Thereafter the war around New York became largely an affair of raids, skirmishes, and constant vigilance on both sides.

Clinton's inaction allowed Washington to attempt to deal with British-inspired Indian attacks. Although Burgoyne's defeat ended the threat of invasion from Canada, the British continued to incite the Indians all along the frontier to bloody raids on American settlements. From Fort Niagara and Detroit they sent out their bands, usually led by Tories, to pillage, scalp, and burn in the Mohawk Valley of New York, the Wyoming Valley of Pennsylvania, and the new American settlements in Kentucky. In August 1779 Washington detached General Sullivan with a force to deal with the Iroquois in Pennsylvania and New York. Sullivan laid waste the Indians' villages and defeated a force of Tories and Indians at Newtown on August 29.

In the winter of 1778–79, the state of Virginia had sponsored an expedition that struck a severe blow at the British and Indians in the northwest. Young Lt. Col. George Rogers Clark with a force of only 175 men, ostensibly recruited for the defense of Kentucky, overran all the British posts in what is today Illinois and Indiana. Neither he nor Sullivan, however, was able to strike at the sources of the trouble—Niagara and Detroit. Indian raids along the frontiers continued, though they were somewhat less frequent and severe.

British Successes in the South

Late in 1778 the British began to turn their main effort to the south. Tory strength was greater in the Carolinas and Georgia and the area was closer to the West Indies, where the British Fleet had to stand guard against the French. The king's ministers hoped to bring the southern states into the fold one by one, and from bases there to strangle the recalcitrant north. A small British force operating from Florida quickly overran thinly populated Georgia in the winter of 1778–79. Alarmed by this development, Congress sent General Benjamin Lincoln south to Charleston in December 1778 to command the Southern Army and organize the southern effort. Lincoln gathered 3,500 Continentals and militiamen, but in May 1779, while he maneuvered along the Georgia border, the British commander, Maj. Gen. Augustine Prevost, slipped around him to lay siege to Charleston. The city barely managed to hold out until Lincoln returned to relieve it. (*Map 10*)

In September 1779 d'Estaing arrived off the coast of Georgia with a strong French Fleet and 6,000 troops. Lincoln then hurried south with 1,350 Americans to join him in a siege of the main British base at Savannah. Unfortunately, the Franco-American force had to hurry its attack because d'Estaing was unwilling to risk his fleet in a position dangerously exposed to autumn storms. The French and Americans mounted a direct assault on Savannah on October 9, abandoning their plan to make a systematic approach by regular parallels. The British in strongly entrenched positions repulsed the attack in what was essentially a Bunker Hill in reverse, the French and Americans suffering

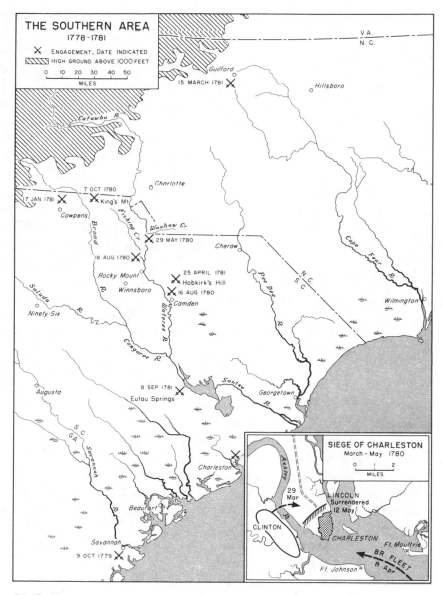

MAP 10

staggering losses. D'Estaing then sailed away to the West Indies, Lincoln returned to Charleston, and the second attempt at Franco-American co-operation ended in much the same atmosphere of bitterness and disillusion as the first.

Meanwhile Clinton, urged on by the British Government, had determined to push the southern campaign in earnest. In October 1779 he withdrew the British garrison from Newport, pulled in his troops from outposts around New York, and prepared to move south against Charleston with a large part of his force. With d'Estaing's withdrawal the British regained control of the sea along the American coast, giving Clinton a mobility that Washington could not match. While Clinton drew forces from New York and Savannah to achieve a decisive concentration of force (14,000 men) at Charleston, Washington was able to send only piecemeal reinforcements to Lincoln over difficult overland routes. Applying the lessons of his experience in 1776, Clinton this time carefully planned a co-ordinated Army-Navy attack. First, he landed his force on John's Island to the south, then moved up to the Ashley River, investing Charleston from the land side. Lincoln, under strong pressure from the South Carolina authorities, concentrated his forces in a citadel defense on the neck of land between the Ashley and Cooper Rivers, leaving Fort Moultrie in the harbor lightly manned. On April 8 British warships successfully forced the passage past Moultrie, investing Charleston from the sea. The siege then proceeded in traditional eighteenth century fashion, and on May 12, 1780, Lincoln surrendered his entire force of 5,466 men, the greatest disaster to befall the American cause during the war. Meanwhile, Col. Abraham Buford with 350 Virginians was moving south to reinforce the garrison. Lt. Col. Banastre Tarleton with a force of British cavalry took Buford by surprise at the Waxhaws, a district near the North Carolina border, and slaughtered most of his men, refusing to honor the white flag Buford displayed.

After the capture of Charleston, Clinton returned to New York with about a third of his force, leaving General Cornwallis with 8,000 men to follow up the victory. Cornwallis established his main seaboard bases at Savannah, Beaufort, Charleston, and Georgetown, and in the interior extended his line of control along the Savannah River westward to Ninety-Six and northward to Camden and Rocky Mount. Cornwallis' force, however, was too small to police so large an area, even with the aid of the numerous Tories who took to the field. Though no organized Continental force remained in the Carolinas and Georgia, American guerrillas, led by Brig. Gens. Thomas Sumter and Andrew Pickens and Lt. Col. Francis Marion, began to harry British posts and lines of communications and to battle the bands of Tories. A bloody, ruthless, and confused civil war ensued, its character determined in no small degree by Tarleton's action at the Waxhaws. In this way, as in the Saratoga campaign, the American grass roots strength began once again to assert itself and to deny the British the fruits of military victory won in the field.

On June 22, 1780, two more understrength Continental brigades from Washington's army arrived at Hillsboro, North Carolina, to form the nucleus of a new Southern Army around which militia could rally and which could serve as the nerve center of guerrilla resistance. In July Congress, without consulting Washington, provided a commander for this army in the person of General Gates, the hero of Saratoga. Gates soon lost his northern laurels. Gathering a force of about 4,000 men, mostly militia, he set out to attack the British post at Camden, South Carolina. Cornwallis hurried north from Charleston with reinforcements and his army of 2,200 British Regulars made contact with Gates outside Camden on the night of August 15. In the battle that ensued the following morning, Gates deployed his militia on the left and the Continentals under Maj. Gen. Johann de Kalb on the right. The militia were still forming in the hazy dawn when Cornwallis struck, and they fled in panic before the British onslaught. De Kalb's outnumbered Continentals put up a valiant but hopeless fight. Tarleton's cavalry pursued the fleeing Americans for 30 miles, killing or making prisoner those who lagged. Gates himself fled too fast for Tarleton, reaching Hillsboro, 160 miles away, in three days. There he was able to gather only about 800 survivors of the Southern Army. To add to the disaster, Tarleton caught up with General Sumter, whom Gates had sent with a detachment to raid a British wagon train, and virtually destroyed his force in a surprise attack at Fishing Creek on August 18. Once more South Carolina seemed safely in British hands.

Nadir of the American Cause

In the summer of 1780 the American cause seemed to be at as low an ebb as it had been after the New York campaign in 1776 or after the defeats at Ticonderoga and Brandywine in 1777. Defeat in the south was not the only discouraging aspect of patriot affairs. In the north a creeping paralysis had set in as the patriotic enthusiasm of the early war years waned. The Continental currency had virtually depreciated out of existence, and Congress was impotent to pay the soldiers or purchase supplies. At Morristown, New Jersey, in the winter of 1779–80 the army suffered worse hardships than at Valley Forge. Congress could do little but attempt to shift its responsibilities onto the states, giving each the task of providing clothing for its own troops and furnishing certain quotas of specific supplies for the entire Army. The system of "specific supplies" worked not at all. Not only were the states laggard in furnishing supplies, but when they did it was seldom at the time or place they were needed. This breakdown in the supply system was more than even General Greene, as Quartermaster General, could cope with, and in early 1780, under heavy criticism in Congress, he resigned his position.

Under such difficulties, Washington had to struggle to hold even a small Army together. Recruiting of Continentals, difficult to begin with, became almost impossible when the troops could neither be paid nor supplied adequately and had to suffer such winters as those at Morristown. Enlistments and drafts from the militia in 1780 produced not quite half as many men for one year's service as had enlisted in 1776 for three years or the duration. While recruiting lagged, morale among those men who had enlisted for the longer terms naturally fell. Mutinies in 1780 and 1781 were suppressed only by measures of great severity.

Germain could write confidently to Clinton: "so very contemptible is the rebel force now . . . that no resistance . . . is to be apprehended that can materially obstruct . . . the speedy suppression of the rebellion . . . the American levies in the King's service are more in number than the whole of the enlisted troops in the service of the Congress." The French were unhappy. In the summer of 1780 they occupied the vacated British base at Newport, moving in a naval squadron and 4,000 troops under the command of Lieutenant General the Comte de Rochambeau. Rochambeau immediately warned his government: "Send us troops, ships and money, but do not count on these people nor on their resources, they have neither money nor credit, their forces exist only momentarily, and when they are about to be attacked in their own homes they assemble . . . to defend themselves." Another French commander thought only one highly placed American traitor was needed to decide the campaign.

Clinton had, in fact, already found his "highly placed traitor" in Benedict Arnold, the hero of the march to Quebec, the naval battle on the lakes, Stanwix, and Saratoga. "Money is this man's God," one of his enemies had said of Arnold earlier, and evidently he was correct. Lucrative rewards promised by the British led to Arnold's treason, though he evidently resented the slights Congress had dealt him, and he justified his act by claiming that the Americans were now fighting for the interests of Catholic France and not their own. Arnold wangled an appointment as commander at West Point and then entered into a plot to deliver this key post to the British. Washington discovered the plot on September 21, 1780, just in time to foil it, though Arnold himself escaped to become a British brigadier.

Arnold's treason in September 1780 marked the nadir of the patriot cause. In the closing months of 1780, the Americans somehow put together the ingredients for a final and decisive burst of energy in 1781. Congress persuaded

Robert Morris, a wealthy Philadelphia merchant, to accept a post as Superintendent of Finance, and Col. Timothy Pickering, an able administrator, to replace Greene as Quartermaster General. Greene, as Washington's choice, was then named to succeed Gates in command of the Southern Army. General Lincoln, exchanged after Charleston, was appointed Secretary at War and the old board was abolished. Morris took over many of the functions previously performed by unwieldy committees. Working closely with Pickering, he abandoned the old paper money entirely and introduced a new policy of supplying the army by private contracts, using his personal credit as eventual guarantee for payment in gold or silver. It was an expedient but, for a time at least, it worked.

Greene's Southern Campaign

It was the frontier militia assembling "when they were about to be attacked in their own homes" who struck the blow that actually marked the turning point in the south. Late in 1780, with Clinton's reluctant consent, Cornwallis set out on the invasion of North Carolina. He sent Maj. Patrick Ferguson, who had successfully organized the Tories in the upcountry of South Carolina, to move north simultaneously with his "American Volunteers," spread the Tory gospel in the North Carolina back country, and join the main army at Charlotte with a maximum number of recruits. Ferguson's advance northward alarmed the "over-mountain men" in western North Carolina, southwest Virginia, and what is now east Tennessee. A picked force of mounted militia riflemen gathered on the Catawba River in western North Carolina, set out to find Ferguson, and brought him to bay at King's Mountain near the border of the two Carolinas on October 7. In a battle of patriot against Tory (Ferguson was the only British soldier present), the patriots' triumph was complete. Ferguson himself was killed and few of his command escaped death or capture. Some got the same "quarter" Tarleton had given Buford's men at the Waxhaws.

King's Mountain was as fatal to Cornwallis' plans as Bennington had been to those of Burgoyne. The North Carolina Tories, cowed by the fate of their compatriots, gave him little support. The British commander on October 14, 1780, began a wretched retreat in the rain back to Winnsboro, South Carolina, with militia harassing his progress. Clinton was forced to divert an expedition of 2,500 men sent to establish a base in Virginia to reinforce Cornwallis.

The frontier militia had turned the tide, but having done so, they returned to their homes. To keep it moving against the British was the task of the new commander, General Greene. When Greene arrived at Charlotte, North Carolina, early in December 1780, he found a command that consisted of 1,500 men fit for duty, only 949 of them Continentals. The army lacked clothing and provisions and had little systematic means of procuring them. Greene decided that he must not engage Cornwallis' army in battle until he had built up his strength, that he must instead pursue delaying tactics to wear down his stronger opponent. The first thing he did was to take the unorthodox step of dividing his army in the face of a superior force, moving part under his personal command to Cheraw Hill, and sending the rest under Brig. Gen. Daniel Morgan west across the Catawba over 100 miles away. It was an intentional violation of the principle of mass. Greene wrote:

I am well satisfied with the movement . . . . It makes the most of my inferior force, for it compels my adversary to divide his, and holds him in doubt as to his own line of conduct. He cannot leave Morgan behind him to come at me, or his posts at Ninety-Six and Augusta would be exposed. And he cannot chase Morgan far, or prosecute his views upon Virginia, while I am here with the whole country open before me. I am as near to Charleston as he is, and as near Hillsborough as I was at Charlotte; so that I am in no danger of being cut off from my reinforcements.

Left unsaid was the fact that divided forces could live off the land much easier than one large force and constitute two rallying points for local militia instead of one. Greene was, in effect, sacrificing mass to enhance maneuver.

Cornwallis, an aggressive commander, had determined to gamble everything on a renewed invasion of North Carolina. Ignoring Clinton's warnings, he depleted his Charleston base by bringing almost all his supplies forward. In the face of Greene's dispositions, Cornwallis divided his army into not two but three parts. He sent a holding force to Camden to contain Green, directed Tarleton with a fast-moving contingent of 1,100 infantry and cavalry to find and crush Morgan, and with the remainder of his army moved cautiously up into North Carolina to cut off any of Morgan's force that escaped Tarleton.

Tarleton caught up with Morgan on January 17, 1781, west of King's Mountain at a place called the Cowpens, an open, sparsely forested area six miles from the Broad River. (*Map 11*) Morgan chose this site to make his stand less by design than necessity, for he had intended to get across the Broad. Nevertheless, on ground seemingly better suited to the action of Regulars, he achieved a little tactical masterpiece, making the most effective use of his heterogeneous force, numerically equal to that of Tarleton but composed of three-fourths militia. Selecting a hill as the center of his position, he placed his Continental infantry on it, deliberately leaving his flanks open. Well out in front of the main line he posted militia riflemen in two lines, instructing the first line to fire two volleys and then fall back on the second, the combined line to fire until the British pressed them, then to fall back to the rear of the Continentals and re-form as a reserve. Behind the hill he placed Lt. Col. William Washing-

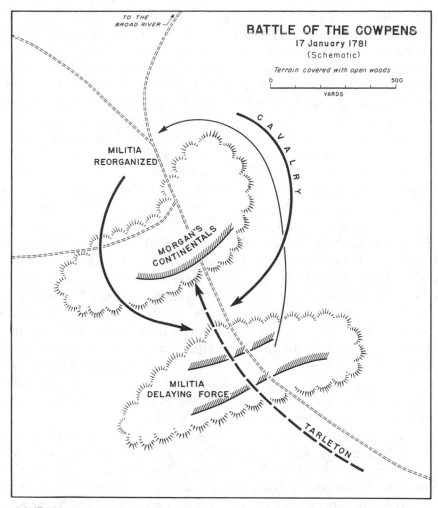

MAP 11

ton's cavalry detachment, ready to charge the attacking enemy at the critical moment. Every man in the ranks was informed of the plan of battle and the part he was expected to play in it.

On finding Morgan, Tarleton ordered an immediate attack. His men moved forward in regular formation, were momentarily checked by the militia rifles, but, taking the retreat of the first two lines to be the beginning of a rout, rushed headlong into the steady fire of the Continentals on the hill. When the British were well advanced, the American cavalry struck them on the right flank and the militia, having re-formed, charged out from behind the hill to hit the British left. Caught in a clever double envelopment, the British surrendered after suffering heavy losses. Tarleton managed to escape with only a small force of cavalry he had held in reserve. It was on a small scale, and with certain significant differences, a repetition of the classic double envelopment of the Romans by a Carthaginian army under Hannibal at Cannae in 216 B.C., an event of which Morgan, no reader of books, probably had not the foggiest notion.

Having struck his fatal blow against Tarleton, Morgan still had to move fast to escape Cornwallis. Covering 100 miles and crossing two rivers in five days, he rejoined Greene early in February. Cornwallis by now was too heavily committed to the campaign in North Carolina to withdraw. Hoping to match the swift movement of the Americans, he destroyed all his superfluous supplies, baggage, and wagons and set forth in pursuit of Greene's army. The American general retreated, through North Carolina, up into southern Virginia, then back into North Carolina again, keeping just far enough in front of his adversary to avoid battle with Cornwallis' superior force. Finally on March 15, 1781, at Guilford Court House in North Carolina, on ground he had himself chosen, Greene halted and gave battle. By this time he had collected 1,500 Continentals and 3,000 militia to the 1,900 Regulars the British could muster. The British held the field after a hard-fought battle, but suffered casualties of about one-fourth of the force engaged. It was, like Bunker Hill, a Pyrrhic victory. His ranks depleted and his supplies exhausted, Cornwallis withdrew to Wilmington on the coast, and then decided to move northward to join the British forces General Clinton had sent to Virginia.

Greene, his army in better condition than six months earlier, pushed quickly into South Carolina to reduce the British posts in the interior. He fought two battles—at Hobkirk's Hill on April 25, and at Eutaw Springs on September 8—losing both but with approximately the same results as at Guilford Court House. One by one the British interior posts fell to Greene's army, or to militia and partisans. By October 1781 the British had been forced to withdraw to their port strongholds along the coast—Charleston and Savannah. Greene had lost battles, but won a campaign. In so doing, he paved the way for the greater victory to follow at Yorktown.

Yorktown: The Final Act

As Howe and Burgoyne went their separate ways in 1777, seemingly determined to satisfy only their personal ambitions, so Clinton and Cornwallis in 1781 paved the road to Yorktown by their disagreements and lack of co-ordination. Clinton was Cornwallis' superior in this case, but the latter enjoyed the confidence of Germain to an extent that Clinton did not. Clinton, believing that without large reinforcements the British could not operate far from coastal bases, had opposed Cornwallis' ventures in the interior of the Carolinas, and when Cornwallis came to Virginia he did so without even informing his superior of his intention.

Since 1779 Clinton had sought to paralyze the state of Virginia by conducting raids up its great rivers, arousing the Tories, and establishing a base in the Chesapeake Bay region. (*Map 12*) He thought this base might eventually be used as a starting point for one arm of a pincers movement against Pennsylvania for which his own idle force in New York would provide the other. A raid conducted in the Hampton Roads area in 1779 was highly successful, but when Clinton sought to follow it up in 1780 the force sent for the purpose had to be diverted to Charleston to bail Cornwallis out after King's Mountain. Finally in 1781 he got an expedition into Virginia, a contingent of 1,600 under the American traitor, Benedict Arnold. In January Arnold conducted a destructive raid up the James River all the way to Richmond. His presence soon proved to be a magnet drawing forces of both sides to Virginia.

In an effort to trap Arnold, Washington dispatched Lafayette to Virginia with 1,200 of his scarce Continentals and persuaded the French to send a naval squadron from Newport to block Arnold's escape by sea. The plan went awry when a British fleet drove the French squadron back to Newport and Clinton sent another 2,600 men to Virginia along with a new commander, Maj. Gen. William Phillips. Phillips and Arnold continued their devastating raids, which Lafayette was too weak to prevent. Then on May 20 Cornwallis arrived from Wilmington and took over from Phillips. With additional reinforcements sent by Clinton he was able to field a force of about 7,000 men, approximately a quarter of the British strength in America. Washington sent down an additional reinforcement of 800 Continentals under General Wayne, but even with Virginia militia Lafayette's force remained greatly outnumbered.

Cornwallis and Clinton were soon working at cross-purposes. Cornwallis proposed to carry out major operations in the interior of Virginia, but Clinton saw as little practical value in this tactic as Cornwallis did in Clinton's plan to establish a base in Virginia for a pincers movement against Pennsylvania. Cornwallis at first turned to the interior and engaged in a fruitless pursuit of Lafayette north of Richmond. Then, on receiving Clinton's positive order to return to the coast, establish a base, and return part of his force to New York, Cornwallis moved back down the Virginia peninsula to take up station at Yorktown, a small tobacco port on the York River just off Chesapeake Bay. In the face of

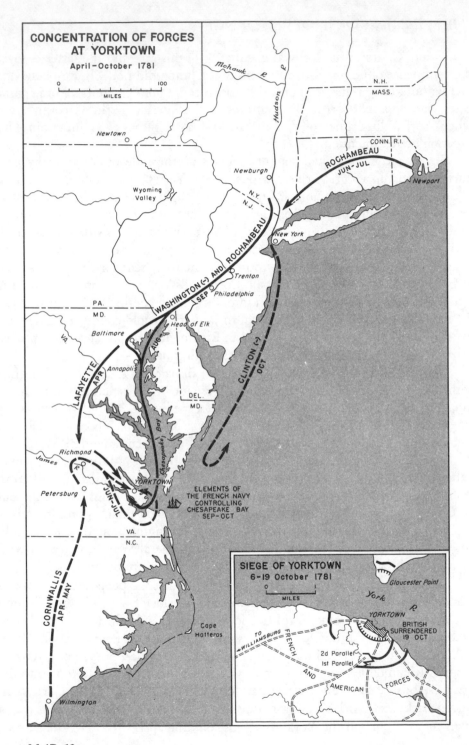

CONCENTRATION OF FORCES AT YORKTOWN
April–October 1781

0   100
MILES

Mohawk R.

Hudson R.

N.H.
MASS.

Newtown

Newburgh

CONN. R.I.

ROCHAMBEAU
JUN–JUL

Newport

Wyoming Valley

N.Y.
N.J.

New York

WASHINGTON (–) AND ROCHAMBEAU

Trenton

SEP Philadelphia

PA.
MD.

CLINTON (–) OCT

VA.

Baltimore

Head of Elk

LAFAYETTE APR

Annapolis

AUG

DEL.
MD.

Chesapeake Bay

Richmond

James R.

YORKTOWN

JUN–JUL

ELEMENTS OF
THE FRENCH NAVY
CONTROLLING
CHESAPEAKE BAY
SEP–OCT

Petersburg

VA.
N.C.

CORNWALLIS APR–MAY

Cape Hatteras

Wilmington

SIEGE OF YORKTOWN
6–19 October 1781

0
MILES

Gloucester Point

York R.

YORKTOWN

BRITISH
SURRENDERED
19 OCT

TO WILLIAMSBURG

FRENCH

2d Parallel

1st Parallel

AND

AMERICAN   FORCES

MAP 12

Cornwallis' insistence that he must keep all his troops with him, Clinton vacillated, reversing his own orders several times and in the end granting Cornwallis' request. Lafayette and Wayne followed Cornwallis cautiously down the peninsula, lost a skirmish with him at Green Spring near Williamsburg on July 6, and finally took up a position of watchful waiting near Yorktown.

Meanwhile, Washington had been trying to persuade the French to co-operate in a combined land and naval assault on New York in the summer of 1781. Rochambeau brought his 4,000 troops down from Newport in April and placed them under Washington's command. The prospects were still bleak since the combined Franco-American force numbered but 10,000 against Clinton's 17,000 in well-fortified positions. Then on August 14 Washington learned that the French Fleet in the West Indies, commanded by Admiral Francois de Grasse, would not come to New York but would arrive in the Chesapeake later in the month and remain there until October 15. He saw immediately that if he could achieve a superior concentration of force on the land side while de Grasse still held the bay he could destroy the British army at Yorktown before Clinton had a chance to relieve it.

The movements that followed illustrate most effectively a successful application of the principles of the offensive, surprise, objective, mass, and maneuver. Even without unified command of Army and Navy forces, Franco-American co-operation this time was excellent. Admiral Louis, Comte de Barras, immediately put out to sea from Newport to join de Grasse. Washington sent orders to Lafayette to contain Cornwallis at Yorktown and then, after making a feint in the direction of New York to deceive Clinton, on August 21 started the major portion of the Franco-American Army on a rapid secret movement to Virginia, via Chesapeake Bay, leaving only 2,000 Americans behind to watch Clinton.

On August 30, while Washington was on the move southward, de Grasse arrived in the Chesapeake with his entire fleet of twenty-four ships of the line and a few days later debarked 3,000 French troops to join Lafayette. Admiral Thomas Graves, the British naval commander in New York, meanwhile had put out to sea in late August with nineteen ships of the line, hoping either to intercept Barras' squadron or to block de Grasse's entry into the Chesapeake. He failed to find Barras, and when he arrived off Hampton Roads on September 5 he found de Grasse already in the bay. The French admiral sallied forth to meet Graves and the two fleets fought an indecisive action off the Virginia capes. Yet for all practical purposes the victory lay with the French for, while the fleets maneuvered at sea for days following the battle, Barras' squadron slipped into the Chesapeake and the French and American troops got past into the James River. Then de Grasse got back into the bay and joined Barras, con-

SURRENDER OF CORNWALLIS

fronting Graves with so superior a naval force that he decided to return to New York to refit.

When Washington's army arrived on September 26, the French Fleet was in firm control of the bay, blocking Cornwallis' sea route of escape. A decisive concentration had been achieved. Counting 3,000 Virginia militia, Washington had a force of about 9,000 Americans and 6,000 French troops with which to conduct the siege. It proceeded in the best traditions of Vauban under the direction of French engineers. Cornwallis obligingly abandoned his forward position on September 30, and on October 6 the first parallel was begun 600 yards from the main British position. Artillery placed along the trench began its destructive work on October 9. By October 11 the zigzag connecting trench had been dug 200 yards forward, and work on the second parallel had begun. Two British redoubts had to be reduced in order to extend the line to the York River. This accomplished, Cornwallis' only recourse was escape across the river to Gloucester Point where the American line was thinly held. A storm on the night of October 16 frustrated his attempt to do so, leaving him with no hope but relief from New York. Clinton had been considering such relief for days, but he acted too late. On the very day, October 17, that Admiral Graves set sail from New York with a reinforced fleet and 7,000 troops for the relief of Yorktown, Cornwallis began negotiations on terms of surrender. On October 19 his entire army marched out to lay down its arms, the British band playing an old tune called "The World Turned Upside Down."

So far as active campaigning was concerned, Yorktown ended the war. Both Greene and Washington maintained their armies in position near New York and Charleston for nearly two years more, but the only fighting that occurred was some minor skirmishing in the South. Cornwallis' defeat led to the overthrow of the British cabinet and the formation of a new government that decided the war in America was lost. With some success, Britain devoted its energies to trying to salvage what it could in the West Indies and in India. The independence for which Americans had fought thus virtually became a reality when Cornwallis' command marched out of its breached defenses at Yorktown.

The Summing Up: Reasons, Lessons, and Meaning

The American victory in the War of the Revolution was a product of many factors, no one of which can be positively assigned first importance. Washington, looking back on the vicissitudes of eight years, could only explain it as the intervention of "Divine Providence." American historians in the nineteenth century saw that "Divine Providence" as having been manifested primarily in the character and genius of the modest Commander in Chief himself. Washington's leadership was clearly one of the principal factors in American success; it seems fair to say that the Revolution could hardly have succeeded without him. Yet in many of the events that led to victory—Bennington, Saratoga, King's Mountain, and Cowpens, to name but a few—his personal influence was remote.

Today many scholars stress not the astonishment that Washington felt at the victory of a weak and divided confederation of American states over the greatest power of the age, but the practical difficulties the British faced in suppressing the revolt. These were indeed great but they do not appear to have been insuperable if one considers military victory alone and not its political consequences. The British forfeited several chances for military victory in 1776–77, and again in 1780 they might have won had they been able to throw 10,000 fresh troops into the American war. American military leaders were more resourceful and imaginative than the British commanders, and they proved quite capable of profiting from British blunders. In addition to Washington, Nathanael Greene, Henry Knox, Daniel Morgan, and Benedict Arnold showed remarkable military abilities, and of the foreign volunteers Steuben and the young Lafayette were outstanding. The resourcefulness of this extraordinary group of leaders was matched by the dedication of the Continental rank and file to the cause. Only men so dedicated could have endured the hardships of the march to Quebec, the crossing of the Delaware, Valley Forge, Morristown, and Greene's forced marches in the southern campaign. British and Hessian professionals never showed the same spirit; their virtues were exhibited principally in situations where discipline and training counted most.

The militia, the men who fought battles and then went home, also exhibited this spirit on many occasions. The militiamen have been generally maligned as useless by one school of thought, and glorified by another as the true victors in the war. In any balanced view it must be recognized that their contributions were great, though they would have counted for little without a Continental Army to give the American cause that continued sustenance that only a permanent force in being could give it. It was the ubiquity of the militia that made British victories over the Continentals in the field so meaningless. And the success with which the militia did operate derived from the firm political control the patriots had established over the countryside long before the British were in any position to challenge it—the situation that made the British task so difficult in the first place.

For all these American virtues and British difficulties and mistakes, the Americans still required French aid—money, supplies, and in the last phase military force—to win a decisive and clear-cut military victory. Most of the muskets, bayonets, and cannon used by the Continental Army came from France. The French contested the control of the seas that was so vital to the British, and compelled them to divert forces from the American mainland to other areas. The final stroke at Yorktown, though a product of Washington's strategic conception, was possible only because of the temporary predominance of French naval power off the American coast and the presence of a French army.

French aid was doubly necessary because the American war effort lacked strong national direction. The Revolution showed conclusively the need for a central government with power to harness the nation's resources for war. It is not surprising that in 1787 nearly all those who had struggled so long and hard as leaders in the Continental Army or in administrative positions under the Congress were to be found in the ranks of the supporters of a new constitution creating such a central government with a strong executive and the power to "raise armies and navies," call out the militia, and levy taxes directly to support itself.

Strictly military lessons of the Revolution were more equivocal. Tactical innovations were not radical but they did represent a culmination of the trend, which started during the French and Indian War, toward employment of light troops as skirmishers in conjunction with traditional linear formations. By the end of the war both armies were fighting in this fashion. The Americans strove to develop the same proficiency as the British in regular line-of-battle tactics, while the British adapted to the American terrain and tactics by themselves employing skirmishers and fighting when possible from behind cover. Washington was himself a military conservative, and Steuben's training program was designed to equip American troops to fight in European fashion with modifications to provide for the increased use of light infantry. The guerrilla tactics that characterized many actions, principally those of the militia, were no product of the design of Washington or his leading subordinates but of circumstances over which they had little control. The American rifle, most useful in guerrilla actions or in the hands of skirmishers, played no decisive role in the Revolution. It was of great value in wooded areas, as at Saratoga and King's Mountain, but for open-field fighting its slow rate of fire and lack of a bayonet made it inferior to the musket.

Since both militia and Continentals played roles in winning the war, the Revolutionary experience provided ammunition for two diametrically opposed schools of thought on American military policy: the one advocating a large Regular Army, the other reliance on the militia as the bulwark of national defense. The real issue, as Washington fully recognized, was less militia versus Regulars—for he never believed the infant republic needed a large standing army—than the extent to which militia could be trained and organized to form a reliable national reserve. The lesson Washington drew from the Revolution was that the militia should be "well regulated," that is, trained and organized under a uniform national system in all the states and subject to call into national service in war or emergency.

The lesson had far greater implications for the future than any of the tactical changes wrought by the American Revolution. It balanced the rights of freedom and equality, proclaimed in the Declaration of Independence, with a corresponding obligation of all citizens for military service to the nation. This concept, which was to find explicit expression in the "nation in arms" during the French Revolution, was also implicit in the American, and it portended the end of eighteenth century limited war, fought by professional armies officered by an aristocratic class. As Steuben so well recognized, American Continentals were not professional soldiers in the European sense, and militia even less so. They were, instead, a people's army fighting for a cause. In this sense then, the American Revolution began the "democratization of war," a process that was eventually to lead to national conscription and a new concept of total war for total victory.

CHAPTER 3

The War of 1812

To Great Britain the War of 1812 was simply a burdensome adjunct of its greater struggle against Napoleonic France. To the Canadians it was clearly a case of naked American aggression. But to the Americans it was neither simple nor clear. The United States entered the war with confused objectives and divided loyalties and made peace without settling any of the issues that had induced the nation to go to war.

Origins of the War

The immediate origins of the war were seizure of American ships, insults and injuries to American seamen by the British Navy, and rapid expansion of the American frontier. The British outrages at sea took two distinct forms. One was the seizure and forced sale of merchant ships and their cargoes for allegedly violating the British blockade of Europe. Although France had declared a counterblockade of the British Isles and had seized American ships, England was the chief offender because its Navy had greater command of the seas. The second, more insulting, type of outrage was the capture of men from American vessels for forced service in the Royal Navy. The pretext for impressment was the search for deserters, who, the British claimed, had taken employment on American vessels.

The reaction in the United States to impressment differed from that aroused by the seizure of ships and cargoes. In the latter case the maritime interests of the eastern seaboard protested vigorously and demanded naval protection, but rather than risk having their highly profitable trade cut off by war with England they were willing to take an occasional loss of cargo. Impressment, on the other hand, presented no such financial hardship to the shipowners, whatever the consequences for the unfortunate seamen, and the maritime interests tended to minimize it.

To the country at large the seizure of American seamen was much more serious than the loss of a few hogsheads of flour or molasses. When a British naval vessel in June 1807 attacked and disabled the USS *Chesapeake* and impressed several members of the crew, a general wave of indignation rose in which even the maritime interests joined. This was an insult to the flag, and had Jefferson chosen to go to war with England he would have had considerable support. Instead he decided to clamp an embargo on American trade. In New England scores of prosperous shipowners were ruined, and a number of thriving little seaports suffered an economic depression from which few recovered. While the rest of the country remembered the *Chesapeake* affair and stored up resentment against Britain, maritime New England directed its anger at Jefferson and his party.

The seat of anti-British fever was in the Northwest and the lower Ohio Valley, where the land-hungry frontiersmen had no doubt that their troubles with the Indians were the result of British intrigue. Stories were circulated after every Indian raid of British Army muskets and equipment being found on the field. By 1812 the westerners were convinced that their problems could best be solved by forcing the British out of Canada.

While the western "war hawks" urged war in the hope of conquering Canada, the people of Georgia, Tennessee, and the Mississippi Territory entertained similar designs against Florida, a Spanish possession. The fact that Spain and England were allies against Napoleon presented the southern war hawks with an excuse for invading Florida. By this time, also, the balance of political power had shifted south and westward; ambitious party leaders had no choice but to align themselves with the war hawks, and 1812 was a Presidential election year.

President Madison's use of economic pressure to force England to repeal its blockade almost succeeded. The revival of the Non-Intercourse Act against Britain, prohibiting all trade with England and its colonies, coincided with a poor grain harvest in England and with a growing need of American provisions to supply the British troops fighting the French in Spain. As a result, on June 16, 1812, the British Foreign Minister announced that the blockade would be relaxed on American shipping. Had there been an Atlantic cable, war might have been averted. President Madison had sent a message to Congress on June 1 listing all the complaints against England and asking for a declaration of war. Dividing along sectional lines the House had voted for war on June 4, but the Senate approved only on June 18 and then by only six votes.

The Opposing Forces

At the outbreak of the war the United States had a total population of about 7,700,000 people. A series of border forts garrisoned by very small Regular Army detachments stretched along the Canadian boundary: Fort Michilimackinac, on the straits between Lake Michigan and Lake Huron; Fort Dearborn, on the site of what is now Chicago; Fort Detroit; and Fort Niagara, at the mouth of the Niagara River on Lake Ontario. (*Map 15*) The actual strength of the Regular Army in June 1812 totaled approximately 11,744 officers and men, including an estimated 5,000 recruits enlisted for the additional force authorized the preceding January, in contrast to an authorized strength of 35,600. The Navy consisted of 20 vessels: the 3 large 44-gun frigates, 3 smaller frigates of the *Constellation* class rated at 38 guns, and 14 others.

Congress did not lack the will to prepare for war. In March 1812 it had tried to place the Army's supply system on a more adequate footing by establishing a Quartermaster Department on the military staff in place of the inefficient and costly military agent system. At the same time Congress created the Office of the Commissary General of Purchases in the War Department, and for the first time since the Revolution the Army's supply system was placed under the exclusive control of the Secretary of War. In May Congress had made provision for an Ordnance Department, responsible for the inspection and testing of all ordnance, cannon balls, shells, and shot, the construction of gun carriages and ammunition wagons, and the preparation and inspection of the "public powder." It enlarged the Corps of Engineers by adding a company of bombardiers, sappers, and miners, and expanded and reorganized the Military Academy at West Point. In addition to increasing the Regular Army, Congress had authorized the President to accept volunteer forces and to call upon the states for militia. The difficulty was not planning for an army, but raising one.

One of the world's major powers was ranged against the United States, but on the basis of available resources the two belligerents were rather evenly matched. Most of Britain's forces were tied up in the war against Napoleon, and for the time being very little military and naval assistance could be spared for the defense of Canada. At the outbreak of the war, there were approximately 7,000 British and Canadian Regulars in Upper and Lower Canada (now the provinces of Ontario and Quebec). With a total white population of only about half a million, Canada itself had only a small reservoir of militia to draw upon. When the war began, Maj. Gen. Isaac Brock, the military commander and civil governor of Upper Canada, had 800 militiamen available in addition to his approximately 1,600 Regulars. In the course of the war, the two provinces put a total of about 10,000 militia in the field, whereas in the United States probably 450,000 of the militia saw active service, although not more than half of them ever got near the front. The support of Indian tribes gave Canada one source of manpower that the United States lacked. After the Battle of Tippe-

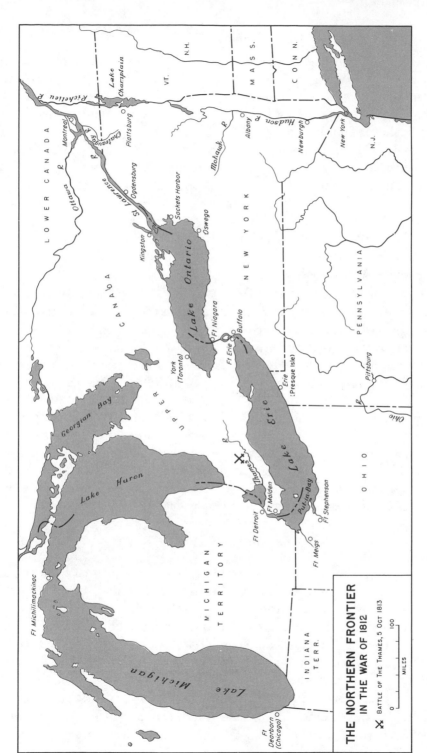

N. H.

MASS.

CONN.

VT.

Lake Champlain

Plattsburg

Richelieu R.

Montreal

LOWER CANADA

Ottawa R.

St. Lawrence R.

Chateaugay R.

Ogdensburg

Sackets Harbor

Oswego

Kingston

Lake Ontario

Mohawk R.

Albany

Hudson R.

Newburgh

New York

N. J.

NEW YORK

CANADA

Ft. Niagara

Buffalo

Ft. Erie

York (Toronto)

Erie (Presque Isle)

PENNSYLVANIA

Pittsburg

Ohio R.

UPPER

Georgian Bay

Lake Erie

Lake Huron

Thames R.

Ft. Malden

Put-in-Bay

Ft. Stephenson

Ft. Detroit

OHIO

Ft. Michilimackinac

MICHIGAN TERRITORY

Ft. Meigs

Lake Michigan

INDIANA TERR.

Ft. Dearborn (Chicago)

THE NORTHERN FRONTIER
IN THE WAR OF 1812

✕ BATTLE OF THE THAMES, 5 OCT 1813

0   100

MILES

MAP 15

canoe, Tecumseh had led his warriors across the border into Canada, where, along with the Canadian Indians, they joined the forces opposing the Americans. Perhaps 3,500 Indians were serving in the Canadian forces during the Thames River campaign in the fall of 1813, probably the largest number that took the field at any one time during the war.

The bulk of the British Navy was also fighting in the war against Napoleon. In September 1812, three months after the outbreak of war with the United States, Britain had no more than eleven ships of the line, thirty-four frigates, and about an equal number of smaller naval vessels in the western Atlantic. These were all that could be spared for operations in American waters, which involved the tremendous task of escorting British merchant shipping, protecting the St. Lawrence River, blockading American ports, and at the same time hunting down American frigates.

A significant weakness in the American position was the disunity of the country. In the New England states public opinion ranged from mere apathy to actively expressed opposition to the war. A good many Massachusetts and Connecticut shipowners fitted out privateers—privately owned and armed vessels that were commissioned to take enemy ships—but New England contributed little else to the prosecution of the war, and continued to sell grain and provisions to the British.

Canada was not faced with the same problem. Nevertheless, many inhabitants of Upper Canada were recent immigrants from the United States who had no great desire to take up arms against their former homeland, and there were other Canadians who thought that the superiority of the United States in men and material made any defense hopeless. That General Brock was able to overcome this spirit of defeatism is a tribute to his leadership.

The Strategic Pattern

The fundamental strategy was simple enough. The primary undertaking would be the conquest of Canada. The United States also planned an immediate naval offensive, whereby a swarm of privateers and the small Navy would be set loose on the high seas to destroy British commerce. The old invasion route into Canada by way of Lake Champlain and the Richelieu River led directly to the most populous and most important part of the enemy's territory. The capture of Montreal would cut the line of communications upon which the British defense of Upper Canada depended, and the fall of that province would then be inevitable. But this invasion route was near the center of disaffection in the United States, from which little local support could be expected. The west, where enthusiasm for the war ran high and where the Canadian forces were weak, offered a safer theater of operations though one with fewer strategic opportunities. Thus, in violation of the principles of objective and economy of force, the first assaults were delivered across the Detroit River and across the Niagara River between Lake Erie and Lake Ontario.

The war progressed through three distinct stages. In the first, lasting until the spring of 1813, England was so hard pressed in Europe that it could spare neither men nor ships in any great number for the conflict in North America. The United States was free to take the initiative, to invade Canada, and to send out cruisers and privateers against enemy shipping. During the second stage, lasting from early 1813 to the beginning of 1814, England was able to establish a tight blockade but still could not materially reinforce the troops in Canada. In this stage the American Army, having gained experience, won its first successes. The third stage, in 1814, was marked by the constant arrival in North America of British Regulars and naval reinforcements, which enabled the enemy to raid the North American coast almost at will and to take the offensive in several quarters. At the same time, in this final stage of the war, American forces fought their best fights and won their most brilliant victories.

The First Campaigns

The first blows of the war were struck in the Detroit area and at Fort Michilimackinac. President Madison gave Brig. Gen. William Hull, governor of the Michigan Territory, command of operations in that area. Hull arrived at Fort Detroit on July 5, 1812, with a force of about 1,500 Ohio militiamen and 300 Regulars, which he led across the river into Canada a week later. (*See Map 15.*) At that time the whole enemy force on the Detroit frontier amounted to about 150 British Regulars, 300 Canadian militiamen, and some 250 Indians led by Tecumseh. Most of the enemy were at Fort Malden, about twenty miles south of Detroit, on the Canadian side of the river. General Hull had been a dashing young officer in the Revolution, but by this time age and its infirmities had made him cautious and timid. Instead of moving directly against Fort Malden, Hull issued a bombastic proclamation to the people of Canada and stayed at the river landing almost opposite Detroit. He sent out several small raiding detachments along the Thames and Detroit Rivers, one of which returned after skirmishing with the British outposts near Fort Malden. In the meantime General Brock, who was both energetic and daring, sent a small party of British Regulars, Canadians, and Indians across the river from Malden to cut General Hull's communications with Ohio. By that time Hull was discouraged by the loss of Fort Michilimackinac, whose sixty defenders had quietly surrendered on July 17 to a small group of British Regulars supported by a motley force of fur traders and Indians that, at Brock's suggestion, had swiftly marched from St. Joseph Island, forty miles to the north. Hull also knew that the enemy in Fort Malden had received reinforcements (which he overestimated tenfold) and feared that Detroit would be completely cut off from its base of supplies. On August 7 he began to withdraw his force across the river into Fort Detroit. The last American had scarcely returned before the first men of Brock's force appeared and began setting up artillery opposite Detroit. By August 15 five guns were in position and opened fire on the fort, and the next morning Brock led his troops across the river. Before Brock could launch his assault, the Americans surrendered. Militiamen were released under parole; Hull and the Regulars were sent as prisoners to Montreal. Later paroled, Hull returned to face a court-martial for his conduct of the campaign, was sentenced to be shot, and was immediately pardoned.

On August 15, the day before the surrender, the small garrison at distant Fort Dearborn, acting on orders from Hull, had evacuated the post and started out for Detroit. The column was almost instantly attacked by a band of Indians who massacred the Americans before returning to destroy the fort.

With the fall of Michilimackinac, Detroit, and Dearborn, the entire territory north and west of Ohio fell under enemy control. The settlements in Indiana lay open to attack, the neighboring Indian tribes hastened to join the winning side, and the Canadians in the upper province lost some of the spirit of defeatism with which they had entered the war.

Immediately after taking Detroit, Brock transferred most of his troops to the Niagara frontier where he faced an American invasion force of 6,500 men. Maj. Gen. Stephen van Rensselaer, the senior American commander and a New York militiaman, was camped at Lewiston with a force of 900 Regulars and about 2,300 militiamen. Van Rensselaer owed his appointment not to any active military experience, for he had none, but to his family's position in New York. Inexperienced as he was in military art, van Rensselaer at least fought the enemy, which was more than could be said of the Regular Army commander in the theater, Brig. Gen. Alexander Smyth. Smyth and his 1,650 Regulars and nearly 400 militiamen were located at Buffalo. The rest of the American force, about 1,300 Regulars, was stationed at Fort Niagara.

Van Rensselaer planned to cross the narrow Niagara River and capture Queenston and its heights, a towering escarpment that ran perpendicular to the river south of the town. From this vantage point he hoped to command the area and eventually drive the British out of the Niagara peninsula. Smyth, on the other hand, wanted to attack above the falls, where the banks were low and the current less swift, and he refused to co-operate with the militia general. With a force ten times that of the British opposite him, van Rensselaer decided to attack alone. After one attempt had been called off for lack of oars for the boats, van Rensselaer finally ordered an attack for the morning of October 13. The assault force numbered 600 men, roughly half New York militiamen; but several boats drifted beyond the landing area, and the first echelon to land, numbering far less than 500, was pinned down for a time on the river bank below the heights until the men found an unguarded path, clambered to the summit, and, surprising the enemy, overwhelmed his fortified battery and drove him down into Queenston.

The Americans repelled a hastily formed counterattack later in the morning, during which General Brock was killed. This, however, was the high point of van Rensselaer's fortunes. Although 1,300 men were successfully ferried across the river under persistent British fire from a fortified battery north of town, less than half of them ever reached the American line on the heights. Most of the militiamen refused to cross the river, insisting on their legal right to remain on American soil, and General Smyth ignored van Rensselaer's request for Regulars. Meanwhile, British and Canadian reinforcements arrived in Queenston, and Maj. Gen. Roger Sheaffe, General Brock's successor, began to advance on the American position with a force of 800 troops and 300 Indian skirmishers. Van Rensselaer's men, tired and outnumbered, put up a stiff resistance on the heights but in the end were defeated—300 Americans were killed or wounded and nearly 1,000 were captured.

After the defeat at Queenston, van Rensselaer resigned and was succeeded by the unreliable Smyth, who spent his time composing windy proclamations. Disgusted at being marched down to the river on several occasions only to be marched back to camp again, the new army that had assembled after the battle of Queenston gradually melted away. The men who remained lost all sense of discipline, and finally at the end of November the volunteers were ordered home and the Regulars were sent into winter quarters. General Smyth's request for leave was hastily granted, and three months later his name was quietly dropped from the Army rolls.

Except for minor raids across the frozen St. Lawrence, there was no further fighting along the New York frontier until the following spring. During the Niagara campaign the largest force then under arms, commanded by Maj. Gen. Henry Dearborn, had been held in the neighborhood of Albany, more than 250 miles from the scene of operations. Dearborn had had a good record in the Revolutionary War and had served as Jefferson's Secretary of War. Persuaded to accept the command of the northern theater, except for Hull's forces, he was in doubt for some time about the extent of his authority over the Niagara front. When it was clarified he was reluctant to exercise it. Proposing to move his army, which included seven regiments of Regulars with artillery and dragoons, against Montreal in conjunction with a simultaneous operation across the Niagara River, Dearborn was content to wait for his subordinates to make the first move. When van Rensselaer made his attempt against Queenston, Dearborn, who was still in the vicinity of Albany, showed no sign of marching toward Canada. At the beginning of November he sent a large force north to Plattsburg and announced that he would personally lead the army into Montreal, but most of his force got no farther than the border. When his advanced guard was driven back to the village of Champlain by Canadian militiamen and Indians, and his Vermont and New York volunteers flatly refused to cross the border, Dearborn quietly turned around and marched back to Plattsburg, where he went into winter quarters.

If the land campaigns of 1812 reflected little credit on the Army, the war at sea brought lasting glory to the infant Navy. Until the end of the year the American frigates, brigs-of-war, and privateers were able to slip in and out of harbors and cruise almost at will, and in this period they won their most brilliant victories. At the same time, American privateers were picking off English merchant vessels by the hundreds. Having need of American foodstuffs, Britain was at first willing to take advantage of New England's opposition to the war by not extending the blockade to the New England coast, but by the beginning of 1814 it was effectively blockading the whole coast and had driven most American naval vessels and privateers off the high seas.

The Second Year, 1813

On land, the objects of the American plan of campaign for 1813 were the recapture of Detroit and an attack on Canada across Lake Ontario. (*See Map 15.*) For the Detroit campaign, Madison picked Brig. Gen. William H. Harrison, governor of the Indian Territory and hero of Tippecanoe. The difficulties of a winter campaign were tremendous, but the country demanded action. Harrison therefore started north toward Lake Erie at the end of October 1812 with some 6,500 men. In January 1813 a sizable detachment, about 1,000, pushed on to Frenchtown, a small Canadian outpost on the Raisin River twenty-six miles south of Detroit. There the American commander, Brig. Gen. James Winchester, positioned his men, their backs to the river with scant natural protection and their movements severely hampered by deep snow. A slightly larger force of British Regulars, militiamen, and Indians under Col. Henry Proctor soundly defeated the Americans, killing over 100 Kentucky riflemen and capturing approximately 500. The brutal massacre of wounded American prisoners by their Indian guards made "Remember the Raisin" the rallying cry of the Northwestern Army, but any plans for revenge had to be postponed, for Harrison had decided to suspend operations for the winter. He built Forts Meigs and Stephenson and posted his army near the Michigan border at the western end of Lake Erie.

The Ontario campaign was entrusted to General Dearborn, who was ordered to move his army from Plattsburg to Sackett's Harbor, where Commodore Isaac Chauncey had been assembling a fleet. Dearborn was to move across the lake to capture Kingston and destroy the British flotilla there, then proceed to York (now Toronto), the capital of Upper Canada, to capture military stores, and finally he was to co-operate with a force from Buffalo in seizing the forts on the Canadian side of the Niagara River.

The American strategy was sound. The capture of Kingston, the only tenable site for a naval station on the Canadian side of Lake Ontario, would give the United States control of the lake and, by cutting the British lines of communications, frustrate enemy plans for operations in the west. After the fall of Kingston, the operations against York and the Niagara forts would be simple mopping-up exercises. When the time came to move, however, Dearborn and Chauncey, hearing a rumor that the British forces in Kingston had been reinforced, decided to bypass that objective and attack York first. About 1,700 men were embarked and sailed up Lake Ontario without incident, arriving off York before daybreak on April 27. Dearborn, who was in poor health, turned over the command of the assault to Brig. Gen. Zebulon Pike, the explorer of the Southwest. The landing, about four miles west of the town, was virtually unopposed. The British garrison of about 600 men, occupying a fortification about halfway between the town and the landing, was overwhelmed after sharp resistance, but just as the Americans were pushing through the fort toward the town, a powder magazine exploded, killing or disabling many Americans and a number of British soldiers. Among those killed was General Pike. Remnants of the garrison fled toward Kingston, 150 miles to the east. The losses were heavy on both sides—almost 20 percent of Dearborn's forces had been killed or wounded. With General Dearborn incapacitated and General Pike dead, the troops apparently got out of hand. They looted and burned the public buildings and destroyed the provincial records. After holding the town for about a week, they recrossed the lake to Niagara to join an attack against the forts on the Canadian side of the Niagara River.

Meanwhile, Sackett's Harbor had been almost stripped of troops for the raid on York and for reinforcing the army at Fort Niagara. At Kingston, across the lake, Sir George Prevost, the Governor-General of Canada, had assembled a force of 800 British Regulars in addition to militia. Taking advantage of the absence of Chauncey's fleet, which was at the other end of the lake, Prevost launched an attack on Sackett's Harbor with his entire force of Regulars on the night of May 26. The town was defended by about 400 Regulars and approximately 750 militiamen, under the command of Brig. Gen. Jacob Brown of the New York militia. Brown posted his men in two lines in front of a fortified battery to cover a possible landing. Coming ashore under heavy fire the British nevertheless pressed rapidly forward, routed the first line, and pushed the second back into the prepared defenses. There the Americans held. The British then tried two frontal assaults, but were repulsed with heavy losses. While they were re-forming for a third attack, General Brown rallied the militia and sent them toward the rear of the enemy's right flank. This was the turning point. Having suffered serious losses and in danger of being cut off, the British hurriedly withdrew to their ships.

On the same day that Prevost sailed against Sackett's Harbor, General Dearborn at the western end of Lake Ontario was invading Canada with an army of 4,000 men. The operation began with a well-executed and stubbornly resisted amphibious assault led by Col. Winfield Scott and Commander Oliver Hazard Perry, USN, with Chauncey's fleet providing fire support. Outnumbered more than two to one, the British retreated, abandoning Fort George and Queenston to the Americans. (*Map 16*) An immediate pursuit might have sealed the victory, but Dearborn, after occupying Fort George, waited several days and then sent about 2,000 men after the enemy. The detachment advanced to within ten miles of the British and camped for the night with slight regard for security and even less for the enemy's audacity. During the night a force of about 700 British attacked the camp and thoroughly routed the Americans. Dearborn withdrew his entire army to Fort George. About two weeks later, a 500-man detachment ventured fifteen miles outside the fort and surrendered to a force of British and Indians that was half as large. After these reverses there was no further action of consequence on the Niagara front for the remainder of the year. Dearborn, again incapacitated by illness, resigned his commission in early July. Both armies were hard hit by disease, and the

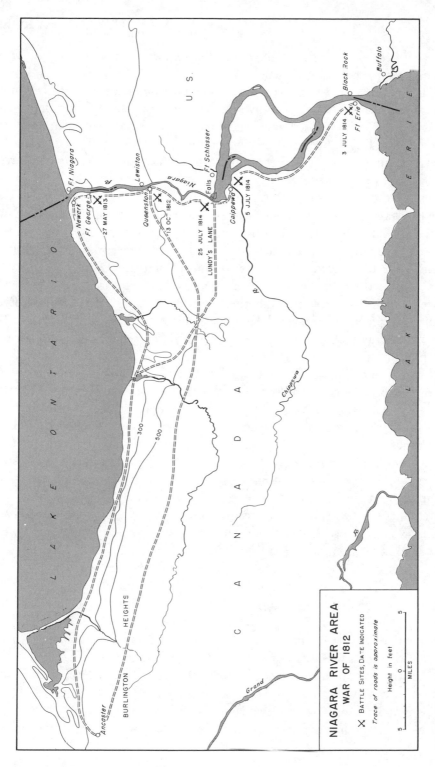

NIAGARA RIVER AREA
WAR OF 1812

X BATTLE SITES, DATE INDICATED

Trace of roads is approximate

Height in feet

MILES

MAP 16

American forces were further reduced by the renewal of the war in the west and by an attempt against Montreal.

Hull's disaster at Detroit in 1812 and Harrison's unsuccessful winter campaign had clearly shown that any offensive action in that quarter depended upon first gaining control of Lake Erie. Commander Perry had been assigned the task of building a fleet and seizing control of the lake. Throughout the spring and summer of 1813, except for the time he had joined Dearborn's force, the 27-year-old Perry had been busy at Presque Isle assembling his fleet, guns, and crews. By the beginning of August his force was superior to that of the British in every respect except long-range armament. Sailing up the lake, he anchored in Put-in-Bay, near the line still held by General Harrison in the vicinity of Forts Meigs and Stephenson, and there on September 10 Perry met the British Fleet, defeated it, and gained control of Lake Erie.

As soon as the damage to Perry's ships and the captured British vessels had been repaired, Harrison embarked his army and sailed against Fort Malden. A regiment of mounted Kentucky riflemen under Col. Richard M. Johnson moved along the shore of the lake toward Detroit. Vastly outnumbered on land and now open to attack from the water, the British abandoned both Forts Malden and Detroit and retreated eastward. Leaving a detachment to garrison the forts, Harrison set out after the enemy with the Kentucky cavalry regiments, five brigades of Kentucky volunteers, and a part of the 27th Infantry, a force of about 3,500 men. On October 5 he made contact with the British on the banks of the Thames River about eighty-five miles from Malden. (See Map 15.) The enemy numbered about 2,900, of whom about 900 were British Regulars and the remainder Indians under Tecumseh. Instead of attacking with infantry in the traditional line-against-line fashion, Harrison ordered a mounted attack. The maneuver succeeded completely. Unable to withstand the charging Kentuckians, the British surrendered in droves. The Indians were routed, and Tecumseh, who had brought so much trouble to the western frontier, was killed. Among those who distinguished themselves on that day was Commander Perry, who had ridden in the front rank of Johnson's charge.

As a result of the victory, which illustrated successful employment of the principles of offensive and mass, Lake Erie became an American lake. The Indian confederacy was shattered. The American position on the Detroit frontier was re-established, a portion of Canadian territory was brought under American control, and the enemy threat in that sector was eliminated. There was no further fighting here for the rest of the war.

The small remnant of the British force that had escaped capture at the Thames—no more than 250 soldiers and a few Indians—made its way overland to the head of Lake Ontario. Harrison, after discharging his Kentucky volunteers and arranging for the defenses of the Michigan Territory, sailed after it with the remainder of his army. He arrived at the Niagara frontier at an opportune time, since the American forces in that theater were being called upon to support a 2-pronged drive against Montreal.

The expedition against Montreal in the fall of 1813 was one of the worst fiascoes of the war. It involved a simultaneous drive by two forces: one, an army of about 4,000 men assembled at Plattsburg on Lake Champlain under the command of Brig. Gen. Wade Hampton and another, of about 6,000 men under the command of Maj. Gen. James Wilkinson, which was to attack down the St. Lawrence River from Sackett's Harbor. Hampton and Wilkinson were scarcely on speaking terms, and there was no one on the spot to command the two of them. Neither had sufficient strength to capture Montreal without the other's aid; each lacked confidence in the other, and both suspected that the War Department was leaving them in the lurch. At first contact with the British, about halfway down the Chateaugay River, Hampton retreated and, after falling back all the way to Plattsburg, resigned from the Army. Wilkinson, after a detachment of about 2,000 men was severely mauled in an engagement just north of Ogdensburg, also abandoned his part of the operation and followed Hampton into Plattsburg.

In the meantime, during December 1813 the British took advantage of the weakened state of American forces on the Niagara frontier to recapture Fort George and to cross the river and take Fort Niagara, which remained in British hands until the end of the war. Before evacuating Fort George the Americans had burned the town of Newark and part of Queenston. In retaliation the British, after assaulting Fort Niagara with unusual ferocity, loosed their Indian allies on the surrounding countryside and burned the town of Buffalo and the nearby village of Black Rock.

During 1813 a new theater of operations opened in the south. Andrew Jackson, an ardent expansionist and commander of the Tennessee militia, wrote the Secretary of War that he would "rejoice at the opportunity of placing the American eagle on the ramparts of Mobile, Pensacola, and Fort St. Augustine." (*Map 17*) For this purpose Tennessee had raised a force of 2,000 men to be under Jackson's command. Congress, after much debate, approved only an expedition into that part of the gulf coast in dispute between the United States and Spain, and refused to entrust the venture to the Tennesseans. Just before he went north to take part in the Montreal expedition, General Wilkinson led his Regulars into the disputed part of West Florida and, without meeting any

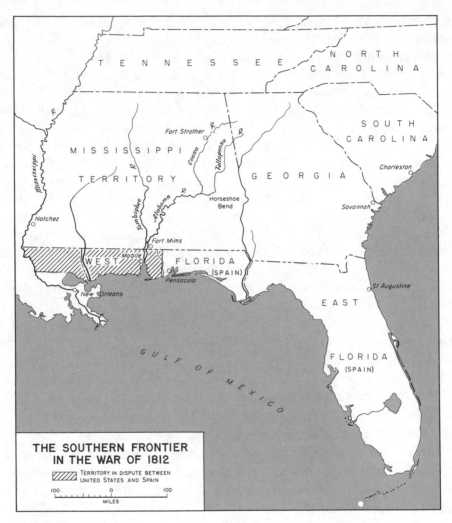

THE SOUTHERN FRONTIER
IN THE WAR OF 1812

Territory in dispute between
United States and Spain

100 ___ 0 ___ 100
MILES

MAP 17

resistance, occupied Mobile, while the Tennessee army was left cooling its heels
in Natchez.

An Indian uprising in that part of the Mississippi Territory soon to become
Alabama saved General Jackson's military career. Inspired by Tecumseh's
earlier successes, the Creek Indians took to the warpath in the summer of 1813
with a series of outrages culminating in the massacre of more than 500 men,
women, and children at Fort Mims. Jackson, with characteristic energy, reas-
sembled his army, which had been dismissed after Congress rejected its services

for an attack on Florida, and moved into the Mississippi Territory. His own energy added to his problems, for he completely outran his primitive supply system and dangerously extended his line of communications. The hardships of the campaign and one near defeat at the hands of the Indians destroyed any enthusiasm the militia might have had for continuing in service. Jackson was compelled to entrench at Fort Strother, on the Coosa River, and remain there for several months until the arrival of a regiment of the Regular Army gave him the means to deal with the mutinous militia. At the end of March 1814 he decided that he had sufficient strength for a decisive blow against the Indians, who had gathered a force of about 900 warriors and many women and children in a fortified camp at the Horseshoe Bend of the Tallapoosa River. Jackson had about 2,000 militia and volunteers, nearly 600 Regulars, several hundred friendly Indians, and a few pieces of artillery. The attack was completely successful. A bayonet charge led by the Regulars routed the Indians, who were ruthlessly hunted down and all but a hundred or so of the warriors were killed. "I lament that two or three women and children were killed by accident," Jackson later reported. The remaining hostile tribes fled into Spanish territory. As one result of the campaign Jackson was appointed a major general in the Regular Army. The campaign against the Creeks had no other effect on the outcome of the war, but for that matter neither had any of the campaigns in the north up to this point.

Fighting also broke out during 1813 along the east coast where a British fleet blockaded the Delaware and Chesapeake Bays, bottling up the American frigates *Constellation* at Norfolk and *Adams* in the Potomac. (*Map 18*) Opposed only by small American gunboats, the British under Admiral Sir John Warren sought "to chastise the Americans into submission," and at the same time to relieve the pressure on Prevost's forces in Canada. With a flotilla, which at times numbered fifteen ships, Rear Adm. Sir George Cockburn, Warren's second-in-command, roamed the Chesapeake during the spring of 1813, burning and looting the prosperous countryside. Reinforced in June by 2,600 Regulars, Warren decided to attack Norfolk, its navy yard and the anchored *Constellation* providing the tempting targets. Norfolk's defenses rested chiefly on Craney Island, which guarded the narrow channel of the Elizabeth River. The island had a 7-gun fortification and was manned by 580 Regulars and militia in addition to 150 sailors and marines from the *Constellation*. The British planned to land an 800-man force on the mainland and, when low tide permitted, march onto the island in a flanking movement. As the tide rose, another 500 men would be rowed across the shoals for a frontal assault. On June 22 the landing party debarked four miles northwest of the island, but the flanking move was

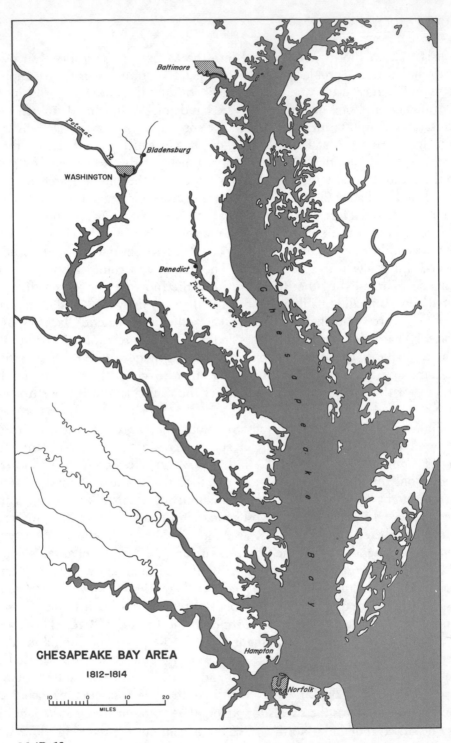

Baltimore

Potomac

Bladensburg

WASHINGTON

Benedict

Patuxent R.

Chesapeake Bay

Hampton

Norfolk

CHESAPEAKE BAY AREA

1812-1814

10   0   10   20
MILES

MAP 18

countered by the highly accurate marksmanship of the *Constellation's* gunners and was forced to pull back. The frontal assault also suffered from well-directed American fire, which sank three barges and threw the rest into confusion. After taking 81 casualties, the British sailed off in disorder. The defenders counted no casualties.

Frustrated at Norfolk, Warren crossed the Roads to Hampton where he overwhelmed the 450 militia defenders and pillaged the town. A portion of the fleet remained in the bay for the rest of the year, blockading and marauding, but the operation was not an unalloyed success. It failed to cause a diversion of American troops from the northern border and, by strengthening popular resentment (Cockburn was vilified throughout the country), helped unite Americans behind the war effort.

The conduct of the war in 1812 and 1813 revealed deficiencies in the administration of the War Department that would plague the American cause to the end. In early 1813 Madison replaced his incompetent Secretary of War William Eustis with John Armstrong, who instituted a reorganization that eventually resulted in the substitution of younger, more aggressive field commanders for the aged veterans of the Revolution. Congress then authorized an expansion of the Army staff to help the Secretary manage the war. In March it re-created the offices of Adjutant General, Inspector General, Surgeon, and Apothecary General and assigned eight topographical Engineers to the staff.

Competent leadership meant little, however, without sufficient logistical support, and logistics, more than any other factor, determined the nature of the military campaigns of the war. Lack of transportation was a major problem. The United States was fighting a war on widely separated fronts that required moving supplies through a wilderness where roads had to be built for wagons and packhorses. For this reason, ammunition and clothing supplies proved inadequate. General Harrison had to depend on homemade cartridges and clothing from Ohio townsmen for his northwestern campaign, and General Scott's Regulars would fight at Chippewa in the gray uniforms of the New York militia. Winter found the troops without blankets, inadequately housed, and without forage for their horses. Most important, the subsistence supply failed so completely that field commanders found it necessary to take local food procurement virtually into their own hands.

Transportation difficulties accounted for only part of the problem. The supply system devised in 1812 proved a resounding failure. Congressional intent notwithstanding, the Quartermaster General had never assumed accountability for the money and property administered by his subordinates or administrative control over his deputies in the south and northwest. Moreover, the functions of his office, never clearly defined, overlapped those of the Commissary General. In a vain attempt to unravel the administrative tangle, Congress created the office of Superintendent General of Military Supplies to keep account of all military stores and reformed the Quartermaster Department, giving the Quartermaster General stricter control over his deputies. In practice, however, the deputies continued to act independently in their own districts.

Both Congress and the War Department overlooked the greatest need for reform as the Army continued to rely on contractors for the collection and delivery of rations for the troops. With no centralized direction for subsistence supply, the inefficient, fraud-racked contract system proved to be one of the gravest hindrances to military operations throughout the war.

The Last Year of the War, 1814

After the setbacks at the end of 1813, a lull descended on the northern frontier. In March 1814 Wilkinson made a foray from Plattsburg with about 4,000 men and managed to penetrate about eight miles into Canada before some 200 British and Canadian troops stopped his advance. It was an even more miserable failure than his attempt of the preceding fall.

In early 1814 Congress increased the Army to 45 infantry regiments, 4 regiments of riflemen, 3 of artillery, 2 of light dragoons, and 1 of light artillery. The number of general officers was fixed at 6 major generals and 16 brigadier generals in addition to the generals created by brevet. Secretary of War Armstrong promoted Jacob Brown, who had been commissioned a brigadier general in the Regular Army after his heroic defense of Sackett's Harbor, to the rank of major general and placed him in command of the Niagara–Lake Ontario theater. He also promoted the youthful George Izard to major general and gave him command of the Lake Champlain frontier. He appointed six new brigadier generals from the ablest, but not necessarily most senior, colonels in the Regular Army, among them Winfield Scott, who had distinguished himself at the battle of Queenston Heights and who was now placed in command at Buffalo.

British control of Lake Ontario, won by dint of feverish naval construction during the previous winter, obliged the Secretary of War to recommend operations from Buffalo, but disagreement within the President's cabinet delayed adoption of a plan until June. Expecting Commodore Chauncey's naval force at Sackett's Harbor to be strong enough to challenge the British Fleet, Washington decided upon a co-ordinated attack on the Niagara peninsula. (See Map 16.) Secretary Armstrong instructed General Brown to cross the Niagara

River in the vicinity of Fort Erie and, after assaulting the fort, either to move against Fort George and Newark or to seize and hold a bridge over the Chippewa River, as he saw fit.

Brown accordingly crossed the Niagara River on July 3 with his force of 3,500 men, took Fort Erie, and then advanced toward the Chippewa River, sixteen miles away. There a smaller British force, including 1,500 Regulars, had gathered to oppose the Americans. General Brown posted his army in a strong position behind a creek with his right flank resting on the Niagara River and his left protected by a swamp. In front of the American position was an open plain, beyond which flowed the Chippewa River; on the other side of the river were the British.

In celebration of Independence Day, General Scott had promised his brigade a grand parade on the plain the next day. On July 5 he formed his troops, numbering about 1,300, but on moving forward discovered British Regulars who had crossed the river undetected, lined up on the opposite edge of the plain. Scott ordered his men to charge and the British advanced to meet them. The two lines approached each other, alternately stopping to fire and then moving forward, closing the gaps torn by musketry and artillery fire. They came together first at the flanks, while about sixty or eighty yards apart at the center. At this point the British line crumbled and broke. By the time a second brigade sent forward by General Brown reached the battlefield, the British had withdrawn across the Chippewa River and were retreating toward Ancaster, on Lake Ontario. Scott's casualties amounted to 48 killed and 227 wounded; British losses were 137 killed and 304 wounded.

Brown followed the retreating British as far as Queenston, where he halted to await Commodore Chauncey's fleet. After waiting two weeks for Chauncey, who failed to co-operate in the campaign, Brown withdrew to Chippewa. He proposed to strike out to Ancaster by way of a crossroad known as Lundy's Lane, from which he could reach the Burlington Heights at the head of Lake Ontario and at the rear of the British.

Meanwhile the British had drawn reinforcements from York and Kingston, and more troops were on the way from Lower Canada. Sixteen thousand British veterans, fresh from Wellington's victories over the French in Europe, had just arrived in Canada, too late to participate in the Niagara campaign but in good time to permit the redeployment of the troops that had been defending the upper St. Lawrence. By the time General Brown decided to pull back from Queenston, the British force at Ancaster amounted to about 2,200 men under General Phineas Riall; another 1,500 British troops were gathered at Fort George and Fort Niagara at the mouth of the Niagara River.

As soon as Brown began his withdrawal, Riall sent forward about 1,000 men along Lundy's Lane, the very route by which General Brown intended to advance against Burlington Heights; another force of more than 600 British moved out from Fort George and followed Brown along the Queenston road; while a third enemy force of about 400 men moved along the American side of the Niagara River from Fort Niagara. Riall's advance force reached the junction of Lundy's Lane and the Queenston road on the night of July 24, the same night that Brown reached Chippewa, about three miles distant. Concerned lest the British force on the opposite side of the Niagara cut his line of communications and entirely unaware of Riall's force at Lundy's Lane, General Brown on July 25 ordered Scott to take his brigade back along the road toward Queenston in the hope of drawing back the British force on the other side of the Niagara; but in the meantime that force had crossed the river and joined Riall's men at Lundy's Lane. Scott had not gone far when much to his surprise he discovered himself face-to-face with the enemy.

The ensuing battle, most of which took place after nightfall, was the hardest fought, most stubbornly contested engagement of the war. For two hours Scott attacked and repulsed the counterattacks of the numerically superior British force, which, moreover, had the advantage in position. Then both sides were reinforced. With Brown's whole contingent engaged the Americans now had a force equal to that of the British, about 2,900. They were able to force back the enemy from its position and capture its artillery. The battle then continued without material advantage to either side until just before midnight, when General Brown ordered the exhausted Americans to fall back to their camp across the Chippewa River. The equally exhausted enemy was unable to follow. Losses on both sides had been heavy, each side incurring about 850 casualties. On the American side, both General Brown and General Scott were severely wounded, Scott so badly that he saw no further service during the war. On the British side, General Riall and his superior, General Drummond, who had arrived with the reinforcements, were wounded, and Riall was taken prisoner.

Both sides claimed Lundy's Lane as a victory, as well they might; but Brown's invasion of Canada was halted. Commodore Chauncey, who failed to prevent the British from using Lake Ontario for supply and reinforcements, contributed to the unfavorable outcome. In contrast to the splendid co-operation between Harrison and Perry on Lake Erie, relations between Brown and Chauncey were far from satisfactory. A few days after the Battle of Lundy's Lane the American army withdrew to Fort Erie and held this outpost on Canadian soil until early in November.

Reinforced after Lundy's Lane, the British laid siege to Fort Erie at the beginning of August but were forced to abandon the effort on September 21 after heavy losses. Shortly afterward General Izard arrived with reinforcements from Plattsburg and advanced as far as Chippewa, where the British were strongly entrenched. After a few minor skirmishes, he ceased operations for the winter. The works at Fort Erie were destroyed, and the army withdrew to American soil on November 5.

During the summer of 1814 the British had been able to reinforce Canada and to stage several raids on the American coast. Eastport, Maine, on Passamaquoddy Bay, and Castine, at the mouth of the Penobscot River, were occupied without resistance. This operation was something more than a raid since Eastport lay in disputed territory, and it was no secret that Britain wanted a rectification of the boundary. No such political object was attached to British forays in the region of Chesapeake Bay. (*See Map 18.*) On August 19 a force of some 4,000 British troops under Maj. Gen. Robert Ross landed on the Patuxent River and marched on Washington. At the Battle of Bladensburg, five days later, Ross easily dispersed 5,000 militia, naval gunners, and Regulars hastily gathered together to defend the Capital. The British then entered Washington, burned the Capitol, the White House, and other public buildings, and returned to their ships.

Baltimore was next on the schedule, but that city had been given time to prepare its defenses. The land approach was covered by a rather formidable line of redoubts; the harbor was guarded by Fort McHenry and blocked by a line of sunken gunboats. On September 13 a spirited engagement fought by Maryland militia, many of whom had run at Bladensburg just two weeks before, delayed the invaders and caused considerable loss, including General Ross, who was killed. When the fleet failed to reduce Fort McHenry, the assault on the city was called off.

Two days before the attack on Baltimore, the British suffered a much more serious repulse on Lake Champlain. After the departure of General Izard for the Niagara front, Brig. Gen. Alexander Macomb had remained at Plattsburg with a force of about 3,300 men. Supporting this force was a small fleet under Commodore Thomas Macdonough. Across the border in Canada was an army of British veterans of the Napoleonic Wars whom Sir George Prevost was to lead down the route taken by Burgoyne thirty-seven years before. Moving slowly up the Richelieu River toward Lake Champlain, he crossed the border and on September 6 arrived before Plattsburg with about 11,000 men. There he waited for almost a week until his naval support was ready to join the attack. With militia reinforcements, Macomb now had about 4,500 men manning a strong line of redoubts and blockhouses that faced a small river. Macdonough had an-chored his vessels in Plattsburg Bay, out of range of British guns, but in a position to resist an assault on the American line. On September 11 the British flotilla appeared and Prevost ordered a joint attack. There was no numerical disparity between the naval forces, but an important one in the quality of the seamen. Macdonough's ships were manned by well-trained seamen and gunners, the British ships by hastily recruited French-Canadian militia and soldiers, with only a sprinkling of regular seamen. As the enemy vessels came into the bay the wind died, and the British were exposed to heavy raking fire from Macdonough's long guns. The British worked their way in, came to anchor, and the two fleets began slugging at each other, broadside by broadside. At the end the British commander was dead and his ships battered into submission. Prevost immedi-ately called off the land attack and withdrew to Canada the next day.

Macdonough's victory ended the gravest threat that had arisen so far. More important it gave impetus to peace negotiations then under way. News of the two setbacks—Baltimore and Plattsburg—reached England simultaneously, aggra-vating the war weariness of the British and bolstering the efforts of the American peace commissioners to obtain satisfactory terms.

New Orleans: The Final Battle

The progress of the peace negotiations influenced the British to continue an operation that General Ross, before his repulse and death at Baltimore, had been instructed to carry out, a descent upon the gulf coast to capture New Orleans and possibly sever Louisiana from the United States. (See Map 17.) Major General Sir Edward Pakenham was sent to America to take command of the expedition. On Christmas Day, 1814, Pakenham arrived at the mouth of the Mississippi to find his troops disposed on a narrow isthmus below New Orleans between the Mississippi River and a cypress swamp. They had landed two weeks earlier at a shallow lagoon some ten miles east of New Orleans and had already fought one engagement. In this encounter, on December 23, General Jackson, who had taken command of the defenses on December 1, almost succeeded in cutting off an advance detachment of 2,000 British, but after a 3-hour fight in which casualties on both sides were heavy, he was compelled to retire behind fortifications covering New Orleans.

Opposite the British and behind a ditch stretching from the river to the swamp, Jackson had raised earthworks high enough to require scaling ladders for an assault. The defenses were manned by about 3,500 men with another 1,000 in reserve. It was a varied group, composed of the 7th and 44th Infantry Regi-

BATTLE OF NEW ORLEANS

ments, Major Beale's New Orleans Sharpshooters, LaCoste and Daquin's battalions of free Negroes, the Louisiana militia under General David Morgan, a band of Choctaw Indians, the Baratorian pirates, and a motley battalion of fashionably dressed sons and brothers of the New Orleans aristocracy. To support his defenses, Jackson had assembled more than twenty pieces of artillery, including a battery of nine heavy guns on the opposite bank of the Mississippi.

After losing an artillery duel to the Americans on January 1, Pakenham decided on a frontal assault in combination with an attack against the American troops on the west bank. The main assault was to be delivered by about 5,300 men, while about 600 men under Lt. Col. William Thornton were to cross the river and clear the west bank. As the British columns appeared out of the early morning mist on January 8, they were met with murderous fire, first from the artillery, then from the muskets and rifles of Jackson's infantry. Achieving mass through firepower, the Americans mowed the British down by the hundreds. Pakenham and one other general were killed and a third badly wounded. More than 2,000 of the British were casualties; the American losses were trifling.

Suddenly, the battle on the west bank became critical. Jackson did not make adequate preparations to meet the advance there until the British began their movement, but by then it was too late. The heavy guns of a battery posted on the west bank were not placed to command an attack along that side of the river and only about 800 militia, divided in two groups a mile apart, were in position to oppose Thornton. The Americans resisted stubbornly, inflicting greater losses than they suffered, but the British pressed on, routed them, and overran the battery. Had the British continued their advance Jackson's position would have been critical, but Pakenham's successor in command, appalled by the repulse of the main assault, ordered Thornton to withdraw from the west bank and rejoin the main force. For ten days the shattered remnant of Pakenham's army remained in camp unmolested by the Americans, then re-embarked and sailed away.

The British appeared off Mobile on February 8, confirming Jackson's fear that they planned an attack in that quarter. They overwhelmed Fort Bowyer, a garrison manned by 360 Regulars at the entrance to Mobile Harbor. Before they could attack the city itself, word arrived that a treaty had been signed at Ghent on Christmas Eve, two weeks before the Battle of New Orleans.

The news of the peace settlement followed so closely on Jackson's triumph in New Orleans that the war as a whole was popularly regarded in the United States as a great victory. Yet at best it was a draw. American strategy had centered on the conquest of Canada and the harassment of British shipping; but the land campaign failed, and during most of the war the Navy was bottled up behind a tight British blockade of the North American coast.

If it favored neither belligerent, the war at least taught the Americans several lessons. Although the Americans were proud of their reputation as the world's most expert riflemen, the rifle played only a minor role in the war. On the other hand, the American soldier displayed unexpected superiority in gunnery and engineering. Artillery contributed to American successes at Chippewa, Sackett's Harbor, Norfolk, the siege of Fort Erie, and New Orleans. The war also boosted the reputation of the Corps of Engineers, a branch which owed its efficiency chiefly to the Military Academy. Academy graduates completed the fortifications at Fort Erie, built Fort Meigs, planned the harbor defenses of Norfolk and New York, and directed the fortifications at Plattsburg. If larger numbers of infantrymen had been as well trained as the artillerymen and engineers, the course of the war might have been entirely different.

Sea power played a fundamental role in the war. In the west both opponents were handicapped in overland communication, but the British were far more dependent on the Great Lakes for the movement of troops and supplies for the defense of Upper Canada. In the east, Lake Champlain was strategically important as an invasion corridor to the populous areas of both countries. Just as Perry's victory on Lake Erie decided the outcome of the war in the far west, Macdonough's success on Lake Champlain decided the fate of the British invasion in 1814 and helped influence the peace negotiations.

The militia performed as well as the Regular Army. The defeats and humiliations of the Regular forces during the first years of the war matched those of the militia, just as in a later period the Kentucky volunteers at the Thames and the Maryland militia before Baltimore proved that the state citizen soldier could perform well. The keys to the militiaman's performance, of course, were training and leadership, the two areas over which the national government had little control. The militia, occasionally competent, was never dependable, and in the nationalistic period that followed the war when the exploits of the Regulars were justly celebrated, an ardent young Secretary of War, John Calhoun, would be able to convince Congress and the nation that the first line of defense should be a standing army.

CHAPTER 4

The Mexican War

Receiving by the new telegraph the news that James K. Polk had been elected to the Presidency in November 1844, President John Tyler interpreted the verdict as a mandate from the people for the annexation of Texas, since Polk had come out strongly in favor of annexation. On March 1, 1845, Congress jointly resolved to admit Texas into the Union and the Mexican Government promptly broke off diplomatic relations. President Polk continued to hope that he could settle by negotiation Mexico's claim to Texas and acquire Upper California by purchase as well. In mid-June, nevertheless, anticipating the Fourth of July acceptance by Texas of annexation, he ordered Bvt. Brig. Gen. Zachary Taylor to move his forces from Fort Jesup on the Louisiana border to a point "on or near" the Rio Grande to repel any invasion from Mexico.

The Period of Watchful Waiting

General Taylor selected a wide sandy plain at the mouth of the Nueces River near the hamlet of Corpus Christi and beginning July 23 sent most of his 1,500-man force by steamboat from New Orleans. Only his dragoons moved overland, via San Antonio. By mid-October, as shipments of Regulars continued to come in from all over the country, his forces had swollen to nearly 4,000, including some volunteers from New Orleans. A company of Texas Rangers served as the eyes and ears of the Army. For the next six months drilling, horse-breaking, and parades, interspersed with boredom and dissipation, went on at the big camp on the Nueces. Then in February Taylor received orders from Washington to advance to the Rio Grande. Negotiations with the Mexican Government had broken down.

The march of more than a hundred miles down the coast to the Rio Grande was led by Bvt. Maj. Samuel Ringgold's battery of "flying artillery," organized in late 1838 on orders from Secretary of War Joel R. Poinsett. It was the last word in mobility, for the cannoneers rode on horseback rather than on limbers and caissons. The rear was brought up by Taylor's supply train of three hundred wagons drawn by oxen. On March 23 the columns came to a road that forked left to Point Isabel, ten miles away on the coast, where Taylor's supply ships were waiting, and led on the right to his destination on the Rio Grande, some eighteen miles southwest, opposite the Mexican town of Matamoros. Sending the bulk of his army ahead, Taylor went to Point Isabel to set up his supply base, fill his wagons, and bring forward four 18-pounder siege guns from his ships.

At the boiling brown waters of the Rio Grande opposite Matamoros he built a strong fort, which he called Fort Texas, mounting his siege guns. At the same time he sent pacific messages to the Mexican commander on the opposite bank. These were countered by threats and warnings, and on April 25, the day after the arrival at Matamoros of General Mariano Arista with two or three thousand additional troops, by open hostilities. The Mexicans crossed the river in some force and attacked a reconnoitering detachment of sixty dragoons under Capt. Seth B. Thornton. They killed eleven men and captured Thornton and the rest, many of whom were wounded.

Taylor reported to President Polk that hostilities had commenced and called on Texas and Louisiana for about 5,000 militiamen. His immediate concern was that his supply base might be captured. Leaving an infantry regiment and a small detachment of artillery at Fort Texas under Maj. Jacob Brown, he set off May 1 with the bulk of his forces for Point Isabel, where he stayed nearly a week strengthening his fortifications. After loading two hundred supply wagons and acquiring two more ox-drawn 18-pounders, he began the return march to Fort Texas with his army of about 2,300 men on the afternoon of May 7. About noon next day near a clump of tall trees at a spot called Palo Alto, he saw across the open prairie a long dark line with bayonets and lances glistening in the sun. It was the Mexican Army.

The Battles of Palo Alto and Resaca de la Palma

General Arista's forces barring the road to Fort Texas stretched out on a front a mile long and were about 4,000 strong. Taylor, who had placed part of his force in the rear to guard the supply wagons, was outnumbered at least two to one; and in terrain that favored cavalry, Arista's cavalry overwhelmingly outnumbered Taylor's dragoons. But the American artillery was superior. Also, among Taylor's junior officers were a number of West Point graduates who were to make their reputations in the Civil War, notably 2d Lt. George G. Meade and 2d Lt. Ulysses S. Grant.

On the advice of the young West Pointers on his staff, Taylor emplaced his two 18-pounder iron siege guns in the center of his line and blasted the advancing Mexicans with canister. His field artillery—bronze 6-pounder guns firing solid shot and 12-pounder howitzers firing shell—in quick-moving attacks threw back Arista's flanks. The Mexicans were using old-fashioned bronze 4-pounders and 8-pounders that fired solid shot and had such short range that their fire did little damage. During the battle Lieutenant Grant saw their cannon balls striking the ground before they reached the American troops and ricocheting so slowly that the men could dodge them.

During the afternoon a gun wad set the dry grass afire, causing the battle to be suspended for nearly an hour. After it was resumed the Mexicans fell back rapidly. By nightfall when both armies went into bivouac, Mexican casualties, caused mostly by cannon fire, numbered about 320 killed and 380 wounded. Taylor lost only 9 men killed and 47 wounded. One of the mortally wounded was his brilliant artilleryman, Major Ringgold.

At daybreak the Americans saw the Mexicans in full retreat. Taylor decided to pursue but did not begin his advance until afternoon, spending the morning erecting defenses around his wagon train, which he intended to leave behind. About two o'clock he reached Resaca de la Palma, a dry river bed about five miles from Palo Alto. There his scouts reported that the Mexicans had taken advantage of his delay to entrench themselves strongly a short distance down the road in a similar shallow ravine known as Resaca de la Guerra, whose banks formed a natural breastwork. Narrow ponds and thick chaparral protected their flanks.

Taylor sent forward his flying artillery, now commanded by Lt. Randolph Ridgely. Stopped by a Mexican battery, Ridgely sent back for help and Taylor ordered in a detachment of dragoons under Capt. Charles A. May. The dragoons overran the Mexican guns but on their return were caught in infantry crossfire from the thickets and could not prevent the enemy from recapturing the guns. The pieces were later captured by American infantrymen. Dense chaparral prevented Taylor from making full use of his artillery. The battle of Resaca de la Palma was an infantry battle of small parties and hand-to-hand fighting.

The Mexicans, still demoralized by their defeat at Palo Alto and lacking effective leadership, gave up the fight and fled toward Matamoros. Their losses at Resaca de la Palma were later officially reported as 547 and were probably much greater. The Americans lost 33 killed and 89 wounded. In the meantime Fort Texas had been attacked by the Mexicans May 3 and had withstood a two-day siege with the loss of only two men, one of them its commander for whom the fort was later renamed Fort Brown.

The panic-stricken Mexicans fleeing to Matamoros crossed the Rio Grande as best they could, some by boats, some by swimming. Many drowned, others were killed by the guns of Fort Texas. If Taylor's Regulars, flushed with victory and yelling as they pursued the enemy, had been able to catch up with Arista, they could probably have taken his demoralized army, complete with guns and ammunition. But Taylor had failed to make any provision for crossing the Rio Grande. He blamed the War Department's failure to provide him with ponton equipment (developed during the Second Seminole War), which he had requested while he was still at Corpus Christi. Since that time, however, he had done nothing to acquire bridge materials or boats, although he had been urged to do so by the West Pointers. Lieutenant Meade reported that "the old gentleman would never listen or give it a moment's attention." Not until May 18, after Taylor had brought up some boats from Point Isabel, was he able to cross into Matamoros. By that time Arista's army had melted away into the interior to rest, recoup, and fight another day.

War Is Declared

On the evening of May 9, the day of the battle of Resaca de la Palma, President Polk received a message from the War Department telling of the attack on Captain Thornton's detachment on April 25. Polk, who was already convinced by the breakdown in negotiations with Mexico that war was justified, immediately drafted a message declaring that a state of war existed between the United States and Mexico. Congress passed the declaration and Polk signed it on May 13. Congress then appropriated $10 million and substantially increased the strength of the Army. After the Second Seminole War the authorized strength had been cut from 12,500 to 8,500. This had been done by reducing the rank and file strength of the regiments, instead of eliminating units, thus firmly establishing the principle of an expansible Army. To meet the needs of the Mexican War the Congress raised the authorized enlisted strength of a company from 64 to 100 men, bringing the rank and file up to 15,540, and added a regiment of mounted riflemen and a company of sappers, miners, and pontoniers. Also, the President was authorized to call for 50,000 volunteers for a term of one year or the duration of the war.

The President went into the war with one object clearly in view—to seize all of Mexico north of the Rio Grande and the Gila River and westward to the Pacific. After discussions with General Scott, the outlines of a three-pronged thrust emerged. (*Map 20*) General Taylor was to advance westward from Matamoros to the city of Monterrey, the key to further progress in northern Mexico. A second expedition under Brig. Gen. John E. Wool was to move from San Antonio to the remote village of Chihuahua in the west, an expedition later directed southward to Saltillo near Monterrey. A third prong under Col. Stephen W. Kearny was to start at Fort Leavenworth

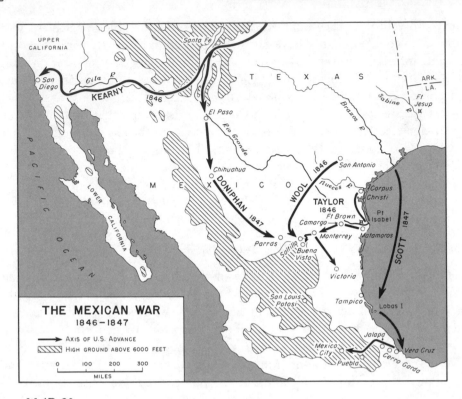

MAP 20

for Santa Fe, ultimately to continue to San Diego on the coast of California; part of Kearny's forces under Col. Alexander W. Doniphan was later sent south through Chihuahua to Parras.

Polk was counting on "a brisk and a short war"; not until July did he and his Secretary of War, William L. Marcy, even begin to consider the possibility of an advance on Mexico City by landing a force on the Gulf near Vera Cruz. General Scott was not so optimistic. He was more aware of the problems of supply, transportation, communications, and mobilization involved in operations against Mexico, a country with a population of seven million and an army of about thirty thousand, many with experience gained by some twenty years of intermittent revolution. Scott's preparations seemed too slow to Polk. Ostensibly for that reason, but also because success in the field might make Scott a too powerful contender for the Presidency, Polk decided not to give him command of the forces in the field. When news came of the victories at Palo Alto and Resaca de la Palma, Polk promoted Zachary Taylor to the brevet rank of major general and gave him command of the army in Mexico.

The Monterrey Campaign

Taylor's plan was to move on Monterrey with about six thousand men via Camargo, a small town on the San Juan River, a tributary of the Rio Grande about 130 miles upriver. From Camargo, where he intended to set up a supply base, a road led southwest about 125 miles to Monterrey in the foothills of the Sierra Madres. His troops were to march overland to Camargo, his supplies to come by steamboat up the Rio Grande. But he could not move immediately because he lacked transportation—partly because of his failure to requisition in time and partly because of the effort required to build more wagons in the United States and to collect shallow-draft steamboats at river towns on the Mississippi and the Ohio and send them across the Gulf of Mexico. Ten steamboats were in operation at the end of July, but wagons did not begin arriving until November, after the campaign was over. To supplement his wagon train, reduced to 175, Taylor had to rely on 1,500 Mexican pack mules and a few native oxcarts.

In manpower Taylor had an embarrassment of riches. May saw the arrival of the first of the three-months militia he had requested on April 26 from the governors of Texas and Louisiana, and with them thousands of additional six-months volunteers from neighboring states recruited by Bvt. Maj. Gen. Edmund P. Gaines, commander of the Department of the West, on his own initiative—a repetition of his impulsive actions in the Second Seminole War. More than 8,000 of these short-term volunteers were sent before Gaines was censured by a court-martial for his unauthorized and illegal recruiting practices and transferred to New York to command the Department of the East. Very few of his recruits had agreed to serve for twelve months. All the rest were sent home without performing any service; in the meantime they had to be fed, sheltered, and transported. In June the volunteers authorized by Congress began pouring into Point Isabel and were quartered in a string of camps along the Rio Grande as far as Matamoros.

By August Taylor had a force of about 15,000 men at Camargo, an unhealthy town deep in mud from a recent freshet and sweltering under heat that rose as high as 112 degrees. Many of the volunteers became ill and more than half were left behind when Taylor advanced toward Monterrey at the end of August with 3,080 Regulars and 3,150 volunteers. The Regulars (with a few volunteers) were organized into the First and Second Divisions, the volunteers mainly into a Field Division, though two regiments of mounted Texans were thought of as the Texas Division. More than a fourth of the troops were mounted, among them the First Mississippi Rifle

Regiment under a West Point graduate recently elected to Congress, Col. Jefferson Davis. The mounted riflemen had percussion rifles; the infantrymen were armed with flintlock muskets. Taylor placed great reliance on the bayonet. He had a low opinion of artillery, and though warned that field pieces were not effective against the stone houses of Mexican towns, he had in addition to his four field batteries only two 24-pounder howitzers and one 10-inch mortar, the latter his only real siege piece.

By September 19 Taylor's army reached Monterrey, a city of stone in a pass of the Sierra Madres leading to the city of Saltillo. It was strongly fortified and defended by more than 7,000 Mexicans with better artillery than the Mexicans had had at Palo Alto—new British 9- and 12-pounder guns. Taylor, encamped on the outskirts of Monterrey, sent out reconnoitering parties accompanied by engineers and on September 20 began his attack. On the north the city was protected by a formidable citadel, on the south by a river; and it was ringed with forts. Taylor sent one of his Regular divisions, with four hundred Texas Rangers in advance, around to the west to cut off the road to Saltillo, and after a miserable night of drenching rain it accomplished its mission the next day, September 21, though at a cost of 394 dead or wounded, a high proportion of them officers. Taylor placed his heavy howitzers and one mortar in position to fire on the citadel and sent the remainder of his forces to close in from the eastern outskirts of the town. By the third day both attacks were driving into the city proper, the men battering down doors of the stone and adobe houses with planks, tossing lighted shells through apertures, and advancing from house to house rather than from street to street—tactics that were to be used a century later by American troops in Italian and German towns.

The climax came when the 10-inch mortar was brought up to lob shells on the great plaza into which the Mexican troops had been driven. On September 24 the Mexican commander offered to surrender on condition that his troops be allowed to withdraw unimpeded and that an eight-week armistice go into effect. Taylor agreed to the proposal. He had lost some 800 men to battle casualties and sickness, besides quantities of arms and ammunition, and he was about 125 miles from his base. Moreover, he believed that magnanimity would advance negotiations for peace which had begun when President Polk allowed General Antonio Lopez de Santa Ana to return to Mexico from exile in Havana to exert his influence in favor of a treaty.

When Polk received the news from Monterrey by courier October 11, he condemned Taylor for allowing the Mexican Army to escape and ordered the armistice terminated. Thereupon, Taylor on November 13 sent a thousand men 68 miles southwestward to occupy Saltillo, an important road center commanding the only road to Mexico City from the north that was practicable for wagons and guns. Saltillo also commanded the road west to Chihuahua and east to Victoria, capital of Tamaulipas, the province that contained Tampico, the second largest Mexican port on the Gulf. The U.S. Navy captured Tampico November 15. On the road to Chihuahua was the town of Parras, where General Wool's expedition of about 2,500 men arrived early in December after a remarkable march from San Antonio. On the way Wool had learned that the Mexican troops holding Chihuahua had abandoned it; accordingly, he joined Taylor's main army. Taylor thus acquired a valuable young engineer who had been scouting with Wool, Capt. Robert E. Lee.

Taylor was planning to establish a strong defensive line, Parras-Saltillo-Monterrey-Victoria, when he learned that most of his troops would have to be released to join General Scott's invasion of Mexico at Vera Cruz, an operation which had been decided upon in Washington in mid-November. Scott arrived in Mexico in late December. He proceeded to Camargo and detached almost all of Taylor's Regulars, about 4,000, and an equal number of volunteers, ordering them to rendezvous at Tampico and at the mouth of the Brazos River in Texas. Taylor, left with fewer than 7,000 men, all volunteers except two squadrons of dragoons and a small force of artillery, was ordered to evacuate Saltillo and go on the defensive at Monterrey.

Enraged, Taylor attributed Scott's motive to politics. Hurrying back to Monterrey from Victoria, he decided to interpret Scott's orders as "advice" rather than as an order. Instead of retiring his forces to Monterrey, he moved 4,650 of his troops (leaving garrisons at Monterrey and Saltillo) to a point about 18 miles south of Saltillo, near the hacienda of Agua Nueva. This move brought him almost 11 miles closer to San Luis Potosi, 200 miles to the south, where General Santa Ana was assembling an army of 20,000. Most of the 200 miles were desert, which Taylor considered impassable by any army; moreover, both he and Scott believed that Santa Ana would make his main effort against Scott's landing at Vera Cruz, the news of which had leaked to the newspapers. On February 8, 1847, Taylor wrote a friend, "I have no fears."

At the time he wrote, Santa Ana was already on the march northward toward Saltillo. Stung by newspaper reports that he had sold out to the Americans, Santa Ana was determined to win a quick victory and he thought he saw his opportunity when his troops brought him a copy of Scott's order depleting Taylor's forces, found on the body of a messenger they had ambushed and killed. Leading his army across barren country through heat, snow, and rain, by February 19 Santa Ana had 15,000 men at a hacienda at the edge of the desert, only 35 miles from Agua Nueva. The hardest battle of the Mexican War was about to begin.

The Battle of Buena Vista

On the morning of February 21 scouts brought the word to General Taylor that a great Mexican army was advancing, preceded by a large body of cavalry swinging east to block the road between Agua Nueva and Saltillo. That afternoon Taylor withdrew his forces up the Saltillo road about 15 miles to a better defensive position near the hacienda Buena Vista, a few miles south of Saltillo. There, about a mile south of the clay-roofed ranch buildings, mountain spurs came down to the road on the east, the longest and highest known as La Angostura; between them was a wide plateau cut by two deep ravines. West of the road was a network of gullies backed by a line of high hills. Leaving General Wool to deploy the the troops, Taylor rode off to Saltillo to look after his defenses there.

By next morning, Washington's Birthday (the password was "Honor to Washington"), the little American army of less than 5,000 troops, most of them green volunteers, was in position to meet a Mexican army more than three times its size. The American main body was east of the road near La Angostura, where artillery had been emplaced, commanding the road. West of the road, the gullies were thought to be sufficient protection.

Santa Ana arrived with his vanguard around eleven o'clock. Disliking the terrain, which by no means favored cavalry, his best arm, he sent a demand for surrender to Taylor, who had returned from Saltillo. Taylor refused. Then Santa Ana planted artillery on the road and the high ground east of it and sent a force of light infantry around the foot of the mountains south of the plateau. About three o'clock a shell from a Mexican howitzer on the road gave the signal for combat; but the rest of the day was consumed mainly in jockeying for position on the mountain spurs, a competition in which the Mexicans came off best, and the placing of American infantry and artillery well forward on the plateau. After a threatening movement on the Mexican left, Taylor sent a Kentucky regiment with two guns of Maj. Braxton Bragg's battery to the high hills west of the road, but no attack occurred there. Toward evening Taylor returned to Saltillo, accompanied by the First Mississippi Rifles and a detachment of dragoons. At nightfall his soldiers, shaken by the size and splendid appearance of the Mexican army, got what sleep they could.

The next day, February 23, the battle opened in earnest at dawn. Santa Ana sent a division up the road toward La Angostura, at the head of the defile, but it was quickly broken up by American artillery and infantrymen, and no further action occurred in that sector. The strongest assault took place on the plateau, well to the east, where Santa Ana launched two divisions, backed by a strong battery at the head of the southernmost ravine. The Americans farthest forward, part of an Indiana regiment supported by three cannons, held off the assault for half an hour; then their commander gave them an order to retreat. They broke and ran and were joined in their flight by adjoining regiments. Some of the men ran all the way back to Buena Vista, where they fired at pursuing Mexican cavalrymen from behind the hacienda walls.

About nine o'clock that morning, when the battle had become almost a rout, General Taylor arrived from Saltillo with his dragoons, Col. Jefferson Davis' Mississippi Rifles, and some men of the Indiana regiment whom he had rallied on the way. They fell upon the Mexican cavalry that had been trying to outflank the Americans north of the plateau. In the meantime Bragg's artillery had come over from the hills west of the road, and the Kentucky regiment also crossed the road to join in the fight. A deafening thunderstorm of rain and hail broke early in the afternoon, but the Americans in the north field continued to force the Mexicans back.

Just when victory for the Americans seemed in sight, Santa Ana threw an entire division of fresh troops, his reserves, against the plateau. Rising from the broad ravine where they had been hidden, the Mexicans of the left column fell upon three regiments—two Illinois and one Kentucky—and forced them back to the road with withering fire, while the right stormed the weak American center. They seemed about to turn the tide of battle when down from the north field galloped two batteries, followed by the Mississippians and Indianans led by Jefferson Davis, wounded, but still in the saddle. They fell upon the Mexicans' right and rear and forced them back into the ravine. The Mexicans' left, pursuing the Illinois and Kentucky regiments up the road, was cut to pieces by the American battery at La Angostura.

That night Santa Ana, having lost 1,500 to 2,000 men killed and wounded, retreated toward San Luis Potosi. The Americans, with 264 men killed, 450 wounded, and 26 missing, had won the battle. A great share of the credit belonged to the artillery; without it, as General Wool said in his report, the army could not have stood "for a single hour." Moving with almost the speed of cavalry, the batteries served as rallying points for the infantry. The fighting spirit of the volunteers, most of them frontiersmen, and the able and courageous leadership of the officers were beyond praise. Perhaps the greatest contribution to the victory had been Zachary Taylor himself. Stationed all day conspicuously

THE MISSISSIPPI RIFLES AT BUENA VISTA

in the center of the battle hunched on his horse "Old Whitey," with one leg
hooked over the pommel of his saddle, disregarding two Mexican bullets that
ripped through his coat, and occasionally rising in his stirrups to shout encouragement, he was an inspiration to his men, who swore by him. Under such a
leader they felt that defeat was impossible.

Taylor knew little of the art of war. He was careless in preparing for battle
and neglected intelligence; he often misunderstood the intention of the enemy
and underestimated the enemy's strength. But he possessed to a superlative
degree physical courage and moral courage, which according to Jomini are the
most essential qualities for a general.

Buena Vista ended any further Mexican threat against the lower Rio
Grande. On the Pacific coast, Colonel Kearny by December 1846 had reached
San Diego after one of the most extraordinary marches in American history,
across deserts and rugged mountains, to find that a naval squadron had already
seized the California ports. Early in February 1847 a force of Missouri volun-
teers detached from Kearny's command and led by Col. Alexander W.
Doniphan had set out from Santa Fe to pacify the region of the upper Rio
Grande. Crossing the river at El Paso, they defeated a large force of Mexicans,

mostly militia, at Chihuahua, less than a week after Taylor's victory at Buena Vista. Thus by March 1847, America's hold on Mexico's northern provinces was secure. All that remained was the capture of Mexico City.

The Landing at Vera Cruz

From a rendezvous at Lobos Island almost 50 miles south of Tampico, General Scott's force of 13,660 men, of whom 5,741 were Regulars, set sail on March 2, 1847, for the landing near Vera Cruz—the first major amphibious landing in the history of the U.S. Army. On March 5 the transports were off the coast of their target, where they met a U.S. naval squadron blockading the city. In a small boat Scott, his commanders, and a party of officers including Robert E. Lee, George G. Meade, Joseph E. Johnston, and Pierre G. T. Beauregard ran close inshore to reconnoiter and came near being hit by a shell fired from the island fortress of San Juan de Ulua opposite Vera Cruz, a shell that might have changed the course of the Mexican War and the Civil War as well.

Scott chose for the landing a beach nearly 3 miles south of the city, beyond the range of the Mexican guns. On the evening of March 9, in four hours more than 10,000 men went ashore in landing craft, consisting of 65 heavy surf boats that had been towed to the spot by steamers. The troops proceeded inland over the sand hills with little opposition from the Mexican force of 4,300 behind the city's walls. The landing of artillery, stores, and horses, the last thrown overboard and forced to swim for shore, was slowed by a norther that sprang up on March 12 and blew violently for four days, but by March 22 seven 10-inch mortars had been dragged inland and emplaced about half a mile south of Vera Cruz. That afternoon the bombardment began.

Town and fort replied, and it was soon apparent that the mortars were ineffective. Scott found himself compelled to ask for naval guns from the commander of the naval force, Commodore Matthew C. Perry. The six naval guns— three 32-pounders firing shot and three 8-inch shell guns—soon breached the walls and demoralized the defenders. On March 27, 1847, Vera Cruz capitulated.

Scott's next objective was Jalapa, a city in the highlands about 74 miles from Vera Cruz on the national highway leading to Mexico City. Because on the coast the yellow fever season was approaching, Scott was anxious to move forward to the uplands at once, but not until April 8 was he able to collect enough pack mules and wagons for the advance. The first elements, under Bvt. Maj. Gen. David E. Twiggs, set out with two batteries. One was equipped with 24-pounder guns, 8-inch howitzers, and 10-inch mortars. The other was a new type of battery equipped with mountain howitzers and rockets, officered and manned by the Ordnance Corps. The rocket section, mainly armed with the Congreve, carried for service tests a new rocket, the Hale, which depended for stability not on a stick but on vents in the rear, which also gave it a spin like that of an artillery projectile. The rockets were fired from troughs mounted on portable stands. In addition to his two batteries, General Twiggs had a squadron of dragoons, in all about 2,600 men. He advanced confidently, though warned by Scott that a substantial army commanded by Santa Ana lay somewhere ahead. On April 11, after Twiggs had gone about 30 miles, his scouts brought word that Mexican guns commanded a pass near the hamlet of Cerro Gordo.

The Battle of Cerro Gordo

Near Cerro Gordo the national highway ran through a rocky defile. On the left of the approaching Americans, Santa Ana with about 12,000 men had emplaced batteries on mountain spurs and on the right of the Americans farther down the road his guns were emplaced on a high hill, El Telegrafo. He thus had firm command of the national highway, the only means he thought Scott had of bringing up his artillery.

Fortunately for Twiggs, advancing on the morning of April 12, the Mexican gunners opened fire before he was within range and he was able to pull his forces back. Two days later Scott arrived with reinforcements, bringing his army up to 8,500. A reconnaissance by Capt. Robert E. Lee showed that the rough country to the right of El Telegrafo, which Santa Ana had considered impassable, could be traversed, enabling the Americans to cut in on the Mexican rear. The troops hewed a path through forest and brush, and when they came to ravines, lowered the heavy siege artillery by ropes to the bottom, then hoisted it up the other side. By April 17 they were able to occupy a hill to the right of El Telegrafo, where they sited the rocket battery. Early on the morning of April 18 the battle began.

Though Santa Ana, by then forewarned, had been able to plant guns to protect his flank, he could not withstand the American onslaught. The Mexicans broke and fled into the mountains. By noon Scott's army had won a smashing victory at a cost of only 417 casualties, including 64 dead. Santa Ana's losses were estimated at more than a thousand.

Scott moved next morning to Jalapa. The way seemed open to Mexico City, only 170 miles away. But now he faced a serious loss in manpower. The term of enlistment of seven of his volunteer regiments was about to expire and only a handful agreed to re-enlist. The men had to be sent home at once to minimize the danger of yellow fever when they passed through Vera Cruz. The departure of the volunteers, added to wounds and sickness among the men remaining, reduced the army to 5,820 effectives.

In May Scott pushed forward cautiously to Puebla, then the second largest city in Mexico. Its citizens were hostile to Santa Ana and had lost hope of winning the war. It capitulated without resistance on May 15 to an advance party under General Worth. Scott stayed there until the beginning of August, awaiting reinforcements from Vera Cruz, which by mid-July more than doubled his forces, and awaiting also the outcome of peace negotiations then under way. A State Department emissary, Nicholas P. Trist, had arrived on the scene and made contact with Santa Ana through a British agent in Mexico City. Trist learned that Santa Ana, elected President of Mexico for the second time, would discuss peace terms for $10,000 down and $1,000,000 to be paid when a treaty was ratified. After receiving the down payment through the intermediary, however, Santa Ana made it known that he could not prevail upon the Mexican Congress to repeal a law it had passed after the battle of Cerro Gordo making it high treason for any official to treat with the Americans. It was clear that Scott would have to move closer to the capital of Mexico before Santa Ana would seriously consider peace terms.

Contreras, Churubusco, Chapultepec

For the advance on Mexico City, Scott had about 10,000 men. He had none to spare to protect the road from Vera Cruz to Puebla; therefore his decision to move forward was daring: it meant that he had abandoned his line of communications, as he phrased it, "thrown away the scabbard." On August 7 Scott moved off with the lead division, followed at a day's march by three divisions with a three-mile-long train of white-topped supply wagons bringing up the rear. Meeting no opposition—a sign that Santa Ana had withdrawn to defend Mexico City—Scott by August 10 was at Ayolta, located on a high plateau 14 miles from the city.

The direct road ahead, entering the capital on the east, was barred by strongly fortified positions. Scott therefore decided to take the city from the west by a wide flanking movement to the south, using a narrow muddy road that passed between the southern shores of two lakes and the mountains and skirted a fifteen-mile-wide lava bed, the Pedregal, before it turned north and went over a bridge at Churubusco to the western gates of Mexico City.

The Pedregal had been considered impassable, but Captain Lee found a mule path across its southwestern tip that came out at the village of Contreras.

Scott sent a force under Bvt. Maj. Gen. Gideon J. Pillow to work on the road, supported by Twiggs's division and some light artillery. They came under heavy fire from a Mexican force under General Valencia. Pillow, manhandling his guns to a high position, attacked on August 19, but his light artillery was no match for Valencia's 68-pounder howitzer, nor his men for the reinforcements Santa Ana brought to the scene. American reinforcements made a night march in pouring rain through a gully the engineers had found through the Pedregal and fell upon the Mexicans' rear on the morning of August 20, simultaneously with an attack from the front. In seventeen minutes the battle of Contreras was won, with a loss to Scott of only 60 killed or wounded; the Mexicans lost 700 dead and 800 captured, including 4 generals.

Scott ordered an immediate pursuit, but Santa Ana was able to gather his forces for a stand at Churubusco, where he placed a strong fortification before the town at the bridge and converted a thick-walled stone church and a massive stone convent into fortresses. When the first American troops rode up around noon on August 20 they were met by heavy musket and cannon fire. The Mexicans fought as never before; not until midafternoon could Scott's troops make any progress. At last the fire of the Mexicans slackened, partly because they were running out of ammunition, and the Americans won the day, a day that Santa Ana admitted had cost him one third of his forces. About 4,000 Mexicans had been killed or wounded, not counting the many missing and captured. The battle had also been costly for Scott, who had 155 men killed and 876 wounded.

The victory at Churubusco brought an offer from Santa Ana to reopen negotiations. Scott proposed a short armistice and Santa Ana quickly agreed. For two weeks Trist and representatives of the Mexican Government discussed terms until it became clear that the Mexicans would not accept what Trist had to offer and were merely using the armistice as a breathing spell. On September 6 Scott halted the discussions and prepared to assault Mexico City.

Though refreshed by two weeks of rest, his forces now numbered only about 8,000 men. Santa Ana was reputed to have more than 15,000 and had taken advantage of the respite to strengthen the defenses of the city. And ahead on a high hill above the plain was the Castle of Chapultepec guarding the western approaches.

Scott's first objective, about half a mile west of Chapultepec, was a range of low stone buildings, containing a cannon foundry, known as El Molino del Rey. It was seized on September 8, though at heavy cost from unexpected resistance. At eight o'clock on the morning of September 13, after a barrage from the 24-pounder guns, Scott launched a three-pronged attack over the causeways leading to Chapultepec and up the rugged slopes. Against a hail of Mexican projectiles from above, his determined troops rapidly gained the summit, and though they were delayed at the moat, waiting for scaling ladders to come up, by half past nine o'clock the Americans were overrunning the castle. Scarcely pausing, they pressed on to Mexico City by the two routes available and by nightfall held two gates to the city. Exhausted and depleted by the 800 casualties suffered that day, the troops still faced house-to-house fighting; but at dawn the next day, September 14, the city surrendered.

Throughout the campaign from Vera Cruz to Mexico City General Scott had displayed not only dauntless personal courage and fine qualities of leadership but great skill in applying the principles of war. In preparing for battle he would order his engineers to make a thorough reconnaissance of the enemy's position and the surrounding terrain. He was thus able to execute brilliant flanking movements over terrain that the enemy had considered impassable, notably at Cerro Gordo and the Pedregal, the latter a fine illustration of the principle of surprise. Scott also knew when to break the rules of warfare, as he had done at Puebla when he deliberately severed his line of communications.

"He sees everything and counts the cost of every measure," said Robert E. Lee. Scott on his part ascribed his quick victory over Mexico, won without the loss of a single battle, to the West Pointers in his army, Lee, Grant, and many others. As for the troops, the trained and disciplined Regulars had come off somewhat better than the volunteers, but the army on the whole had fought well. Scott had seen to it that the men fought at the right time and place. Grant summed it up: "Credit is due to the troops engaged, it is true, but the plans and strategy were the general's."

Occupation and Negotiation in Mexico City

For two months the only responsible government in Mexico was the American military government under Scott. The collection of revenues, suppression of disorder, administration of justice, all the details of governing the country were in the hands of the Army. When the Mexicans finally organized a government with which Commissioner Trist could negotiate a peace treaty, dispatches arrived from Washington instructing Trist to return to the United States and ordering Scott to resume the war. Knowing that the Mexicans were now sincerely desirous of ending the war and realizing that the government in Washington was unaware of the situation, both Trist and Scott decided to continue the negotiations.

On February 2, 1848, the Treaty of Guadalupe Hidalgo was signed. It was ratified by the U.S. Senate on March 10, but powerful opposition to it developed in Mexico. Not until May 30 were ratifications exchanged by the two govern-ments. Preparations began immediately to evacuate American troops from Mexico. On June 12 the occupation troops marched out of Mexico City, and on August 1, 1848, the last American soldiers stepped aboard their transports at Vera Cruz and quitted Mexican soil.

By the Treaty of Guadalupe Hidalgo the United States agreed t6 pay Mexico $15 million and to assume the unpaid claims by Americans against Mexico. In return Mexico recognized the Rio Grande as the boundary of Texas and ceded New Mexico (including the present states of Arizona, New Mexico, Utah, and Nevada, a small corner of present-day Wyoming, and the western and southern portions of Colorado) and Upper California (the present state of California) to the United States.

CHAPTER 5

The Civil War, 1861

During the administration of President James Buchanan, 1857–61, tensions over the issue of extending slavery into the western territories mounted alarmingly and the nation ran its inexorable course toward disunion. Along with slavery, the shifting social, economic, political, and constitutional problems of the fast-growing country fragmented its citizenry. After open warfare broke out in Kansas Territory among slaveholders, abolitionists, and opportunists, the battle lines of opinion hardened rapidly. President Buchanan quieted Kansas by using the Regular Army, but it was too small and too scattered to suppress the struggles that were almost certain to break out in the border states.

In 1859 John Brown, who had won notoriety in "Bleeding Kansas," seized the federal arsenal at Harpers Ferry in a mad attempt to foment a slave uprising within a slaveholding state. Again federal troops were called on to suppress the new outbreak, and pressures and emotions rose on the eve of the 1860 elections. Republican Abraham Lincoln was elected to succeed Buchanan; although he failed to win a majority of the popular vote, he received 180 of the 303 electoral votes. The inauguration that was to vest in him the powers of the Presidency would take place March 4, 1861. During this lame-duck period, Mr. Buchanan was unable to control events and the country continued to lose its cohesion.

Secession, Sumter, and Standing to Arms

Abraham Lincoln's election to the Presidency on November 6, 1860, triggered South Carolina on December 20 to enact an ordinance declaring "the union now subsisting between South Carolina and other States, under the name of the 'United States of America,' is hereby dissolved." Within six weeks, six other deep-South states seceded from the Union and seized federal property inside their borders, including military installations, save Fort Pickens outside Pensacola and Fort Sumter in Charleston Harbor. (*Map 21*) To the seven states that formed the Confederate States of America on February 18, 1861, at Montgomery, Alabama, retention of the forts by the U.S. Government was equivalent to a warlike act. To provide his fledgling government with a military force, on

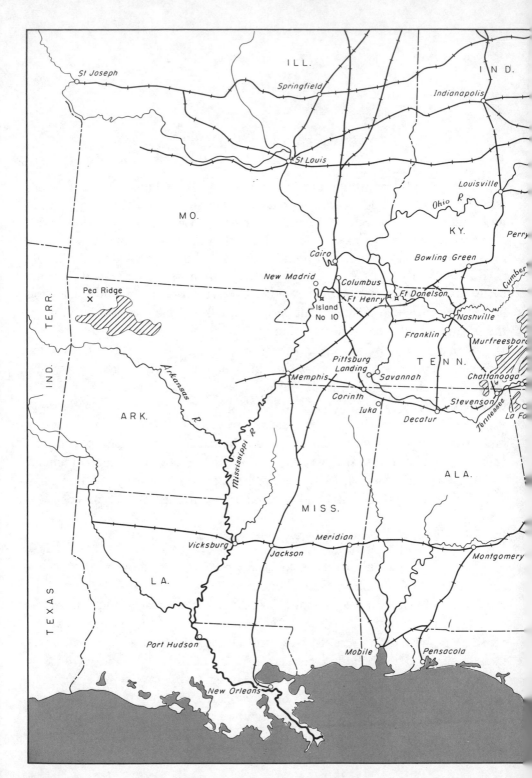

MAP 21

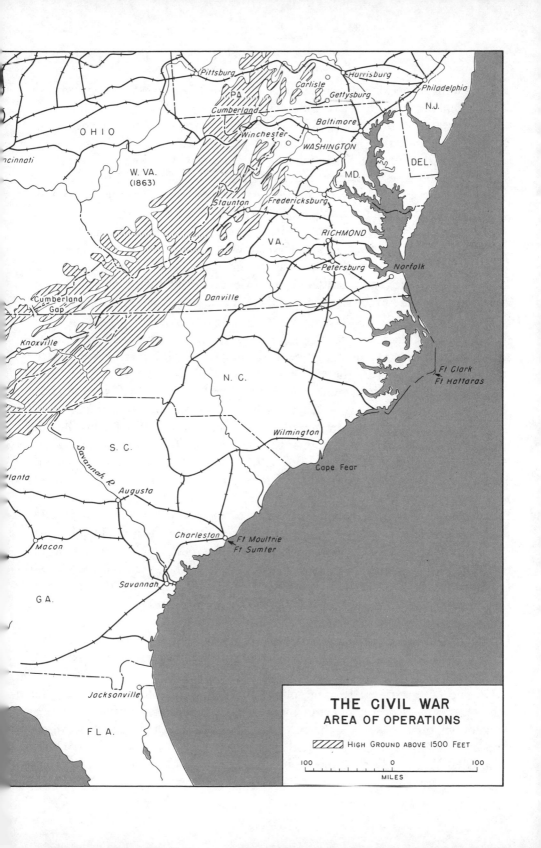

THE CIVIL WAR
AREA OF OPERATIONS

///// HIGH GROUND ABOVE 1500 FEET

100   0   100
MILES

March 6 the new Confederate Executive, Jefferson Davis, called for a 100,000-man volunteer force to serve for twelve months.

The creation of a rival War Department south of the 35th parallel on February 21 shattered the composition of the Regular Army and disrupted its activities, particularly in Texas, where Maj. Gen. David E. Twiggs surrendered his entire command. With an actual strength of 1,080 officers and 14,926 enlisted men on June 30, 1860, the Regular Army was based on 5-year enlistments. Recruited heavily from men of foreign birth, the United States Army consisted of 10 regiments of infantry, 4 of artillery, 2 of cavalry, 2 of dragoons, and 1 of mounted riflemen. It was not a unified striking force. The Regular Army was deployed within seven departments, six of them west of the Mississippi. Of 198 line companies, 183 were scattered in 79 isolated posts in the territories. The remaining 15 were in garrisons along the Canadian border and on the Atlantic coast.

Created by Secretary of War John C. Calhoun and expanded by Secretary of War Davis in 1853, the departments of the United States Army had become powerful institutions by the eve of the Civil War. Within each of the trans-Mississippi departments a senior colonel or general officer by brevet commanded some 2,000 officers and men. All the states east of the Mississippi constituted the Department of the East, where Bvt. Maj. Gen. John E. Wool controlled 929 Regulars. A department commander was responsible for mobilizing and training militia and volunteer forces called into federal service, and for co-ordinating his resources with any expeditionary force commander who operated inside his territory or crossed through his department. A department commander often doubled in command. He was responsible for the administration of his department as well as for conduct of operations in the field. He often had a dual staff arrangement, one departmental and another for the campaign. For strategic guidance and major decisions he looked to the President and General in Chief; for administrative support he channeled his requirements through the Secretary of War to the appropriate bureau chief. In the modern sense he had no corps of staff experts who could assist him in equating his strategic goals with his logistical needs. In many respects the departmental system was a major reason why the Union armies during the Civil War operated like a team of balky horses.

The 1,676 numbered paragraphs of the U.S. Army Regulations governed the actions of a department commander. The provisions concerning Army organization and tactics were archaic in most cases despite Davis' efforts in 1857 to update the Regulations to reflect the experience of the Mexican War. During the Civil War the Regulations would be slightly modified to incorporate the military laws passed by two wartime Congresses. In the South these same Regulations would govern the policy and procedures of the Confederate forces.

The roster of the Regular Army was altered considerably by Davis' action in creating a Confederate Army. Of the active officer corps numbering 1,080, 286 resigned or were dismissed and entered the Confederate service. (At least 26 enlisted men are known to have violated their oaths.) West Point graduates on the active list numbered 824; of these, 184 were among the officers who offered their swords to the Confederacy. Of the approximately 900 graduates then in civil life, 114 returned to the Union Army and 99 others sought southern commissions. General in Chief Scott and Col. George H. Thomas of Virginia were southerners who fought for the Union. More serious than their numbers, however, was the high caliber of the officers who joined the Confederacy; many were regimental commanders and three had commanded at departmental level.

With military preparations under way, Davis dispatched commissioners to Washington a few days after Lincoln's inauguration on March 4, 1861, to treat for the speedy takeover of Forts Sumter and Pickens. Informally reassured that the forts would not be provisioned without proper notice, the envoys returned to Montgomery expecting an uneventful evacuation of Sumter. President Lincoln had to move cautiously, for he knew Sumter's supplies were giving out. As each March day passed, Sumter aggravated the harshness of Lincoln's dilemma. In case of war, the fort had no strategic value. If Lincoln reinforced it, Davis would have his act of provocation and Lincoln might drive eight more slaveholding states out of the Union. If Sumter was not succored, the North might cool its enthusiasm for the Union concept and become accustomed to having a confederation south of the Mason-Dixon line.

President Lincoln spent a fortnight listening to the conflicting counsel of his constitutional advisers, and made up his own mind on March 29 to resupply Fort Sumter with provisions only. No effort would be made to increase its military power. By sea he soon dispatched a token expedition and on April 8 notified South Carolina's governor of his decision. The next move was up to the local Confederate commander, Brig. Gen. Pierre G. T. Beauregard. On the 11th, Maj. Robert Anderson, Sumter's commander, politely but firmly rejected a formal surrender demand. At 4:30 the next morning Confederate batteries began a 34-hour bombardment. Anderson's 90-man garrison returned it in earnest, but Sumter's guns were no match for the concentric fire from Confederate artillery. Offered honorable terms on April 14,

Anderson surrendered the federal fort, saluted his U.S. flag with fifty guns, and, with his command, was conveyed to the fleet outside the harbor to be taken to New York City.

Unquestionably, the Confederates fired the first shot of the war, and with that rash act removed many difficulties from Lincoln's path to preserve the Union. On the 15th Lincoln personally penned a proclamation declaring the seven southern states in insurrection against the laws of the United States. To strangle the Confederacy, on the 19th Lincoln declared the entire coast from South Carolina to Texas under naval blockade. To augment the reduced Regular Army, Lincoln asked the governors of the loyal states for 75,000 militiamen to serve for three months, the maximum time permissible under existing laws. With a unanimity which astonished most people, the northern states responded with 100,000 men. Within the eight slave states still in the Union, the militia call to suppress the rebellion was angrily and promptly rejected, and the President's decision to coerce the Confederacy moved Virginia, North Carolina, Tennessee, and Arkansas to join it.

As spring changed into summer the magnitude of the job that the Union had proclaimed for itself—the conquest of an area the size of western Europe, save Scandinavia and Italy, defended by a plucky and proud people and favored by military geography—was imperfectly understood. Although Lincoln later emerged as a diligent student of warfare, he was as yet unversed in the art. His rival, Davis, from the outset knew his military men quite well and thoroughly understood the mechanics of building a fighting force. Yet, as time passed, Davis was to mismanage his government and its military affairs more and more.

Virginia's secession caused Col. Robert E. Lee, Scott's choice to be the Union's field leader, to resign his commission and offer his services to his state. The Confederates moved their capital to Richmond, Virginia, site of the largest iron works in the south and one hundred miles south of the Union capital, Washington. On May 23, Union forces crossed into northern Virginia, occupying Arlington Heights and Alexandria. With Virginia and North Carolina in rebellion, Lincoln extended the naval blockade and called for a large volunteer army backed by an increased Regular force.

Correctly anticipating that Congress in its session to open July 4 would approve his actions, Lincoln, on his own authority, established 40 regiments of U.S. Volunteers (42,034 men) to serve three years or for the duration of the war. He ordered the Regular Army increased by 1 regiment of artillery, 1 of

INSIDE FORT SUMTER *the day after its surrender.*

cavalry, and 8 of infantry (actually, 9 regiments were added), or 22,714 men, and the Navy by 18,000 sailors. The new Regular infantry regiments were each to have 3 battalions of about 800 men, in contrast to the 1-battalion structure in the existing Regular and volunteer regiments. Because the recruits preferred the larger bonuses, laxer discipline, and easy-going atmosphere of the volunteers, most of the newly constituted regiments were never able to fill their additional battalions to authorized strength.

The enthusiastic response to Lincoln's various calls had forced him to ask the governors to scale down the induction of men. The overtaxed camps could not handle the increased manpower. In raising the Army Lincoln used methods that dated back to Washington's day. The combat efficiency and state of training of the new units varied from good to very poor. Some militia regiments were well trained and equipped, others were regiments in name only. The soldiers often elected their own company officers, and the governors commissioned majors and colonels. The President appointed generals. Although many of the newly commissioned officers proved to be enthusiastic, devoted to duty, and eager to learn, incompetents were also appointed. Before the end of 1861, however, officers were being required to prove their qualifications before examining boards; those found unfit were allowed to resign.

Frequently advised by governors and congressmen, Mr. Lincoln selected generals from among leading politicians in order to give himself a broader base of political support. Some political generals, such as John A. Logan and Francis P. Blair, Jr., distinguished themselves, whereas others proved military hindrances. Lincoln gave a majority of the commissions in the first forty volunteer units to Regulars on active duty, to former West Pointers like George B. McClellan who had resigned to pursue a business career, or to those who had held volunteer commissions during the Mexican War. On the other hand, Davis never gave higher than a brigade command to a Confederate volunteer officer until he had proved himself in battle.

Both North and South failed to develop a good system of replacement of individuals in volunteer units. The Confederacy, though hamstrung by its insistence that Texans be commanded by Texans and Georgians by Georgians and by governors' demands for retaining home guards, did devise a regimental system that stood up well until the closing days of the war. Except for Wisconsin, Illinois, and Vermont, the Union armies never had an efficient volunteer replacement system. As battle losses mounted and the ranks of veteran regiments thinned, commanders were forced to send men back to their home states on recruiting duty or face the disbandment of their regiments. Northern governors with patronage in mind preferred to raise new regiments, allowing battle-tested ones to decline to company proportions.

GENERAL LEE. (*Photograph taken after his promotion to lieutenant general.*)

The enlisted Regular Army was kept intact for the duration of the war. Many critics believed that the Regulars should have been used to cadre the volunteer units. But this practice was initially impossible during the summer of 1861 for at least two reasons. Lincoln did not foresee a long war, and the majority of Regulars were needed on the frontier until trained men could replace them. In addition, Lincoln's critics overlooked the breakdown in morale that would have accompanied the breakup of old line regiments, many of which had histories and honors dating back to the War of 1812. An officer holding a Regular commission in 1861 had to resign to accept a commission in the volunteers unless the War Department specifically released him. Most Regulars were loath to resign, uncertain that they would be recalled to active duty after the war. Thus, during 1861 and part of 1862, promotion in the Regular Army was slow. All Regulars could accept commissions in the volunteers by 1862, and in many cases the year that they had spent in small unit command seasoning had its reward in advancing them to higher commands. Ulysses S. Grant and William T. Sherman, both U.S. Military Academy graduates returning from civilian life, asked specifically for volunteer regimental commands at first and soon advanced rapidly to general officer posts.

The Opponents

As North and South lined up for battle, clearly the preponderance of productive capacity, manpower, and agricultural potential lay on the side of the North. Its crops were worth more annually than those of the South, which had concentrated on growing cotton, tobacco, and rice. Between February and May 1861 the Confederate authorities missed the opportunity of shipping baled cotton to England and drawing bills against it for the purchase of arms. In seapower, railroads, material wealth, and industrial capacity to produce iron and munitions the North was vastly superior to the South. This disparity became even more pronounced as the ever-tightening blockade gradually cut off the Confederacy from foreign imports. The North had more mules and horses, a logistical advantage of great importance since supplies had to be carried to the troops from rail and river heads.

According to the census of 1860 the population of the United States numbered 31,443,321 persons. Approximately 23,000,000 of them were in the twenty-two northern states and 9,000,000 in the eleven states that later seceded. Of the latter total, 3,500,000 were slaves. The size of the opposing armies would reflect this disparity. At one time or another about 2,100,000 men would serve in the northern armies, while some 800,000 to 900,000 men would serve the South. Peak strength of the two forces would be about 1,000,000 and 600,000, respectively.

Yet not all the advantages lay with the North. The South possessed good interior lines of communications, and its 3,550-mile coast line, embracing 189 harbors and navigable river mouths, was most difficult to blockade effectively. Possessors of a rich military record in wars against the British, Spanish, Mexicans, and Indians, the southerners initially managed to form redoubtable cavalry units more easily than the North and used them with considerable skill against the invading infantry. As the war moved along, the armies on both sides demonstrated high degrees of military skill and bravery. Man for man they became almost evenly matched, and their battles were among the bloodiest in modern history.

Jefferson Davis hoped that the sympathy or even intervention of European powers might more than compensate for the Confederacy's lack of material resources. This hope, largely illusory from the start, became less and less likely of realization with the emancipation of the slaves, with every Union victory, and with the increasing effectiveness of the blockade.

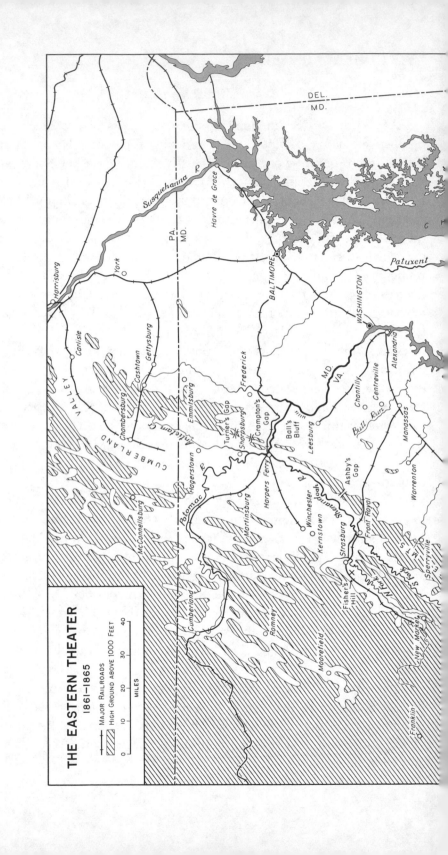

THE EASTERN THEATER
1861–1865

MAJOR RAILROADS
HIGH GROUND ABOVE 1000 FEET

MILES
0   10   20   30   40

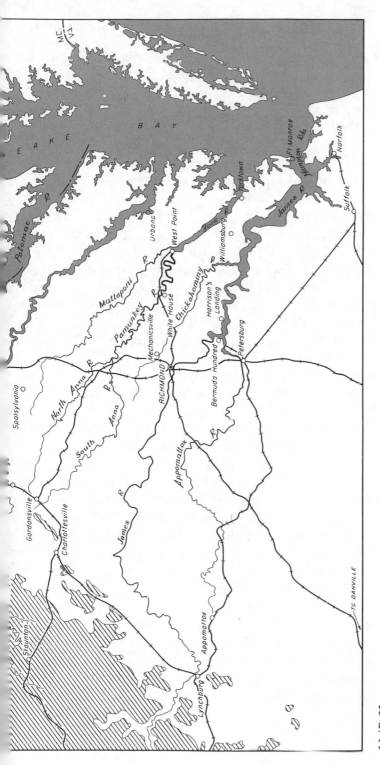

Labels visible on map:

MD.
VA.

C H E S A P E A K E   B A Y

Potomac R.

Norfolk
Ft Monroe
Hampton Rds
Suffolk

James R.
Yorktown
Williamsburg R.
West Point
Urbana

Mattaponi R.
Pamunkey R.
Mechanicsville
White House
Chickahominy
Harrison's Landing
Petersburg
Bermuda Hundred

Spotsylvania
North Anna R.
South Anna R.
RICHMOND

Gordonsville
Charlottesville
James R.
Appomattox R.

Staunton

Appomattox
Lynchburg

TO DANVILLE

MAP 22

Militarily, the South's greatest advantage over the North was simply the fact that if not attacked it could win by doing nothing. To restore the Union the Federal forces would have to conquer the Confederacy. Thus the arena of action lay below the strategic line of the Potomac and Ohio Rivers. Here geography divided the theater of war into three interrelated theaters of operations. The eastern theater lay between the Atlantic Ocean and the Appalachian Mountains; the western theater embraced the area from the Appalachians to the Mississippi; and the trans-Mississippi theater ran westward to the Pacific Ocean. (*Map 22*)

In the east, the strategic triangle of northern Virginia shielded invasion routes. Its apex aimed arrowlike at the Federal capital; the Potomac River and the lower Chesapeake Bay formed its right leg; its left bounded on the Blue Ridge and the adjacent Shenandoah Valley; and the base of the triangle followed the basin of the James and Appomattox Rivers, whereon stood Richmond, halfway between the bay and the valley. For three and a half years Federal commanders would be defeated on the legs and in the center of this triangle as they tried to take Richmond and defeat the Army of Northern Virginia under Lee. In three neighboring counties within this triangle more than half a million men would clash in mortal combat; more would die in these counties than in the Revolutionary War, the War of 1812, the War with Mexico, and all the Indian wars combined. To bring the Confederates out of this triangle the North would have to execute an operation aimed at breaking through the base line along the James and Appomattox Rivers.

The hammer for swinging against the anvil of Virginia came from the line of the Ohio River as Union forces moved along the invasion routes of the Green, Cumberland, Tennessee, and Mississippi Rivers. To breach the lower reaches of the Appalachians, the Federals needed the railroad centers at Nashville, Chattanooga, and Atlanta; with them they could strike northward through the Carolinas toward the line of the James. But in the spring of 1861, the anvil and hammer concept had not yet occurred to the military leaders in Washington. Only the General in Chief, Winfield Scott, had a concrete strategic proposal for waging total war. He recommended to Lincoln that time be taken to train an army of 85,000 men and that the naval blockade of the Confederacy be enforced. Then the Army was to advance down the Mississippi to divide and conquer the South. The press ridiculed the strategy, calling it the Anaconda Plan. But few leaders examined the South in terms of its military geography or concentrated on a strategy to prevail over it. Instead, most thought in terms of political boundaries and a short war that would end with the capture of Richmond.

Manassas (Bull Run)

In the early summer of 1861 the partly trained 90-day militia, the almost untrained volunteers, and one newly organized battalion of Regulars—a total force of 50,000 Federals commanded by Brig. Gen. Irvin McDowell—defended the nation's capital. Thirty miles to the southwest, covering the rail and road hub at Manassas, Virginia, General Beauregard posted some 20,000 Confederates, to be joined by 2,000 more within a few days. To the left, on their defensive line along the Potomac, the Confederates stationed another 11,000 men under Brig. Gen. Joseph E. Johnston in the Shenandoah Valley town of Winchester. Opposing Johnston around Martinsburg, with the mission of keeping the Confederates in place, was Maj. Gen. Robert Patterson with 18,000 Federals. On the extreme right of the Confederate northern Virginia defense line was Col. Joseph B. Magruder's force, which had recently repulsed Maj. Gen. Benjamin F. Butler's Union troops at Big Bethel, Virginia, on 10 June, and forced them back into their sanctuary at Fort Monroe.

Big Bethel, the first large-scale meeting engagement of the Civil War, demonstrated that neither opponent was as yet well trained. The Confederates had started preparations earlier to protect northern Virginia and therefore might have had a slight edge on their opponents. General McDowell, only recently a major of Regulars, had less than three months to weld his three types of units—militia, volunteer, and Regular—into a single fighting force. He attempted to do too much himself, and there were few competent staff officers in the vicinity to help him. McDowell's largest tactical unit was a regiment until just before he marched out of Alexandria. Two to four brigades, plus a battery of Regular artillery—the best arm against raw infantry—formed a division. In all, thirteen brigades were organized into five divisions. McDowell parceled out his forty-nine guns among his brigade commanders, who in turn attached them to their regiments. His total force for the advance was 35,732 men, but of these one division of 5,752 men dropped off to guard roads to the rear.

McDowell's advance against Beauregard, on four parallel routes, was hastened by northern opinion, expressed in editorials and Congressional speeches, demanding immediate action. Scott warned Lincoln against undertaking the "On to Richmond" campaign until McDowell's troops had become disciplined units. But Lincoln, eager to use the 90-day militia before they departed, demanded an advance, being aware that the Confederates were also unseasoned and cherishing the belief that one defeat would force the South to quit. Scott, influenced by false intelligence that Beauregard would move immediately on Washington, acceded. Accordingly, McDowell's battle plan and preparations were expedited. The plan, accepted in late June, called for Butler and Patterson to prevent the Confederates facing them from reinforcing Beauregard, while McDowell advanced against Manassas to outflank the southern position. Scott called it a good plan on paper but knew Johnston was capable of frustrating it if given the chance. McDowell's success against the Confederate center depended upon a rapid 30-mile march, if 35,000 Federals were to keep 22,000 Confederates from being reinforced.

On July 16, 1861, the largest army ever assembled on the North American continent up to that time advanced slowly on both sides of the Warrenton pike toward Bull Run. McDowell's march orders were good, but the effect was ruined by one unwise caution to the brigade commanders: "It will not be pardonable in any commander . . . to come upon a battery or breastwork without a knowledge of its position." The caution recalled to McDowell's subordinates the currently sensationalized bugbear of the press of being fooled by "masked batteries," a term originating at Sumter where a certain battery was constructed, masked by a house which was demolished just before the guns opened fire. Accordingly, 35,000 men moved just five miles on the 17th. Next day the Federals occupied Centreville, some four miles east of Stone Bridge, which carried the Warrenton pike over Bull Run. (*Map 23*)

Beauregard's advanced guards made no effort to delay the Federals, but fell back across the battle line, now extending some three miles along the west bank of Bull Run, which meandered from Stone Bridge southeast until it joined the Occoquan stream. The country was fairly rough, cut by streams, and thickly wooded. It presented formidable obstacles to attacking raw troops, but a fair shelter for equally raw troops on the defensive. On the 18th, while McDowell's main body waited at Centreville for the trains to close up, the leading division demonstrated against Beauregard's right around Mitchell's Ford. The Federal infantry retired after a sharp musketry fight, and a 45-minute artillery duel ensued. It was the first exchange of four standard types of artillery ammunition for all muzzle-loading guns, whether rifled or smoothbore. Solid shot, shell, spherical case or shrapnel, and canister from eight Federal guns firing 415 rounds were answered by seven Confederate pieces returning 310 rounds. Steadily withdrawing its guns, the oldest and best drilled unit of the South, the Washington Light Artillery of New Orleans, broke off the fight against well-trained U.S. Regular artillery. Both sides had used rifled artillery, which greatly increased the accuracy and gave a range more than double that of the smoothbores. Yet rifled guns never supplanted the new, easily loaded Napoleons. In the fight, defective Confederate ammunition fired from three new 3-inch iron rifles

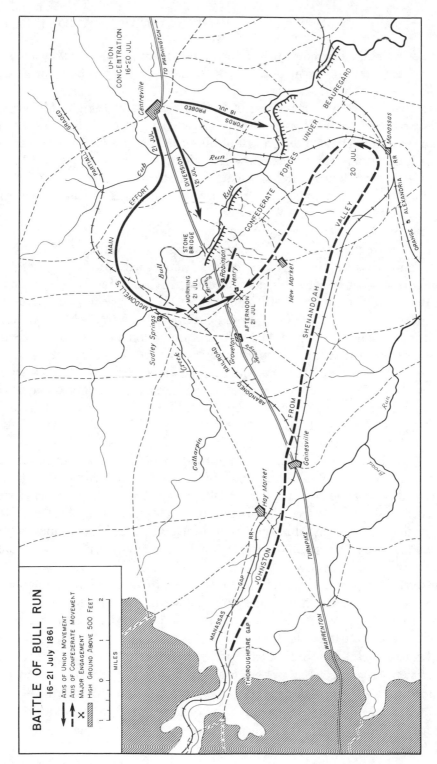

BATTLE OF BULL RUN
16-21 July 1861

Axis of Union Movement
Axis of Confederate Movement
X   Major Engagement
High Ground Above 500 Feet

MILES
2 1 0 1 2

MAP 23

would not fly point foremost but tumbled and lost range against McDowell's gunners. That the error went undetected for days reveals the haste in which Davis had procured his ordnance.

Sure that his green troops could not flank the Confederate right, McDowell tarried two more fateful days before he attacked in force. Engineers reconnoitered for an undefended ford north of Stone Bridge. Finding no vedettes at the ford near Sudley Springs, McDowell decided to envelop the Confederate left on July 21 and destroy the Manassas Gap Railroad to keep Johnston from reinforcing the outnumbered Beauregard. The idea was excellent, but the timing was slow.

While McDowell frittered away four and a half days before he was ready to envelop in force, new tools of warfare swung the advantages of mobility, surprise, and mass at critical points toward Beauregard. On July 17 spies in Washington told of McDowell's departure from Alexandria. By electric telegraph Beauregard in turn alerted Richmond. Davis, also telegraphing, ordered commanders around Richmond, at Aquia Creek, and at Winchester to concentrate their available strength at Manassas. Johnston lost no time in deceiving Patterson by using Col. J. E. B. Stuart's cavalry as a screen and adroitly maneuvering his infantry away from the valley. Johnston selected the best overland routes for his artillery and cavalry marches and arranged for railroad officials to move his four infantry brigades. Brig. Gen. Thomas Jackson's lead brigade, accompanied by Johnston himself, covered fifty-seven miles in twenty-five hours by road and rail, reaching Beauregard on the 20th.

At daylight on the 21st, McDowell unmasked the first phase of his attack plan. Three brigades of Brig. Gen. Daniel Tyler's division appeared before Stone Bridge, and a huge, 30-pounder Parrott rifle dragged into place by ten horses commenced a slow fire, directed by six cannoneers of the 2d U.S. Artillery. Five brigades in two divisions directly under McDowell's command meanwhile marched on an 8-mile circuitous route toward the undefended ford at Sudley Springs. McDowell's goal was the Confederate left rear and a chance to cut the railroad. At 9:00 a.m. a signal flag wigwag from the Henry house announced the point of the enveloping columns at Sudley's crossing, and the intelligence was immediately relayed to Beauregard and Johnston, who were three miles away on the Confederate right.

The first weight of the Federal attack fell against eleven Confederate companies and two guns. For an hour McDowell's regiments, firing one by one and moving forward cautiously in piecemeal fashion, tried to overrun Beauregard's left flank. The timid tactics gave Beauregard time to redeploy ten regiments across a 3-mile front to form a second defensive line across the north face of the hill behind the Henry house. At 10:30 a.m., as the summer sun grew hotter, a portentous dust cloud, rising ten miles northwest of Manassas, heralded the arrival of Kirby Smith's brigade, the tail of Johnston's reinforcements from the Shenandoah Valley.

For two hours the roar of the battle swelled in volume. Federal musketry crashes and the thunder from the heavier pieces indicated that McDowell was now committing whole brigades, supported by four batteries of artillery. North of the Warrenton turnpike, the Confederate infantry began to lose its brigade cohesion and fall back in disorder. As Beauregard and Johnston rode to the sound of battle, some 10,000 Federals were punishing 7,000 Confederates in the vicinity of the Henry and Robinson houses. Johnston, though senior in command, turned the battle over to Beauregard and galloped off toward Manassas to direct the arrival of reinforcements. Brig. Gen. Barnard E. Bee's brigade was pushed back from its advanced position toward the flat-crested hill behind the Henry house, where Jackson's newly arrived brigade had formed. In rallying his routed troops, Bee shouted: "Look at Jackson's Brigade; it stands like a stone wall! Rally behind the Virginians!" (Out of these words came a nickname that Jackson would carry to his grave, and after his death in 1863 the Confederate War Department officially designated his unit the Stonewall Brigade.) Screened by a wooded area, three brigades regrouped behind Jackson's lines, and the rally became a great equalizer as McDowell's strength dissipated to 9,000 men, with no immediate infantry reserves in sight.

The cloud of dust moved closer to Manassas Junction, but McDowell ignored it and allowed a lull to settle over his front for almost two hours. At 2:00 p.m., having deployed two batteries of Regular artillery directly to his front around the Henry house with insufficient infantry protection, McDowell renewed the battle. By midafternoon the dust had blended sweaty uniforms into a common hue, and more and more cases of mistaken identity were confusing both sides in the smoke of the battle. Then, as part of the confusion, came a fateful episode. To the right front of McDowell's exposed artillery, a line of advancing blue-clad infantry, the 33d Regiment, Virginia Volunteers, suddenly appeared through the smoke. The Federal artillery commander ordered canister, but the chief artillery officer on McDowell's staff overruled the order, claiming that the oncoming blue uniforms belonged to friendly infantry arriving in support. The Virginians advanced to within seventy yards of the Federal guns, leveled their muskets, and let loose. The shock of their volley cut the artillery to shreds, and for the remainder of the day nine Federal guns stood silent, unserved, and helpless between the armies.

About 4:00 p.m., Beauregard, with two additional fresh brigades, advanced his entire line. Shorn of their artillery, the faltering Federal lines soon lost cohesion and began to pull back along the routes they knew; there was more and more confusion as they retired. East of Bull Run, Federal artillery, using Napoleon smoothbores in this initial pullback from the field, proved to the unsuspecting Confederate cavalry, using classic saber-charging tactics, that a determined line of artillerymen could reduce cavalry to dead and sprawling infantry in minutes.

As in so many battles of the Civil War yet to come, there was no organized pursuit in strength to cut the enemy to ribbons while he fled from the immediate area of the battlefield. At Bull Run the Federal withdrawal turned into a panic-stricken flight about 6:30 p.m., when Cub Run bridge, about a mile west of Centreville, was blocked by overturned wagons. Sunset would fall at 7:15 p.m., and President Davis, just arrived from Richmond, had two daylight hours to arrive at a decision for pursuit. In council with Johnston and Beauregard, Davis instructed the whole Confederate right to advance against the Centreville road, but apparently his orders were never delivered or Beauregard neglected to follow them. Davis thus lost a splendid opportunity for seeing in person whether the unused infantry and artillery on the right of his line could have made a concerted effort to destroy McDowell's fleeing forces. Logistically, Federal booty taken over the next two days by the Confederates would have sustained them for days in an advance against Washington.

Strategically, Bull Run was important to the Confederates only because the center of their Virginia defenses had held. Tactically, the action highlights many of the problems and deficiencies that were typical of the first year of the war. Bull Run was a clash between large, ill-trained bodies of recruits, who were slow in joining battle; masked batteries frightened commanders; plans called for maneuvering the enemy out of position, but attacks were frontal; security principles were disregarded; tactical intelligence was nil; and reconnaissance was poorly executed. Soldiers were overloaded for battle. Neither commander was able to employ his whole force effectively. Of McDowell's 35,000 men, only 18,000 crossed Bull Run and casualties among these, including the missing, numbered about 2,708. Beauregard, with 32,000 men, ordered only 18,000 into action and lost 1,982.

Both commanders rode along the front, often interfering in small unit actions. McDowell led his enveloping column instead of directing all his forces from the rear. Wisely, Johnston left the battlefield and went to the rear to hasten up his Shenandoah Valley reserves. Regiments were committed piecemeal. Infantry failed to protect exposed artillery. Artillery was parceled out under infantry command; only on the retreat was the Union senior artillery officer on the scene allowed to manage his guns. He saved 21 guns of the 49 that McDowell had. Beauregard's orders were oral, vague, and confusing. Some were delivered, others were never followed.

The Second Uprising in 1861

The southern victory near Manassas had an immediate and a long-range effect on the efforts of both the northern and the southern states. First, it compelled northern leaders to face up to the nature and scope of the struggle and to begin the task of putting the Union on a full war footing. Second, it made them more willing to give heed to the advice of professional soldiers charged with the task of directing military operations along a vast continental land front extending from Point Lookout, Maryland, to Fort Craig in central New Mexico. Third, Confederate leaders, after their feeling of invincibility quickly wore off, called for 400,000 volunteers, sought critical military items in Europe, and turned to planning operations that might swing the remaining slaveholding states and territories into the Confederacy. Finally, the most potent immediate influence of Bull Run was upon the European powers, which eyed the Confederacy as a belligerent with much potential for political intervention and as a source of revenue. Unless the Federal Navy could make it unprofitable for private merchant ships to deliver arms to southern ports and depart with agricultural goods, speculative capital would flow increasingly into the contraband trade.

Strategically, in 1861 the U.S. Navy made the most important contribution toward an ultimate Union victory. At considerable expense and in haste to make the blockade effective, the Navy by the end of the year had assembled 200 ships of every description, armed them after a fashion, and placed them on station. With new Congressional acts regarding piracy, revenue, confiscation, and enforcement in hand, commanders of this motley fleet intercepted more and more swift blockade runners steaming out of Nassau, Bermuda, and Havana on their three-day run to Wilmington, North Carolina, Charleston, South Carolina, or Savannah, Georgia. In two round trips a blockade runner, even if lost on its third voyage, still produced a considerable profit to its owner. By the end of 1861 such profit was no longer easy, because the Navy had many new fast ships in service, specially fitted for blockade duty.

After 1861 the naval character of the war changed. There was no Civil War on the high seas except for the exciting exploits of three or four Confederate cruisers which raided commercial shipping. As the war progressed, both opponents perfected the nature and construction of ships and naval ordnance for a war that would be fought in coastal waters or inside defensible harbors. The three main weapons, the rifled naval gun, the armored ram, and the torpedo mine, were developed and used in novel ways. To offset the defensive use of these weapons by the South, the Federal Navy beginning in August 1861 landed more and more Army expeditionary forces and gradually obtained footholds in the vicinity of Mobile, Savannah, Charleston, and Wilmington. By the end of the war, joint Navy-Army expeditions would convert the sea blockade into a military occupation and would seal off all major ports in the South.

The defeat at Bull Run was followed by "a second uprising" in the North, greatly surpassing the effort after Sumter's surrender. President Lincoln and Congress set to with a will to raise and train the large Federal armies that would be required to defeat the South, to select competent Army field commanders, and to reorganize and strengthen the War Department. On July 22, 1861, Lincoln called for a 500,000-man force of 3-year volunteers and during the rest of July quickly disbanded the 90-day militiamen. The more experienced entered the newly authorized volunteer force. Meanwhile, the volunteer quota and the increase of Regulars, mobilized after Sumter, had so far progressed that camps and garrisons, established at strategic points along the 1,950-mile boundary with the border states and territories, were bustling with activity. As July ended, Congress authorized the volunteers to serve for the duration of the war and perfected their regimental organization. Four regiments were grouped into a brigade, and three brigades formed a division. The infantry corps structure would be fixed when the President directed. In effect, the Lincoln administration was building a federal force, as opposed to one based on joint state-federal control and support. State governors, given a quota according to a state's population, raised 1,000-man volunteer regiments, bought locally whatever the units needed, shipped them to federal training centers, and presented all bills to the U.S. Government. Accordingly, Congress floated a national loan of $250 million.

Pending the transformation of their volunteer forces, both opponents necessarily suspended major military operations for the remainder of 1861. President Lincoln conferred frequently with General Scott and his military advisers about steps already taken to strengthen Union forces along the continental front. Regular Army units were consolidating their position at Forts Craig and Union to protect the upper Rio Grande valley against any Confederate columns coming from Texas. To protect communication lines to the Pacific and the southwest and to guard federal supplies at Fort Leavenworth, Kansas, and St. Louis, Missouri, Union troops were deployed in eastern Kansas and across central Missouri. In August Union troops fought a drawn battle at Wilson's Creek,

UNION VOLUNTEERS IN CAMP

and Missouri became a state divided against itself. The loss of Kentucky, in Lincoln's judgment, would be "nearly the same as to lose the whole game"; so he carefully respected Kentucky's decision of May to remain neutral. After Bull Run, Illinois, Indiana, and Ohio volunteers were assembled north of the Ohio at exposed river towns to keep watch on the situation in Kentucky. In western Virginia forty counties elected to secede from Virginia and asked for federal troops to assist them in repelling any punitive expeditions emerging from the Shenandoah Valley. Between May and early July 1861, Ohio volunteers, under the command of Maj. Gen. George B. McClellan, occupied the Grafton area of western Virginia, hoping to protect the railroad that linked the Ohio Valley with Baltimore. In a series of clashes at Philippi, Beverly, and along the Cheat River, McClellan's forces checked the invading Confederates, paving the way for West Virginia's entrance into the Union.

Although the border strife intensified in the west, Scott attended to the more important front facing Virginia. The nation's capital was imperiled, the Potomac was directly under Confederate guns, and Maryland and Delaware were being used as recruiting areas for the southern cause. On July 22, Lincoln, following Scott's advice, had summoned McClellan, who was thirty-five years old at the time, to Washington, and assigned him command, under Scott, of all the troops in the Washington area. McClellan's reputation was unrivaled, and the public had acclaimed him for his victories in western Virginia. On August 21 McClellan named his force the Army of the Potomac, and commenced molding it into a formidable machine.

McClellan organized the Army of the Potomac into eleven 10,000-man divisions, each with three brigades of infantry, a cavalry regiment, and four 6-gun batteries. In general this structure was adopted by the other Union armies, and the Confederates deviated from the model only in their cavalry organization. In the Army of Northern Virginia, for example, General Lee treated his cavalry as a tactical arm, grouped first as a division, and later as a cavalry corps. Union cavalry consisted of little more than mounted infantry, carrying out a multitude of duties for the division commander, such as serving as pickets, wagon train escorts, and couriers. McClellan planned, once Lincoln activated corps, to withdraw one-half of the artillery pieces from each infantry division and center them at corps level as a reserve to be deployed under army command. He insisted that the .58-caliber single-shot, muzzle-loading Springfield rifle be the standard weapon of the infantry, and most of the Army of the Potomac possessed it when corps were organized on March 8, 1862.

McClellan completely transformed the military atmosphere around Washington before the end of 1861. But, although he was an able administrator, his critics doubted his abilities as a top field commander. And from the day he activated the Army of the Potomac, McClellan was politically active in trying to oust Scott. Finally, on November 1, the aged and harassed General in Chief, taking advantage of a new law, retired from the Army. That same day, acting on assurances that McClellan could handle two tasks concurrently, Lincoln made McClellan the General in Chief and retained him in command of the Army of the Potomac. By the 9th, basing his action on Scott's earlier groundwork, McClellan carved out five new departments in the west, all commanded by Regular Army officers. In addition, he continued the work of the new Department of New England, where General Butler was already forming volunteer regiments for scheduled seaborne operations off the Carolina capes and in the Gulf of New Mexico.

For the Union cause in Kentucky, the new General in Chief's move came none too soon. As early as September 4, a Confederate force from Tennessee had violated Kentucky's neutrality by occupying the Mississippi River town and railroad terminal of Columbus. The next day Illinois troops under Brig. Gen. Ulysses S. Grant seized Paducah and Smithland, strategic river towns in Kentucky at the confluence of the Tennessee and Cumberland Rivers with the Ohio. After Kentucky declared for the Union on September 20, both sides rapidly concentrated forces in western Kentucky. Maj. Gen. Albert S. Johnston, recently appointed to command Confederate forces in the west, fortified Bowling Green, Kentucky, and extended his defensive line to Columbus. Union troops immediately occupied Louisville and planned advances down the railroad to Nashville and eastward into the Appalachians. By November 15, the commanders of the Department of the Ohio and the Department of the Missouri, dividing their operational boundaries in Kentucky along the Cumberland River, were exchanging strategic plans with McClellan in anticipation of a grand offensive in the spring of 1862.

The outpouring of troops and their preparations for battle disrupted the leisurely pace of the War Department. In their haste to supply, equip, and deploy the second quota of volunteers, a score or more of states competed not only against one another but against the federal government as well. Profiteers demanded exorbitant prices for scarce items, which frequently turned out to be worthless. Unbridled graft and extravagance were reflected in the bills which the states presented to the War Department for payment. After Bull Run a concerted, widespread movement emerged for the dismissal of Secretary of War Simon Cameron, who had failed to manage his office efficiently. Cameron selected Edwin M. Stanton, former Attorney General in President Buchanan's cabinet, as his special counsel to handle all legal arguments justifying the War Department's purchasing policies. Knowing that the cabinet post had considerable potential, Stanton worked hard to restore the War Department's prestige. Behind the scenes Stanton aided his fellow Democrat, McClellan, in outfitting the Army of the Potomac. As the summer faded Stanton, having once scoffed at Lincoln early in the war, ingratiated himself with the President and his key cabinet members by urging his pro-Union views. In January 1862 Lincoln replaced Cameron with Stanton, who immediately set out to make his cabinet position the most powerful in Lincoln's administration.

Self-confident, arrogant, abrupt, and contemptuous of incompetent military leaders, Stanton was also fiercely energetic, incorruptible, and efficient. Respecting few men and fearing none, he did his best to eliminate favoritism and see to it that war contracts were honestly negotiated and faithfully filled. Few men liked Stanton, but almost all high officials respected him. Stanton insisted that the Army receive whatever it needed, and the best available, and no campaign by any Union army would ever fail for want of supplies.

From the day that Stanton took office, the structure of the War Department was centralized to handle the growing volume of business. Each bureau chief reported directly to Stanton, but the responsibility became so heavy that he delegated procurement and distribution matters to three assistant secretaries. Because the Quartermaster General's Department transported men and matériel, operated the depot system, constructed camps, and handled the largest number of contracts, it soon became the most important agency of the general staff. Hard-working, efficient, and loyal, Montgomery C. Meigs as Quartermaster General was an organizing genius, and was one of the few career officers to whom Stanton would listen. To complete his department, Stanton added three major bureaus during the war: the Judge Advocate General's Office in 1862; the Signal Department in 1863; and the Provost Marshal General's Bureau, established in 1863 to administer the draft (enrollment) act. In the same year the Corps of Topographical Engineers was merged with the Corps of Engineers.

Stanton faced mobilization problems and home front crises of unprecedented magnitude. Loyal states were bringing half a million men under arms. Grain, wool, leather, lumber, metals, and fuel were being turned into food, clothing, vehicles, and guns, and thousands of draft animals were being purchased and shipped from every part of the North. A well-managed federal authority was needed to assume the states' obligations, to train volunteer units in the use of their tools of war, and then to deploy them along a vast continental front. By exploiting the railroad, steamship, and telegraph, the War Department provided field commanders a novel type of mobility in their operations. Stanton's major task was to control all aspects of this outpouring of the nation's resources. If war contracts were tainted, the Union soldiers might despair. Moral as well as financial bankruptcy could easily wreck Union hopes of victory. In addition, Stanton had the job of suppressing subversion, of timing the delicate matter of putting Negroes in the Army, and of co-operating with a radical-dominated Congress, a strong-willed cabinet, and a conservative-minded Army. With a lawyer's training, Stanton, like Lincoln, knew little about military affairs, and there was little time for him to learn. Anticipating that President Lincoln would soon call for War Department plans for the spring 1862 offensives, Stanton researched every document he could find on Army administration, consulted his bureau chiefs about readiness, and prepared himself to work with the General in Chief on strategic matters.

When he took office, Stanton found that the War Department had a rival in the form of the Joint Congressional Committee on the Conduct of the War. It had its origins in an investigation of a badly executed reconnaissance at Ball's Bluff on the Potomac, October 21, 1861, in which a volunteer officer and popular former senator, Col. Edward D. Baker, was killed. By subsequently searching out graft and inefficiency, the committee did valuable service, but it also vexed the President, Stanton, and most of the generals during the war. Composed of extreme antislavery men without military knowledge and experience, the committee probed the battles, tried to force all its views regarding statecraft and strategy on the President, and put forward its own candidates for high command. Suspicious of proslavery men and men of moderate views, it considered that the only generals fit for office were those who had been abolitionists before 1861.

As the year ended both North and South were earnestly preparing for a hard war. Both opponents were raising and training huge armies totaling nearly a million men. Fort Sumter and bloody Bull Run were over and each side was gathering its resources for the even bloodier struggles to come.

CHAPTER 6

The Civil War, 1862

In 1862 the armed forces of the United States undertook the first massive campaigns to defeat the southern Confederacy. Better organization, training, and leadership would be displayed on both sides as the combat became more intense. Young American citizen soldiers would find that war was not a romantic adventure and their leaders would learn that every victory had its price.

As the winter of 1861–62 wore on, McClellan exaggerated his difficulties and the enemy's strength, and discounted the Confederacy's problems. He drilled and trained the Army of the Potomac while western forces under his general command accomplished little. Lincoln and the Union waited impatiently for a conclusive engagement. But neither the Union nor the Confederate Army showed much inclination to move, each being intent on perfecting itself before striking a heavy blow.

The President was particularly eager to support Unionist sentiment in east Tennessee by moving forces in that direction. Above all he wanted a concerted movement to crush the rebellion quickly. In an effort to push matters Lincoln issued General War Order No. 1 on January 27, 1862. This order, besides superfluously telling the armies to obey existing orders, directed that a general movement of land and sea forces against the Confederacy be launched on February 22, 1862. Lincoln's issuance of an order for an offensive several weeks in advance, without considering what the weather and the roads might be like, has been scoffed at frequently. But apparently he issued it only to get McClellan to agree to move. Even before Lincoln sent the directive his intentions were overtaken by events in the western theater.

The Twin Rivers Campaign

Students of the Civil War often concentrate their study upon the cockpit of the war in the east—Virginia. The rival capitals lay only a hundred miles apart and the country between them was fought over for four years. But it was the Union armies west of the Appalachians that struck the death knell of the Confederacy.

GENERAL GRANT. (*Photograph taken after his promotion to lieutenant general.*)

These Union forces in late 1861 were organized into two separate commands. Brig. Gen. Don Carlos Buell commanded some 45,000 men from a headquarters at Louisville, Kentucky, while Maj. Gen. Henry W. Halleck with headquarters at St. Louis, Missouri, had 91,000 under his command. These troops were generally raw, undisciplined western volunteers. Logistical matters and training facilities were undeveloped and as Halleck once wrote in disgust to his superior in Washington, "affairs here are in complete chaos."

Affairs were no better among Confederate authorities farther south. Facing Buell and Halleck were 43,000 scattered and ill-equipped Confederate troops under General Albert Sidney Johnston. Charged with defending a line which stretched for more than 500 miles from western Virginia to the border of Kansas, Johnston's forces mostly lay east of the Mississippi River. They occupied a system of forts and camps from Cumberland Gap in western Virginia through Bowling Green, Kentucky, to Columbus, Kentucky, on the Mississippi. Rivers and railroads provided Johnston with most of his interior lines of communications since most of the roads were virtually impassable in winter. To protect a lateral railroad where it crossed two rivers in Tennessee and yet respect Kentucky's neutrality, the Confederates had built Fort Henry on the Tennessee River and Fort Donelson on the Cumberland River just south of the boundary between the two states. On the other hand, hampering the Confederate build-up were southern governors whose states' rights doctrine led them to believe that defense of their respective states had higher priority than pushing forward the needed men and munitions to a Confederate commander, Johnston, at the front.

At the beginning of 1862, Halleck and Buell were supposed to be co-operating with each other but had yet to do so effectively. On his own, Buell moved in mid-January to give token response to Lincoln's desire to help the Unionists in east Tennessee. One of his subordinates succeeded in breaching the

Confederate defense line in eastern Kentucky in a local action near Mill Springs, but Buell failed to exploit the victory.

In Halleck's department, Brig. Gen. Ulysses S. Grant, at the time an inconspicuous district commander at Cairo, Illinois, had meanwhile proposed a river expedition up the Tennessee to take Fort Henry. After some hesitancy and in spite of the absence of assurance of support from Buell, Halleck approved a plan for a joint Army-Navy expedition. On January 30, 1862, he directed 15,000 men under Grant, supported by armored gunboats and river craft of the U.S. Navy under Flag Officer Andrew H. Foote, to "take and hold Fort Henry." The actions of subordinate commanders were at last prodding the Union war machine to move.

Capture of Forts Henry and Donelson

Grant landed his troops below Fort Henry and together with Foote's naval force moved against the Confederate position on February 6. At the Federals' approach the Confederate commander sent most of his men to Fort Donelson. Muddy roads delayed the Union Army's advance, but Foote's seven gunboats plunged ahead and in a short fire fight induced the defenders of Fort Henry to surrender. Indeed, the Confederates had lowered their colors before Grant's infantry could reach the action. The Tennessee River now lay open to Foote's gunboats all the way to northern Alabama.

General Grant was no rhetorician. Sparing with words, he never bombarded his troops with Napoleonic manifestos as McClellan did. After the capture of Fort Henry he simply telegraphed the somewhat surprised Halleck: "I shall take and destroy Fort Donelson on the 8th and return to Fort Henry." But inclement weather delayed the Federal movement until February 12. Then river craft carried some of the troops by water around to Fort Donelson. The rest of the troops moved overland under sunny skies and unseasonably mild temperatures. The springlike weather caused the youthful soldiers to litter the roadside with overcoats, blankets, and tents.

But winter once more descended upon Grant's forces (soon to swell to nearly 27,000 men) as they invested Fort Donelson. Johnston, sure that the fall of this fort would jeopardize his entrenched camp at Bowling Green, hurried three generals and 12,000 reinforcements to Fort Donelson and then retired toward Nashville with 14,000 men. Even without reinforcements, Fort Donelson was a strong position. The main earthwork stood 100 feet above the river and with its outlying system of rifle pits embraced an area of 100 acres. The whole Confederate position occupied less than a square mile. Grant and Foote first attempted to reduce it by naval bombardment, which had succeeded at Fort

Henry. But this time the Confederate defenders handled the gunboats so roughly that they withdrew. Grant then prepared for a long siege, although the bitter cold weather and lack of assault training among his troops caused him to have some reservations.

The Confederates, sensing they were caught in a trap, essayed a sortie on February 15, and swept one of Grant's divisions off the field. But divided Confederate command, not lack of determination or valor on the part of the fighting men, led to ultimate defeat of the attack. The three Confederate commanders could not agree upon the next move, and at a critical moment, Grant ordered counterattacks all along the line. By the end of the day Union troops had captured a portion of the Confederate outer works. Now surrounded by Union forces that outnumbered them almost two to one, the Confederate leaders decided they were in a hopeless situation. In a scene resembling *opéra bouffe,* Brig. Gen. John B. Floyd, who had been Buchanan's Secretary of War and feared execution as a traitor, passed the command to Brig. Gen. Gideon Pillow. Pillow passed the command immediately to Brig. Gen. Simon B. Buckner, who asked Grant, an old friend, for terms. Soon afterward Grant sent his famous message: "No terms except unconditional and immediate surrender can be accepted. I propose to move immediately upon your works."

Some Confederates escaped with Floyd and Pillow, and Col. Nathan Bedford Forrest led his cavalry through frozen backwaters to safety. But the bulk of the garrison "from 12,000 to 15,000 prisoners . . . also 20,000 stand of arms, 48 pieces of artillery, 17 heavy guns, from 2,000 to 4,000 horses, and large quantities of commissary stores" fell into Federal hands.

Poor leadership, violation of the principle of unity of command, and too strict adherence to position defense had cost the South the key to the gateway of the Confederacy in the west. The loss of the two forts dealt the Confederacy a blow from which it never fully recovered. Johnston had to abandon Kentucky and most of middle and west Tennessee. The vital industrial and transportation center of Nashville soon fell to Buell's advancing army. Foreign governments took special notice of the defeats. For the North the victories were its first good news of the war. They set the strategic pattern for further advance into the Confederacy. In Grant the people had a new hero and he was quickly dubbed "Unconditional Surrender" Grant.

Confederate Counterattack at Shiloh

As department commander, Halleck naturally received much credit for these victories. President Lincoln decided to unify command of all the western armies, and on March 11 Halleck received the command. Halleck, nicknamed "Old Brains," was well known as a master of the theory and literature of war. Lincoln's decision gave him jurisdiction over four armies—Buell's Army of the Ohio, Grant's Army of the Tennessee, Maj. Gen. Samuel Curtis' Army of the Southwest in Missouri and Arkansas, and Maj. Gen. John Pope's Army of the Mississippi. While Pope, in co-operation with Foote's naval forces, successfully attacked New Madrid and Island No. 10 on the Mississippi River, Halleck decided to concentrate Grant's and Buell's armies and move against Johnston at Corinth in northern Mississippi. Grant and Buell were to meet at Shiloh (Pittsburgh Landing) near Savannah on the Tennessee River. Well aware of the Federal movements, Johnston decided to attack Grant before Buell could join him. (*Map 24*) The Confederate army, 40,000 strong, marched out of Corinth on the afternoon of April 3. Muddy roads and faulty staff co-ordination made a shambles of Confederate march discipline. Mixed up commands, artillery and wagons bogged down in the mud, and green troops who insisted upon shooting their rifles at every passing rabbit threatened to abort the whole expedition. Not until late in the afternoon of April 5 did Johnston's army complete the 22-mile march to its attack point. Then the Confederate leader postponed his attack until the next morning and the delay proved costly.

Grant's forces were encamped in a rather loose battle line and apparently anticipated no attack. The position at Shiloh itself was not good, for the army was pocketed by the river at its back and a creek on each flank. Because the army was on an offensive mission, it had not entrenched. Grant has often been criticized for this omission, but entrenchment was not common at that stage of the war. The fact that the principle of security was disregarded is inescapable. Very little patrolling had been carried out, and the Federals were unaware that a Confederate army of 40,000 men was spending the night of April 5 just two miles away. The victories at Forts Henry and Donelson had apparently produced overconfidence in Grant's army, which like Johnston's, was only partly trained. Even Grant reflected this feeling, for he had established his headquarters at Savannah, nine miles downstream.

Johnston's men burst out of the woods early on April 6, so early that Union soldiers turned out into their company streets from their tents to fight. Some fled to the safety of the landing, but most of the regiments fought stubbornly and yielded ground slowly. One particular knot of Federals rallied along an old sunken road, named the Hornet's Nest by Confederates because of the stinging shot and shell they had to face there. Although this obstacle disrupted Johnston's timetable of attack, by afternoon the Confederates had attained local success elsewhere all along the line. At the same time the melee of battle badly

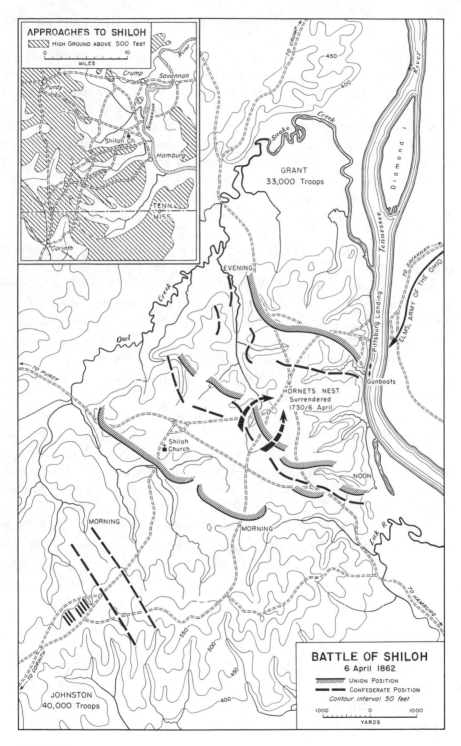

APPROACHES TO SHILOH

High Ground above 500 feet

0   MILES   10

River

Crump

Savannah

Purdy

Tennessee

Shiloh Ch.

Hamburg

TENN.

MISS.

Corinth

TO CRUMP

450

400

Snake   Creek

Creek

GRANT
33,000 Troops

Diamond I.

Tennessee   River

EVENING

Owl

Creek

TO PURDY

TO SAVANNAH

ELMS, ARMY OF THE OHIO

Pittsburg Landing

Gunboats

HORNETS NEST
Surrendered
1730/6 April

Shiloh
Church

NOON

Lick R.

MORNING

MORNING

TO HAMBURG

TO CORINTH

550

500

450

400

JOHNSTON
40,000 Troops

BATTLE OF SHILOH
6 April 1862

Union Position
Confederate Position
Contour Interval 50 feet

1000   0   1000
YARDS

MAP 24

disorganized the attackers. Johnston's attack formation had been awkward from the beginning. He had formed his three corps into one column with each corps deployed with divisions in line so that each corps stretched across the whole battlefront, one behind the other. Such a formation could be effectively controlled neither by army nor corps commanders.

Then, almost at the moment of victory, Johnston himself was mortally wounded while leading a local assault. General Beauregard, Johnston's successor, suspended the attack for the day and attempted to straighten out and reorganize his command. As the day ended, Grant's sixth division, which had lost its way while marching to the battlefield, reached Shiloh along with advance elements of Buell's army.

Next morning Grant counterattacked to regain the lost ground and the Confederates withdrew to Corinth. There was no pursuit. Shiloh was the bloodiest battle fought in North America up to that time. Of 63,000 Federals, 13,000 were casualties. The Confederates lost 11,000. Fortunate indeed for the Federals had been Lincoln's decision to unify the command under Halleck, for this act had guaranteed Buell's presence and prevented Johnston from defeating the Union armies separately. Grant came in for much denunciation for being surprised, but President Lincoln loyally sustained him. "I can't spare this man; he fights."

Halleck was a master of military maxims, but he had failed to concentrate all his forces immediately for a final defeat of Beauregard. As it was, Pope and Foote took Island No. 10 in April, opening the Mississippi as far as Memphis. Halleck, taking personal command of Grant's and Buell's forces, then ponderously advanced toward Corinth. Remembering Shiloh, he proceeded cautiously, and it was May 30 before he reached his objective. Beauregard had already evacuated the town. Meanwhile Capt. David G. Farragut with a naval force and Maj. Gen. Benjamin F. Butler's land units cracked the gulf coast fortifications of the Mississippi and captured New Orleans. By mid-1862, only strongholds at Vicksburg and Port Hudson on the Mississippi blocked complete Federal control of that vital river.

Perryville to Stones River

Despite these early setbacks the Confederate armies in the west were still full of fight. As Federal forces advanced deeper into the Confederacy it became increasingly difficult for them to protect the long lines of river, rail, and road supply and communications. Guerrilla and cavalry operations by colorful

Confederate "wizards of the saddle" like John Hunt Morgan, Joseph Wheeler, and Nathan Bedford Forrest followed Forrest's adage of "Get 'em skeered, and then keep the skeer on 'em." Such tactics completely disrupted the timetable of Federal offensives.

By summer and fall rejuvenated Confederate forces under General Braxton Bragg, Lt. Gen. Edmund Kirby Smith, and Maj. Gen. Earl Van Dorn were ready to seize the initiative. Never again was the South so close to victory, nor did it ever again hold the initiative in every theater of the war.

Over-all Confederate strategy called for a three-pronged advance from the Mississippi River all the way to Virginia. Twin columns under Bragg and Smith were to bear the brunt of the western offensive by advancing from Chattanooga into east Tennessee, then northward into Kentucky. They were to be supported by Van Dorn, who would move north from Mississippi with the intention of driving Grant's forces out of west Tennessee. The western columns of the Confederacy were then to unite somewhere in Kentucky.

At the same time, these movements were to be co-ordinated with the planned invasion of Maryland, east of the Appalachians, by General Robert E. Lee's Army of Northern Virginia. Much depended upon speed, good co-ordination of effort and communications, and attempts to woo Kentucky and Maryland into the arms of the Confederacy. Victory could stimulate peace advocates and the Copperheads in the North to bring peace. Furthermore there was always the possibility that a successful invasion might induce Great Britain and France to recognize the Confederacy and to intervene forcibly to break the blockade. This last hope was a feeble one. Emperor Napoleon III was primarily interested in advancing his Mexican schemes; he considered both recognition and intervention but would not move without British support. Britain, which pursued the policy of recognizing *de facto* governments, would undoubtedly have recognized the Confederacy eventually had it won the war. But the British Government only briefly flirted with the idea of recognition and throughout the war adhered to a policy of neutrality and respect for the Union blockade.

At first things went well for the Confederates in the west. Bragg caught Buell off guard and without fighting a battle forced Federal evacuation of northern Alabama and central Tennessee. But when Bragg entered Kentucky he became engaged in "government making" in an effort to set up a state regime which would bind Kentucky to the Confederacy. Also, the Confederate invasion was not achieving the expected results since few Kentuckians joined Bragg's forces and an attempt at conscription in east Tennessee failed completely.

Buell finally caught up with Bragg's advance at Perryville, Kentucky, on October 7. Finding the Confederates in some strength, Buell began concentrating his own scattered units. The next morning fighting began around Perryville over possession of drinking water. Brig. Gen. Philip H. Sheridan's division forced the Confederates away from one creek and dug in. The battle as a whole turned out to be a rather confused affair as Buell sought to concentrate units arriving from several different directions upon the battlefield itself. Early in the afternoon, Maj. Gen. Alexander M. McCook's Union corps arrived and began forming a line of battle. At that moment Maj. Gen. Leonidas Polk's Confederate corps attacked and drove McCook back about a mile, but Sheridan's troops held their ground. Finally a Union counterattack pushed the Confederates out of the town of Perryville. Buell himself remained at headquarters, only two and a half miles from the field, completely unaware of the extent of the engagement until it was nearly over. The rolling terrain had caused an "acoustic shadow" whereby the sounds of the conflict were completely inaudible to the Federal commander. While the battle ended in a tactical stalemate, Bragg suffered such severe casualties that he was forced to retreat. Coupled with Van Dorn's failure to bypass Federal defenses at Corinth, Mississippi, and carry out his part of the strategic plan, this setback forced the Confederates to abandon any idea of bringing Kentucky into the Confederacy.

By Christmas Bragg was back in middle Tennessee, battered but still anxious to recoup his losses by recapturing Nashville. Buell had been dilatory in pursuing Bragg after Perryville and had been replaced in command of the Army of the Ohio (now restyled the Army of the Cumberland) by Maj. Gen. William S. Rosecrans. In spite of urgent and even threatening letters from the War Department, the new commander would not move against Bragg until he had collected abundant supplies at Nashville. Then he would be independent of the railroad line from Nashville to Louisville, a line of communications continually cut by Confederate cavalry.

On December 26 Rosecrans finally marched south from Nashville. Poorly screened by Union cavalry, his three columns in turn knew little about Confederate concentrations near Murfreesboro, thirty miles southeast of the Tennessee capital. Here Bragg had taken a strong position astride Stones River on the direct route to Chattanooga and proposed to fight it out. Rosecrans moved into line opposite Bragg on the evening of December 30. Both army commanders proceeded to develop identical battle plans—each designed to envelop the opponent's right flank. Bragg's objective was to drive Rosecrans off his communications line with Nashville and pin him against the river. Rosecrans' plan had the same objective in reverse, that of pinning the Confederates against the stream. Victory would probably belong to the commander who struck first and hard.

Insufficient Federal security and Rosecrans' failure to insure that the pivotal units in his attack plan were also properly posted to thwart Confederate counterattacks resulted in Confederate seizure of the initiative as the battle of Stones River opened on December 31. (*Map 25*) At dawn, Maj. Gen. William J. Hardee's corps with large cavalry support began the drive on the Federal right. Undeceived by their opponent's device of extra campfires to feign a longer

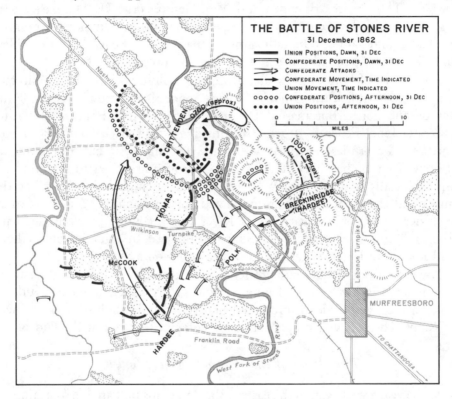

MAP 25

battle line, Confederate attacking columns simply pushed farther around the Union flank and promptly rolled the defenders back. Applying the principles of mass and surprise to achieve rapid success, Bragg's battle plan forced Rosecrans to modify his own. The Union leader pulled back his left flank division, which had jumped off to attack Maj. Gen. John C. Breckinridge's Confederate units north of Stones River. While Sheridan's division, as at Perryville, provided stubborn resistance to General Polk's corps in the center, Hardee's units continued their drive, which by noon saw the Union battle line bent back against the Nashville pike. Meanwhile the Confederate cavalry had wrought havoc among Rosecrans' rear area elements. As was typical of many Civil War battles the attacking columns of Polk and Hardee became badly intermingled. Their men began to tire, and by afternoon repeated Confederate assaults against the constricted Union line along the Nashville pike had bogged down.

That night Rosecrans held a council of war. Some of the subordinate commanders wanted to retreat. Rosecrans and two of his corps commanders, Maj. Gen. Thomas L. Crittenden and Maj. Gen. George H. Thomas, vetoed the scheme. Brigades were then returned to their proper divisions, stragglers rounded up, and various other adjustments made in the Federal position. New Year's Day, 1863, dawned quiet and little action occurred that day.

The sunrise of January 2 revealed Rosecrans still in position. Bragg directed Breckinridge to attack the Union left wing, once more thrown across Stones River on the north. But massed Union artillery shattered the assaults and counterattacking Federals drove Breckinridge's men back to their line of departure. The armies remained stationary on January 3 but Bragg finally withdrew from the battlefield that evening, permitting victory to slip from his grasp. Tactically a draw, Stones River so badly mangled the Army of the Cumberland that it would be immobilized for six months. Yet, more than most other battles of the war, Stones River was a conflict between the wills of the opposing army leaders. Rosecrans, supported by Thomas and others, would not admit himself beaten and in the end won a victory of sorts.

The great Confederate counteroffensives of 1862 had failed in the west, yet Chattanooga, the key to east Tennessee and Georgia, remained in southern hands. Farther west Federal forces had penetrated only slightly into northern Mississippi. The war was simply on dead center in the west at the end of the year.

The Army of the Potomac Moves South

As the year 1862 began in the eastern theater, plans prepared in Washington were aimed at the capture of Richmond rather than destruction of the army commanded by Joseph E. Johnston, now a full general. Precise methods for reaching the Confederate capital differed. President Lincoln favored an overland advance which would always keep an army between the Confederates and Washington. McClellan agreed at first, then changed his views in favor of a waterborne move by the Army of the Potomac to Urbana on the Rappahannock. From there he could drive to Richmond before Johnston could retire from the Manassas area to intercept him. The Washington fortifications, an elaborate system of earthen forts and battery emplacements then in advanced stages of construction, would adequately protect the capital while the field army was away. Johnston, however, rendered this plan obsolete; he withdrew from Manassas to Fredericksburg, halfway between the two capitals and astride McClellan's prospective route of advance. Early in March McClellan moved his army out to the deserted Confederate camps around Manassas to give his troops some field experience. While he was in the field President Lincoln relieved him as General in Chief, doubtless on the ground that he could not command one army in the field and at the same time supervise the operations of all the armies of the United States. Lincoln did not appoint a successor. For a time he and Stanton took over personal direction of the Army, with the advice of a newly constituted Army board consisting of the elderly Maj. Gen. Ethan A. Hitchcock and the chiefs of the War Department bureaus.

When events overtook the Urbana scheme, McClellan began to advocate a seaborne move to Fort Monroe, Virginia (at the tip of the peninsula formed by the York and James Rivers), to be followed by an overland advance up the peninsula. If the troops moved fast, he maintained, they could cover the seventy-five miles to Richmond before Johnston could concentrate his forces to stop them. This plan had promise, for it utilized Federal control of the seas and a useful base of operations at Fort Monroe and there were fewer rivers to cross than by the overland route. Successful neutralization of the *Merrimac* by the *Monitor* on March 9 had eliminated any naval threat to supply and communications lines, but the absence of good roads and the difficult terrain of the peninsula offered drawbacks to the plan. Lincoln approved it, providing McClellan would leave behind the number of men that his corps commanders considered adequate to insure the safety of Washington. McClellan gave the President his assurances, but failed to take Lincoln into his confidence by pointing out that he considered the Federal troops in the Shenandoah Valley to be covering Washington. In listing the forces he had left behind, he counted some men twice and included several units in Pennsylvania not under his command.

Embarkation began in mid-March, and by April 4 advance elements had moved out of Fort Monroe against Yorktown. The day before, however, the commander of the Washington defenses reported that he had insufficient forces to protect the city. In addition, Stonewall Jackson had become active in the Shenandoah Valley. Lincoln thereupon told Stanton to detain one of the two corps which were awaiting embarkation at Alexandria. Stanton held back McDowell's corps, numbering 30,000 men, seriously affecting McClellan's plans.

Jackson's Valley Campaign

While a small Confederate garrison at Yorktown made ready to delay McClellan, Johnston hurried his army to the peninsula. In Richmond Confederate authorities had determined on a spectacularly bold diversion. Robert E. Lee, who had rapidly moved to the rank of general, had assumed the position of military adviser to Jefferson Davis on March 13. Charged with the conduct of operations of the Confederate armies under Davis' direction, Lee saw that any threat to Washington would cause progressive weakening of McClellan's advance against Richmond. He therefore ordered Jackson to begin a rapid campaign in the Shenandoah Valley close to the northern capital. The equivalent of three Federal divisions was sent to the valley to destroy Jackson. Lincoln and Stanton, using the telegraph and what military knowledge they had acquired, devised plans to bottle Jackson up and destroy him. But Federal forces in the valley were not under a locally unified command. They moved too slowly; one force did not obey orders strictly; and directives from Washington often neglected to take time, distance, or logistics into account. Also, in Stonewall Jackson, the Union troops were contending against one of the most outstanding field commanders America has ever produced. Jackson's philosophy of war was:

Always mystify, mislead, and surprise the enemy, if possible; and when you strike and overcome him, never give up the pursuit as long as your men have strength to follow; for an army routed, if hotly pursued, becomes panic-stricken and can then be destroyed by half their number.

By mobility and maneuver, achieved by rapid marches, surprise, deception, and hard fighting, Jackson neutralized and defeated in detail Federal forces three times larger than his own. In a classic campaign between March 23 and June 9, 1862, he fought six battles: Kernstown, McDowell, Front Royal, Winchester, Cross Keys, and Port Republic. All but Kernstown were victories. His presence alone in the Shenandoah immobilized McDowell's corps by keeping these reinforcements from joining McClellan before Richmond.

The Peninsular Campaign: Fair Oaks

When McClellan reached the peninsula in early April he found a force of ten to fifteen thousand Confederates under Maj. Gen. John B. Magruder barring his path to Richmond. Magruder, a student of drama and master of deception, so dazzled him that McClellan, instead of brushing the Confederates aside, spent a month in a siege of Yorktown. But Johnston, who wanted to fight the decisive action closer to Richmond, decided to withdraw slowly up the peninsula. At Williamsburg, on May 5, McClellan's advance elements made contact with the Confederate rear guard under Maj. Gen. James Longstreet, who successfully delayed the Federal advance. McClellan then pursued in leisurely fashion. By May 25, two corps of the Army of the Potomac had turned southwest toward Richmond and crossed the sluggish Chickahominy River.

The remaining three corps were on the north side of the stream with the expectation of making contact with McDowell, who would come down from Fredericksburg. Men of the two corps south of the river could see the spires of the Confederate capital, but Johnston's army was in front of them. (*Map 26*)

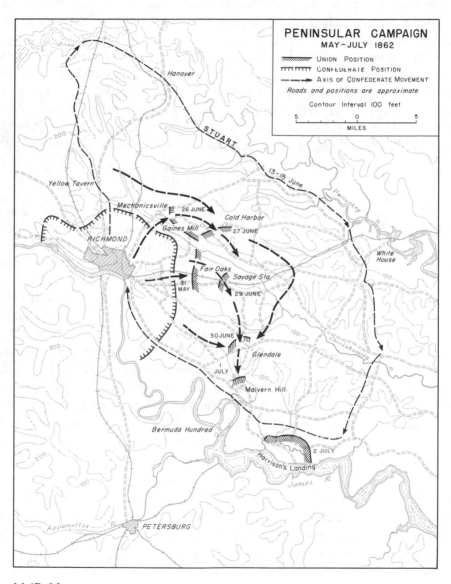

MAP 26

Drenching rains on May 30 raised the Chickahominy to flood stage and seriously divided McClellan's army. Johnston decided to grasp this chance to defeat the Federals in detail. He struck on May 31 near Fair Oaks. His plans called for his whole force to concentrate against the isolated corps south of the river, but his staff and subordinate commanders were not up to the task of executing them. Assaulting columns became confused, and attacks were delivered piecemeal. The Federals, after some initial reverses, held their ground and bloodily repulsed the Confederates.

When Johnston suffered a severe wound at Fair Oaks, President Davis replaced him with General Lee. Lee for his part had no intention of defending Richmond passively. The city's fortifications would enable him to protect Richmond with a relatively small force while he used the main body of his army offensively in an attempt to cut off and destroy the Army of the Potomac. He ordered Jackson back from the Shenandoah Valley with all possible speed.

The Seven Days' Battles

McClellan had planned to utilize his superior artillery to break through the Richmond defenses, but Lee struck the Federal Army before it could resume the advance. Lee's dispositions for the Battle of Mechanicsville on June 26 present a good illustration of the principles of mass and economy of force. On the north side of the Chickahominy, he concentrated 65,000 men to oppose Brig. Gen. Fitz-John Porter's V Corps of 30,000. Only 25,000 were left before Richmond to contain the remainder of the Union Army. When Lee attacked, the timing and co-ordination were off; Jackson of all people was slow and the V Corps defended stoutly during the day. McClellan thereupon withdrew the V Corps southeast to a stronger position at Gaines' Mill. Porter's men constructed light barricades and made ready. Lee massed 57,000 men and assaulted 34,000 Federals on June 27. The fighting was severe but numbers told, and the Federal line broke. Darkness fell before Lee could exploit his advantage, and McClellan took the opportunity to regroup Porter's men with the main army south of the Chickahominy.

At this point McClellan yielded the initiative to Lee. With his line of communications cut to White House—his supply base on the York River—and with the James River open to the U.S. Navy, the Union commander decided to shift his base to Harrison's Landing on the south side of the peninsula. His rear areas had been particularly shaky since Confederate cavalry under Brig. Gen. J. E. B. Stuart had ridden completely around the Federal Army in a daring raid in early June. The intricate retreat to the James, which involved

90,000 men, the artillery train, 3,100 wagons, and 2,500 head of cattle, began on the night of June 27 and was accomplished by using two roads. Lee tried to hinder the movement but was held off by Federal rear guards at Savage Station on June 29 and at Frayser's Farm (Glendale) on the last day of the month.

By the first day of July McClellan had concentrated the Army of the Potomac on a commanding plateau at Malvern Hill, northwest of Harrison's Landing. The location was strong, with clear fields of fire to the front and the flanks secured by streams. Massed artillery could sweep all approaches, and gunboats on the river were ready to provide fire support. The Confederates would have to attack by passing through broken and wooded terrain, traversing swampy ground, and ascending the hill. At first Lee felt McClellan's position was too strong to assault. Then, at 3:00 p.m. on July 1, when a shifting of Federal troops deceived him into thinking there was a general withdrawal, he changed his mind and attacked. Again staff work and control were poor. The assaults, which were all frontal, were delivered piecemeal by only part of the army against Union artillery, massed hub to hub, and supporting infantry. The Confederate formations were shattered because Lee failed to carry out the principle of mass. On the following day, the Army of the Potomac fell back to Harrison's Landing and dug in. After reconnoitering McClellan's position, Lee ordered his exhausted men back to the Richmond lines for rest and reorganization.

The Peninsular Campaign cost the Federal Army some 15,849 men killed, wounded, and missing. The Confederates, who had done most of the attacking, lost 20,614. Improvement in the training and discipline of the two armies since the disorganized fight at Bull Run was notable. Also significant was the fact that higher commanders had not yet thoroughly mastered their jobs. Except in McClellan's defensive action at Malvern Hill, which was largely conducted by his corps commanders, neither side had been able to bring an entire army into co-ordinated action.

Second Manassas

Failure of the Union forces to take Richmond quickly forced President Lincoln to abandon the idea of exercising command over the Union armies in person. On July 11, 1862, he selected as new General in Chief Henry W. Halleck, who had won acclaim for the victories in the west. The President did not at once appoint a successor in the west, which was to suffer from divided command for a time. Lincoln wanted Halleck to direct the various Federal armies in close concert to take advantage of the North's superior strength. If all Federal armies co-ordinated their efforts, Lincoln reasoned, they could strike where the Confederacy was weak or force it to strengthen one army at the expense of another, and eventually they could wear the Confederacy down, destroy the various armies, and win the war.

Halleck turned out to be a disappointment. He never attempted to exercise field command or assume responsibility for strategic direction of the armies. But, acting more as military adviser to the President, he performed a valuable function by serving as a channel of communication between the Chief Executive and the field commanders. He adeptly translated the President's ideas into terms the generals could comprehend, and expressed the soldier's views in language that Mr. Lincoln could understand.

Shortly before Halleck's appointment, Lincoln also decided to consolidate the various Union forces in the Shenandoah Valley and other parts of western Virginia—some 45,000 men—under the victor at Island No. 10, Maj. Gen. John Pope. Pope immediately disenchanted his new command by pointing out that in the west the Federal armies were used to seeing the backs of their enemies. Pope's so-called Army of Virginia was ordered to divert pressure from McClellan on the peninsula. But Jackson had left the valley and Federal forces were scattered. On August 3, Halleck ordered McClellan to withdraw by water from the peninsula to Aquia Creek on the Potomac and to effect a speedy junction at Fredericksburg with Pope. Meanwhile Pope began posting the Army of Virginia along the Orange and Alexandria Railroad to the west of Fredericksburg.

Lee knew that his Army of Northern Virginia was in a dangerous position between Pope and McClellan, especially if the two were to unite. On July 13, he sent Jackson, with forces eventually totaling 24,000 men, to watch Pope. After an initial sparring action at Cedar Mountain on August 9, Jackson and Pope stood watching each other for nearly a week. Lee, knowing that McClellan was leaving Harrison's Landing, had departed Richmond with the remainder of the Army of Northern Virginia and joined Jackson at Gordonsville. The combined Confederate forces outnumbered Pope's, and Lee resolved to outflank and cut off the Army of Virginia before the whole of McClellan's force could be brought to bear.

A succession of captured orders enabled both Lee and Pope to learn the intentions of the other. Pope ascertained Lee's plan to trap him against the Rappahannock and withdrew to the north bank astride the railroad. Lee, learning that two corps from the Army of the Potomac would join Pope within days, acted quickly and boldly. He sent Jackson off on a wide turning movement

TRESTLE OF THE ORANGE AND ALEXANDRIA RAILROAD *built by soldiers.*

through Thoroughfare Gap in the Bull Run Mountains around the northern flank of Pope's army and subsequently followed the same route with the divisions commanded by General Longstreet.

Pope took note of Jackson's move, but first assumed that it was pointed toward the Shenandoah Valley. Then Jackson, covering nearly sixty miles in two days, came in behind Pope at Manassas on August 26, destroyed his supply base there, and slipped away unmolested. Pope marched and counter-marched his forces for two days trying to find the elusive Confederates. At the same time the Union commander failed to take Lee's other forces into account. As a result he walked into Lee's trap on the site of the old battlefield of Manassas, or Bull Run. Pope attacked Jackson, posted behind an abandoned railroad embankment, but again the attack consisted of a series of piecemeal frontal assaults which were repulsed with heavy casualties. By then Porter's V Corps from the Army of the Potomac had reached the field and was ordered to attack Jackson's right (south) flank. By this time also, Longstreet's column had burst through Thoroughfare Gap, and deploying on Jackson's right, it blocked Porter's move.

Next day, August 30, Pope renewed his attacks against Jackson, whom he thought to be retreating. Seizing the opportunity to catch the Federal columns in an exposed position, Lee sent Longstreet slashing along the Warrenton turnpike to catch Pope's flank in the air. The Federal army soon retired from the field and Pope led it back to Washington, fighting an enveloping Confederate force at Chantilly on the way.

Lee, by great daring and rapid movement, and by virtue of having the Confederate forces unified under his command, had successfully defeated one formidable Union army in the presence of another even larger one. Halleck, as General in Chief, had not taken the field to co-ordinate Pope and McClellan, and Pope lost the campaign despite the advantage of interior lines.

President Lincoln, desiring to use McClellan's admitted talents for training and reorganizing the battered eastern armies, had become convinced that bitter personal feelings between McClellan and Pope prevented them from working effectively in the same theater. On September 5, Halleck, upon the President's order, dissolved the Army of Virginia and assigned its units to the Army of the Potomac. He sent Pope to a command in Minnesota. The Union authorities expected that McClellan would be able to devote several months to training and reorganization, but Lee dashed these hopes.

Lee Invades Maryland

Up to this point the Confederates in the east had been following defensive strategy, though tactically they frequently assumed the offensive. But Davis and Lee, for a complicated set of political and military reasons, determined to take the offensive and invade the North in co-ordination with Bragg's drive into Kentucky. Militarily, in the east, an invasion of Maryland would give Lee a chance to defeat or destroy the Army of the Potomac, uncovering such cities as Washington, Baltimore, and Philadelphia, and to cut Federal communications with the states to the west.

The Army of Northern Virginia, organized into 2 infantry commands (Longstreet's consisting of 5 divisions, and Jackson's of 4 divisions) plus Stuart's 3 brigades of cavalry, and the reserve artillery, numbered 55,000 effectives. Lee did not rest after Manassas but crossed the Potomac and encamped near Frederick, Maryland, from which he sent Jackson to capture an isolated Federal garrison at Harpers Ferry. The remainder of Lee's army then crossed South Mountain and headed for Hagerstown, about twenty-five miles northwest of Frederick, with Stuart's cavalry screening the right flank. In the meantime

McClellan's rejuvenated Army of the Potomac, 90,000 men organized into 6 corps, marched northwest from Washington and reached Frederick on September 12.

At this time McClellan had a stroke of luck. Lee, in assigning missions to his command, had detached Maj. Gen. D. H. Hill's division from Jackson and attached it to Longstreet and had sent copies of his orders, which prescribed routes, objectives, and times of arrival, to Jackson, Longstreet, and Hill. But Jackson was not sure that Hill had received the order. He therefore made an additional copy of Lee's order and sent it to Hill. One of Hill's orders, wrapped around some cigars, was somehow left behind in an abandoned camp where it was picked up on September 13 by Union soldiers and rushed to McClellan. This windfall gave the Federal commander an unmatched opportunity to defeat Lee's scattered forces in detail if he pushed fast through the gaps. McClellan vacillated for sixteen hours. Lee, informed of the lost order, sent all available forces to hold the gaps, so that it was nightfall on the 14th before McClellan fought his way across South Mountain.

Lee retreated to Sharpsburg on Antietam Creek where he turned to fight. Pinned between Antietam Creek and the Potomac with no room for maneuver, and still outnumbered since Jackson's force had yet to return to the main body after capturing Harpers Ferry, Lee relied on the advantage of interior lines and the boldness and the fighting ability of his men.

McClellan delayed his attack until September 17, when he launched an un-co-ordinated series of assaults which drove back the Confederates in places but failed to break their line. Heavy fighting swelled across ripe fields and up through rocky glens that became known to history as the West Wood, the Cornfield, the East Wood, Bloody Lane, and Burnside's Bridge. One southerner remembered the attacking Union columns: "With flags flying and the long unfaltering lines rising and falling as they crossed the rolling fields, it looked as though nothing could stop them." But when the massed fire of field guns and small arms struck such human waves, a Union survivor recalled, it "was like a scythe running through our line."

McClellan, like too many leaders during the Civil War, could not bring himself to commit his reserve (the V Corps under Porter) at the strategic moment. Although adored by his men, as one of the veterans wrote after the war, he "never realized the metal that was in his grand Army of the Potomac." Jackson's last division arrived in time to head off the final assaults by Maj. Gen. Ambrose Burnside's corps, and at the end of the day Lee still held most of his line. Casualties were heavy. Of 70,000 Federal troops nearly 13,000 were killed, wounded, or missing, and the 40,000 or more Confederates engaged lost almost as many. Although Lee audaciously awaited new attacks on September 18, McClellan left him unmolested, and that night the Army of Northern Virginia withdrew across the Potomac.

Lincoln's Emancipation Proclamation

Antietam was tactically a draw, but the fact that Lee was forced to call off the invasion made it a strategic victory and gave President Lincoln an opportunity to strike at the Confederacy psychologically and economically by issuing the Emancipation Proclamation on September 22, 1862. Lincoln, while opposed to slavery and its extension to the western territories, was not an abolitionist. He had stated publicly that the war was being fought over union or secession, with the slavery question only incidental, and had earlier overruled several generals who were premature emancipators. But anticipating the total psychological warfare techniques of the twentieth century, he had for some time desired to free the slaves of the Confederate states in order to weaken their economies and to appeal to antislavery opinion in Europe. He had awaited the opportune moment that a Union victory would give him and decided that Antietam was suitable. Acting on his authority as Commander in Chief he issued the Proclamation which stated that all slaves in states or districts in rebellion against the United States on January 1, 1863, would be thenceforward and forever free. The Proclamation set no slaves free on the day it took effect. Negroes in the four slave states still in the Union were not touched, nor were the slaves in those Confederate areas that had been subjugated by Union bayonets. It had no immediate effect behind the Confederate lines, except to cause a good deal of excitement. But thereafter, as Union forces penetrated the South, the newly freed people deserted the farms and plantations and flocked to the colors.

Negroes had served in the Revolution, the War of 1812, and other early wars, but they had been barred from the Regular Army and, under the Militia Act of 1792, from the state militia. The Civil War marks their official debut in American military forces. Recruiting of Negroes began under the local auspices of Maj. Gen. David Hunter in the Department of the South as early as April 1862. There was a certain appeal to the idea that Negroes might assure their freedom by joining in the battle for it even if they served for lower pay in segregated units under white officers. On July 17, 1862, Congress authorized recruitment of Negroes while passing the antislavery Second Confiscation Act. The Emancipation Proclamation put the matter in a new light, and on May 22, 1863, the War Department established a Bureau of Colored Troops, another innovation of the Civil War since it was an example of Federal volunteer formations without official ties to specific states (others being the various U.S. sharp-shooter regiments and the invalid Veteran Reserve Corps). By the end of the war 100,000 Negroes were enrolled as U.S. Volunteers. Many other Negroes served in state units, elsewhere in the armed forces, and as laborers for the Union Army.

Fiasco at Fredericksburg

After Antietam both armies returned to face each other in Virginia, Lee situated near Culpeper and McClellan at Warrenton. But McClellan's slowness, his failure to accomplish more at Antietam, and perhaps his rather arrogant habit of offering gratuitous political advice to his superiors, coupled with the intense anti-McClellan views of the joint Congressional Committee on the Conduct of the War, convinced Lincoln that he could retain him in command no longer. On November 7 Lincoln replaced him with Burnside, who had won distinction in operations that gained control of ports on the North Carolina coast and who had led the IX Corps at Antietam. Burnside accepted the post with reluctance.

Burnside decided to march rapidly to Fredericksburg and then advance along the railroad line to Richmond before Lee could intercept him. (*Map 27*) Such a move by the army—now 120,000 strong—would cut Lee off from his main base. Burnside's advance elements reached the north bank of the Rappahannock on November 17, well ahead of Lee. But a series of minor failures delayed the completion of ponton bridges, and Lee moved his army to high ground on the south side of the river before the Federal forces could cross. Lee's situation resembled McClellan's position at Malvern Hill which had proved the folly of frontal assaults against combined artillery and infantry strongpoints. But Burnside thought the sheer weight of numbers could smash through the Confederates.

To achieve greater ease of tactical control, Burnside had created three headquarters higher than corps—the Right, Center, and Left Grand Divisions under Maj. Gens. Edwin V. Sumner, Joseph Hooker, and William B. Franklin, respectively—with two corps plus cavalry assigned to each grand division. Burnside originally planned to make the main thrust by Center and Left Grand Divisions against Jackson's positions on a long, low-wooded ridge southeast of the town. The Right Grand Division would cross three ponton bridges at Fredericksburg and attack Marye's Heights, a steep eminence about one mile from the river where Longstreet's men were posted. On the morning of December 13, he weakened the attack on the left, feeling that under cover of

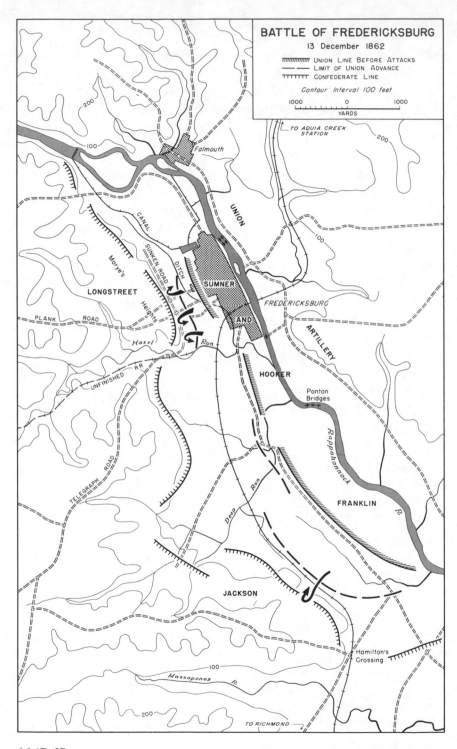

BATTLE OF FREDERICKSBURG
13 December 1862

mmmmm UNION LINE BEFORE ATTACKS
— — — LIMIT OF UNION ADVANCE
TTTTTT CONFEDERATE LINE

Contour Interval 100 feet

1000   0   1000
YARDS

TO AQUIA CREEK STATION

Falmouth

UNION

CANAL

SUNKEN ROAD

DITCH

Marye's

Heights

LONGSTREET

PLANK ROAD

Hazel Run

UNFINISHED RR

SUMNER

AND

FREDERICKSBURG

ARTILLERY

HOOKER

Ponton Bridges

TELEGRAPH ROAD

Deep Run

Rappahannock R.

FRANKLIN

JACKSON

Hamilton's Crossing

Massaponax R.

TO RICHMOND

MAP 27

147 heavy siege and field guns on the heights on the Union side of the river much could be achieved by a better-balanced attack along the whole line.

Burnside's engineers had begun laying the bridges as early as December 11. But harassment from Confederate sharpshooters complicated the operation, and it was not until the next day that all the assault units were over the river. After an artillery duel on the morning of the 13th, fog lifted to reveal dense Union columns moving forward to the attack. Part of the Left Grand Division, finding a weakness in Jackson's line, drove in to seize the ridge, but as Burnside had weakened this part of the assault the Federals were not able to hold against Confederate counterattacks. On the right, the troops had to cross a mile of open ground to reach Marye's Heights, traverse a drainage canal, and face a fusillade of fire from the infamous sunken road and stone wall behind which Longstreet had placed four ranks of riflemen. In a series of assaults the Union soldiers pushed to the stone wall but no farther. As a demonstration of valor the effort was exemplary; as a demonstration of tactical skill it was tragic. Lee, observing the shattered attackers, commented: "It is well that war is so terrible—we should grow too fond of it."

The Army of the Potomac lost 12,000 men at Fredericksburg while the Army of Northern Virginia suffered only 5,300 casualties. Burnside planned to renew the attack on the following day and Jackson, whose enthusiasm in battle sometimes approached the point of frenzy, suggested that the Confederates strip off their clothes for better identification and strike the Army of the Potomac in a night attack. But Lee knew of Burnside's plans from a captured order and vetoed the scheme. When the Federal corps commanders talked Burnside out of renewing the attack, both armies settled into winter quarters facing each other across the Rappahannock. Fredericksburg, a disastrous defeat, was otherwise noteworthy for the U.S. Army in that the telegraph first saw extensive battlefield use, linking headquarters with forward batteries during the action—a forerunner of twentieth century battlefield communications.

West of the Mississippi

If the major fighting of the Civil War occurred in the "older" populated sections of the United States, the youthful area of the American frontier across the Mississippi saw its share of action also. Missouri and Kansas, and indeed the distant New Mexico Territory (all areas involved in the root causes for the conflict), were touched by the Civil War.

The Southwest was a particularly rich plum, for as one Confederate commander observed: "The vast mineral resources of Arizona, in addition to its

affording an outlet to the Pacific, makes its acquisition a matter of some importance to our Govt." Also it was assumed that Indians and the Mormons in Utah
would readily accept allegiance to almost any government other than that in
Washington.

It was with these motives in mind that early in 1862 Confederate forces
moved up the Rio Grande valley and proceeded to establish that part of New
Mexico Territory north of the 34th parallel as the Confederate territory of
Arizona. Under Brig. Gen. Henry H. Sibley, inventor of a famous tent bearing
his name, the Confederates successfully swept all the way to Santa Fe, capital of
New Mexico, bypassing several Union garrisons on the way. But Sibley was
dangerously overextended, and Federal troops, reinforced by Colorado volunteers, surprised the advancing Confederates in Apache Canyon on March 26
and 28, as they sought to capture the largest Union garrison in the territory at
Fort Union.

One of the bypassed Federal columns under Col. Edward R. S. Canby from
Fort Craig meanwhile joined the Fort Union troops against the Confederates.
Unable to capture the Union posts, unable to resupply his forces, and learning
of yet a third Federal column converging on him from California, Sibley began
a determined retreat down the Rio Grande valley. By May he was back in Texas
and the Confederate invasion of New Mexico was ended. The fighting, on a
small scale by eastern standards, provided valuable training for Federal troops
involved later in Indian wars in this area. Indeed, while the Confederate dream
of a new territory and an outlet to the Pacific was shattered by 1862, Indian
leaders in the mountain territories saw an opportunity to reconquer lost land
while the white men were otherwise preoccupied. In 1863 and 1864 both Federal
and Confederate troops in the southwest were kept busy fighting hostile tribes.
(Map 28)

In Missouri and Arkansas, fighting had erupted on a large scale by the early
spring of 1862. Federal authorities had retained a precarious hold over Missouri
when Maj. Gen. Samuel R. Curtis with 11,000 men chased disorganized Confederates back into Arkansas. But under General Van Dorn and Maj. Gen. Sterling
Price, the Confederates regrouped and embarked upon a counteroffensive which
only ended at Pea Ridge on March 7 and 8. Here Van Dorn executed a double
envelopment as half his army stole behind Pea Ridge, marched around three-
fourths of Curtis' force, and struck Curtis' left rear near Elkhorn Tavern while
the other half attacked his right rear. But in so doing the Confederates uncovered
their own line of communications and Curtis' troops turned around and fought
off the attacks from the rear. After initial success, Van Dorn and Price were

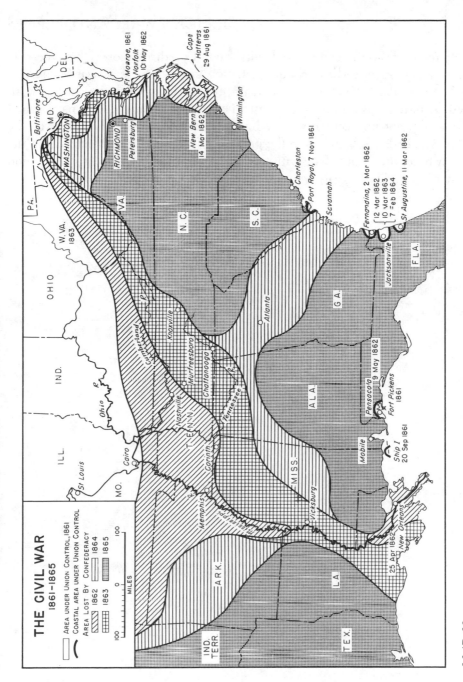

THE CIVIL WAR
1861-1865

- ☐ AREA UNDER UNION CONTROL, 1861
- ⌒ COASTAL AREA UNDER UNION CONTROL

AREA LOST BY CONFEDERACY

1862	1864
1863	1865

MILES
100   0   100

Baltimore

DEL.

Ft Monroe, 1861
Norfolk
10 May 1862

Cape
Hatteras
29 Aug 1861

MD.

WASHINGTON

PA.

RICHMOND
Petersburg

VA.

Wilmington

New Bern
14 Mar 1862

W. VA.
1863

N.C.

S.C.

Charleston

Port Royal, 7 Nov 1861

Savannah

Fernandina, 2 Mar 1862
12 Mar 1862
10 Mar 1863
7 Feb 1864
St Augustine, 11 Mar 1862

OHIO

Jacksonville

FLA.

IND.

Knoxville

Cumberland R.

Murfreesboro

Chattanooga

Atlanta

GA.

ILL.

Nashville

TENN.

Tennessee R.

ALA.

Pensacola
9 May 1862

Fort Pickens
1861

St Louis

MO.

Cairo

Ohio R.

Memphis

Corinth

Mississippi R.

Vicksburg

MISS.

Mobile

Ship I
20 Sep 1861

New Orleans
25 Apr 1862

ARK.

LA.

IND.
TERR.

TEX.

MAP 28

unable to continue the contest and withdrew. For three more years guerrilla warfare would ravage Missouri but the Union grip on the state was secure.

The year 1862, which began with impressive Union victories in the west, ended in bitter frustration in the east. Ten full-scale and costly battles had been fought, but no decisive victory had yet been scored by the forces of the Union. The Federals had broken the great Confederate counteroffensives in the fall only to see their hopes fade with the advent of winter. Apparently the Union war machine had lost its earlier momentum.

CHAPTER 7

The Civil War, 1863

At the beginning of 1863 the Confederacy seemed to have a fair chance of ultimate success on the battlefield. But during this year three great campaigns would take place that would shape the outcome of the war in favor of the North. One would see the final solution to the control of the Mississippi River. A second, concurrent with the first, would break the back of any Confederate hopes for success by invasion of the North and recognition abroad. The third, slow and uncertain in its first phases, would result eventually in Union control of the strategic gateway to the South Atlantic region of the Confederacy—the last great stronghold of secession and the area in which the internecine conflict would come of age as modern total war.

Confusion Over Clearing the Mississippi

When Halleck went east in September 1862 to become General in Chief, his splendid army was divided between Grant and Buell. Grant, with over 60,000 men, remained in western Tennessee guarding communication lines. Buell's army of 56,000, after containing Bragg's invasion of Kentucky, had been taken over by Rosecrans, whose hard-won victory at Murfreesboro at the end of 1862 nevertheless immobilized the Army of the Cumberland for nearly half a year. To the west, only the posts at Vicksburg and Port Hudson prevented the Union from controlling the entire length of the Mississippi and splitting the Confederacy in two. Naval expeditions, under Capt. David G. Farragut, supported by the army, tried to seize Vicksburg in May and again in July 1862, but the Confederates easily repulsed the attempts. In the autumn Grant pressed Halleck to let him get on with the campaign down the Mississippi and finally received the response: "Fight the enemy where you please." But while Halleck and Grant were planning to move against Vicksburg by water and land, Lincoln and Stanton also outlined a similar move, but without consulting the military leaders.

The Chief Executive had long seen the importance of controlling the Mississippi, and in the fall of 1862 he and the Secretary of War prepared plans for a simultaneous advance northward from New Orleans and southward from Tennessee. Somewhat vague orders were drawn up giving command of the northbound expedition to Maj. Gen. Nathaniel Banks, who had replaced Butler as commander of the Department of the Gulf. Command of the southbound expedition was to go to Maj. Gen. John A. McClernand. Both officers were relatively untried, unstable, volunteer officers and politicians who often dabbled in intrigue in order to gain favors. Further, McClernand was to operate within Grant's department but independently of him. When Halleck found out about the Lincoln-Stanton plan, he persuaded the President to put Grant in command of the southbound expedition and to make McClernand one of his subordinates.

Grant's Campaign Against Vicksburg

Grant first tried a combined land and water expedition against Vicksburg in December 1862–January 1863. He sent Maj. Gen. William T. Sherman down river from Memphis, but the Confederates under Van Dorn and Forrest raided and cut the 200-mile-long line of communications. Sherman himself bogged down before Vicksburg, and Grant, perhaps also wishing to keep close rein on McClernand, who ranked Sherman, then determined on a river expedition which he would lead in person. Late in January Grant arrived before Vicksburg. He had upwards of 45,000 men, organized into three corps, the XIII Corps under McClernand, the XV Corps under Sherman, and Maj. Gen. James B. McPherson's XVII Corps. During the ensuing campaign Grant received two more corps as reinforcements to bring his total strength to 75,000 men.

Vicksburg had almost a perfect location for defense. (*Map 29*) At that point on the river, bluffs rose as high as 250 feet above the water and extended for about 100 miles from north to south. North of Vicksburg lay the Yazoo River and its delta, a gloomy stretch of watery, swampy bottom land extending 175 miles from north to south, 60 miles from east to west. The ground immediately south of Vicksburg was almost as swampy and impassable. The Confederates had fortified the bluffs from Haynes' Bluff on the Yazoo, some 10 miles above Vicksburg, to Grand Gulf at the mouth of the Big Black River about 40 miles below. Vicksburg could not be assaulted from the river, and sailing past it was extremely hazardous. The river formed a great U here, and Vicksburg's guns threatened any craft that tried to run by. For the Union troops to attack successfully, they would have to get to the high, dry ground east of town. This would put them in Confederate territory between two enemy forces. Lt. Gen. John C. Pemberton commanded some 30,000 men in Vicksburg, while the Confederate area commander, General Joseph E. Johnston (now recovered from his wound at Fair Oaks), concentrated the other scattered Confederate forces in Mississippi at Jackson, the state capital, 40 miles east of Vicksburg.

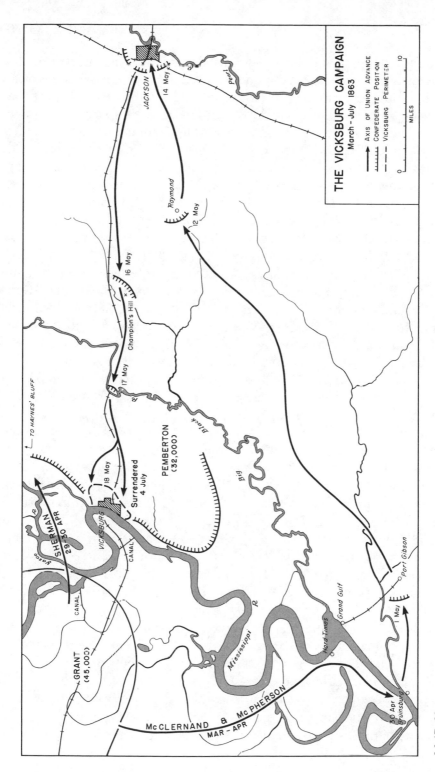

THE VICKSBURG CAMPAIGN
March – July 1863

AXIS OF UNION ADVANCE
CONFEDERATE POSITION
VICKSBURG PERIMETER

MILES

JACKSON

14 May

Pearl

Raymond

12 May

16 May

Champion's Hill

17 May

TO HAYNES' BLUFF

18 May

Surrendered
4 July

PEMBERTON
(32,000)

Black

Big

SHERMAN
29-30 APR

VICKSBURG

CANAL

CANAL

Yazoo R

Port Gibson

Grand Gulf

1 May

Hard Times

Mississippi R

GRANT
(45,000)

McCLERNAND & McPHERSON
MAR – APR

30 Apr
Bruinsburg

MAP 29

During late winter and early spring, with the rains falling, the streams high, and the roads at their wettest and muddiest, overland movement was impossible. Primarily to placate discontented politicians and a critical press, Grant made four attempts to reach high ground east of Vicksburg. All four were unsuccessful, foiled either by Confederate resistance or by natural obstacles. One of the more spectacular efforts was digging canals. These projects had as their objective the clearing of an approach by which troops could sail to a point near the high ground without being fired on by Vicksburg's guns, and all failed. That Grant kept on trying in the face of such discouragement is a tribute to his dogged persistence, and that Lincoln supported him is a tribute to his confidence in the general. The trouble was that Grant had been on the river for two months, and by early spring, Vicksburg was no nearer falling than when he came.

On April 4 in a letter to Halleck, Grant divulged his latest plan to capture Vicksburg. Working closely with the local naval commander, Flag Officer David D. Porter, Grant evolved a stroke of great boldness. He decided to use part of his force above Vicksburg to divert the Confederates while the main body marched southward on the west side of the Mississippi, crossed to the east bank, and with only five days' rations struck inland to live off a hostile country without a line of supply or retreat. As he told Sherman, the Union troops would carry "what rations of hard bread, coffee, and salt we can and make the country furnish the balance." Porter's gunboats and other craft, which up to now were on the river north of Vicksburg, were to run past the batteries during darkness and then ferry the troops over the river. Sherman thought the campaign too risky, but the events of the next two months were to prove him wrong.

While Sherman demonstrated near Vicksburg in March, McClernand's and McPherson's corps started their advance south. The rains let up in April, the waters receded slightly, and overland movement became somewhat easier. On the night of April 16 Porter led his river fleet past Vicksburg, whose guns, once the move was discovered, lit up the black night with an eerie bombardment. All but one transport made it safely, and starting on April 30, Porter's craft ferried the troops eastward over the river at Bruinsburg below Grand Gulf. The final march against Vicksburg was ready to begin.

At this time the Confederates had more troops in the vicinity than Grant had but never could make proper use of them. Grant's swift move had bewildered Pemberton. Then too, just before marching downstream, Grant had ordered a brigade of cavalry to come down from the Tennessee border, riding between the parallel north-south railroad lines of the Mississippi Central and Mobile and Ohio. Led by Col. Benjamin H. Grierson, this force sliced the length of the state, cutting railroads, fighting detachments of Confederate cavalry, and finally reaching Union lines at Baton Rouge, Louisiana. Most important, for the few days that counted most, it drew Pemberton's attention away from Grant and kept the Confederate general from discerning the Union's objectives.

Once more divided counsel hampered co-ordination of Confederate strategy. Johnston had been sent west by Davis to take over-all command, an imposing task, for Pemberton's army in Mississippi and Bragg's in Tennessee were widely separated. Things were further confused by Davis' directive to Pemberton to hold Vicksburg at all costs while Johnston recognized the potential trap and ordered him to move directly against Grant. In such a situation Pemberton could do little that was right. He tried to defend too wide an area; he had not concentrated but dispersed his forces at Vicksburg, the Big Black River, and along the railroad line to Jackson, where Johnston was gathering more troops.

After Grant had captured Port Gibson on May 1, and Sherman's corps had rejoined the main force, the Union commander decided that he must defeat Johnston before turning on Vicksburg. He moved northeastward and fought his way into Raymond on May 12, a move which put him squarely between Johnston and Pemberton and in a position to cut the Confederate line of communications. Next day Sherman and McPherson marched against the city of Jackson, with McClernand following in reserve, ready to hold off Pemberton. The leading corps took Jackson on May 14 and drove its garrison eastward. While Sherman occupied the state capital to fend off Johnston, the other two corps turned west against Pemberton and Vicksburg. Pemberton tried too late to catch Grant in open country. He suffered severe defeats at Champion's Hill (May 16) and Black River Bridge (May 17) and was shut up in Vicksburg. In eighteen days' Grant's army had marched 200 miles, had won four victories, and had finally secured the high ground along the Yazoo River that had been the goal of all the winter's fruitless campaigning.

Grant assaulted the Vicksburg lines on May 18 and 22, but as Sherman noted of the attacks: "The heads of columns have been swept away as chaff from the hand on a windy day." The only recourse now was a siege. Grant settled down, and removed McClernand from command after the attack of May 22 during which the corps commander sent a misleading report, then later slighted the efforts of the other corps and publicly criticized the army commander. Grant replaced him with Maj. Gen. Edward O. C. Ord, and ordered the army to implant batteries and dig trenches around the city.

The rest was now a matter of time, as Sherman easily kept Johnston away and the Federals advanced their siegeworks toward the Confederate fortifications. Food became scarce and the troops and civilians inside Vicksburg were

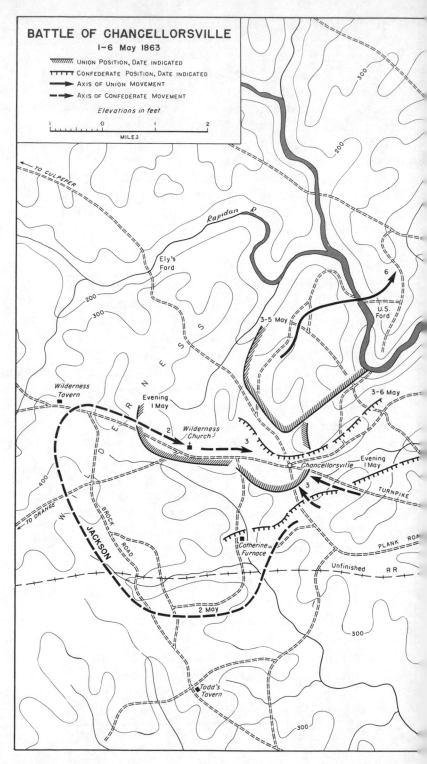

BATTLE OF CHANCELLORSVILLE
1–6 May 1863

Union Position, Date indicated
Confederate Position, Date indicated
Axis of Union Movement
Axis of Confederate Movement

Elevations in feet

0   1   2
MILES

TO CULPEPER

Rapidan R.

Ely's Ford

300
200

3–5 May

U.S. Ford

6

W I L D E R N E S S

200
300

Wilderness Tavern

Evening 1 May

2   Wilderness Church

3–6 May

3

Chancellorsville

Evening 1 May

TURNPIKE

3

400

TO ORANGE

JACKSON

BROCK ROAD

Catherine Furnace

PLANK ROAD

Unfinished   R R

2 May

300

Todd's Tavern

300

MAP 30

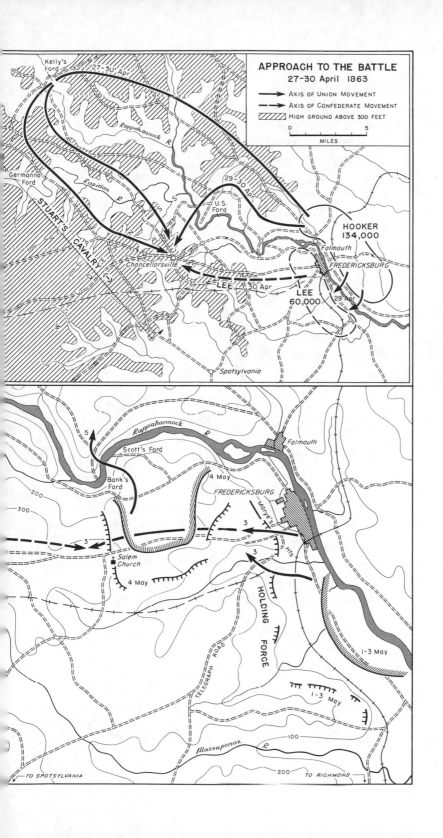

APPROACH TO THE BATTLE
27–30 April 1863

→ AXIS OF UNION MOVEMENT
⇢ AXIS OF CONFEDERATE MOVEMENT
▧ HIGH GROUND ABOVE 300 FEET

0   5
MILES

Kelly's Ford

27–30 Apr

Rappahannock R.

Germanna Ford

Rapidan R.

29–30 Apr

U.S. Ford

STUART'S CALVARY

HOOKER
134,000

Falmouth

FREDERICKSBURG

Chancellorsville

LEE 30 Apr

LEE
60,000

29 Apr

Spotsylvania

Rappahannock R.

Scott's Ford

Falmouth

4 May

Bank's Ford

FREDERICKSBURG

200

300

Marye's

Hts.

3

3

3

3

Salem Church

4 May

4 May

HOLDING FORCE

1–3 May

TELEGRAPH ROAD

1–3 May

100

Massaponax R.

TO SPOTSYLVANIA

200

TO RICHMOND

soon reduced to eating mules and horses. Shells pounded the city, and the Federal lines were drawn so tight that one Confederate soldier admitted that "a cat could not have crept out of Vicksburg without being discovered." The front lines were so close that the Federals threw primitive hand grenades into the Confederate works. By July 1 the Union troops had completed their approaches and were ready for another assault. But Vicksburg was starving and Pemberton asked for terms. Grant offered to parole all prisoners, and the city surrendered on Independence Day. Since Grant was out of telegraphic contact with Washington, the news reached the President via naval channels on July 7, the day before General Banks' 15,000-man army, having advanced up river from New Orleans, captured Port Hudson. The whole river was now repossessed by the Union, the Confederacy sliced in two. Once more Grant had removed an entire Confederate army from the war—40,000 men—losing only one-tenth that number in the process.

Hooker Crosses the Rappahannock

Events in the western theater in the spring and early summer of 1863 were impressive. Those in the east during the same period were fewer in number but equally dramatic. After the battle of Fredericksburg, Burnside's Army of the Potomac went into winter quarters on the north bank of the Rappahannock, while the main body of Lee's Army of Northern Virginia held Fredericksburg and guarded the railway line to Richmond. During January, Burnside's subordinates intrigued against him and went out of channels to present their grievances to Congress and the President. When Burnside heard of this development, he asked that either he or most of the subordinate general officers be removed. The President accepted the first alternative, and on January 25, 1863, replaced Burnside with Maj. Gen. Joseph Hooker. The new commander had won the sobriquet of "Fighting Joe" for his intrepid reputation as a division and corps commander. He was highly favored in Washington, but in appointing him the President took the occasion to write a fatherly letter in which he warned the general against rashness and overambition, reproached him for plotting against Burnside, and concluded by asking for victories.

Under Hooker's able administration, discipline and training improved. Morale, which had fallen after Fredericksburg, rose as Hooker regularized the furlough system and improved the flow of rations and other supplies to his front-line troops. Abolishing Burnside's grand divisions Hooker returned to the orthodox corps, of which he had seven, each numbering about 15,000 men. One of Hooker's most effective innovations was the introduction of distinctive corps and division insignia. He also took a long step toward improving the cavalry arm of the army, which up to this time had been assigned many diverse duties and was split up into small detachments. Hooker regarded cavalry as a combat arm of full stature, and he concentrated his units into a cavalry corps of three divisions under Brig. Gen. George Stoneman. On the other hand Hooker made a costly mistake in decentralizing tactical control of his artillery to his corps commanders. As a result Union artillery would not be properly massed in the coming action at Chancellorsville.

Hooker had no intention of repeating Burnside's tragic frontal assault at Fredericksburg. With a strength approaching 134,000 men, Hooker planned a double envelopment which would place strong Union forces on each of Lee's flanks. (*Map 30*) He ordered three of his infantry corps to move secretly up the Rappahannock and ford the stream, while two more corps, having conspicuously remained opposite Fredericksburg, were to strike across the old battlefield there. Two more corps were in reserve. The cavalry corps, less one division which was to screen the move up river, was to raid far behind Lee's rear to divert him. Hooker's plan was superb; his execution faulty. The three corps moved quickly up the river and by the end of April had crossed and advanced to the principal road junction of Chancellorsville. They were now in the so-called "Wilderness," a low, flat, confusing area of scrub timber and narrow dirt roads in which movement and visibility were extremely limited. Maj. Gen. John Sedgwick crossed the Rappahannock at Fredericksburg on the 29th, and the two remaining corps moved to within supporting distance of Hooker at Chancellorsville. So far everything had gone according to plan, except that Stoneman's diversion had failed to bother Lee. One of Stuart's brigades kept Stoneman under surveillance while the main body of cavalry shadowed Hooker so effectively that the southern commander knew every move made by the Union army. By the morning of April 30, Lee was aware of what was afoot and knew that he was threatened by double envelopment. Already Hooker was sending his columns eastward toward the back door to Fredericksburg. A less bold and resolute man than Lee would have retreated southward at once, and with such ample justification that only the captious would have found fault. But the southern general, his army numbering only 60,000, used the principles of the offensive, maneuver, economy of force, and surprise to compensate for his inferior numbers. Instead of retreating, he left a part of his army to hold the heights at Fredericksburg and started west for Chancellorsville with the main body.

Chancellorsville: Lee's Finest Battle

When Lee began to move, Hooker simply lost his courage. Over protests of his corps commanders, he ordered the troops back into defensive positions around Chancellorsville. The Federals established a line in the forest, felled trees for an abatis, and constructed earth-and-log breastworks. Their position faced generally south, anchored on the Rappahannock on the east; but in the west it was weak, unsupported, and hanging in the air. Lee brought his main body up and on May 1 made contact with Hooker's strong left. That day Stuart's cavalry discovered Hooker's vulnerable right flank and promptly reported the intelligence to Lee. Conferring that night with Stonewall Jackson, Lee made another bold decision. Facing an army much greater than his own, he decided to divide his forces and further envelop the envelopers. Accordingly, Lee committed about 17,000 men against Hooker's left to hold it in place while Jackson with some 26,000 men made a wide 15-mile swing to get beyond the right flank. At first glance Lee's decision might appear a violation of the principles of mass and concentration, but while Lee's two forces were initially separated their common objective was the Army of the Potomac, and their ultimate routes converged on a common center.

Jackson's force, in a 10-mile-long column, moved out at daybreak of May 2, marching southwest first, then swinging northwest to get into position. The Federals noted that something was happening off to the south but were unable to penetrate the defensive screen; Hooker soon began to think Lee was actually retreating. In late afternoon Jackson turned onto the Orange turnpike near Wilderness Tavern. This move put him west of Hooker's right flank, and since the woods thinned out a little at this point it was possible to form a line of battle. Because time was running short and the hour of the day was late, Jackson deployed in column of divisions, with each division formed with brigades abreast, the same kind of confusing formation Johnston had used at Shiloh. Shortly after 5:00 p.m. Jackson's leading division, shrieking the "rebel yell" and driving startled rabbits and deer before it, came charging out of the woods, rolling up Maj. Gen. Oliver O. Howard's XI Corps in wild rout. The Confederates pressed forward, but fresh Union troops, disorganization of his own men, and oncoming darkness stymied the impatient Jackson. While searching for a road that would permit him to cut off Hooker from United States Ford across the Rappahannock, Jackson fell prey to a mistaken ambush by his own men. The Confederate leader was wounded and died eight days later. During the night of May 2, Stuart, Jackson's successor as corps commander, re-formed his lines. Against Stuart's right, Hooker launched local counterattacks which at first gained some success, but the next morning withdrew his whole line. Once more Hooker yielded the initiative at the moment he had a strong force between Lee's two divided and weaker forces.

Stuart renewed the attack during the morning as Hooker pulled his line back. Hooker was knocked unconscious when a shell struck the pillar of the Chancellor house against which he was leaning. Until the end of the battle he was dazed and incapable of exercising effective command, but he did not relinquish it nor would the army's medical director declare him unfit. Meanwhile Sedgwick, who shortly after Jackson's attack had received orders to proceed through Fredericksburg to Chancellorsville, had assaulted Marye's Heights. He carried it about noon on May 3, but the next day Lee once more divided his command, leaving Stuart with 25,000 to guard Hooker, and moved himself with 21,000 to thwart Sedgwick. In a sharp action at Salem Church, Lee forced the Federals off the road and northward over the Rappahannock. Lee now made ready for a full-scale assault against the Army of the Potomac huddled with its back against the river on May 6, but Hooker ordered retirement to the north bank before the attack. Confederate losses were approximately 13,000; Federal losses, 17,000. But Lee lost far more with the death of Jackson. Actually, Lee's brilliant and daring maneuvers had defeated only one man—Hooker—and in no other action of the war did moral superiority of one general over the other stand out so clearly as a decisive factor in battle. Chancellorsville exemplified Napoleon's maxim: "The General is the head, the whole of the army."

Hooker was a talented tactical commander with a good reputation. But in spite of Lincoln's injunction, "This time, put in all your men," he allowed nearly one-third of his army to stand idle during the heaviest fighting. Here again was a general who could effectively lead a body of troops under his own eyes, but could not use maps and reports to evaluate and control situations that were beyond his range of vision. Hooker, not the Army of the Potomac, lost the battle of Chancellorsville. Yet for the victors, Chancellorsville was a hollow triumph. It was dazzling, a set piece for the instruction of students of the military art ever since, but it had been inconclusive, winning glory and little more. It left government and army on both sides with precisely the problems they had faced before the campaign began.

Lee's Second Invasion of the North

By 1863 the war had entered what Sherman called its professional phase. The troops were well trained and had ample combat experience. Officers had generally mastered their jobs and were deploying their forces fairly skillfully in accordance with the day's tactical principles. Furthermore, the increased range and accuracy of weapons, together with the nature of the terrain, had induced some alterations in tactics, alterations which were embodied in a revised infantry manual published in 1863. Thus, by the third year of the war, battles had begun to take on certain definite characteristics. The battle of Gettysburg is a case in point.

Gettysburg was, first of all, an act of fate—a 3-day holocaust, largely unplanned and uncontrollable. Like the war itself, it sprang from decisions that men under pressure made in the light of imperfect knowledge. It would someday symbolize the war with all the blunders and heroism, hopes and delusions, combativeness and blinding devotion of the American man in arms of that period. With its enormous destruction, tactical maneuvers, and use of weapons, Gettysburg was one of the most dramatic and most typical of the 2,000-odd land engagements of the Civil War.

After the great victory at Chancellorsville, the Confederate cause in the eastern theater looked exceptionally bright. If 60,000 men could beat 134,000, then the Confederacy's inferiority in manpower was surely offset by superior generalship and skill at arms. Vicksburg was not yet under siege, although Grant had ferried his army over to the east bank of the Mississippi. If Davis and Lee were overly optimistic, they could hardly be blamed. Both men favored another invasion of the North for much the same political and military reasons that led to invasion in 1862. Longstreet, on the other hand, was concerned over the Federal threats in the west. He proposed going on the defensive in Virginia and advised taking advantage of the Confederacy's railroads and interior lines to send part of the Army of Northern Virginia to Tennessee to relieve pressure on Vicksburg. But he was overruled and Lee made ready to move into Pennsylvania. By this time Union strategy in the east was clearly defined: to continue operations against Confederate seaports—an attempt to seize Fort Sumter on April 7 had failed—and to destroy Lee's army. President Lincoln's orders made clear that the destruction of the Army of Northern Virginia was the major objective of the Army of the Potomac. Richmond was only incidental.

On June 30, 1863, the Army of the Potomac numbered 115,256 officers and enlisted men, with 362 guns. It consisted of 51 infantry brigades organized into 19 divisions, which in turn formed 7 infantry corps. The cavalry corps had 3 divisions. The field artillery, 67 batteries, was assigned by brigades to the corps, except for army reserve artillery. The Army of Northern Virginia, numbering 76,224 men and 272 guns in late May, comprised 3 infantry corps, each led by a lieutenant general, and Stuart's cavalry division. (The Confederacy was much more generous with rank than was the U.S. Army.) In each corps were 3 divisions, and most divisions had 4 brigades. Of the 15 field artillery battalions of 4 batteries each, 5 battalions were attached to each corps under command of the corps' artillery chiefs.

In early June Lee began moving his units away from Fredericksburg. In his advance he used the Shenandoah and Cumberland Valleys, for by holding the east-west mountain passes he could readily cover his approach route and line of communications. Hooker got wind of the move; he noted the weakening of the Fredericksburg defenses, and on June 9 his cavalry, commanded by Brig. Gen. Alfred Pleasonton, surprised Stuart at Brandy Station, Virginia. Here on an open plain was fought one of the few mounted, saber-swinging, cut-and-thrust cavalry combats of the Civil War. Up to now the Confederate cavalry had been superior, but at Brandy Station the Union horsemen "came of age," and Stuart was lucky to hold his position.

When the Federals learned that Confederate infantrymen were west of the Blue Ridge heading north, Hooker started to move to protect Washington and Baltimore and to attempt to destroy Lee. Earlier, Lincoln had vetoed Hooker's proposal to seize Richmond while Lee went north. As the Army of Northern Virginia moved through the valleys and deployed into Pennsylvania behind cavalry screens, the Army of the Potomac moved north on a broad front to the east, crossing the Potomac on June 25 and 26. Lee, forced to disperse by the lack of supplies, had extended his infantry columns from McConnellsburg and Chambersburg on the west to Carlisle in the north and York on the east.

After Brandy Station, and some sharp clashes in the mountain passes, Stuart set forth on another dramatic ride around the Union army. With only vague instructions and acting largely on his own initiative, he proved of little use to Lee. It was only on the afternoon of July 2 with his troopers so weary that they were almost falling from their saddles, that Stuart rejoined Lee in the vicinity of Gettysburg, too late to have an important influence on the battle. His absence had deprived Lee of prompt, accurate information about the Army of the Potomac. When Lee learned from Longstreet on June 28 that Hooker's men were north of the Potomac, he ordered his widespread units to concentrate at once between Gettysburg and Cashtown.

After Chancellorsville, Lincoln, though advised to drop Hooker, had kept him in command of the Army of the Potomac on the theory that he would not throw away a gun because it has misfired once. But Hooker soon became embroiled with Halleck and requested his own relief. He was replaced by a corps commander, Maj. Gen. George G. Meade, who before dawn on June 28 received word of his promotion and the accompanying problems inherent in assuming command of a great army while it was moving toward the enemy. Meade, who was to command the Army of the Potomac for the rest of the war, started north on a broad front at once but within two days decided to fight a defensive action in Maryland and issued orders to that effect. However, not all his commanders received the order, and events overruled him.

Gettysburg

Outposts of both armies clashed during the afternoon of June 30 near the quiet little Pennsylvania market town of Gettysburg. The terrain in the area included rolling hills and broad shallow valleys. Gettysburg was the junction of twelve roads that led to Harrisburg, Philadelphia, Baltimore, Washington, and the mountain passes to the west which were controlled by Lee. The rest was inevitable; the local commanders sent reports and recommendations to their superiors, who relayed them upward, so that both armies, still widely dispersed, started moving toward Gettysburg. (*Map 31*)

On July 1, Union cavalrymen fought a dismounted delaying action against advance troops of Lt. Gen. Ambrose P. Hill's corps northwest of town. By this stage of the war cavalrymen, armed with saber, pistol, and breech-loading carbine, were often deployed as mounted infantrymen, riding to battle but fighting on foot. The range and accuracy of the infantry's rifled muskets made it next to impossible for mounted men to attack foot soldiers in position. With their superior speed and mobility, cavalrymen, as witnessed in the Gettysburg campaign, were especially useful for screening, reconnaissance, and advance guard actions in which they seized and held important hills, river crossings, and road junctions pending the arrival of infantry. During the morning hours of July 1, this was the role played by Union horsemen on the ridges north and west of Gettysburg.

By noon both the I and the XI Corps of the Army of the Potomac had joined in the battle, and Lt. Gen. Richard S. Ewell's Corps of Confederates had moved to support Hill. The latter, advancing from the north, broke the lines of the XI Corps and drove the Federals back through Gettysburg. The Union infantry rallied behind artillery positioned on Cemetery and Culp's Hills south of the town. Lee, who reached the field about 2:00 p.m. ordered Ewell to take Cemetery Hill, "if possible." But Ewell failed to press his advantage, and the Confederates settled into positions extending in a great curve from northeast of Culp's Hill, westward through Gettysburg, thence south on Seminary

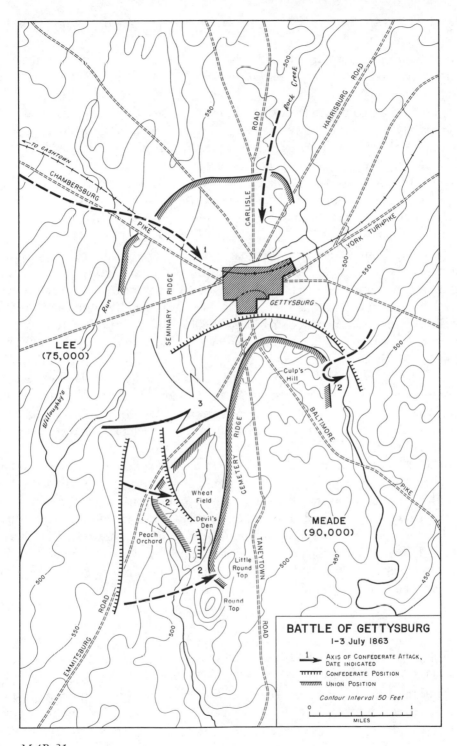

TO CASHTOWN

CHAMBERSBURG

PIKE

CARLISLE ROAD

Rock Creek

HARRISBURG ROAD

500

550

YORK TURNPIKE

500

550

1

SEMINARY RIDGE

Willoughby's Run

LEE
(75,000)

GETTYSBURG

Culp's Hill

3

CEMETERY RIDGE

BALTIMORE PIKE

2

500

450

Wheat Field

Devil's Den

Peach Orchard

MEADE
(90,000)

TANEYTOWN ROAD

500

Little Round Top

2

Round Top

EMMITSBURG ROAD

550

500

450

BATTLE OF GETTYSBURG

1–3 July 1863

1 → AXIS OF CONFEDERATE ATTACK, DATE INDICATED

⊤⊤⊤⊤ CONFEDERATE POSITION

⊤⊤⊤⊤ UNION POSITION

Contour Interval 50 Feet

0 _____ 1

MILES

MAP 31

Ridge. During the night the Federals, enjoying interior lines, moved troops onto the key points of Culp's Hill, Cemetery Hill, Cemetery Ridge, and Little Round Top.

Meade had completed his dispositions by the morning of July 2, and his line was strong except in two places. In the confusion, Little Round Top was occupied only by a signal station when the supporting cavalry was dispatched to guard the army trains and not replaced; and the commander of the III Corps, Maj. Gen. Daniel E. Sickles, on his own responsibility moved his line forward from the south end of Cemetery Ridge to higher ground near the Peach Orchard, so that his corps lay in an exposed salient. By early afternoon, seven corps were arrayed along the Union battle line.

On the Confederate side, Lee had not been able to attack early; reconnaissance took time, and Longstreet's leading division did not arrive until afternoon. Generals in the Civil War tried to combine frontal assaults with envelopments and flanking movements, but the difficulty of timing and coordinating the movements of such large bodies of men in broken terrain made intricate maneuvers difficult. The action on the second day at Gettysburg graphically illustrates the problem. Lee wanted Longstreet to outflank the Federal left, part of Hill's corps was to strike the center, while Ewell's corps was to envelop the right flank of Meade's army. The attack did not start until 3:00 p.m. when Longstreet's men, having deployed on unfamiliar ground, under a corps commander that preferred to take a defensive stance, advanced toward Little Round Top. The brigade was the basic maneuver element, and it formed for the attack with regiments in a two-rank line. Divisions usually attacked in columns of brigades, the second 150 to 300 yards behind the first, the third a similar distance behind the second. Skirmishers protected the flanks if no units were posted on either side. But such textbook models usually degenerated under actual fighting conditions, and so it was with Longstreet's attack. Divisions and brigades went in piecemeal, but with savage enthusiasm. Attacks started in close order as most men were using single-shot muzzle-loaders and had to stand shoulder to shoulder in order to get enough firepower and shock effect. But intervals between units soon increased under fire, troops often scattered for cover and concealment behind stone walls and trees, and thereafter units advanced by short rushes supported by fire from neighboring units. Thus, by late afternoon the smoke of battle was thick over the fields south of Gettysburg and the cries of the wounded mingled with the crash of musketry. The whole sector had become a chaos of tangled battle lines.

At this point Meade's chief engineer, Brig. Gen. Gouverneur Warren, discovering that no infantry held Little Round Top, persuaded the commander of the V Corps, Maj. Gen. George Sykes, to send two brigades and some artillery to the hill. They arrived just in time to hold the summit against a furious Confederate assault. When this attack bogged down, Longstreet threw a second division against Sickles' troops in the Peach Orchard and Wheatfield; this cracked the Federal line and drove as far as Cemetery Ridge before Meade's reserves halted it. Lee then ordered his troops to attack progressively from right to left and one of Hill's divisions assaulted Cemetery Ridge in piecemeal fashion, but was driven off. On the north Ewell attacked about 6:00 p.m. and captured some abandoned trenches, but Federals posted behind stone walls proved too strong. As the day ended the Federals held all their main positions. The Confederates had fought hard and with great bravery, but the progressive attack, which ignored the principle of mass, never engaged the Union front decisively at any point. The assaults were delivered against stoutly defended, prepared positions; Malvern Hill and Fredericksburg had shown this tactic to be folly, although perhaps Lee's successes against prepared positions at Chancellorsville led him to overoptimism.

Meade, after requesting the opinions of his corps commanders, decided to defend, rather than attack, on July 3. He also estimated that Lee, having attacked his right and left, would try for his center. He was right. Lee had planned to launch a full-scale, co-ordinated attack all along the line but then changed his mind in favor of a massive frontal assault by 10 brigades from 4 divisions of Longstreet's and Hill's corps against the Union center, which was held by Maj. Gen. Winfield Scott Hancock's II Corps. The assault was to be preceded by a massive artillery barrage.

The infantry's main support during the war was provided by field artillery. Rifled guns of relatively long range were available, but the soldiers preferred the 6-pounder and 12-pounder smoothbores. Rifled cannon were harder to clean; their projectiles were not as effective; their greater range could not always be effectively used because development of a good indirect fire control system would have to await the invention of the field telephone and the radio; and, finally, the rifled guns had flat trajectories, whereas the higher trajectories of the smoothbores enabled gunners to put fire on reverse slopes. Both types of cannon were among the artillery of the two armies at Gettysburg.

At 1:00 p.m. on July 3 Confederate gunners opened fire from approximately 140 pieces along Seminary Ridge in the greatest artillery bombardment witnessed on the American continent up to that time. For two hours the barrage continued, but did little more than tear up ground, destroy a few caissons, and expend ammunition. The Union artillery in the sector, numbering only 80 guns, had not been knocked out. It did stop firing in order to conserve ammunition,

PICKETT'S CHARGE

and the silence seemed to be a signal that the Confederates should begin their attack.

Under command of Maj. Gen. George E. Pickett, 15,000 men emerged from the woods on Seminary Ridge, dressed their three lines as if on parade, and began the mile-long, 20-minute march toward Cemetery Ridge. The assault force—47 regiments altogether—moved at a walk until it neared the Union lines, then broke into a run. Union artillery, especially 40 Napoleons on the south end of the ridge and some rifled guns on Little Round Top, opened fire, enfiladed the gray ranks, and forced Pickett's right over to the north. Despite heavy casualties the Confederates kept their formation until they came within rifle and canister range of the II Corps, and by then the lines and units were intermingled. The four brigades composing the left of Pickett's first line were heavily hit but actually reached and crossed the stone wall defended by Brig. Gen. John Gibbon's 2d Division of the II Corps, only to be quickly cut down or captured. Pickett's survivors withdrew to Seminary Ridge, and the fighting was over except for a suicidal mounted charge by Union cavalry, which Longstreet's right flank units easily halted. Both sides had fought hard and with great valor, for among 90,000 effective Union troops and 75,000 Confederates there were more than 51,000 casualties. The Army of the Potomac lost 3,155 killed, 14,529 wounded, and 5,365 prisoners and missing. Of the Army of Northern Virginia, 3,903 were killed, 18,735 wounded, and 5,425 missing and prisoners. If Chancellorsville was Lee's finest battle, Gettysburg was clearly his worst; yet the reverse did not unnerve him or reduce his effectiveness as a commander. The invasion had patently failed, and he retired at once toward the Potomac. As that river was flooded, it was several days before he was able to cross. Mr. Lincoln, naturally pleased over Meade's defensive victory and elated over Grant's capture of Vicksburg, thought the war could end in 1863 if Meade launched a resolute pursuit and destroyed Lee's army on the north bank of the Potomac. But Meade's own army was too mangled, and the Union commander moved cautiously, permitting Lee to return safely to Virginia on July 13.

Gettysburg was the last important action in the eastern theater in 1863. Lee and Meade maneuvered against each other in Virginia, but there was no more fighting. After Gettysburg and Vicksburg the center of strategic gravity shifted to Tennessee.

The Chickamauga Campaign

One week before the surrender of Vicksburg and the Union victory at Gettysburg, General Rosecrans moved out of Murfreesboro, Tennessee, and headed for Chattanooga, one of the most important cities in the south because of its location. (*See Map 21.*) It was a main junction on the rail line linking Richmond with Knoxville and Memphis. President Lincoln had long recognized the importance of railroads in this area. In 1862 he said, "To take and hold the railroad at or east of Cleveland [near Chattanooga], in East Tennessee, I think fully as important as the taking and holding of Richmond." Furthermore, at Chattanooga the Tennessee River cuts through the parallel ridges of the Appalachian Mountains and forms a natural gateway to either north or south. By holding the city, the Confederates could threaten Kentucky and prevent a Union penetration of the southeastern part of the Confederacy. If the Union armies pushed through Chattanooga, they would be in position to attack Atlanta, Savannah, or even the Carolinas and Richmond from the rear. As Lincoln told Rosecrans in 1863, "If we can hold Chattanooga and East Tennessee I think the rebellion must dwindle and die."

After the spring and summer campaigns in the east, the Davis government in Richmond approved a movement by Longstreet's corps of Lee's army to the west to reinforce the hard-pressed Bragg. Longstreet's move—a 900-mile trip by rail—involving some 10,000–15,000 men and six batteries of artillery, began on September 9. But a force under Burnside, now commanding the Department of the Ohio, which was not part of Rosecrans' command, had penetrated the Cumberland Gap and driven the Confederates from Knoxville; Longstreet had to go around by way of Savannah and Augusta to Atlanta, Georgia, and did not reach Bragg until September 18. The rail network was rickety, and Longstreet's soldiers quipped that such poor rolling stock had never been intended to carry such good soldiers. Movement of Longstreet's troops from Virginia was nevertheless an outstanding logistical achievement for the Confederacy.

Rosecrans had meanwhile reached the north bank of the Tennessee River near Stevenson, Alabama, on August 20. By September 4 his forces were across and on their way toward Chattanooga. After months of delay Rosecrans had accomplished the feat of completely outmaneuvering Bragg without a major battle. He planned to get in behind Bragg from the southwest and bottle him up in Chattanooga, but the Confederate general saw through the scheme and slipped away southward, carefully planting rumors that his army was demoralized and in flight. Rosecrans then resolved to pursue, a decision that would have been wise if Bragg has been retreating in disorder.

There were few passes through the mountains and no good lateral roads. Rosecrans' army was dispersed in three columns over a 40-mile front in order to make use of the various passes. Bragg concentrated his army about September 10 at Lafayette, Georgia, some twenty miles south of Chattanooga. As his force was three times as large as any one of the Union columns, Bragg hopefully anticipated that he could defeat Rosecrans in detail. But his intelligence service failed him: he thought there were two, rather than three Union columns, and prepared plans accordingly. He first planned to strike what he thought was Rosecrans' right—actually the center—then the left, but his subordinates did not support him promptly, and the attacks were made in desultory fashion. Thus, twice in three days Bragg missed a fine opportunity to inflict a serious reverse upon the Federals because of his subordinates' failure to carry out orders.

By September 12 Rosecrans was at last aware that Bragg was not retreating in disorder but was preparing to fight. The Union commander ordered an immediate concentration, but this would take several days and in the meantime his corps were vulnerable. Although Bragg was usually speedy in executing attacks, this time he delayed, awaiting the arrival of Longstreet's corps. He intended to push Rosecrans southward away from Chattanooga into a mountain cul-de-sac where the Federals could be destroyed.

By September 17 Bragg was poised just east of Chickamauga Creek. (*Map 32*) (Chickamauga, translated from Cherokee into English, means "River of Death.") When Longstreet's three leading brigades arrived on September 18, Bragg decided to cross the Chickamauga and attack. But the Federals, with two corps almost concentrated, defended the fords so stoutly that only a few units got over that day. During the night more Confederates slipped across, and by morning of the 19th about three-fourths of Bragg's men were over.

Rosecrans' third corps went into the line on the 19th, and now Bragg faced a much stronger force than he had expected. The heavily wooded battlefield had few landmarks, and some units had difficulty maintaining direction. Fighting continued throughout much of the day, but by nightfall the Federals still controlled the roads to Chattanooga. That night Lee's "Warhorse," Longstreet, arrived in person with two more brigades. He went looking for Bragg to report to him and lost his way in the woods. Encountering some soldiers, he asked them to identify their unit. When they replied with numbers—Confederate divisions were named for their commanders—he realized he was within

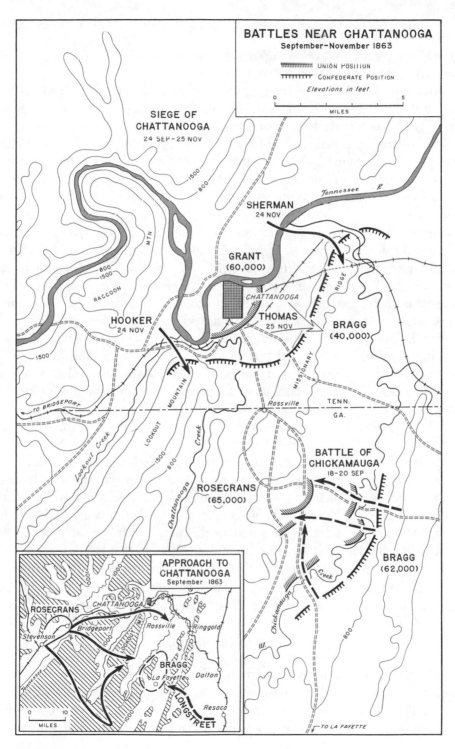

MAP 32

Union lines, hastily rode off in the darkness, and eventually found Bragg. During the night Rosecrans regrouped and dug in.

Bragg decided to renew the attack the next day and to attack progressively from his right to left (sometimes known in military parlance as "oblique order"). He reorganized the Army of Tennessee into two wings under Polk and Longstreet with little regard for its existing corps organization. The attack began about 9:00 a.m. and hit Thomas' corps first. The Union line held until Rosecrans received an erroneous report that one of his units was not supported, and ordered another unit to move in and help. In the ensuing confusion, orders designated a unit which was already in line of battle. When this force obediently abandoned its position, Longstreet, just beginning his attack, saw the hole and drove into it at once. Thomas' right flank was bent back and most of the Union right wing simply melted from the field and streamed in rout back toward Chattanooga. Rosecrans, considering himself defeated, retired to Chattanooga to organize it for defense. Thomas, with about two-thirds of the disorganized army, stood fast and checked vicious attacks by Longstreet and Polk until nightfall. This resolute stand and the valorous performance of the U.S. 19th Infantry won for Thomas and that unit the title "Rock of Chickamauga." A Confederate remembered that afternoon how "the dead were piled upon each other in ricks, like cord wood, to make passage for advancing columns. The sluggish Chickamauga ran red with human blood."

Bragg concluded that no decisive results could be attained that day. Polk, Longstreet, and Forrest pleaded with him to push the routed Federals and recapture Chattanooga. But 18,000 casualties (the Federals had lost only 1,500 less) so unnerved Bragg that he permitted Thomas to withdraw unmolested from the field to a blocking position extending from Missionary Ridge west to Lookout Mountain. Next day Thomas retired into Chattanooga. Polk wrote to President Davis of Bragg's "criminal negligence," and Forrest a week later insubordinately told the army commander, "You have played the part of a damned scoundrel, and are a coward and if you were any part of a man I would slap your jaws." Yet nothing could erase completely the fact that the Confederates had won a great victory and had Rosecrans' army bottled up in a trap.

Grant at Chattanooga

Rosecrans' army, having started out offensively, was now shut up in Chattanooga, as Bragg took up positions on Lookout Mountain and Missionary Ridge. The Union commander accepted investment and thus surrendered his freedom of action. Burnside, at Knoxville, was too far away to render immediate aid. There were no strong Confederate units north of Chattanooga, but Rose-crans' line of communications was cut away. The Nashville and Chattanooga Railroad, instead of running directly into the city, reached the river at Stevenson, crossed at Bridgeport southwest of Chattanooga, and ran through Confederate territory into town. River steamers could get to within only eight miles of Chattanooga; beyond, the Tennessee River was swift and narrow. Supplies therefore came over the mountains in wagons, but starting September 30 Confederate cavalry under Maj. Gen. Joseph Wheeler, one of Bragg's cavalry corps commanders, raided as far north as Murfreesboro. Though heavily and effectively opposed in his effort to tear up the railroad, he managed to destroy many precious Union supply wagons. With the mountain roads breaking down under the heavy traffic in wet weather, rations within Chattanooga ran short. Men went hungry, and horses and mules began to die of starvation. Rosecrans prepared to reopen his line of communications by means of an overland route to the west. But this route was dominated by Confederate troops on Raccoon and Lookout Mountains. Additional troops to clear these strongpoints were required if the Army of the Cumberland was to survive.

Washington finally awoke to the fact that an entire Union army was trapped in Chattanooga and in danger of capture. In a midnight council meeting on September 23, the President met with Secretary Stanton, General Halleck, and others to determine what could be done. As General Meade was not then active in the east, they decided to detach two corps, or about 20,000 men, from the Army of the Potomac and send them by rail to Tennessee under the command of General Hooker, who had been without active command since his relief in June. The forces selected included 10 artillery batteries with over 3,000 mules and horses. The 1,157–mile journey involved four changes of trains, owing to differing gauges and lack of track connections, and eclipsed all other such troop movements by rail up to that time. The troops began to entrain at Manassas Junction and Bealton Station, Virginia, on September 25 and five days later the first trains arrived at Bridgeport, Alabama. Not all of the troops made such good time—for the majority of the infantry the trip consumed about nine days. And movement of the artillery, horses, mules, baggage, and impedimenta was somewhat slower. Combined with a waterborne movement of 17,000 men under Sherman from Mississippi, the reinforcement of the besieged Rosecrans was a triumph of skill and planning.

Chickamauga had caused Stanton and his associates to lose confidence in Rosecrans. For some time Lincoln had been dubious about Rosecrans, who, he said, acted "like a duck hit on the head" after Chickamauga, but he did not immediately choose a successor. Finally, about mid-October, he decided to

UNION TRANSPORTS ON THE TENNESSEE RIVER

unify command in the west and to vest it in General Grant, who still commanded the Army of the Tennessee. In October Stanton met Grant in Louisville and gave him orders which allowed him some discretion in selecting subordinates. Grant was appointed commander of the Military Division of the Mississippi, which embraced the Departments and Armies of the Ohio, the Cumberland, and the Tennessee, and included the vast area from the Alleghenies to the Mississippi River north of Banks' Department of the Gulf. Thomas replaced Rosecrans, and Sherman was appointed to command Grant's old army.

Now that Hooker had arrived, the line of communications, or the "cracker line" to the troops, could be reopened. Rosecrans had actually shaped the plan, and all that was needed was combat troops to execute it. On October 26 Hooker crossed the Tennessee at Bridgeport and attacked eastward. Within two days he had taken the spurs of the mountains, other Union troops had captured two important river crossings, and the supply line was open once more. Men, equipment, and food moved via riverboat and wagon road, bypassing Confederate strongpoints, to reinforce the besieged Army of the Cumberland.

In early November Bragg weakened his besieging army by sending Longstreet's force against Burnside at Knoxville. This move reduced Confederate strength to about 40,000 at about the same time that Sherman arrived with two army corps from Memphis. The troops immediately at hand under Grant—Thomas' Army of the Cumberland, two corps of Sherman's Army of the Tennessee, and two corps under Hooker from the Army of the Potomac—now numbered about 60,000. Grant characteristically decided to resume the offensive with his entire force.

The Confederates had held their dominant position for so long that they seemed to look on all of the Federals in Chattanooga as their ultimate prisoners. One day Grant went out to inspect the Union lines and he reached a point where Union and Confederate picket posts were not far apart. Not only did his own troops turn out the guard, but a smart set of Confederates came swarming out, formed a neat military rank, snapped to attention, and presented arms. Grant returned the salute and rode away. But plans were already afoot to divest the Confederates of some of their cockiness.

Grant planned to hit the ends of the Confederates' line at once. Hooker would strike at Lookout Mountain, and Sherman moving his army upstream, across the river from Chattanooga, and crossing over by pontons, would hit the upper end of Missionary Ridge. While they were breaking the Confederate flanks, Thomas' men could make limited attacks on the center, and the Army of the Cumberland's soldiers, already nursing a bruised ego for the rout at Chickamauga, realized that in the eyes of the commanding general they were second-class troops.

Hooker took Lookout Mountain on November 24. On the same day Sherman crossed the Tennessee at the mouth of Chickamauga Creek and gained positions on the north end of Missionary Ridge. The next day his attacks bogged down as he attempted to drive southward along the Ridge. To help Sherman, Grant directed the Army of the Cumberland to take the rifle pits at the foot of the west slope of Missionary Ridge. These rifle pits were the first of three lines of Confederate trenches. Thomas' troops rushed forward, seized the pits, and then, having a score to settle with the Confederates positioned above them, took control of this phase of the battle. Coming under fire from the pits above and in front of them, the Federals simply kept on going. When Grant observed this movement he muttered that someone was going to sweat for it if the charge ended in disaster. But Thomas' troops drove all the way to the top, and in the afternoon Hooker swept the southern end of the ridge. The Federals then had the unusual experience of seeing a Confederate army disintegrate into precipitate retreat and beckoned to their Northern comrades: "My God! Come and see them run!" Grant pursued Bragg the next day, but one Confederate division skillfully halted the pursuit while Bragg retired into Georgia to regroup.

The battles around Chattanooga ended in one of the most complete Union victories of the war. Bragg's army was defeated, men and matériel captured, and the Confederates driven south. The mountainous defense line which the Confederates had hoped to hold had been pierced; the rail center of Chattanooga was permanently in Union hands; and the rich, food-producing eastern Tennessee section was lost to the Confederacy. Relief had come at last for the Union sympathizers in eastern Tennessee. With Chattanooga secured as a base, the way was open for an invasion of the lower South.

CHAPTER 8

The Civil War, 1864–1865

From Bull Run to Chattanooga, the Union armies had fought their battles without benefit of either a grand strategy or a supreme field commander. During the final year of the war the people of the North grew restless, and as the election of 1864 approached, many of them advocated a policy of making peace with the Confederacy. President Lincoln never wavered. Committed to the policy of destroying the armed power of the Confederacy, he sought a general who could pull all the threads of an emerging strategy together, and then concentrate the Union armies and their supporting naval power against the secessionists. After Vicksburg in July 1863, Lincoln leaned more and more toward Grant as the man whose strategic thinking and resolution would lead the Union armies to final victory.

It is the strategic moves of the armies during the last year of the war, rather than the tactical details, that are most instructive.

Strategy of Annihilation and Unity of Command

Acting largely as his own General in Chief after McClellan's removal in early 1862, Mr. Lincoln had watched the Confederates fight from one ephemeral victory to another inside their cockpit of northern Virginia. In the western theater, Union armies, often operating independently of one another, had scored great victories at key terrain points. But their hold on the communications base at Nashville was always in jeopardy as long as the elusive armies of the Confederacy could escape to fight another day at another key point. The twin, un-co-ordinated victories at Gettysburg and Vicksburg, 900 airline miles apart, only pointed up the North's need for an over-all strategic plan and a general who could carry it out.

Having cleared the Mississippi River, Grant wrote to Halleck and the President about the opportunities now open to his army. Grant first called for the consolidation of the autonomous western departments and the co-ordination of their individual armies. After this great step, he proposed to isolate the area west of the line Chattanooga-Atlanta-Montgomery-Mobile. Within this region, Grant urged a "massive rear attack" that would take Union armies in the Gulf Department under Maj. Gen. Nathaniel P. Banks and Grant's Army of the Tennessee to Mobile and up the Alabama River to Montgomery. The U.S. Navy would play a major role in this attack. Simultaneously, Rosecrans was to advance overland through Chattanooga to Atlanta. All military resources within this isolated area would be destroyed.

Lincoln vetoed Grant's plan in part by deferring the Mobile-Montgomery phase. The President favored a demonstration by Banks up the Red River to Shreveport in order to show the American flag to Napoleon III's interlopers in Mexico, and Banks' Department of the Gulf was left out of the consolidation of the other western commands under Grant in October 1863.

After his own victory at Chattanooga in November, Grant wasted few hours in writing the President what he thought the next strategic moves should be. As a possible winter attack, Grant revived the touchy Mobile campaign while the Chattanooga victors were gathering strength for a spring offensive to Atlanta. Grant reasoned that Lee would vacate Virginia and shift strength toward Atlanta. For the Mobile-Montgomery plan, Grant asked for Banks' resources in the Gulf Department. Lincoln again balked because the Texas seacoast would be abandoned. Grant's rebuttal explained that Napoleon III would really be impressed with a large Army-Navy operation against Mobile Bay. The Red River campaign, Grant believed, would not deter Napoleon III. The President told Grant again that he had to heed the demands of Union diplomacy, but at the same time he encouraged Grant to enlarge his strategic proposals to include estimates for a grand Federal offensive for the coming spring of 1864.

Grant's plan of January 1864 projected a four-pronged continental attack. In concert, the four armies were to move on Atlanta, on Mobile—after Banks took Shreveport—on Lee's communications by a campaign across the middle of North Carolina on the axis New Bern–Neuse River–Goldsboro–Raleigh–Greensboro, and on Lee's Army of Northern Virginia in the hope of defeating it in an open battle. Lincoln opposed the North Carolina phase, fearing that Grant's diversion of 60,000 effective bayonets from formations covering Washington was too dangerous. Lincoln knew that Lee's eyes were always fixed on the vast amount of supplies in the depots around the Washington area.

Though Lincoln scuttled some of Grant's professional schemes, he never lost his esteem for Grant's enthusiasm and intelligence. In February 1864 Congress revived Scott's old rank of lieutenant general, to which Grant was promoted on March 9. Lincoln relieved Halleck as General in Chief, ordered Grant to Washington to assume Halleck's post, and during March the President, the new General in Chief, and the Secretary of War ironed out top-level command arrangements which had plagued every President since the

War of 1812. Lincoln and Stanton relinquished powerful command, staff, and communications tools to Grant. Stanton, greatly impressed with Grant's public acclaim, cautioned his General Staff Bureau chiefs to heed Grant's needs and timetables.

In twentieth century terms, Grant was a theater commander. As General in Chief, he reported directly to the President and Secretary of War, keeping them informed about the broad aspects of his strategic plans and telling them in advance of his armies' needs. Grant removed himself from the politics of Washington and established his headquarters in northern Virginia. Though he planned to go quickly to troubled spots, Grant elected to accompany Meade's Army of the Potomac in order to assess Lee's moves and their effects on the other columns of the Union Army. By rail or steamboat, Grant was never far from Lincoln, and in turn the President visited Grant frequently. To tie his far-flung commands together, Grant employed a vast telegraph system.

In a continental theater of war larger than Napoleon's at its zenith, Grant's job, administratively, eventually embraced four military divisions, totaling seventeen subcommands, wherein 500,000 combat soldiers would be employed. At Washington, Halleck operated a war room for Grant and eased his heavy burden of studying the several Army commanders' detailed field directives by preparing brief digests, thus saving the General in Chief many hours of reading detailed reports. Bearing the then nebulous title of "Chief of Staff, U.S. Army," Halleck had a major job in keeping Grant informed about supply levels at base depots and advance dumps in Nashville, St. Louis, City Point, Washington, Philadelphia, Louisville, and New York City. Under Stanton, Quartermaster General Montgomery C. Meigs, the most informed logistician and supply manager of his day, dispatched men and munitions to Grant's subcommands according to a strategic timetable. As the spring offensive progressed, Stanton, Halleck, and Meigs gave Grant a rear-area team that grasped the delicate balance between theater objectives and the logistical support required to achieve them.

Grant spent the month of April on the Rapidan front developing his final strategic plan for ending the war. In essence, he recapped all of his views on the advantages to be gained from his victories in the western theater. He added some thoughts about moving several Federal armies, aided by naval power when necessary, toward a common center in a vast, concentrated effort. He planned to stop the Confederates from using their interior lines. He intended to maneuver Lee away from the Rapidan Wilderness and defeat the Army of Northern Virginia in open terrain by a decisive battle. Another Union force collected from the Atlantic seaport towns of the deep South was to cut the James-Appomattox River line to sever Lee's rail and road links with the other parts of the Confederacy. Simultaneously, Sherman's group of armies would execute a wide wheeling movement through the South to complete the envelopment of the whole country east of the Mississippi. Banks was still scheduled to make the attack through Mobile. As Lincoln described the plan, "Those not skinning can hold a leg."

By mid-April 1864 Grant had issued specific orders to each commander of the four Federal armies that were to execute the grand strategy. In round numbers the Union armies were sending 300,000 combat troops against 150,000 Confederates defending the invasion paths. Meade's Army of the Potomac and Burnside's independent IX Corps, a combined force of 120,000 men, constituted the major attack column under Grant's over-all direction. The enemy had 63,000 troops facing Grant along the Rapidan. Two subsidiary thrusts were to support Meade's efforts. Commanding a force of 33,000 men, Butler with his Army of the James was to skirt the south bank of the James, menace Richmond, take it if possible, and destroy the railroads below Petersburg. Acting as a right guard in the Shenandoah Valley, Maj. Gen. Franz Sigel's 23,000 Federals were to advance on Lee's rail hub at Lynchburg, Virginia. With the northern Virginia triangle under attack, in the continental center of the line Sherman's 100,000 men were to march on Atlanta, annihilating Joseph E. Johnston's 65,000 soldiers, and devastating the resources of central Georgia. On the continental right of the line, Banks was to disengage as soon as possible along the Red River and with Rear Adm. David C. Farragut's blockading squadron in the Gulf of Mexico make a limited amphibious landing against Mobile. The day for advance would be announced early in May.

In rising from regimental command to General in Chief, Grant had learned much from experience, and if he sometimes made mistakes he rarely repeated them. Not a profound student of the literature of warfare, he had become, by the eve of his grand campaign, one of those rare leaders who combine the talents of the strategist, tactician, and logistician and who marry those talents to the principle of the offensive. His operations, especially the "rear mass attack," were models of the execution of the principles of war. He was calm in crisis; reversals and disappointments did not unhinge his cool judgment. He mastered the dry-as-dust details of a logistical system and used common sense in deciding when to use the horse-drawn wagon, the railroad, or the steamboat in his strategic moves. Above all, Grant understood and applied the principle of modern war that the destruction of the enemy's economic resources is as necessary as the annihilation of the enemy's armies.

Lee Cornered at Richmond

On the morning of May 4, 1864, Meade and Sherman moved out to execute Grant's grand strategy. The combat strength of the Army of the Potomac, slimmed down from seven unwieldy corps, consisted of three infantry corps of 25,000 rifles each and a cavalry corps. Commanding the 12,000-man cavalry corps was Maj. Gen. Philip H. Sheridan, an energetic leader brought east by Grant on Halleck's recommendation. Meade again dispersed his cavalry, using troopers as messengers, pickets, and train guards, but young Sheridan, after considerable argument, eventually succeeded in concentrating all of his sabers as a separate combat arm. Grant reorganized Burnside's IX Corps of 20,000 infantrymen, held it as a strategic reserve for a time, and then assigned the IX Corps to Meade's army. Lee's army, now 70,000 strong, was also organized into a cavalry and three infantry corps.

Grant and Lee were at the height of their careers and this was their first contest of wills. Having the initiative, Grant crossed the Rapidan and decided to go by Lee's right, rather than his left. (*Map 33*) First, Grant wanted to rid himself of the need to use an insecure railroad with limited capacity back to Alexandria, Virginia. Second, he wanted to end the Army of the Potomac's dependence on a train of 4,000 wagons; the Army's mobility was hobbled by having to care for 60,000 animals. Finally, Grant wanted to use the advantages of Virginia's tidewater rivers and base his depots on the Chesapeake Bay. He was willing to accept the risk inherent in moving obliquely across Lee's front in northern Virginia.

With little room for maneuver, Grant was forced to advance through the Wilderness, where Hooker had come to grief the year before. As the army column halted near Chancellorsville to allow the wagon trains to pass the Rapidan, on May 5 Lee struck at Meade's right flank. Grant and Meade swung their corps into line and hit hard. The fighting in the battle of the Wilderness, consisting of assault, defense, and counterattack, was close and desperate in tangled woods and thickets. Artillery could not be brought to bear. The dry woods caught fire and some of the wounded died miserably in the flame and smoke. On May 6 Lee attacked again. Longstreet's I Corps, arriving late in battle but as always in perfect march order, drove the Federals back. Longstreet himself received a severe neck wound, inflicted in error by his own men, that took him out of action until October 1864. Lee, at a decisive moment in the battle, his fighting blood aroused to a white heat, attempted to lead an assault in person; but men of the Texas brigade with whom Lee was riding persuaded

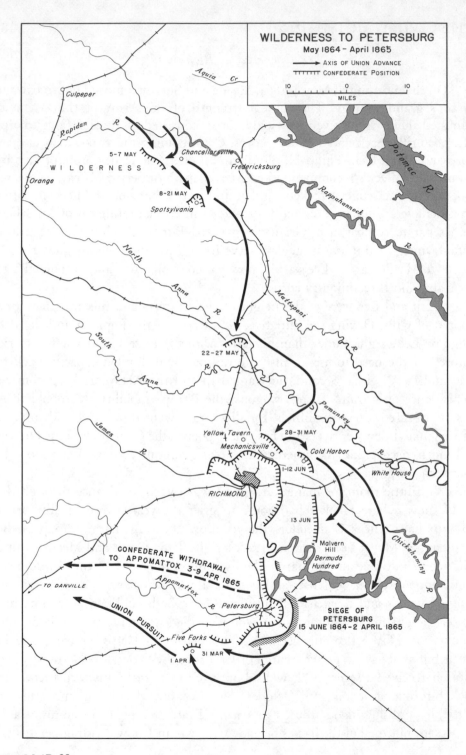

WILDERNESS TO PETERSBURG
May 1864 – April 1865

→ AXIS OF UNION ADVANCE
⊤⊤⊤⊤⊤ CONFEDERATE POSITION

10   0   10
MILES

Aquia Cr

Culpeper

Rapidan R

5-7 MAY   Chancellorsville

WILDERNESS   Fredericksburg

Orange

8-21 MAY

Spotsylvania

Rappahannock

Potomac R

North Anna R

South Anna

Mattaponi

James R

22-27 MAY

Pamunkey

Yellow Tavern   28-31 MAY
Mechanicsville   Cold Harbor
1-12 JUN   White House

RICHMOND

13 JUN   Chickahominy R

Malvern Hill
Bermuda Hundred

CONFEDERATE WITHDRAWAL
TO APPOMATTOX 3-9 APR 1865

TO DANVILLE   Appomattox R   Petersburg   SIEGE OF
PETERSBURG
15 JUNE 1864-2 APRIL 1865

UNION PURSUIT

Five Forks

1 APR   31 MAR

MAP 33

the southern leader to go to the rear and direct the battle as their Army commander. On May 7 neither side renewed the battle.

Now came the critical test of Grant's execution of strategy. He had been worsted, though not really beaten, by Lee, a greater antagonist than Bragg, Joseph E. Johnston, and Pemberton. After an encounter with Lee, each of the former Army of the Potomac commanders, McClellan, Burnside, and Hooker, had retired north of the Rappahannock River and postponed any further clashes with that great tactician. But Grant was of a different breed. He calmly ordered his lead corps to move south toward Spotsylvania as rapidly as possible to get around Lee's flank and interpose the Army of the Potomac between Lee and Richmond.

Lee detected Grant's march and, using roads generally parallel to Grant's, also raced toward the key road junction at Spotsylvania. J.E.B. Stuart's cavalry harassed and slowed Grant; Lee arrived first and quickly built strong earth-and-log trenches over commanding ground which covered the roads leading to Richmond. In this crossroads race, Sheridan's cavalry would have been useful, but Meade had dissipated the cavalry corps' strength by deploying two divisions of horse to guard his already well-protected trains. Sheridan and Meade argued once again over the use of cavalry, and the General in Chief backed Sheridan, allowing him now to concentrate his cavalry arm. Grant gave Sheridan a free hand in order to stop Stuart's raids. Leading his corps southward in a long ride toward Richmond, its objective a decisive charge against Stuart, Sheridan did the job. He fought a running series of engagements that culminated in a victory at Yellow Tavern, in which the gallant Stuart was mortally wounded. The South was already short of horses and mules, and Sheridan's 16-day raid ended forever the offensive power of Lee's mounted arm.

For four days beginning May 9 Meade struck repeatedly at Lee's roadblock at Spotsylvania but was beaten back. Twice the Federals broke through the trenches and divided Lee's army, but in each case the attackers became disorganized. Supporting infantry did not or could not close in, and Confederate counterattacks were delivered with such ferocity that the breakthroughs could be neither exploited nor held. On the morning of the 11th, Grant wrote Halleck: "I propose to fight it out on this line if it takes all summer." On May 20, having decided the entrenchments were too strong to capture, Grant sideslipped south again, still trying to envelop Lee's right flank.

With smaller numbers, Lee skillfully avoided Grant's trap and refused to leave entrenched positions and be destroyed in open battle. Lee retired to the North Anna River and dug in. Grant then continued to move south, to his left, in a daring and difficult tactical maneuver. Butler had meanwhile advanced

up the peninsula toward Richmond, but
Beauregard outmaneuvered him in May
and bottled up Butler's men at Bermuda
Hundred between the James and Appomattox Rivers. Eventually Butler and
Banks, who did not take Mobile, were
removed from command for their failure to carry out their assignments in the
grand strategy.

Lee easily made his way into the
Richmond defenses with his right flank
on the Chickahominy and his center
at Cold Harbor, the site of the Gaines'
Mill action in 1862. The front extended
for eight miles. On June 3 Grant assaulted Lee's center at Cold Harbor.
Though bravely executed, the attack was
badly planned. The Confederates re-

Guns and Ammunition *stored at
City Point.*

pulsed it with gory efficiency, and Grant later regretted that he had ever
made the attempt. Cold Harbor climaxed a month of heavy fighting in which
Grant's forces had casualties totaling about 55,000 as against about 32,000 for
those of Lee. After Cold Harbor, Grant executed a brilliant maneuver in the
face of the enemy. All Union corps were on the north bank of the deep, wide
James by June 14 and crossed over a 2,100-foot ponton bridge, the longest up to
that time in modern history. Having established a new and modern base depot
at City Point, complete with a railroad line to the front, Grant on June 18, 1864,
undertook siege operations at Petersburg below Richmond, an effort which
continued into the next year.

After forty-four days of continuous fighting, Lee was fixed finally in
position warfare, a war of trenches and sieges, conducted ironically enough
by two masters of mobile warfare. Mortars were used extensively, and heavy
siege guns were brought up on railway cars. Grant still sought to get around
Lee's right and hold against Lee's left to prevent him from shortening his line
and achieving a higher degree of concentration. When Lee moved his lines to
counter Grant, the two commanders were, in effect, maneuvering their
fortifications.

Now that Lee was firmly entrenched in front of Grant, and could spare
some men, he decided to ease the pressure with one of his perennial raids up
the Shenandoah Valley toward Washington. Confederate Maj. Gen. Jubal A.

Early's corps in early July advanced against Maj. Gen. David Hunter, who had replaced Sigel. Hunter, upon receiving confused orders from Halleck, retired up the valley. When he reached the Potomac, he turned west into the safety of the Appalachians and uncovered Washington. Early saw his chance and drove through Maryland. Delayed by a Union force on July 9 near Frederick, he reached the northern outskirts of Washington on July 11 and skirmished briskly in the vicinity of Fort Stevens. Abraham Lincoln and Quartermaster General Meigs were interested spectators. At City Point, Grant had received the news of Early's raid calmly. Using his interior waterway, he embarked the men of his VI Corps for the capital, where they landed on the 11th. When Early realized he was engaging troops from the Army of the Potomac, he managed to escape the next day.

Grant decided that Early had eluded the Union's superior forces because they had not been under a single commander. He abolished four separate departments and formed them into one, embracing Washington, western Maryland, and the Shenandoah Valley. In August, Sheridan was put in command with orders to follow Early to the death. Sheridan spent the remainder of the year in the valley, employing and co-ordinating his infantry, cavalry, and artillery in a manner that has won the admiration of military students ever since. He met and defeated Early at Winchester and Fisher's Hill in September and shattered him at Cedar Creek in October. To stop further raids and prevent Lee from feeding his army on the crops of that fertile region, Sheridan devastated the Shenandoah Valley.

Sherman's Great Wheel to the East

On March 17, 1864, Grant had met with Sherman at Nashville and told him his role in the grand strategy. Sherman, like Grant, held two commands. As Division of the Mississippi commander, he was responsible for the operation and defense of a vast logistical system that reached from a communications zone at St. Louis, Louisville, and Cincinnati to center on a large base depot at Nashville. Strategically, Nashville on the Cumberland River rivaled Washington, D.C., in importance. A 90-mile military railroad, built and operated by Union troops, gave Nashville access to steamboats plying the Tennessee River. Connected with Louisville by rail, Nashville became one vast storehouse and corral. If the city was destroyed, the Federal forces would have to fall back to the Ohio River line. Wearing his other hat, Sherman was a field commander, with three armies under his direction.

With the promise of the return of his two crack divisions from the Red River expedition by May 1864 and with a splendid administrative system working behind him, Sherman was ready to leave Chattanooga in the direction of Atlanta. (*Map 34*) His mission was to destroy Johnston's armies and capture Atlanta, which after Richmond was the most important industrial center in the Confederacy. With 254 guns, Sherman matched his three small armies, and a separate cavalry command—a total force of more than 100,000 men—against Joseph E. Johnston's Army of Tennessee and the Army of Mississippi including Wheeler's cavalry, consisting of 65,000 men.

Sherman moved out on May 4, 1864, the same day the Army of the Potomac crossed the Rapidan. Johnston, realizing how seriously he was outnumbered, decided to go on the defensive, preserve his forces intact, hold Atlanta, and delay Sherman as long as possible. There was always the hope that the North would grow weary of the costly struggle and that some advocate of peaceful settlement might defeat Abraham Lincoln in the election of 1864. From May 4 through mid-July, the two forces maneuvered against each other. There were daily fights but few large-scale actions. As Sherman pushed south, Johnston would take up a strong position and force Sherman to halt, deploy, and reconnoiter. Sherman would then outflank Johnston, who in turn would retire to a new line and start the process all over again. On June 27 Sherman, unable to maneuver because the roads were muddy and seriously concerned by the unrest in his armies brought about by constant and apparently fruitless marching, decided to assault Johnston at Kennesaw Mountain. This attack against prepared positions, like the costly failure at Cold Harbor, was beaten back. Sherman returned to maneuver and forced Johnston back to positions in front of Atlanta.

Johnston had done his part well. He had accomplished his missions and had so slowed Sherman that Sherman covered only 100 miles in 74 days. Johnston, his forces intact, was holding strong positions in front of Atlanta, his main base; but by this time Jefferson Davis had grown impatient with Johnston and his tactics of cautious delay. In July he replaced him with Lt. Gen. John B. Hood, a much more impetuous commander.

On July 20, while Sherman was executing a wide turning movement around the northeast side of Atlanta, Hood left his fortifications and attacked at Peach Tree Creek. When Sherman beat him off, Hood pulled back into the city. While Sherman made ready to invest, Hood attacked again and failed again. Sherman then tried cavalry raids to cut the railroads, just as Johnston had during the advance from Chattanooga, but Sherman's raids had as little success as Johnston's. Sherman then began extending fortifications on August 31. Hood, who had dissipated his striking power in his assaults, gave up and retired to

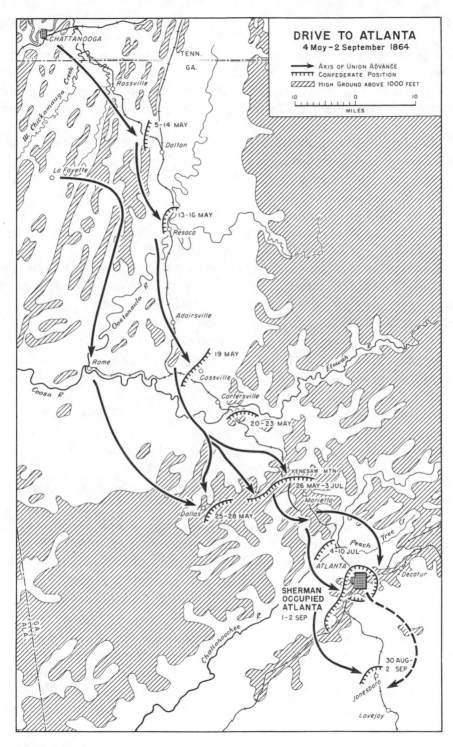

DRIVE TO ATLANTA
4 May – 2 September 1864

Axis of Union Advance
Confederate Position
High Ground above 1000 Feet

MAP 34

northwest Alabama, and Sherman marched into Atlanta on the first two days of September. Sherman hoped that Mobile had fallen, and a shorter line for his supplies by way of Montgomery, Alabama, or still better by the lower Chattahoochee to Columbus, Georgia, was open. Admiral Farragut had entered Mobile Bay on August 5, 1864, but had no troops to take Mobile itself.

The fall of Atlanta gave President Lincoln's campaign for re-election in 1864 a tremendous boost. In addition, the psychological lift given the Union by Admiral Farragut's personal heroism in the battle of Mobile Bay greatly added to Lincoln's prestige.

Atlanta was only a halfway point in Sherman's vast wheel from the western theater toward the rear of Lee's Army of Northern Virginia. Abandoning the idea of catching up with Hood, Sherman by telegraph outlined his next strategic move to Lincoln and Grant in early September 1864. Sherman's two proposals proved him an able strategist as well as a consummately bold and aggressive commander. To defend Nashville, he suggested that he send two corps, 30,000 men, back to Thomas, where that commander would raise and train more men and be in position to hold Tennessee if Hood came north. To carry the offensive against the economic heart of the Confederacy, Sherman recommended that he himself take four corps—62,000 men—cut his own communications, live off the country, and march to the seacoast through Georgia, devastating and laying waste all farms, railways, and storehouses in his path. Whether he arrived at Pensacola, Charleston, or Savannah, Sherman reasoned he could hold a port, make contact with the U.S. Navy, and be refitted by Stanton and Meigs. Meigs promised to do the logistical job, and Lincoln and Grant, though their reaction to the plan was less than enthusiastic, accepted it in a show of confidence in Sherman.

Before marching out of Atlanta, Sherman's engineers put selected buildings to the torch and destroyed all railroads in the vicinity. On November 12, moving away from the Nashville depots toward Savannah, the Division of the Mississippi troops broke telegraphic contact with Grant. They had twenty days' emergency rations in their wagons, but planned to replenish them by living off the country. Operating on a 60-mile-wide front, unimpeded by any Confederate force, Sherman's army systematically burned and destroyed what it did not need. The march became something of a rowdy excursion. Sherman's campaign, like Sheridan's in the Shenandoah, anticipated the economic warfare and strategic aerial bombardments of the twentieth century. Yet the victims of his methods could hardly be blamed if they regarded Sherman's strategy as an excuse for simple thievery.

On December 10 Sherman, having broken the classic pattern by moving away from his logistical base, arrived in front of Savannah. Confederate forces evacuated the seaport on December 21 and Sherman offered it to the nation as a Christmas present. Awaiting him offshore was Meigs' floating seatrain, which enabled him to execute the last phase of Grant's strategy, a thrust north toward the line of the James River.

Thomas Protects the Nashville Base

Sherman, as the western theater commander, did not learn of Nashville's fate until he reached Savannah. He had planned Nashville's defense well enough by sending his IV and XXII Corps under Maj. Gen. John M. Schofield to screen Hood's northward move from Florence, Alabama. Schofield was to allow Thomas some time to assemble 50,000 men and strengthen Nashville. The aggressive Hood with his 30,000 men had lost a golden opportunity to trap Schofield at Spring Hill, Tennessee, on November 29, 1864. Unopposed, the Union troops made a night march across Hood's front to escape capture. Bitterly disappointed, Hood overtook Schofield the next day at Franklin.

Grant's continental timetable could have at this point been upset by Hood. Booty at Nashville might carry Hood to the Ohio or allow him to concentrate with Lee before Richmond. But Franklin turned into one of the Confederacy's most tragic battles. It commenced about 3:30 p.m. on November 30 and ended at dusk as Hood threw 18,000 of his veterans against a solidly entrenched force of Federals. Like Pickett's charge at Gettysburg, Hood's frontal assault gained nothing. He lost over 6,000 men, including 13 general officers. At nightfall Schofield brought his troops in behind Thomas' defenses at Nashville.

Hood was in a precarious position. He had been far weaker than Thomas to begin with; the battle of Franklin had further depleted his army; and, even worse, his men had lost confidence in their commander. The Federals in Nashville were securely emplaced in a city which they had been occupying for three years. Hood could do little more than encamp on high ground a few miles south of Nashville and wait. He could not storm the city; his force was too small to lay siege; to sidestep and go north was an open invitation to Thomas to attack his flank and rear; and to retreat meant disintegration of his army. He could only watch Thomas' moves.

Thomas, the Rock of Chickamauga, belonged to the last bootlace school of soldiering. In comparison with Grant and Sherman, he was slow; but he was also thorough. He had gathered and trained men and horses and was prepared to attack Hood on December 10, but an ice storm the day before made movement impossible. Grant and his superiors in Washington fretted at the delay, and the General in Chief actually started west to remove Thomas. But on December 15 Thomas struck like a sledgehammer in an attack that militarily students have regarded as virtually faultless.

Thomas' tactical plan was a masterly, co-ordinated attack. His heavily weighted main effort drove against Hood's left flank while a secondary attack aimed simultaneously at Hood's right. Thomas provided an adequate reserve and used cavalry to screen his flank and extend the envelopment of the enemy left. Hood, on the other hand, was overextended and his thin line was concave to the enemy, denying him the advantage of interior lines. Hood's reserve was inadequate, and his cavalry was absent on a minor mission.

The two-day battle proceeded according to Thomas' plan as the Federals fixed Hood's right while slashing savagely around the Confederate left flank. They broke Hood's first line on December 15, forcing the southerners to retire to a new line two miles to the rear. The Federals repeated their maneuver on the 16th, and by nightfall the three-sided battle had disintegrated into a rout of Hood's army. Broken and defeated, it streamed southward, protected from hotly pursuing Union cavalry only by the intrepid rear-guard action of Forrest's horsemen. The shattered Army of the Tennessee reached Tupelo, Mississippi, on January 10, 1865. It no longer existed as an effective fighting force; Hood was relieved of command and his scattered units were assigned to other areas of combat. The decisive battle of Nashville had eliminated one of the two great armies of the Confederacy from a shrinking chessboard.

Lee's Last 100 Days

President Lincoln was delighted with Savannah as a Christmas present, and in his congratulatory letter to Sherman and Grant the Commander in Chief said that he would leave the final phases of the war to his two leading professional soldiers. Accordingly, from City Point, Grant directed Sherman, on December 27, 1864, to march overland toward Richmond. At 3:00 p.m. on December 31, Sherman agreed to execute this last phase of Grant's continental sweep. In the final 100 days of the war, the two generals would clearly demonstrate the art of making principles of warfare come alive and prove that each principle was something more than a platitude. Each commander had a common objective: Grant and Meade would continue to hammer Lee. Sherman was to execute a devastating invasion northward through the Carolinas toward a juncture with Meade's Army of the Potomac, then on the line of the James River. Their strategy was simple. It called for the massing of strength and exemplified an economy of force. It would place Lee in an unmaneuverable position, cutting him off from all other Confederate commanders. Surprise would be achieved by reuniting all of Sherman's original corps when Schofield, moving from central Tennessee by rail, river, and ocean transport, arrived at the Carolina capes. Solidly based on a centralized logistical system with protected Atlantic sea trains at their side, Grant and Sherman were ready to end Lee's stay in Richmond.

Robert E. Lee, the master tactician, divining his end, wrote to Davis that the Confederates would have to concentrate their forces for a last-ditch stand. In February 1865 the Confederate Congress conferred supreme command of all Confederate armies on Lee, but it was an empty honor. Lee could no longer control events. Sherman moved through Columbia, South Carolina, in February, took Wilmington, North Carolina, the Confederacy's last port, then pushed on. Johnston, newly reappointed to a command, had the mission of stopping Sherman's forces, but could not. At Richmond and Petersburg toward the end of March, Grant renewed his efforts along a thirty-eight-mile front to get at Lee's right (west) flank. By now Sheridan's cavalry and the VI Corps had returned from the Shenandoah Valley, and the total force immediately under Grant numbered 101,000 infantry, 14,700 cavalry, and 9,000 artillery. Lee had 46,000 infantry, 6,000 cavalry, and 5,000 artillery.

On March 29 Grant began his move to the left. Sheridan and the cavalry pushed out ahead by way of Dinwiddie Court House in order to strike at Burke's Station, the intersection of the Southside and Danville Railroads, while Grant's main body moved to envelop Lee's right. But Lee, alerted to the threat, moved west. General A.P. Hill, who never stood on the defense if there was a chance to attack, took his corps out of its trenches and assaulted the Union left in the swampy forests around White Oak Road. He pushed General Warren's V Corps back at first, but Warren counterattacked and by March 31 had driven Hill back to his trenches. Next day Sheridan advanced to Five Forks, a road junction southwest of Petersburg, and there encountered a strong Confederate force under General Pickett—cavalry plus two infantry divisions—which Lee had dispatched to forestall Sheridan. Pickett attacked and drove Sheridan back to Dinwiddie Court House, but there Sheridan dug in and halted him. Pickett then entrenched at Five Forks instead of pulling back to make contact with Hill, whose failure to destroy Warren had left a gap between him and Pickett, with Warren's corps in between. Sheridan, still formally the commander of the Army of the Shenandoah, had authority from Grant to take control of any nearby infantry corps of the Army of the Potomac. He wanted Warren to fall upon Pickett's exposed rear and destroy him, but Warren moved too slowly, and Pickett consolidated his position. Next day Sheridan attacked again but failed to destroy Pickett because Warren had moved his corps too slowly and put most of it in the wrong place. Sheridan, another devotee of the offensive principle who would not tolerate failure to engage the enemy, summarily relieved Warren of command.

Grant renewed his attack against Lee's right on April 2. The assault broke the Confederate line and forced it back northward. The Federals took the line of the Southside Railroad, and the Confederates withdrew toward Petersburg. Lee then pulled Longstreet's corps away from the shambles of Richmond to hold the line, and in this day's action Hill was killed. With his forces stretched thin, Lee had to abandon Richmond and the Petersburg fortifications. He struck out and raced west toward the Danville Railroad, hoping to get to Lynchburg or Danville, break loose, and eventually join forces with Johnston. But Grant had him in the open at last. He pursued relentlessly and speedily, with troops behind (east of) Lee and south of him on his left flank, while Sheridan dashed ahead with the cavalry to head Lee off. A running fight ensued from April 2 through 6. Ewell's corps was surrounded and captured at Sayler's Creek. Lee's rations ran out; his men began deserting and straggling. Finally, Sheridan galloped his men to Appomattox Court House, squarely athwart Lee's line of retreat.

Lee resolved that he could accomplish nothing more by fighting. He met Grant at the McLean House in Appomattox on April 9, 1865. The handsome, well-tailored Lee, the very epitome of southern chivalry, asked Grant for terms. Reserving all political questions for his own decision, Lincoln had authorized Grant to treat only on purely military matters. Grant, though less impressive in his bearing than Lee, was equally chivalrous. He accepted Lee's surrender, allowed 28,356 paroled Confederates to keep their horses and mules, furnished rations to the Army of Northern Virginia, and forbade the soldiers of the Army of the Potomac to cheer or fire salutes in celebration of victory over their old antagonists. Johnston surrendered to Sherman on April 26, twelve days after the assassination of the President. The last major trans-Mississippi force gave up the struggle on May 26, and the grim fighting was over.

Attrition in manpower had forced both South and North to turn from volunteers to conscription in order to keep their armies up to effective strength. The Confederate government had enacted a draft law as early as April 1862. Late in that year Union governors were no longer able to raise enough troops for the Federal armies and on March 3, 1863, Congress passed the Enrollment Act, an outright assertion of national conscription by the central government. This law made able-bodied males between 20 and 45 years of age liable for national

TRENCHES BEFORE PETERSBURG

military service. The Enrollment Act was not popular, as bloody draft riots in New York demonstrated after Gettysburg. Both the Confederate and the U.S. laws were undemocratic in that they did not apply equally to all individuals. They provided for exemptions that allowed many to escape military service entirely. Comparatively few men were ever drafted into the Federal service, but by stimulating men to volunteer the Enrollment Act had its desired effect.

The principal importance of the Enrollment Act of 1863, however, does not lie in the effect it had on manpower procurement for the Civil War. This measure established firmly the principle that every citizen is obligated to defend the nation and that the Federal government can impose that obligation directly on the citizen without mediation of the states. In addition, the act recognized that the previous system of total reliance on militia and volunteers would not suffice in a modern, total war.

Dimensions of the War

Viewing the war in its broadest context, a historian could fairly conclude that a determined general of the North had bested a legendary general of the South, probably the most brilliant tactician on either side, because the Union could bring to bear a decisive superiority in economic resources and manpower.

Lee's mastery of the art of warfare staved off defeat for four long years, but the outcome was never really in doubt. Grant—and Lincoln—held too many high cards. And during the last year of the war, the relations between the Union's Commander in Chief and his General in Chief set an unexcelled example of civil-military co-ordination.

In this costly war, the Union Army lost 138,154 men killed in battle. This figure seems large, but it is scarcely half the number—221,374—who died of other causes, principally disease, bringing the total Union dead to 359,528. Men wounded in action numbered 280,040. Figures for the Confederacy are incomplete, but at least 94,000 were killed in battle, 70,000 died of other causes, and some 30,000 died in northern prisons.

With the advent of conscription, mass armies, and long casualty lists, the individual soldier seemed destined to lose his identity and dignity. These were the days before regulation serial numbers and dog tags (although some soldiers made individual tags from coins or scraps of paper). But by the third year of the war various innovations had been introduced to enhance the soldier's lot. Union forces were wearing corps badges which heightened unit identification, *esprit de corps*, and pride in organization. The year 1863 saw the first award of the highest United States decoration, the Medal of Honor. Congress had authorized it on July 12, 1862, and the first medals were given by Secretary Stanton in 1863 to Pvt. Jacob Parrott and five other soldiers. They had demonstrated extraordinary valor in a daring raid behind the Confederate lines near Chattanooga. The Medal of Honor remains the highest honor the United States can bestow upon any individual in the armed services.

Throughout the western world, the nineteenth century, with its many humanitarian movements, evidenced a general improvement in the treatment of the individual soldier, and the U.S. soldier was no exception. The more severe forms of corporal punishment were abolished in the U.S. Army in 1861. Although Civil War medical science was primitive in comparison with that of the mid-twentieth century, an effort was made to extend medical services in the Army beyond the mere treatment of battle wounds. As an auxiliary to the regular medical service, the volunteer U.S. Sanitary Commission fitted out hospital ships and hospital units, provided male and, for the first time in the U.S. Army, female nurses, and furnished clothing and fancier foods than the regular rations. Similiarly, the U.S. Christian Commission augmented the efforts of the regimental chaplains and even provided, besides songbooks and Bibles, some coffee bars and reading rooms.

The Civil War forced changes in the traditional policies governing the burial of soldiers. On July 17, 1862, Congress authorized the President to establish national cemeteries "for the soldiers who shall die in the service of the country." While little was done during the war to implement this Congressional action, several battlefield cemeteries—Antietam, Gettysburg, Chattanooga, Stones River, and Knoxville—were set up, ". . . as a final resting place for those who here gave their lives . . ." in lieu of some nameless corner of a forgotten field.

As the largest and longest conflict of the nineteenth century in the western world, save for the Napoleonic struggle, the American Civil War has been argued and analyzed for the more than a hundred years since the fighting stopped. It continues to excite the imagination because it was full of paradox. Old-fashioned, in that infantry attacked in the open in dense formations, it also foreshadowed modern total war. Though not all the ingredients were new, railroads, telegraph communications, steamships, balloons, armor plate, rifled weapons, wire entanglements, the submarine, large-scale photography, and torpedoes—all products of the burgeoning industrial revolution—gave new and awesome dimensions to armed conflict.

CHAPTER 9

The Spanish American War
1898

In the latter part of the nineteenth century the United States, hitherto largely provincial in thought and policies, began to emerge as a new world power. Beginning in the late 1880's more and more Americans displayed a willingness to support involvement of the nation in frankly imperialistic ventures, justifying this break with traditional policy on strategic, economic, religious, and emotional grounds. Much of the energy that had been channeled earlier into internal development of the country, and especially into westward expansion along the frontier (which, according to the Census Bureau, ceased to exist as of 1890), was now diverted to enterprises beyond the continental limits of the United States. It was only a matter of time before both the Army and the Navy were to be called upon to support and protect the new American interests overseas.

A New Manifest Destiny

This new manifest destiny first took the form of vigorous efforts to expand long-established American trade and naval interests overseas, especially in the Pacific and Caribbean. Thus, in the Pacific the United States took steps to acquire control of coaling and maintenance stations for a growing steam-propelled fleet. In 1878 the United States obtained the right to develop a coaling station in Samoa and in 1889, to make this concession more secure, recognized independence of the islands in a tripartite pact with Great Britain and Germany. In 1893, when a new native government in Hawaii threatened to withdraw concessions, including a site for a naval station at Pearl Harbor, American residents tried unsuccessfully to secure annexation of the islands by the United States. Development of a more favorable climate of opinion in the United States in the closing years of the century opened the way for annexation of Hawaii in 1898 and Eastern Samoa (Tutuila) in 1899.

In the same period, the Navy endeavored with little success to secure coaling stations in the Caribbean, and Americans watched with interest abortive efforts of private firms to build an isthmian canal in Panama. American businessmen promoted establishment of better trade relations with Latin American countries, laying the groundwork for the future Pan American Union. And recurrent diplomatic crises, such as that with Chile in 1891–92, arising from a mob attack on American sailors in Valparaiso, and with Great Britain over the Venezuelan–British Guiana boundary in 1895, drew further attention to the southern continent.

Trouble in Cuba

While economic and strategic motives contributed significantly to the new manifest destiny, it was traditional American humanitarian concern for the oppressed peoples of Cuba that ultimately proved most important in launching the United States on an imperialistic course at the turn of the century. Cuba's geographic proximity to the United States and strategic location had long attracted the interest of American expansionists. Yet they were a small minority, and only when the Cubans rebelled against the repressive colonial policies of Spain did the attention of most Americans turn to the Caribbean island. This was true in 1868, when Cubans revolted against the Spanish regime in a rebellion destined to last for a decade, and again in 1895, when they rose up once more against continuing repression by the mother country. Many Americans soon favored some kind of intervention, but President Grover Cleveland was determined that the United States should adhere to a policy of strict neutrality. Events in Cuba, however, soon were to make this position increasingly difficult to maintain.

When after almost a year of costly fighting the Spanish had failed to suppress the rebellion, they turned to harsher measures. To carry these out the Madrid Government appointed a new Captain-General for Cuba, Valeriano Weyler, an officer with a reputation as an able soldier. Weyler arrived in Havana in early February 1896 with additional troops and immediately instituted new tactics designed to isolate the insurrectionist forces—entrenchments, barbed-wire fences, and, at narrow parts of the island, lines of blockhouses. Simultaneously, he inaugurated a policy of *reconcentrado,* herding women, children, and old people from the countryside into detention camps and garrisoned towns, where thousands died from disease and starvation. Weyler's methods gave newspapers in the United States, especially those practicing a newly fashionable yellow journalism, opportunity for renewed attacks on Spanish policies in Cuba. They portrayed the Spanish general as an inhuman "butcher" inflicting his cruel tactics on high-minded patriots struggling bravely for freedom from the oppression of an out-dated Old World authoritarianism.

In early 1896 both houses of Congress adopted by overwhelming majorities concurrent resolutions proposing that the United States grant belligerent status to the insurgents and employ its good offices to gain Spain's recognition of Cuban independence. Politicians, both in and out of Congress, saw in the Cuban situation an opportunity to gain popular support in the upcoming election of 1896. And a few expansion-minded American leaders perceived the insurrection as a chance to acquire naval bases in the Caribbean and open the way further for the country to play a more prominent role in world affairs. But neither Cleveland, nor his successor as President in 1897, William McKinley, wanted a war with Spain.

The Republican party platform of 1896, however, committed McKinley to a policy of using the nation's "influences and good offices to restore peace and give independence . . ." to Cuba. Consistent with this pledge, the newly elected President, in the face of a crescendo of demands for immediate American intervention, worked courageously and patiently, seeking to find a diplomatic solution that would satisfy the Cuban insurrectionists yet avoid a conflict between the United States and Spain.

In early February 1898, after serious rioting in Havana, the jingoistic New York *Journal* published a private letter written by Enrique Dupuy de Lôme, the Spanish Minister in Washington, to a Spanish editor then traveling in the United States. This communication, which a Cuban official in the Havana Post Office had stolen and passed on to the newspaper, expressed de Lôme's adverse personal reaction to McKinley's message to Congress in December 1897. The President was, he thought, "weak and a bidder for admiration of the crowd . . . a would-be politician who tries to leave a door open behind himself while keeping on good terms with the jingoes in his party." For the majority of Americans this unprecedented insult to a President was only further confirmation of the arrogance and insolence with which they felt Spain regularly conducted its Cuban policies. Even de Lôme's prompt resignation did little to calm the storm of indignation that swept the country. Nevertheless when Spain, at American insistence, somewhat reluctantly offered an apology, McKinley was inclined to accept it. Privately he was horrified at the possibility that what he viewed as a strictly personal matter might lead to war.

Despite this development McKinley still might have achieved a diplomatic solution had the American battleship *Maine* not been sunk on February 15, 1898, in Havana harbor as a result of a mysterious explosion, with a loss of 260 lives. The vessel was in the port ostensibly on a courtesy call—but actually to provide closer protection for American citizens in Cuba—dispatched there rather reluctantly by McKinley upon the advice of the American consul in Havana.

A naval investigating commission appointed by the President announced on March 25 that the *Maine* had gone down as a result of an external explosion, which to most Americans indicated Spanish treachery. But McKinley, in reporting to Congress on the commission's verdict, once again counseled "deliberate consideration" and, on March 27, sent to Madrid a new plan for peaceful settlement of the Cuban problem. The Spanish reply on March 31 agreed to end the *reconcentrado* policy and arbitrate the *Maine* disaster, but procrastinated on granting the insurrectionists an immediate armistice and refused to accept mediation by McKinley or to promise eventual independence for Cuba.

In spite of this discouraging response from Spain, the President continued to move slowly, leaving the door open for last-minute negotiations. Twice he postponed his war message to Congress before finally delivering it on April 11. Eight days later Congress passed a joint resolution proclaiming Cuba independent and authorizing the President to take necessary measures to expel the Spanish from the island. It included a significant amendment by Senator Teller of Colorado forbidding annexation of Cuba. With this authorization McKinley immediately ordered a blockade of Cuba, and an American naval squadron promptly took up a position off Havana. On April 25 Congress declared a state of war had existed since April 21. So began the conflict with Spain which McKinley and Cleveland had tried so hard to avoid—a war for which, despite the months of negotiation preceding its outbreak, the country was militarily most ill prepared.

Mobilizing for War

The extent of unpreparedness for overseas combat varied considerably in the two military services. In the decade preceding the war, the Navy, thanks to the efforts of career officers such as Rear Adm. Stephen B. Luce and Capt. Alfred T. Mahan, and to Benjamin Tracy, Secretary of the Navy in Harrison's administration, and also to the willingness of Congress, in a period of expanding overseas interests and relative prosperity, to appropriate the necessary funds, had carried out an extensive construction and modernization program. During the same period, the Naval War College at Newport, Rhode Island (established in 1885 through the efforts of Admiral Luce), had provided the Navy with a strong corps of professional officers trained in the higher levels of warfare and strategy, including the far-ranging doctrines of Mahan.

The Army was not so fortunate. With an average size in the quarter of a century preceding 1898 of only about 26,000 officers and men, most of whom were scattered widely across the country in company- and battalion-size organizations, the Army never had an opportunity for training and experience in the operation of units larger than a regiment. And while the individual soldier was well trained, the Army lacked a mobilization plan, a well-knit higher staff, and experience in carrying on joint operations with the Navy. The National Guard, with somewhat more than 100,000 members, was composed mostly of infantry units. Still lacking a consistent program of supervision by the Regular forces, most Guard units were poorly trained and disciplined, understrength, and inadequately equipped. Thus, typically, although most Regulars by 1898 were armed with Krag-Jörgensen rifles firing smokeless powder cartridges, most Guardsmen were still equipped with Springfield rifles which could fire only black powder ammunition.

Despite obvious deficiencies, the Guard might have supplied many of the units used in the conflict had it not been for other factors that made it difficult to employ Guardsmen on short notice in overseas theaters of war. Under existing law, there was some question as to whether it was legal for Guard units to serve abroad. Furthermore, Guard organization varied greatly from state to state, and most Guardsmen objected to any move that would place them under control of the Regular Army for the sake of achieving greater uniformity in organization. The War Department proposed to form a new federal volunteer force with officers appointed by the President. But again the Guard opposed this, and Congress in the mobilization act of April 22, 1898, settled for a make-shift arrangement providing for a wartime force composed of both Regular and volunteer units organized into brigades, divisions, and army corps. Some Guard units did, in effect, serve under an arrangement whereby if enough members of a state unit volunteered for service, they were kept together to form a comparable federal volunteer unit.

Although the act of April 22 provided for 125,000 volunteers, popular demand soon led Congress to increase this number by 75,000 and authorize additional special volunteer forces, including 10,000 enlisted men "possessing immunity from diseases incident to tropical climates"—the so-called Immunes. Simultaneously it also authorized more than doubling the size of the Regular Army to nearly 65,000. By war's end in August 1898, the Regular forces numbered 59,000 and the volunteers, 216,000, a total of 275,000.

Mobilizing, equipping, and supplying these wartime forces placed a severe burden upon the War Department. With neither a military planning staff nor the funds necessary to plan for war in peacetime, the department inevitably was ill prepared for any kind of major mobilization or military operation.

Further complicating matters was a basic disagreement within the department concerning the strategy to be followed and the way mobilization should be carried out.

To the extent the United States had a strategy for conduct of the war against Spain in the Caribbean, it consisted of maintaining a naval blockade of Cuba while native insurgent forces carried on a harassing campaign against Spanish troops on the island. Supporters of this policy—Captain Mahan was among its more articulate advocates—believed that it would lead eventually to surrender of the Spanish forces and the freeing of Cuba. No direct clash between American and Spanish troops was visualized; American land forces would simply occupy Cuba as soon as the Spanish departed.

More or less in conformity with this strategy, Maj. Gen. Nelson Miles, Commanding General of the Army, proposed to assemble, train, and equip a small force of about 80,000, using the Regular Army as a nucleus. There would be ample time for mobilizing this force, since Miles deemed it unwise to land any troops in Cuba before the end of the unhealthy rainy season in October. The first step was to concentrate the entire Regular Army at Chickamauga Park, Georgia, where it could receive much-needed instruction in combined arms operations.

So deliberate and cautious a plan, however, was, by mid-April 1898, not in harmony with the increasing public demand for immediate action against the Spanish. With an ear to this demand, Secretary of War Russell M. Alger, who had been a general officer in the Civil War and subsequently had pursued a political career for thirty years, ignored the advice of General Miles. He ordered the Regular infantry regiments to go to New Orleans, Tampa, and Mobile, where presumably they would be ready for an immediate descent on Cuba. (*Map 36*) (Later some infantry troops did go to Chickamauga Park, where they trained with the Regular cavalry and artillery concentrated there.)

The decision to mobilize large volunteer forces compounded the problems of equipping, training, and supplying the wartime Army. In the spring and summer of 1898, thousands of enthusiastic volunteers, a few with some militia training but most only raw recruits, poured into newly established camps in the South—located there so as to be near Cuba and, at the same time, help the soldiers to become accustomed to semitropical climatic conditions. But a taste of military life in the training camps soon curbed the enthusiasm of most volunteers, for there they found chronic shortages of the most essential equipment—even of such basic items as underwear, socks, and shoes—a steady diet of badly prepared food, unbelievably poor sanitary conditions, inadequate

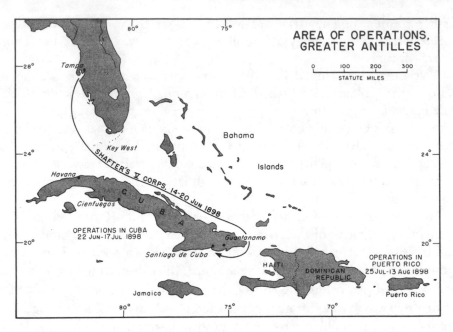

MAP 36

medical facilities, and a lack of up-to-date weapons. Red tape and poor management in the War Department's supply bureaus (the Ordnance Department possibly excepted) continued to delay correction of some of the worst deficiencies and combined with the shortage of capable volunteer officers to limit the effectiveness and quality of training received in the camps.

A similar general inefficiency characterized the War Department's conduct of actual operations against Spain. Since Congress had provided no machinery in the department for peacetime co-ordination of foreign policy with the country's military posture, the nation went to war without any kind of over-all plan of operations or even adequate intelligence about the enemy or the Cuban insurgents. Suddenly confronted in April 1898 with the necessity for launching overseas amphibious attacks on hostile shores—under the best circumstances always a difficult type of operation, requiring careful planning and close interservice co-operation—the War Department bureaus and the Army high command found themselves almost totally unprepared. Given time, they might have devised at least adequate operational plans; but public opinion, political pressures, and the trend of events demanded the launching of an immediate expedition against the Spanish in Cuba.

Victory at Sea: Naval Operations in the Caribbean and Pacific

Fortunately, it turned out that the really decisive fighting of the war fell to the much better prepared Navy, although last-minute alterations in its strategic plan for dealing with the Spanish Fleet seriously threatened to reduce its effectiveness. Shortly after the war began, rumors circulated that an enemy fleet under Admiral Pascual Cervera y Topete was approaching the Atlantic coast of the United States. An alarmed public demanded that measures be taken to defend the Atlantic seaboard. In deference to this demand, the Navy Department in late April 1898 withheld some of its best fighting ships from Rear Adm. William T. Sampson's North Atlantic Squadron, sent to blockade Cuba. These ships, formed into a "flying squadron" under Commodore Winfield S. Schley, set up a watch for Cervera. This move was in conflict with the provisions in the Navy's strategical plan for a war with Spain. Based upon Mahan's doctrines, the plan called for maintaining Sampson's squadron at full strength in the Caribbean, ready to intercept any Spanish fleet sent out to relieve Cuba.

In the western Pacific, meantime, the Navy was able to adhere to its strategical plan—the latest version of which had been completed in June 1897. Worked out after 1895 by officers at the Naval War College in collaboration with the Office of Naval Intelligence, this plan, known to President McKinley and the high officials in the Navy Department, provided for an attack on the Philippines, leading to destruction of Spanish warships there, capture of Manila, and blockade of the principal Philippine ports. The basic objectives of the plan were to weaken Spain by cutting off revenues from the Philippines and to place the United States in the position of having something to offer the Spanish as an inducement to make peace after Cuba had been freed.

Active Navy preparation for war began in January 1898, and in late February Theodore Roosevelt, as Acting Secretary of the Navy (Secretary John D. Long was ailing), cabled orders to American naval commanders, instructing them to get their squadrons in readiness to carry out existing war plans against Spain. Commodore George Dewey of the Asiatic Squadron received instructions to assemble his ships at Hong Kong, where they could take on coal and supplies preparatory to an attack on the Philippines.

Thus, on April 24, when McKinley finally ordered the Asiatic Squadron to execute the war plan against the Philippines Dewey was ready. He sailed into Manila Bay on the night of April 30 and next morning located the Spanish warships at Cavite. In a few hours and without loss of a single

American life, he sank or disabled the entire Spanish Fleet. In the days immediately following, he also silenced the land batteries defending Manila harbor, but the city itself continued to resist. (*See Map 44.*)

Since Dewey's 1,700 men were barely sufficient to maintain his own naval squadron, he requested dispatch of land forces from the United States to take Manila. In the two months before their arrival, he blockaded the port and gave assistance to Emilio Aguinaldo, Filipino insurgent leader, who, with Dewey's aid, had returned to the Philippines from exile in Hong Kong. Aguinaldo undertook guerrilla operations to keep the Spanish land forces in the vicinity of Manila. Dewey had to deal as well with the ticklish problem of British, French, and German naval contingents in Manila Bay, which arrived ostensibly to protect their nationals from the insurgents, but actually also to help uphold any claims their governments might advance to Filipino territory should the United States fail to take control over the islands. Most troublesome was the German squadron under Rear Adm. Otto von Diederichs, but Dewey's patience and firmness prevented a serious incident, and Berlin withdrew its fleet when it became apparent that the United States was not going to abandon the Philippines.

Operations in the Caribbean

As in the Pacific so also in the Caribbean the course of naval developments would determine when and where the Army undertook operations against Spanish land forces. During the early part of May 1898, the whereabouts of the Spanish Fleet under Admiral Cervera remained a mystery. Lacking this information, the Army could not fix precisely the point where it would launch an attack. Nevertheless, the War Department pushed preparations at Tampa, Florida, for an expedition under General Miles to be put ashore somewhere near Havana. But persistent rumors of the approach of the Spanish Fleet to Cuban waters delayed this expedition while the Navy searched further for Cervera. News at last reached Washington near the end of May that the Spanish admiral had skillfully evaded the American naval blockade and, on the 19th of the month, had slipped into the bay at Santiago de Cuba. (*See Map 36.*)

The Navy, at first not at all certain that it was actually Cervera's fleet in Santiago, sent Admiral Sampson to inspect the harbor. As soon as the American naval commander had ascertained that the four cruisers and several smaller war vessels were indeed Spanish, he bombarded the forts at the entrance to Santiago Bay. Unable to silence them, Sampson decided against trying to run the heavily mined harbor entrance. Instead, he sent Lt. (jg) Richmond P. Hobson to bottle up the enemy fleet by sinking the collier *Merrimac* athwart the channel. When this bold project failed, Sampson requested land forces to seize the Spanish batteries, at the same time dispatching marines ashore to secure a site for a naval base east of Santiago. In the first land skirmish of the Cuban campaign, the marines quickly overcame enemy resistance and established the base at Guantánamo Bay.

Upon receipt of Sampson's request for land forces, the War Department, already under strong public pressure to get the Army into action, ordered Maj. Gen. William R. Shafter to embark with the V Corps from Tampa as soon as possible to conduct operations against Santiago in co-operation with the Navy. This corps was the only one of the eight that the War Department had organized for the war that was anywhere near ready to fight. Composed chiefly of Regular Army units, it had been assembling at Tampa for weeks when the order came on May 31 for its embarkation; it would require another two weeks to get the corps and its equipment on board and ready to sail for Cuba.

The slow pace of preparation and loading of the expedition was attributable to many factors. There was no over-all plan and no special staff to direct it. Although selected because of its port facilities and proximity to Cuba, Tampa, from the logistical point of view, proved to be a poor choice for marshaling a major military expedition. With only one pier for loading ships and a single-track railroad connecting with mainline routes from the north, the resulting backup of freight cars for miles delayed shipment of much needed supplies and equipment. Incoming soldiers waited interminably in uncomfortable railroad cars. When freight cars finally did reach the port area, there were no wagons to unload them and no bills of lading to indicate what was in them. When it came to loading the ships, of which there were not enough to carry the entire corps, supplies and equipment were put on board with little regard for unloading priorities in the combat zone should there be enemy resistance during the landings.

In spite of the confusion and inefficiency at Tampa, by June 14 nearly 17,000 men were ready to sail. On board were 18 Regular and 2 volunteer infantry regiments; 10 Regular and 2 volunteer cavalry squadrons, serving dismounted; 1 mounted cavalry squadron; 6 artillery batteries; and a machine gun (Gatling gun) company. The expedition comprised a major part of the Regular forces, including all of the Regular Negro combat regiments. Moving out from Tampa on the morning of the 14th, the V Corps joined its naval convoy next day off the Florida Keys and by June 20 had reached the vicinity of Santiago.

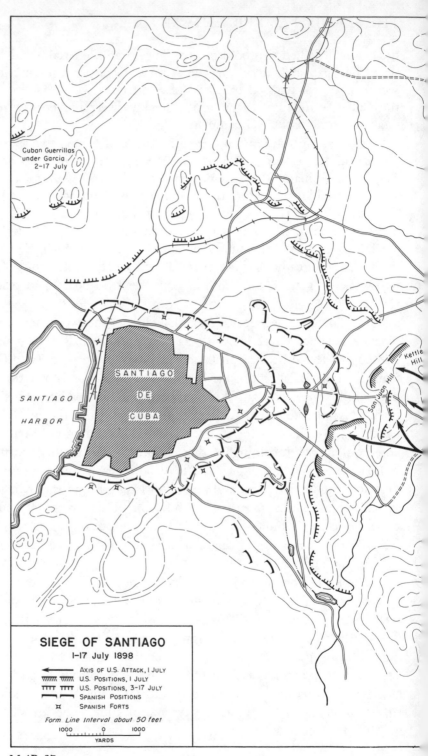

Cuban Guerrillas
under Garcia
2-17 July

SANTIAGO
DE
CUBA

SANTIAGO

HARBOR

San Juan Hill

Kettle
Hill

SIEGE OF SANTIAGO
1-17 July 1898

⟵——— Axis of U.S. Attack, 1 July
🙰🙰🙰 🙰🙰🙰 U.S. Positions, 1 July
🙰🙰🙰 🙰🙰🙰 U.S. Positions, 3-17 July
◖◗ Spanish Positions
⋈ Spanish Forts

Form Line Interval about 50 feet

1000   0   1000
|⊥⊥⊥⊥⊥|⊥⊥⊥⊥⊥|
YARDS

MAP 37

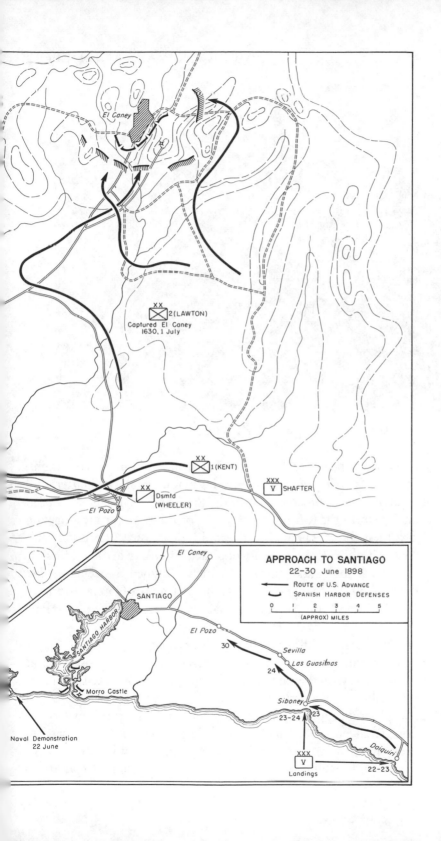

El Caney

XX
2 (LAWTON)
Captured El Caney
1630, 1 July

XX
1 (KENT)

XXX
V SHAFTER

XX
Dsmtd
(WHEELER)

El Pozo

APPROACH TO SANTIAGO
22–30 June 1898

→ ROUTE OF U.S. ADVANCE
Ↄ SPANISH HARBOR DEFENSES

0   1   2   3   4   5
(APPROX) MILES

El Caney

SANTIAGO

SANTIAGO HARBOR

El Pozo

30

Sevilla

Las Guasimas

Morro Castle

24

Siboney

Naval Demonstration
22 June

23–24   23

XXX
V

Landings

Daiquiri

22–23

TRANSPORTS AT TAMPA

While the troops on board endured tropical heat, unsanitary conditions, and cold rations—the canned beef was especially unpalatable—Shafter and Sampson conferred on how to proceed against the Spanish in Santiago. Sampson wanted the Army to storm the fort on the east side of the bay entrance, driving the Spanish from their guns. Then his fleet could clear away the mines and enter Santiago Bay to fight Cervera's squadron. Lacking heavy artillery, Shafter was not sure his troops could take the fort, which crowned a steep hill. He decided instead to follow the suggestion of General Calixto Garcia, the local insurgent leader, and land his forces at Daiquirí, east of Santiago Bay. (*Map 37*)

On June 22, after heavy shelling of the landing areas, the V Corps began disembarking amid circumstances almost as confused and hectic as those at Tampa. Captains of many of the chartered merchant ships resisted bringing their vessels close inshore. Their reluctance slowed the landing of troops and equipment, already handicapped by a shortage of lighters (the Navy could not spare the additional ones needed). Horses, simply dropped overboard to get ashore on their own, swam out to sea in some instances and were lost. An alert enemy defense might well have taken advantage of the chaotic conditions to oppose the landings effectively. But the Spanish, though they had more than 200,000 troops in Cuba—some 36,000 of them in Santiago Province—did nothing to prevent Shafter's men from getting ashore. Some 6,000 landed on June 22 and most of the remaining 11,000 on the two days following. In addition, some 4,000 to 5,000 insurgents under General Garcia supplemented the American force.

The Battle of Santiago

Once ashore, elements of the V Corps moved westward toward the heights of San Juan, a series of ridge lines immediately east of Santiago, where well-entrenched enemy troops guarded the land approaches to the city. On June 23, Brig. Gen. Henry W. Lawton, commanding the vanguard, advanced along the coast from Daiquirí to occupy Siboney, which then became the main base of operations. The next day, Brig. Gen. Joseph Wheeler, the Confederate Army veteran, pushed inland along the road to Santiago with dismounted cavalry to seize Las Guásimas, after a brief skirmish with rear guard elements of a retiring Spanish force. This move brought American units within five miles of the San Juan Heights, where they paused for a few days while General Shafter assembled the rest of his divisions and brought up supplies. Even in this short time, Shafter could observe the debilitating effects of tropical climate and disease on his men. He was aware, too, that the hurricane season was approaching. Consequently, he decided in favor of an immediate attack on the defenses of Santiago.

Shafter's plan was simple: a frontal attack on the San Juan Heights. For this purpose, he deployed Brig. Gen. Jacob F. Kent's infantry division on the left and Wheeler's dismounted cavalry on the right, the entire force with supporting elements comprising some 8,000 troops. But before he made the main advance on the heights Lawton's infantry division with a supporting battery of artillery—more than 6,500 men—was to move some two miles north to seize the fortified village of El Caney, cutting off Santiago's water supply and, if necessary, intercepting rumored Spanish reinforcements. This action completed—Shafter thought it would take about two hours—Lawton was to turn southwestward and form on the right flank of Wheeler's division for participation in the main assault. A brigade which had just landed at Siboney was to advance meanwhile along the coast in a feint to deceive the enemy.

The attack, which moved out at dawn on July 1, soon became badly disorganized because of poor co-ordination, difficult terrain, and tropical heat. The corpulent Shafter, virtually prostrated by the heat, had to leave the direction of the battle to others. At a stream crossing on the crowded main trail to

San Juan Heights enemy gunners scored heavily when a towed Signal Corps balloon pinpointed the front of the advancing line of troops. And Lawton's division, delayed in its seizure of El Caney by a stubborn enemy defense, misplaced artillery, and the necessity of withdrawing a volunteer unit armed only with telltale black powder, did not rejoin the main force until after the assault had ended. Despite these unexpected setbacks, Kent's and Wheeler's divisions at midday launched a strong frontal attack on the Spanish forward defensive positions. Cavalry units of Wheeler's division, including the 9th Cavalry and part of the 10th, both Negro regiments, and the volunteer Rough Riders, who were commanded by Lt. Col. Theodore Roosevelt, seized Kettle Hill, separate from the central heights. Then Kent's infantry regiments, sup-

THE SIGNAL CORPS BALLOON *at Santiago.*

ported by the unorthodox employment of Gatling guns in the attack, stormed up San Juan Hill in the main ridge line, driving the Spanish from blockhouse and trench defenses and compelling them to retire to a strongly fortified inner line. Thus the day ended with the Americans having achieved most of their initial objectives. But the cost was high—nearly 1,700 casualties sustained since the start of operations against Santiago.

Concerned with the increasing sickness that was further thinning the ranks of the V Corps and faced by a well-organized Spanish second line of defense, General Shafter cabled Secretary Alger on July 3 that he was considering withdrawing about five miles to higher ground between the San Juan River and Siboney. The shift would place his troops in a position where they would be less exposed to enemy fire and easier to supply. Alger replied that "the effect upon the country would be much better" if Shafter continued to hold his advanced position.

The V Corps commander then again sought to get the Navy to enter Santiago Bay and attack the city. But neither the Navy Department nor President McKinley was willing to sanction this move. Just when the whole matter threatened to become an embarrassing public debate between the two services, the Spanish themselves resolved the issue.

Deteriorating conditions within Santiago—lack of food and ammunition were seriously affecting the health and morale of the defending forces—convinced the defenders that the city must soon fall. While Cervera considered flight from the port hopeless, he had no recourse but to attempt it. Officials in both Havana and Madrid had ordered him, for reasons of honor, to escape when Santiago appeared about to surrender. Finally, on the morning of July 3, while Sampson and Shafter conferred ashore, Cervera made his dash for the open sea, hoping to reach the port of Cienfuegos on the south coast of Cuba. As soon as the Spanish Fleet appeared, Sampson's squadron, temporarily under command of Commodore Schley, gave chase and in less than two hours destroyed Cervera's fleet; four cruisers were crippled and run ashore and one destroyer was beached and another sunk.

A few days later, General Shafter persuaded the Spanish leaders in Santiago that they had no choice except to surrender. On July 16 they signed the unconditional terms demanded by the McKinley administration, which provided for surrender of 11,500 troops in the city and some 12,000 others in the vicinity of Santiago. The formal surrender ceremony took place on the following day.

During preparations for the Santiago campaign, General Miles personally had been overseeing organization of a second expedition to seize Puerto Rico. On July 21 he sailed from Guantánamo with more than 3,000 troops. His original strategy was to land first at Cape Fajardo in the northeast part of the island, where he could establish a base of operations for a subsequent advance westward to the capital, San Juan. For reasons not entirely clear, but probably because of a desire not to have to co-operate with the Navy in the attack on San Juan, Miles, while still at sea, changed his plans and on July 25 landed forces first at Guánica on the southeastern coast. Meeting virtually no opposition, the Americans shortly occupied the port of Ponce. In early August, after arrival of more than 10,000 additional troops from ports in the United States, General Miles, using Ponce as a base of operations, launched a four-column drive toward San Juan. There was little bloodshed—casualties for the campaign totaled fewer than fifty—and, in fact, most Puerto Ricans welcomed the American troops. The campaign ended on August 13 when word reached the island that Spain had signed a peace protocol the previous day.

Back in Cuba, meanwhile, conditions for the Army were much less pleasant. Spread of malaria, typhoid, and yellow fever among Shafter's troops at Santiago threatened to have far deadlier consequences than had the actual fighting. Concern over this problem led to the drafting of a joint letter by a number of Shafter's senior officers, proposing immediate evacuation of the Army from Cuba. Addressed to the commanding general, this round robin letter unfortunately came to the attention of the press before it reached Shafter. Hence, Washington officials read it in the newspapers before learning of its content from the general himself. Naturally the whole episode, coming at the time when peace negotiations were beginning, caused a sensation. Although acutely embarrassing for the Army and General Shafter, the incident did have the salutary effect of hastening measures to evacuate thousands of troops to Montauk Point, Long Island, where the Army Medical Department already had taken steps to establish an isolated detention camp. Here those who had contracted tropical infections received the necessary treatment. And out of the Army's nearly disastrous experience with the debilitating effects of disease and climate in Cuba came the impetus for the Medical Corps' notable project to determine the causes of yellow fever, inaugurating a long-term program of research and study into what henceforth would be a permanent concern of the Army—the maintenance of the health and effectiveness of American troops in a tropical environment.

The Fall of Manila

In another tropical setting halfway around the world from Cuba the final military episode of the war took place. During May and June 1898 Admiral Dewey, while awaiting the arrival in the Philippines of land forces from the United States, kept in contact with the insurgent leader, General Aguinaldo. The Filipino forces occupied lines on the land side of Manila, preventing the Spanish garrison from moving beyond the immediate outskirts of the city.

Although the Americans and the Philippine insurgents shared a common interest in bringing about the defeat of the Spanish, relations between them tended to deteriorate during the period of waiting. The most important reason was a fundamental difference in objectives. The goal of the insurgents, who controlled most areas outside the towns and cities on Luzon and the other important islands, was immediate independence for the Philippines. But after some hesitation the McKinley administration and more and more Americans were coming around to the view that the United States ought to retain the islands. Once Aguinaldo became aware of this he endeavored to counteract it by taking steps to establish a revolutionary government with himself as president. On August 6 he appealed to foreign governments to recognize the independence of the Philippines. Hence by late summer there was serious doubt as to just what might be expected from the increasingly hostile insurgent forces.

In the interim, the long-awaited ground forces needed to complete the campaign in the Philippines began arriving in the Manila area. By the end of July 1898, some 13,000 volunteer and 2,000 Regular troops, constituting the VIII Corps under Maj. Gen. Wesley Merritt, had reached the islands. These troops had embarked from west coast ports (chiefly San Francisco) with a minimum of the confusion and difficulty that had characterized the launching of the Cuban expedition. In spite of the long voyage across the Pacific, they were in good condition and ready to start operations against the Spanish as soon as enough troops could be moved into the vicinity of Manila.

By early August General Merritt had 11,000 troops of the VIII Corps in lines immediately to the rear of those occupied by the insurgents, ready to attack the city. Inside the Philippine capital and in fortified lines just beyond the city walls were about 10,000 to 15,000 Spanish troops. Although their leaders were fully aware of the relative hopelessness of the situation, efforts of Dewey and Merritt to secure a peaceful surrender failed because the Spanish Government in Madrid insisted that the garrison should make at least a token show of resistance.

On the morning of August 13 the VIII Corps launched an assault on Manila. As the tide receded, American units moved quickly to the beaches on the south side of the city and then, supported by concentrated fire from Dewey's ships, advanced through the insurgent lines. By prior arrangement, somewhat reluctantly agreed to by Aguinaldo, the insurgents were to retire as the Americans moved toward the Spanish entrenchments. But in carrying out this difficult maneuver, Americans and insurgents unintentionally became intermixed and some troops—presumably for the most part insurgents—began firing on the Spanish lines. Momentarily, this flare-up threatened to thwart the enemy's plan to offer only token resistance, but quick action by American officers brought the firing under control and the garrison surrendered. Operations at Manila cost the Americans a total of 17 killed and 105 wounded.

Formal surrender ceremonies came the following day—actually two days after the government in Madrid had signed a peace protocol ending hostilities. News of the protocol had not yet reached Manila because the cable Dewey cut when he first entered Manila Bay still had not been repaired.

After negotiations in Paris in the fall of 1898, the United States and Spain signed a treaty on December 10 ending the war. By its terms Spain gave up sovereignty over Cuba, which became an independent state, ceded Puerto Rico and Guam to the United States, and accepted $20 million in payment for the Philippines. Thus fatefully did Americans commit the nation to a new role as a colonial power in the Far East, with momentous future consequences that few at the turn of the century could anticipate.

CHAPTER 10

World War I: The U.S. Army Overseas

Included in the orders General Pershing received from the Secretary of War before he left for France was a stipulation "to cooperate with the forces of the other countries . . . but in so doing the underlying idea must be kept in view that the forces of the United States are a separate and distinct component of the combined forces, the identity of which must be preserved." This was a requirement that influenced many of Pershing's early decisions in regard to the American Expeditionary Forces and was to be for long months a recurring source of contention between Pershing and Allied commanders who were nearing the end of their manpower resources.

Training and Organizing U.S. Troops

For assembling American troops, Pershing chose the region southeast of Paris. Since the British were committed to that part of the front north of Paris and since the French had achieved their greatest concentration in protection of the capital, they had tied up the Channel ports and the railroads north and northeast of Paris. By locating southeast of the city, U.S. forces would be close to the Lorraine portion of the front, a likely spot for committing an independent American force. The French had few troops there and important objectives lay within reasonable striking distance—coal and iron mines and railroads vital to the Germans. This part of the front could be served by the ports of southern and southwestern France and by rail lines less committed to French and British requirements. Pershing set up his headquarters near the source of the Marne in Chaumont.

To Pershing, the training not only of the hastily assembled 1st Division but also of the others that followed before the end of 1917 (the 2d—half Regular Army, half Marine; 26th—New England National Guard; and 42d—called the "Rainbow Division" because it was a composite of Guardsmen from many states) was seriously inadequate. Many of the men in these divisions were recruits, replacements for those pulled out to help train newly forming units.

Pershing devised an intensive training schedule for the 1st Division and planned to follow a similar program for the other three with the idea of withholding all four from active sectors until all were ready, whereupon, late in 1918, they might be committed as the nucleus of an independent American force. Reinforced by other units arriving in 1918, Pershing in 1919 could open an offensive aimed at victory.

For training in trench warfare, Pershing gratefully accepted the help of experienced Allied officers. He also followed the Allied system of setting up special training centers and schools to teach subjects such as gas warfare, demolitions, and the use of the hand grenade and the mortar. Yet in the belief that the French and British had become too imbued with trench warfare to the exclusion of the open maneuvers that eventually would be necessary to achieve victory, he insisted on additional training in offensive tactics, including detailed work in rifle marksmanship and use of the bayonet.

Not until late October 1917 did Pershing submit the 1st Division to trial experience in the line. One battalion at a time from each regiment spent ten days with a French division. The first U.S. Army casualties of the war resulted from this deployment when early in November the Germans staged a trench raid against the same battalion that had paraded in Paris. With a loss of 3 of their own men, the Germans killed 3 Americans and captured 11.

The cycle in the trenches completed, Pershing submitted the 1st Division to further training to correct the deficiencies observed at the front. Only in mid-January of 1918, six months after its arrival in France, was the division ready in Pershing's view to move as a unit into a quiet sector of the trenches.

General Pershing had in the meantime been setting up the staff and logistical organization for managing the growing American force. Reflecting a strong similarity to the French system, his General Staff ultimately included a chief of staff, a deputy chief, and five assistant chiefs supervising five sections: G–1 (Personnel), G–2 (Intelligence), G–3 (Operations), G–4 (Supply), and G–5 (Training). Staffs for divisions and later for corps and armies followed a similar organization, while to fill the new staff positions Pershing set up a General Staff College with a 3-month course.

To provide logistical support, Pershing created a Line of Communications under a single commander responsible directly to him. It was organized into base sections, each with one or more ports, an intermediate section for storage and classification of supplies, and an advanced section for distribution to the zone of operations. After American units entered combat, depots in the advanced section made up supplies for each division in trains which moved to division railheads, whence the divisions moved the supplies to the front in wagons and trucks. The designation Line of Communications was later changed to Services of Supply under command of Pershing's original chief of staff, Maj. Gen. James G. Harbord.

Pressure From French and British

Carrying out the comprehensive training program required all the determination at Pershing's disposal, for once the first exultation accompanying the arrival of American troops in France had predictably passed, practical French and British commanders saw that it would be a long time before independent American units could assume any appreciable portion of the combat burden. They began to insist almost immediately that American soldiers be fed into Allied divisions as replacements.

The Allies felt their request was logical. They had the experienced commanders and units, the necessary artillery, aviation, and tank support, but they lacked men. The American situation was the reverse. Their way, they argued, the power of the American soldier could be quickly brought to bear and hasten the victory. Yet this was reckoning without a sense of national pride that existed among both the soldiers themselves and the American people.

Pershing refused.

Although the Allied governments tried to bypass Pershing by going directly to Washington, they found the Secretary of War and the President firmly behind their field commander. When General Tasker H. Bliss, who had served briefly as the U.S. Army Chief of Staff, was sent as the American representative to the Supreme War Council, Allied governments tried this channel to break Pershing's adamant resolve; but although Bliss was inclined to be more conciliatory than Pershing, he yielded nothing on the principle of a separate American force.

The issue arose again early in 1918 when the British offered to provide the shipping to transport 150 battalions of infantry, which would be used to fill out British divisions that because of the manpower shortage had been reduced from 12 battalions of infantry to 9. After four or five months, according to the British plan, Pershing might withdraw the battalions to form them into American divisions.

This too Pershing refused, but well aware that a lack of ships was slowing the American build-up, he suggested that the British transport divisions instead. Because the same shipping that could move 150 infantry battalions could accommodate only about 3 divisions, which would mean only 36 infantry battalions, the British declined, but eventually they agreed to transport 6 divisions without equipment on the condition that Pershing outfit and train them in the British zone. Ten divisions would eventually arrive under this program.

The matter of a separate American force stood for the moment with Pershing still in unqualified control, yet in view of Allied persistence and of pending developments at the front the question was bound to arise again and again.

The German Offensive, March 1918

As the year 1918 opened, two more U.S. divisions were destined for early arrival in France, but if Pershing kept to his training schedule the American presence was a long way from assertion on the battlefield. The original excitement among the French and British over America's entry into the war had given way to renewed pessimism, for the Allied position appeared less favorable than at any time since the opening battle of the Marne. To the weary French and British, President Wilson's January proclamation of a 14-point peace proposal, however statesmanlike, appeared too idealistic.

So perturbed by the shocking losses of Passchendaele was the British Prime Minister, Lloyd George, that he withheld replacements to assure that his field commander, Sir Douglas Haig, would have to remain on the defensive. Nor could a French Army not yet fully recovered from the mutinies be expected to swing to the attack. The Allies appeared to have no alternative for 1918 but to hold on grimly until enough American troops arrived to assure the numerical superiority essential to victory.

Aside from the calamities of the Nivelle offensive, Passchendaele, and Caporetto, the Allies faced the prospect of sharply increased German numbers made available by the Russian defection. The number of German divisions shifted from east to west would have been even greater had the new Bolshevik government not reneged on its decision to get out of the war and had the Germans not blundered in response. The Bolsheviks had come to Brest-Litovsk in December 1917 to talk only of a peace that would restore Russia's prewar boundaries and impose no indemnities, a concept that strained German credulity. What came of the first encounter at Brest-Litovsk was neither peace nor war but a bizarre new confrontation between Germany and Russia that still tied down eighty German divisions.

Russia, said the Bolsheviks, would not make peace; neither would its forces continue the war even if the Germans still fought. In response, the German armies in the east began in February 1918 to march deeper into Russia. They marched on even after the Bolsheviks at last agreed to real peace, only to become involved eventually in guerrilla warfare against their rear. Throughout the spring and summer of 1918 a million Germans that might have been decisive on the Western Front remained embroiled in Russia.

Within Germany, by the start of 1918, the duo of Hindenburg and Ludendorff had gradually accumulated almost dictatorial powers, with Ludendorff dominating more than ever. They decided that they had to strike early in 1918 in a final grand effort to achieve victory in the west before American manpower could be brought to bear. Germany, possibly more than France and Britain, was hurting gravely from the long war: on the home front, starvation was becoming a stark reality, and the previous summer there had been Marxist-inspired mutinies in the German Navy. The replacements going to German divisions were old men and boys.

By recalling divisions from Italy and some from the east, Ludendorff managed to assemble over 3,500,000 men on the Western Front, including 192 divisions. He planned to attack in early spring with 62 divisions along the Somme against the British, whose armies had little space for recoil before they would find themselves with their backs on the Channel. Having split the British and French, he then would turn to defeat the French. (*Map 39*)

For success Ludendorff counted on numerical superiority (4 to 1), surprise, and the first mass application of new tactics developed originally in the east by Lt. Gen. Oscar von Hutier. The so-called "Hutier tactics" involved a relatively short (several hours) but intensive artillery preparation, heavy on gas and smoke, followed by a rolling barrage creeping ahead of the infantry at a predetermined rate. Organized in small battle groups built around a light machine gun, the infantry infiltrated to cut off strongpoints rather than assault them, leaving that task to others who came behind. The enemy's forward positions ruptured, the infantry advanced swiftly to overrun the enemy artillery and break into the clear. In both these phases, light artillery was attached to assault battalions, a tactical use of horse-drawn field pieces heretofore considered suicidal in trench warfare.

The new tactics put a premium on courage, stamina, initiative, and co-ordination, qualities which, for lack of time, the Germans could instill in only about two dozen specially selected divisions. These were pulled from the line, filled out with men from other divisions, and put through an intensive training program.

Despite elaborate efforts to achieve surprise, a new confidence radiating from Berlin and intelligence gathered from prisoners at the front made it clear to the Allies that the Germans were readying a major offensive. The British even determined the general strength, place, and finally the date of the attack, and they had a strong indication of the tactics the Germans would employ. But Haig, short of reserves, could do little in advance to prepare to counter the blow,

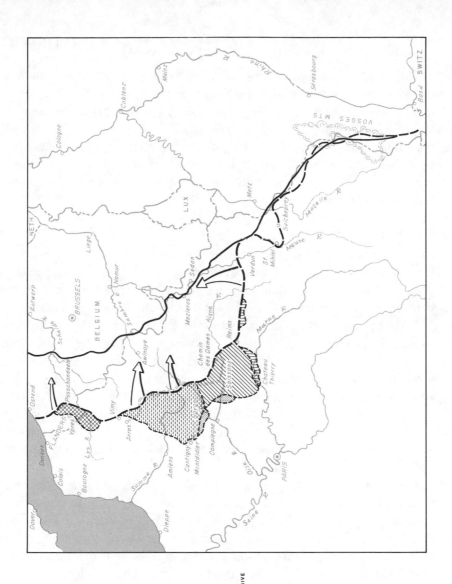

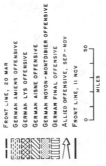

WESTERN FRONT
20 Mar – 11 Nov 1918

FRONT LINE, 20 MAR
GERMAN AMIENS OFFENSIVE
GERMAN LYS OFFENSIVE
GERMAN AISNE OFFENSIVE
GERMAN NOYON-MONTDIDIER OFFENSIVE
GERMAN FINAL OFFENSIVE
ALLIED OFFENSIVE, SEP-NOV
FRONT LINE, 11 NOV

0   50
MILES

MAP 39

while the French High Command refused to believe that if Ludendorff intended a decisive offensive he would strike the British rather than the French.

The big blow came on March 21 in a fog with the main effort against the British right wing. When night fell, the Germans had achieved a penetration along a 50-mile front and were pointing toward Amiens, a communications hub on the Somme that in German hands would effectively split the French and British armies. The only question remaining was, did Ludendorff have the means to exploit his success.

If Ludendorff's success or failure depended on early commitment of Allied reserves, he had little cause for concern. Despite a mutual pledge by Haig and Pétain to go to each other's aid in event of crisis, so imbued was Pétain with the belief that the Germans were bound to strike a harder blow against the French that he was slow to send help. Although he gradually dispatched six divisions to the south flank of the penetration, these acted less to stem the German tide than to screen against any German turn toward Paris.

Ludendorff nevertheless was running into trouble. To broaden the penetration at the northern shoulder, he threw in 20 more divisions; but these were untrained in the Hutier tactics and failed to pierce a solid British defense. The long-fought-over terrain along the Somme slowed the advance of the main effort, and a hastily created British defensive force composed mainly of rear-echelon service troops occupied old trenches east of Amiens to halt the advance on that critical city. The German divisions in the lead were becoming exhausted, and supplies failed to get forward.

By the end of March, Ludendorff's offensive had bogged down. He had achieved a brilliant tactical victory—an advance of forty miles in eight days, 70,000 prisoners, 200,000 other Allied casualties; but strategically the result was empty. He had failed either to destroy the British armies or to separate them from the French, and he had taken as many casualties as he had inflicted, most of them in the highly trained shock divisions, losses he could not replace.

Unity of Command

A combination of the crisis and of Pétain's dilatory response to Haig's pleas for help also harmed German chances of ultimate victory. Although Haig himself had vitiated an earlier attempt to create a 30-division reserve for the Supreme War Council by pleading inability to spare his quota, he was so shaken by the crisis on the Somme that he volunteered to subordinate British troops around Amiens to a Frenchman, General (later Marshal of France) Ferdinand Foch. As an instructor in prewar years at the École de Guerre, Foch had established a reputation as a military theorist and earlier in the war had successfully co-ordinated British, French, and Belgian operations in Flanders. Out of this agreement to subordinate all troops around the Amiens salient to Foch grew a broader understanding to subordinate, first, all British and French troops on the Western Front, then, later, all Allied forces.

The Allies at last had a unified command, even though they qualified it with weakening provisos: one that Foch had only "strategic direction" while "tactical control" remained with national commanders, another that each national commander could appeal a decision of the supreme commander to his home government. These qualifications, in theory, sharply diminished Foch's authority; but through military acumen, determination, and force of personality, Foch would make the arrangement work.

The Lys Offensive, April 1918

Ludendorff, meanwhile, clung to a belief that with another blow he could shatter the British armies. This time he chose a point a few miles north of the Amiens salient along the Lys River in Flanders, close by the scene of the bloody British offensive known as Passchendaele. Now he had 35 divisions.

Following an intensive bombardment, mainly with gas shells, eight German divisions attacked early on April 9 along the south bank of the Lys and quickly took advantage of the collapse of a Portuguese division to plunge five miles past the last of the trenches into open country. The next day other divisions attacking along the north bank of the Lys also achieved a penetration.

By the fourth day of the attack, the British were in serious danger. Putting the new unified command to a test, Field Marshal Haig called on Foch for help, but having long observed the tenacity of the British soldier on defense, Foch was convinced Haig could hold without involving reserves that could be better saved for a counteroffensive once the Germans had exhausted their resources. Although Haig fumed, Foch would agree to send only a few divisions.

Haig at that point issued what became known as his "backs to the wall" order: "There is no other course open to us but to fight it out. . . . With our backs to the wall and believing in the justice of our cause, each one of us must fight on to the end."

As the British soldier responded nobly, hungry German troops often slowed their attack to forage for food. In the end, Ludendorff had no choice but to call off the offensive. As April drew to a close, he held another vulnerable salient that included the Passchendaele Ridge but little else of tactical importance, this at a cost to the British of 305,000 casualties of all types but to the Germans even more, 350,000.

The first major action involving an American division had developed in the meantime far from the flaming Somme and Lys on a quiet sector in Lorraine, not far from the town of St. Mihiel. Here the 26th Division on April 20 came under a heavy bombardment, followed by a German attack in regimental strength aimed at seizing the village of Seicheprey. Boxing in the defenders with artillery barrages, the Germans took the village, only to lose it in the afternoon to a U.S. counterattack. The Germans held on to a nearby wood through the day, but American riflemen, cut off and scattered early in the fighting, regrouped to regain their positions the next day. The Germans left behind 160 dead, but they took 136 prisoners and inflicted 634 casualties.

During these weeks, General Pershing came under renewed pressure from the British and French to make up losses in Allied divisions with individual American replacements. While Pershing at the height of the crisis on the Somme had offered to place U.S. troops at Foch's disposal, he had been thinking only of the existing crisis while remaining faithful in the long run to the concept of an autonomous American army. Long and sometimes tempestuous were the arguments, voluminous the cables between Allied capitals, but in the end Pershing would go only so far as to agree that infantry and engineers of the divisions being transported in British shipping might be brought to France ahead of their artillery. Allied commanders, including Foch, finally endorsed the principle of forming as soon as possible an independent American force.

The Aisne Offensive, May 1918

As these arguments proceeded, the front was for a few weeks relatively quiet. It was a quiet before a storm, for Ludendorff was determined to persist in his struggle in Flanders to pin the British armies against the Channel.

To draw off Allied reserves from Flanders, Ludendorff decided on a diversionary attack against the Chemin des Dames, an elongated, commanding ridgeline northeast of Paris covering Soissons. Although this was the sector where Pétain had feared attack in March, with no attack forthcoming he had progressively thinned the defense. So imbued with the natural strength of the position was the local commander that he had neglected to erect a defense in depth, concentrating his men instead on the forward slope of the Chemin des Dames. In the face of heavy bombardment combined with the Hutier tactics, he was inviting disaster.

It was not long in coming. Although forewarned by an American intelligence analysis that an attack was in the offing, the French refused to heed the signs until the day before the attack was to begin. All the French troops could do in the time remaining was to stand warily at their posts while Foch belatedly began moving reserves.

With 17 divisions forward and 13 in follow-up reserve, the Germans attacked early on May 27 behind a barrage by close to 5,000 guns. German infantry plunged quickly over and beyond the Chemin des Dames, jumping the Aisne and Vesle Rivers, and gaining up to 20 miles in the first 24 hours.

Although this was to have been but a diversionary attack, Ludendorff was too elated by the breakthrough, too tempted by the open road to Paris to bring it to a halt. Three days later, on the last day of May, his troops would reach the Marne at Château-Thierry, less than fifty miles from the French capital, almost as close as Moltke had come in 1914.

Under pressure of this new crisis, General Pershing again went to Foch, this time to offer 5 American divisions to be used along the Marne as Foch deemed necessary. By the night of May 31, the machine gun battalion of the 3d Division, moved up swiftly in trucks, was in position to help French troops hold the bridge site over the Marne at Château-Thierry, and the rest of the division was on the way to help hold the river line. The next day the 2d Division (which included a Marine brigade) took up defensive positions north of the Marne and west of Château-Thierry astride the main highway to Paris.

Despair gripped not only the French stragglers falling back from the front but also the Allied High Command. What they could not know was that again Ludendorff was overextended, that he could strike in earnest for Paris only after broadening the wings of his narrow salient and bringing up supplies and reserves.

For two days Ludendorff's advance troops beat vainly against a hastily dug American line. At last they desisted, but the infantrymen and marines of the 2d Division would give them no rest. Beginning on June 6, the 2d Division attacked in costly but intrepid strikes against Belleau Wood and the villages of Bouresches and Vaux. Although this fighting would continue for three weeks, it was apparent from the first that the sudden, dramatic introduction of a new force had brought Ludendorff's thrust to a halt. For the Americans it was a costly debut—9,777 casualties, including 1,811 dead—but the moral effect on both sides was great.

The moral effect was all the more pronounced because of another action that antedated the 2d Division's achievement, the first offensive by an American division in the war. It began as a preliminary to a planned French counterattack against the Amiens salient, a counterattack that because of Ludendorff's break-through to the Marne failed to come off. It was an attack by the 1st Division against the village of Cantigny on commanding ground near the tip of the salient.

Supported by American and French artillery and by French tanks, one regiment took the village in a swift maneuver early on May 28, then held on grimly as counterattack followed counterattack into the next day. The Americans lost 1,607 men, including 199 killed, but in the process they achieved a victory presaging greater events to follow.

The German Offensive, June 1918

Conscious of this new force entering the battle, conscious too of the necessity to maintain the initiative if ever the British armies were to be broken, Ludendorff wanted to pull back from the highly vulnerable Marne salient, but the effect on German morale would have been too adverse. Denied use of these troops for renewing the offensive against the British in Flanders, he decided on still another diversionary attack. By taking ground that might serve as a buffer for a railroad passing through Soissons, Ludendorff would improve supply into the Marne salient and at the same time pose a new threat to Paris that would, he hoped, pull Allied reserves from Flanders.

Ludendorff on June 9 sent one army westward from Soissons, another southward from the south flank of the Amiens salient between the towns of Noyon and Montdidier. As the two thrusts joined, they would merge the Amiens and Marne salients into one big, less vulnerable bulge in the line and release divisions to move to Flanders.

Yet this time there was no surprise and this time the French were ready with a defense in depth. They held the Germans to a tortuous advance of nine miles, then stopped them with counterattacks. By the fifth day, the attack had run its course.

A Growing American Force

As a temporary lull settled over the front, General Pershing on July 4 announced that a million Americans had arrived in France. Nine divisions had had some combat experience, mainly in quiet sectors; 2 others were completing their training; and 8 more had recently arrived. The total was 19, each one double the size of an Allied or German division.

In June Pershing had created three corps headquarters. The I Corps under Maj. Gen. Hunter Liggett first took responsibility for a sector near Château-

Thierry, while the II Corps under Maj. Gen. George W. Read controlled the 27th and 30th Divisions that were destined to fight through the rest of the war with the British. The III Corps under Maj. Gen. Robert L. Bullard had yet to enter the line.

With 250,000 U.S. troops arriving every month, the effect of the American presence on Allied troops and the French population was stimulating, electric. Winston Churchill saw it this way:

> The impression made upon the hard-pressed French by this seemingly inexhaustible flood of gleaming youth in its first maturity of health and vigour was prodigious. None were under twenty, and few over thirty. As crammed in their lorries they clattered along the roads, singing the songs of a new world at the tops of their voices, burning to reach the bloody field, the French Headquarters were thrilled with the impulse of new life. . . . Half trained, half organized, with only their courage, their numbers and their magnificent youth behind their weapons, they were to buy their experience at a bitter price. But this they were quite ready to do.

For all the influx of new strength, no one yet saw any quick ending of the war, any indication that the Germans might have only one more offensive left in them.

The Last German Offensive, July 1918

The meager gains of Ludendorff's diversionary attack in June having failed either to secure the railroad at Soissons or to draw Allied reserves from Flanders, Ludendorff planned yet another diversionary attack before returning to the offensive in Flanders. A month in preparation, the new offensive began on July 15, one army driving southeast from the Marne salient, another attacking south from positions east of the city of Reims, a total of 52 divisions. Meeting on the Marine, the two armies were to cut a sizable segment from the Allied line and in the process solve the supply problem in the Marne salient by taking the railroads at Reims.

Ludendorff called this the *Friedensturm*—Peace Offensive. That was a mistake, for should failure occur in an offensive associated with such a grandiose aim, the German soldier would be in no condition to recover from the despair that was bound to follow. The slackening of discipline among troops too long denied all but the barest necessities had first emerged in the Lys offensive, but it had become even more apparent during the drive to the Marne as many men deserted the battle to loot wine cellars in the champagne country around Soissons. Weak from malnutrition, the soldiers were peculiarly susceptible to an influenza epidemic that swept the trenches in June and was to keep recurring into November. On the eve of each new offensive, hundreds were deserting to the enemy.

A wave of desertions combined with information gleaned from aerial photographs, observation posts, and patrols told the French what was coming, when, and where. East of Reims, the French commander, whose troops included the 42d U.S. Division, elected to pull the bulk of his men from the forward trenches, leaving only outposts in what was known as a "sacrifice line." While the vacated positions absorbed the German artillery bombardment, the French laid down a counterbarrage. As German troops battered by shellfire neared the "sacrifice line," French and American troops fell back to an intermediate position. After repeating the delaying tactics, French and Americans again withdrew, this time to a main line of resistance. At this third line they held. By noon of the first day the issue was no longer in doubt.

Anxious to deny any German foothold across the Marne, the French opposite the other prong of the German attack had opted against these tactics. Here German gains were greater—up to four miles beyond the Marne at some points—and a French division, occupying a re-entrant formed by a bend in the river, folded, leaving four attached American companies of the 28th Division in a desperate plight. Most of these men were killed or captured. Yet the 3d Division on the French left held, its 38th Infantry, beset on three sides, executing such a steadfast defense that the regiment earned a nickname, "Rock of the Marne."

By noon of the second day, Ludendorff recognized that this prong of his attack also had been blunted. He called off the offensive.

Allied Counteroffensive

Even as the Germans were preparing what turned out to be their last offensive, General Foch had been assembling Allied divisions to launch a counteroffensive directed at first toward a limited objective—cutting the highway leading from Soissons to Château-Thierry, the main supply route of German troops in the Marne salient—but with the certainty that, if successful, the attack would be extended to erase the entire salient. In the forefront of the attack were two U.S. divisions—the 1st and 2d—operating under a French corps command.

A heavy rain fell as the troops moved to their jump-off positions the night of July 17, providential, as it turned out, since it helped conceal Allied preparations. After only a short but intensive artillery preparation early on the 18th, Allied infantry moved to the attack from near Soissons in the north to Château-Thierry in the south. In the corps with U.S. divisions, 350 French tanks early

MEN OF THE 26TH DIVISION NEAR CHÂTEAU-THIERRY, *July 1918.*

took the lead. When night fell, the two armies had advanced in some places up to five miles.

Although these two U.S. divisions were soon relieved by French and British units, the drive continued and expanded to the east, bringing in the 3d, 4th, 26th, and 28th Divisions and eventually the 32d, 42d, and 77th Divisions, and headquarters of the I and III Corps. The Germans began abandoning their Marne salient, though deliberately and in good order, retiring to successive defensive positions all the way to the Vesle River with the Chemin des Dames at their backs.

A Separate American Army

As the Allied drive came to a halt at the end of the first week of August, new hope of victory stirred in the ranks. The drive had carried no more than 20 miles, but the results were infinitely more important than the amount of territory regained. The counteroffensive had eliminated the threat to Paris, spoiled Ludendorff's cherished ambition of striking a deathblow in Flanders, and so dimmed German chances of victory that even Ludendorff could no longer hope for more than a stalemate. Furthermore, the initiative had passed to the Allies, whose fresh force had proven beyond doubt (though at a cost of 50,000 casualties) its ability on the offensive. In the bid to win before the Americans could intervene in force, Ludendorff had failed.

As this counteroffensive (sometimes called, in conjunction with the last German offensive, the Second Battle of the Marne) neared an end, General Pershing pressed his case for an independent American army and a separate

1ST LT. SAMUEL H. ULANOFF *with the American Expeditionary Forces (A.E.F.) in France,* *1918.*

sector of the front. Foch was sympathetic, for a separate American force fitted in with plans he was formulating to eliminate three other German-held salients on the front. British and French together were to reduce the Amiens salient, then the British would erase the Lys salient while the Americans eliminated another salient in Lorraine that had stood for four years and took its name from a town at the tip, St. Mihiel.

With Pershing himself as commander, headquarters of the First Army officially opened on August 10. The new command encompassed the I and III Corps and 19 U.S. divisions.

As demonstrated earlier in making American units available to Allied armies, Pershing for all his adamant resolve to create an independent American force never objected to allowing some U.S. divisions to fight under Allied command; he objected instead to the use of American troops as individual replacements or in small increments to fill out depleted Allied units. Even as he formed the First Army he left the II Corps and its two divisions with the British, while he allowed several other divisions to serve under French command.

The one division whose employment violated Pershing's principle was the 93d, which had only infantry regiments without trains or artillery. This was a Negro division, one of only two organized and sent to France during the war, although thousands of other Negroes served overseas in the Services of Supply. The 93d's regiments were assigned to the French, reorganized according to French tables, and used as integral parts of French divisions. The other Negro division, the 92d, served in the First Army.

The Somme Offensive

As Pershing was forming the First Army, French and British armies under Haig launched converging attacks from the northwest and southwest against the Amiens salient. They achieved as much surprise as had the Germans against the Chemin des Dames. Using 300 tanks in the lead, ten British divisions, including Australians and Canadians, scored a swift breakthrough, brushing aside German units in rout, gaining seven miles in the first few hours, and making of August 8, in Ludendorff's words, a "black day" for the German Army.

Yet the slow, ponderous tanks could not long sustain such a pace, and horse cavalry was of no use when the enemy stiffened. Coming against a strong German stand in old trenches dating from 1915, Haig paused, shifted the emphasis of his attack farther north, then in a methodical campaign gradually pushed the Germans back. By the end of August the Germans were retiring into the positions whence they had begun their big March offensive, the Hindenburg Line. The Amiens salient, like that on the Marne, was a thing of the past. Meanwhile, other British units helped by the U.S. II Corps with the 27th and 30th Divisions had almost finished erasing the Lys salient.

On the German side, the events of 8 August had cast a pall over the High Command. "We have nearly reached the limit of our power to resist," said Hindenburg. "The war must be ended." When Ludendorff agreed, Wilhelm II instructed his Foreign Secretary to find a way out of the war, but the underlying idea was to retain as much as possible of the territory that the German armies had conquered. Under such a condition, there was little real hope for peace.

The St. Mihiel Offensive

As the British drive progressed, General Pershing and his staff shifted divisions to Lorraine. Their goal was to push beyond the St. Mihiel salient to seize Metz or at least to cut the highway running from Metz all the way to Antwerp, the enemy's main line of lateral communications. When Foch saw the plan, he was so enthusiastic that he increased the French participation from 4 to 10 divisions.

Foch's endorsement of the American plan preceded the British success in pushing the Germans into the Hindenburg Line. Planning an early attack along the Somme to break that line, Marshal Haig suggested to Foch that instead of attacking toward Metz the Americans should be employed from

FRENCH TANKS RETURNING FROM THE FRONT

positions west of Verdun to attack northward toward Mézières along the French-Belgian frontier northeast of Reims. Such an attack would serve not only to cut the enemy's railroad but also to converge with the British attack.

Seeing in Haig's proposal a possibility of victory before the year was out, Foch endorsed the idea. Presenting it to General Pershing, he directed that once the St. Mihiel salient was eliminated the American objective should be changed from Metz to Mézières. In the drive on Mézières, Foch was to employ two armies, one wholly American under Pershing, the other Franco-American under French command.

Foch's proposal for a Franco-American army under French command appeared to Pershing as a threat to the long-sought independent American force which he had so recently achieved. He insisted that, while the American army "will fight wherever you may decide, it will not fight except as an independent American army." Foch declined to press the issue.

Reducing the scope of the attack on the St. Mihiel salient to nine U.S. and five French divisions, Pershing and his staff began to prepare two offensives to be mounted within 23 days in areas 40 miles apart. That was something no single army had yet attempted on the Western Front.

The Germans, fortunately, were to make the task easier. Conscious of the vulnerability of the St. Mihiel salient and of a major Allied offensive in the making, they began to pull out of the salient two days before Pershing planned to attack.

Under Pershing's plan, a French corps was to press the tip of the salient while the V Corps under Maj. Gen. George H. Cameron, in its first combat action, hit the west flank. Meanwhile General Liggett's I Corps and the IV Corps under Maj. Gen. Joseph T. Dickman, also new in the line, was to attack the south flank, the two American thrusts to meet in the center of the salient at the town of Vigneulles. French and British provided the bulk of the artillery support—3,000 guns—while the only tanks available were 267 light French Renaults. Although the French furnished many of the tank crews, others were Americans of the 304th Tank Brigade, commanded by Lt. Col. George S. Patton, Jr. An Allied air force controlled by an exponent of air power, Col. William Mitchell, consisted of almost 1,500 planes (600 piloted by Americans), the largest concentration of aircraft yet assembled.

Following a four-hour artillery bombardment, the tank-infantry advance began before daylight on September 12. Most of the tanks fell victim early to mechanical failure or mud, but they were hardly needed. Resistance was from the first surprisingly moderate, particularly on the southern flank where the Germans had already thinned their forward troops as a step in the general withdrawal. By nightfall of the first day a gap of only ten miles separated the two converging American forces.

When Pershing learned that roads leading out of the salient were filled with withdrawing Germans, he urged continued attack through the night to block all escape routes. A regiment of the 26th Division pushed swiftly from the west to enter Vigneulles two hours after midnight, there to be joined soon after dawn by a regiment of the 1st Division.

This first victory of the war by an American army netted 15,000 prisoners at a cost of only 7,000 casualties. It was so easy that some have referred to it as the action in which the Americans relieved the Germans, but the observation fails to take into account that the Germans had begun to pull back because they dreaded what was coming.

The Meuse-Argonne Offensive

Even as Pershing had been preparing and launching this first big American attack, Foch's original plan had been growing by bounds. No longer was the offensive to be confined to a British strike along the Somme and an American drive on Mézières. The new plan also included a Belgian-British-French attack along the Lys and French attacks in between British and Americans. It was to be a grand assault all along the front—said Foch: "Tout le monde à la bataille!". The aim was to cut the enemy's rail line at Mézières and Aulnoye, the latter in front of the British, and thereby force the Germans to retire inside their frontier before winter set in. For the offensive Foch had 220 divisions—160 in line, 60 in reserve. They included 42 of the big American divisions, although some of these had only recently arrived and Pershing would be forced to cannibalize others to obtain replacements. Ten American divisions would still serve with British and French armies.

Assisted by the French Fourth Army on the left, the American attack was to begin first, on September 26. It posed a tremendous logistical effort involving rapid transfer of some 800,000 men, 200,000 French moving out of the new American sector west of Verdun, and 600,000 Americans moving in. That it was completed in secrecy and in time for the jump-off was attributable in large measure to the planning of a young officer on Pershing's staff, Col. George C. Marshall. Again the British and French furnished most of the artillery and tanks (190 French lights) and some of the 800 aircraft supporting the attack.

The terrain over which the advance was to pass was studded with natural and man-made obstacles. From high ground east of the Meuse River, which formed the right boundary for the attack, and from densely wooded high ground of the Argonne Forest in the left of the attack zone, German eyes could look down on much of the battlefield; and in the center, between the forest and the river, the Germans held a hogback ridge replete with fortified spurs and stone-walled villages. The Germans had established three lines with trenches, barbed wire, deep dugouts, and concrete fighting posts, while a fourth was under construction farther back. Particularly formidable were strongpoints at Montfaucon, Cunel, and Barricourt.

In a sector approximately twenty miles wide, Pershing massed three corps, each to employ two divisions forward, one in reserve. With a superiority in men of 8 to 1, he hoped to make the ten miles through the first three German positions in one sustained drive.

The infantry began to advance before daylight after a 3-hour artillery bombardment. Achieving surprise, they caught the Germans with only four divisions in the line. General Bullard's III Corps on the right pushed five miles through both the first and second German positions, but General Cameron's V Corps in the center ground to a halt before the bristling defenses of Montfaucon, and General Liggett's I Corps on the left could advance little more than a mile through the thick, almost trackless Argonne Forest.

During the next few days, the troops plodded slowly forward, at last carrying Montfaucon and putting the V Corps through the second German line, but progress amid the trees and dank ravines of the Argonne Forest still was slow. Flanking fire from east of the Meuse and from uncleared portions of the Argonne harried units on the right and in the center. Most of the supporting tanks succumbed to the usual troubles of mud and mechanical failure. Congestion and muddy roads hampered resupply. Most serious of all was the inexperience of the troops, for having used his experienced divisions in the St. Mihiel salient Pershing had had to withhold them from the first assault. Units got lost, message traffic broke down, some commanders failed.

Any hope that an advance by the French Fourth Army on the left might unhinge the Germans in front of the U.S. troops went for naught, for the French were making no more rapid gains. As September came to an end, Pershing had no choice but to pause to reorganize.

Elsewhere on the Western Front, progress was, with one exception, not much more encouraging. The Belgian-French-British effort on the Lys bogged down in rain and mud, as had every offensive in that region, while the French in the center of the Allied line were not to begin their attack until British and Americans on their flanks had driven deep enough to threaten the Germans opposite them with entrapment. Only the British along the Somme provided any indication of decisive success, scoring a deep penetration of the Hindenburg Line with the help of the 27th and 30th Divisions of the U.S. II Corps. The penetration was soon expanded to create a gap all the way through the fortifications, but the effort left British troops temporarily spent.

Despite the disappointing progress of the grand offensive from an Allied viewpoint, it was enough to start a collapse within the German High Command. On September 28, Ludendorff mused at such length on the miseries besetting him that he worked himself into a rage, foamed at the mouth, and fell to the floor. That evening he called on Hindenburg. The situation, the two agreed, was infinitely worse than in August when they had first urged the kaiser to seek peace, advice that had produced no results. They had no alternative now but to agree to surrender all conquered territory in the west and try to negotiate a peace on the basis of President Wilson's Fourteen Points.

On October 4 the German chancellor cabled Wilson asking for an armistice. Without informing the Allied governments, Wilson answered with a request for clarification. The German chancellor replied on October 12 that the Germans agreed to all Fourteen Points; but by this time word of the peace feeler had reached the French and British, who for their part were in no mood to accept Wilson's unilateral actions. Furthermore, Ludendorff himself had recovered from his convulsive fit, had seen that the Allied offensive had imposed no rout, and had come to believe the Germans could get terms that would allow them to withdraw behind their own frontier, reorganize their armies, and resist any peace proposals they deemed unacceptable.

Yet events were taking place that were destined to tie Ludendorff's hands and harden Wilson's resolve. Not the least of these were continued fierce German resistance and the revelation, in those areas where the Germans were forced to retire, of wanton destruction and a barbaric disregard for human life more flagrant than those excesses of 1917 when they had left behind a wasteland in retiring into the Hindenburg Line.

On the Meuse-Argonne front, Pershing's First Army renewed its offensive on October 4 after inserting experienced divisions into the line, but during the brief pause in operations Ludendorff had brought in reinforcements. The fight to clear the rest of the Argonne Forest and pierce the third German line progressed no more swiftly than before.

In the Argonne a "lost battalion" of the 77th Division was surrounded for five days before other troops could break through to free 194 survivors out of an original 600. In the Argonne, too, an American patrol took about 75 Germans by surprise and was herding them toward the rear when German machine gunners opened fire, killing and wounding 9 out of 17 in the patrol. When a German lieutenant led a charge aimed at the survivors, Pfc. Alvin C. York, a Tennessee sharpshooter, cut down 15 Germans one by one until at last surviving members of this group too surrendered. When a count could be taken, it revealed that York had captured 132 of the enemy.

To dispense with the troublesome German flanking fire from heights on the other side of the Meuse, General Pershing broadened his attack to include the east bank. To control that phase, Pershing created the Second Army under General Bullard. Relinquishing command of the First Army to General Liggett, Pershing himself moved up to the level of army group.

Despite the added strength on the east bank, the fight continued slow and costly, for Ludendorff looked on the offensive as such a threat to the vital railroad through Mézières that he eventually committed 27 of his reserve divisions to this sector. Some help developed on the left when on October 5 the U.S. 2d Division, attacking with the French, captured high ground known as Blanc Mont, prompting a slow German withdrawal before the Fourth Army back to the Aisne River. On the 10th, the I Corps finally cleared the last of the Argonne Forest, but bitter fighting continued through the rest of the month for the fortified hills between the forest and the Meuse. Not until the last day of October was the third German position broken all along the line.

The British in the meantime had renewed their offensive, driving forward inexorably as the Germans fell back grudgingly from one prepared position to another. It was in this section that much of the evidence of German destruction and barbarity was found.

At the same time, continuing activities of the U-boats also helped to crystallize Allied resolve. On the 10th, a submarine torpedoed a passenger steamer off the coast of Ireland with a loss of 300 lives. A few days later another U-boat sank an Irish mail boat taking the lives of 520 passengers, mostly women and children.

Affected by the public outcry over these incidents, President Wilson made clear in his reply to the second German note that the Allied military leaders would set the terms of the armistice, that there was no other way to deal with a government that persisted in illegal and inhumane acts. The note concluded that if the United States had to deal "with the military masters and the monarchial autocrats of Germany now, or if it is likely to have to deal with them later in regard to the international obligations of the German Empire, it must demand, not peace negotiations but surrender."

Confidence restored, Ludendorff called on his government to reject the terms; but the government was by this time listening to the voices of a disillusioned people, the noise of riots in the streets, and to the threat of Marxist revolution. On October 27 the kaiser dismissed Ludendorff, who repaired in disguise to Sweden, and events strode swiftly toward a climax. The German naval commander tried to take the High Seas Fleet to sea in a last bid for glory, but the crews mutinied and brought the ships back into port with revolutionary flags flying. Revolutionary councils formed among the soldiers in the trenches. Bulgaria in late September had already dropped out of the war; Turkey followed on October 30; Austria-Hungary on November 3. On November 6 Ludendorff's successor, General Wilhelm Groener, urged the government to conclude an armistice within three days or face chaos.

All along the front, meanwhile, the Allied armies had renewed their offensives in what became a general advance. In the far north two U.S. divisions—the 37th and 91st—fought with the Belgian-French-British force under the Belgian king. Haig's British troops entered their objective of Aulnoye on November 5, while the French armies maintained steady pressure against the German center.

Beginning on the first of November, the U.S. First Army renewed the attack with the V Corps in the center driving six miles the first day to take heights just south of the fourth German line near Barricourt. This feat assured success of the whole operation, for it prompted German withdrawal behind the Meuse. On November 5 the III Corps forced a crossing of the Meuse, and three days later American troops held high ground overlooking the city of Sedan, a few miles east of Mézières, and brought the lateral railroad under artillery fire. There the advance stopped as Marshal Foch shifted the American boundary eastward to allow the French the honor of retaking Sedan, scene of a disastrous French defeat in 1870.

The Meuse-Argonne was the greatest battle yet fought by the U.S. Army. Almost 1,250,000 American troops had participated during the course of the offensive. Casualties were high—120,000 of all types—but the results impressive. Until the last, this battle had worried German commanders most; unlike other sectors of the front, here they had little space short of a vital objective that they could afford to trade for time.

The German Surrender

Under pressure of continuing Allied attack and of public agitation at home, the Germans early on November 8 sent delegates to a railroad siding in the Compiègne Forest west of Soissons to discuss armistice terms. The next day the kaiser abdicated, fleeing to the Netherlands in exile, and the Germans proclaimed a republic.

Under terms of the armistice, the Germans were to withdraw from all occupied territory, including Alsace and Lorraine; retire all armies to the east bank of the Rhine; provide the Allies with bridgeheads beyond the Rhine; and relinquish specific amounts of military equipment that would preclude their continuing the war.

The fighting ended at the eleventh hour of the eleventh day of the eleventh month, 1918.

Men died right up to the last, but finally, after more than four grim years, it was over. Of the men of all nations in uniform, more than 8,500,000 died, and total casualties exceeded 37,500,000, a price that would forever invite criticism of the way commanders on both sides fought the war. American casualties alone totaled 320,710.

So ended the first adventure of the United States in departing from its traditional policy of noninvolvement in European affairs. That the nation could make such a decisive contribution in so short a time hardly could have been conceived in advance.

That there would be mistakes, blunders, shortcomings under such a rapid expansion and commitment was perhaps inevitable. Until mid-1918, for example, when separate replacement training camps were at last established, units both in the United States and overseas had to be broken up to provide replacements. This practice was damaging to morale and damaging too in that it sent many poorly trained men into the lines. So close did the American supply system in France come to breaking down that in the summer of 1918, under threat of intervention from Washington, Pershing had to exert special efforts to rescue it. Pershing himself was overburdened with command responsibilities—theater, line of communications, and tactical. The dependence on the Allies for air, artillery, and tank support, however inevitable in such a rapid deployment, did nothing for efficiency on the battlefield. On the home front some Americans vented their hostility on other Americans for no more valid reason than their ancestry.

Yet countless other things were done effectively. The nation handled conscription with minimum friction and without disruption of the economy. The Army expanded with almost incredible speed while still maintaining efficiency. The Navy performed invaluable service in defeating the submarine and, with British help, in getting the Army safely overseas. Although the war ended before American industry could demonstrate its full wartime potential, the record, with some exceptions, was impressive nevertheless.

Most important of all, the nation and its Army had provided a force that reached embattled Europe in time to rejuvenate flagging Allied fortunes and provide sufficient advantage to assure victory for the Allied side.

1ST LT. EDWARD V. RICKENBACKER, FIRST AMERICAN ACE, *with his Spad plane, France, 1918.*

CHAPTER 11

World War II: The Defensive Phase

About one o'clock in Washington on the afternoon of December 7, 1941, the first news of the Japanese attack on Pearl Harbor, Hawaii, reached the War Department. The news came as a shock, even as the attack itself had come. It caught by surprise not only the American people at large, who learned of the attack a short while later, but also their leaders, including the very officers who had earlier been so much concerned over the possibility of just such an attack. One explanation is that these officers and their political superiors were momentarily expecting the Japanese to use all their forces against weakly held British and Dutch positions in the Far East (and probably, but not certainly, against the Philippines). But without warning in the early morning of December 7, powerful carrier-borne air forces had smashed the U.S. Pacific Fleet at anchor in Pearl Harbor. The same day (December 8 in the Philippines), about noon, Formosa-based bombers caught the bulk of the U.S. Far East Air Force lined up on Clark and Iba fields not far from Manila in central Luzon and virtually destroyed it. For the second time within a quarter-century, Americans found themselves fully involved in a war they had not sought—this time in the first truly global conflict.

The Outbreak of War: Action and Reaction

The attack on Pearl Harbor was one of the most brilliant tactical feats of the war. From 6 carriers which had advanced undetected to a position 200 miles north of Oahu, some 350 aircraft came in through the morning mist, achieving complete tactical surprise. They bombed and strafed the neatly aligned Army planes on Hickam and Wheeler Fields, as well as Navy and Marine Corps aircraft, and they carefully singled out as targets major units of the Navy's battle force at anchor in the harbor. Fortunately, the fleet's 3 carriers were away at the time, and the attackers failed to hit the oil tanks and naval repair shops on shore. But the blow was devastating enough. About 170 aircraft were destroyed and 102 damaged, all 8 battleships were sunk or badly damaged, besides many other vessels, and total casualties came to about 3,400, including 2,402 service men and civilians killed. Japanese losses were about 49 aircraft and 5 midget submarines. In an astonishing achievement, the enemy managed to apply in one shattering operation a combination of the principles of surprise, objective, mass, security, and maneuver. In its larger strategic context, the Pearl Harbor attack also exemplifies the principles of the offensive and economy of force. The joint Congressional committee investigating the attack called it the "greatest military and naval disaster in our Nation's history."

These two attacks—on Pearl Harbor and on the Philippines—effectively crippled American striking power in the Pacific. The Philippines and other American possessions in the western Pacific were isolated, their loss a foregone conclusion. The Hawaiian Islands and Alaska lay open to invasion; the Panama Canal and the cities, factories, and shipyards of the west coast were vulnerable to raids from the sea and air. Months would pass before the United States could regain a capacity for even the most limited kind of offensive action against its oriental enemy. As Japanese forces moved swiftly southward against the Philippines, Malaya, and the Netherlands Indies, Japan's Axis partners, Germany and Italy, promptly declared war on the United States, thus ending the uncertainty as to whether the United States would become a full-fledged belligerent in the European war. For the first time in its history, the United States was embarked upon an all-out, two-front war.

Meanwhile Britain was battling to maintain its hold on the eastern Mediterranean region which lay athwart the historic lifeline to possessions and Commonwealth associates in the Far East. Late in 1940 small British forces based in Egypt gained important successes against Italian armies in Libya, and the Greeks in the winter of 1940–41 resoundingly defeated an invading Italian army and chased it back into Albania. But German armies quickly came to the aid of their Italian ally. In April 1941 the famous panzer divisions, supported by overwhelming air power, swept through the Balkans, crushing the Yugoslav and Greek armies, and a British expeditionary force hastily dispatched to aid the latter. The following month German airborne forces descended on the island of Crete and swamped British and Greek defenders in a spectacular, though costly, attack. In Libya a powerful German-Italian army under General Erwin Rommel drove the British back across the Egyptian border, isolating a large garrison in Tobruk and threatening the Nile Delta. Against these disasters Britain could count only the final expulsion of the Italians from the Red Sea area and of the Vichy French from Syria, the suppression of pro-German uprisings in Iraq, and the achievement of a precarious naval ascendancy in the eastern and western portions of the Mediterranean. During the remainder of

1941 the British gradually built up strength in eastern Libya, and late in the year they succeeded in relieving Tobruk and pushing Rommel back to his original starting point at El Agheila.

Since mid-1940 the military fortunes of the anti-Axis powers had declined as the European war expanded. Germany had crushed all its continental European opponents in the west, and then attempted to destroy Britain's air forces as a prelude to an invasion across the English Channel. In the air battles over Britain in August and September 1940 the Royal Air Force won a brilliant victory. But during the following winter and spring the waning threat of invasion had been replaced by the equally deadly and more persistent menace of economic strangulation. German aircraft pulverized Britain's ports and inland cities, while U-boats, surface raiders, and mines decimated shipping. By 1941 the imports on which the United Kingdom depended for existence had dwindled to less than two-thirds of their prewar volume, and the British people faced the prospect of ultimate starvation.

In June 1941, however, the storm center of the war had moved elsewhere. Only slightly delayed by the conquest of the Balkans, Hitler on June 22, 1941, hurled German might against the Soviet Union, the only remaining power on the European continent capable of challenging his dominance. By early December, when the onset of winter and stiffening Soviet resistance finally brought the advance to a halt, the German armies had driven to the suburbs of Moscow, inflicted huge losses on the Red Army, and occupied a vast expanse of European Russia embracing its most densely populated and industrialized regions. This, as it turned out, was the high tide of German success in World War II; Hitler, like Napoleon, was to meet disaster on the wind-swept plains of Russia. But in December 1941 few were willing to predict this outcome. British and United States leaders assembling in Washington at the end of that month to make plans for dealing with the crisis had to reckon with the probability that in the year to come, unless the Western Allies could somehow force Germany to divert substantial forces from the eastern front, the German steamroller would complete the destruction of the Soviet armies. Hitler would then be able, with the resources and enslaved peoples of all Europe at his feet, to throw his full power against the West.

American military leaders had already given thought to this grim prospect, and to the implications it held for America's role in the war. In the Victory Program, drawn up by the Army and Navy at the President's behest during the summer of 1941, the leaders of the two services had set forth in some detail the strategy and the means they considered necessary to win ultimate victory if, as they expected, Soviet Russia succumbed to the Axis onslaught. The strategy was the one laid down in the RAINBOW 5 war plan—wear Germany down by bombing, blockade, subversion, and limited offensives, while mobilizing the strength needed to invade the European continent and to defeat Germany on its own ground. Japan meanwhile would be contained by air and sea power, local defense forces, China's inexhaustible manpower, and the Soviet Union's Siberian divisions. With Germany out of the running, Japan's defeat or collapse would soon follow. As for the means, the United States would have to provide them in large part, for the British were already weary and their resources limited. The United States would serve not merely, to use the President's catchy phrase, as the "arsenal of democracy," supplying weapons to arm its allies, but also as the main source of the armies without which wars, above all this war, could not be won. Army leaders envisaged the eventual mobilization of 215 divisions, 61 of them armored, and 239 combat air groups, requiring a grand total, with supporting forces, of 8.8 million men. Five million of these would be hurled against the European Axis. It was emphasized that victory over the Axis Powers would require a maximum military effort and full mobilization of America's immense industrial resources.

Yet the Victory Program was merely an expression of professional military views, not a statement of national military policy. That policy, on the eve of Pearl Harbor, was still ostensibly hemisphere defense. The pace of rearmament and mobilization, in the summer and fall of 1941, was actually slowing down. Signs pointed to a policy of making the American contribution to the defeat of the Axis, as columnist Walter Lippmann put it, one "basically of Navy, Air, and manufacturing," something a great deal less than the all-out effort envisaged in the Victory Program. Public and Congressional sentiment, moreover, still clung to the hope that an immediate showdown with the Axis Powers could be avoided and that the country would not be forced into full belligerent participation in the war, as evidenced by a near defeat of the bill to extend Selective Service, continuation of a prohibition against sending selectees outside the Western Hemisphere, and apathetic public response to submarine attacks on American destroyers in September and October.

The Japanese attack on Pearl Harbor and the Philippines changed the picture. A wave of patriotic indignation over Japanese duplicity and brutality swept the country. Isolationism virtually evaporated as a public issue, and all parties closed ranks in support of the war effort. Indeed, in retrospect, despite the immediate tactical success the Japanese achieved at Pearl Harbor, that attack proved to be a great blunder for them, politically and strategically. The President, early in January, dramatized the magnitude of the effort now demanded by proclaiming a new set of production goals—60,000 airplanes in

1942 and 125,000 in 1943; 45,000 tanks in 1942 and 75,000 in 1943; 20,000 anti-aircraft guns in 1942 and 35,000 in 1943; half a million machine guns in 1942 and as many more in 1943; and 8 million deadweight tons of merchant shipping in 1942 and 10 million in 1943. Vanished were the two illusions that America could serve only as an arsenal of democracy, contributing weapons without the men to wield them, or, conversely, that the nation could rely solely on its own fighting forces, leaving other anti-Axis nations to shift for themselves. "We must not only provide munitions for our own fighting forces," Roosevelt advised Secretary of War Henry L. Stimson, "but vast quantities to be used against the enemy in every appropriate theater of war." A new Victory Program boosted the Army's ultimate mobilization goal to 10 million men, and the War Department planned to have 71 divisions and 115 combat air groups organized by the end of 1942, with a total of 3.6 million men under arms. As an Army planner had predicted back in the spring of 1941, the United States now seemed destined to become "the final reserve of the democracies both in manpower and munitions."

Late in December 1941 President Roosevelt and Prime Minister Churchill met with their advisers in Washington (the ARCADIA Conference) to establish the bases of coalition strategy and concert immediate measures to meet the military crisis. They faced an agonizing dilemma. Prompt steps had to be taken to stem the spreading tide of Japanese conquest. On the other hand, it seemed likely that the coming year might see the collapse of Soviet resistance and of the British position in the Middle East. In this difficult situation the Allied leaders made a far-reaching decision that shaped the whole course of the war. Reaffirming the principle laid down in Anglo-American staff conversations in Washington ten months earlier, they agreed that the first and main effort must go into defeating Germany, the more formidable enemy. Japan's turn would come later. Defeating Germany would involve a prolonged process of "closing and tightening the ring" about Fortress Europe. Operations in 1942 would have to be defensive and preparatory, though limited offensives might be undertaken if the opportunity offered. Not until 1943 at the earliest could the Allies contemplate a return to the European continent "across the Mediterranean, from Turkey into the Balkans, or by landings in Western Europe."

Another important action taken at the ARCADIA Conference was the establishment of the Combined Chiefs of Staff (CCS). This was a committee consisting of the professional military chiefs of both countries, responsible to the President and Prime Minister for planning and directing the grand strategy of the coalition. Its American members were the Army Chief of Staff, General Marshall; the Chief of Naval Operations, Admiral Harold R. Stark (replaced early in 1942 by Admiral Ernest J. King); and the Chief (later Commanding General) of the Army Air Forces, Lt. Gen. Henry H. Arnold. In July 1942 a fourth member was added, the President's personal Chief of Staff, Admiral William D. Leahy. Since the CCS normally sat in Washington, the British Chiefs of Staff, making up its British component, attended in person only at important conferences with the heads of state. In the intervals they were represented in Washington by the four senior members of the permanent British Joint Staff Mission, headed until late in 1944 by Field Marshal Sir John Dill, the former Chief of the British Imperial General Staff. Under the CCS a system of primarily military subordinate committees grew up, specifically designated to handle such matters as strategic and logistical planning, transportation, and communications.

By February 1942 the Joint Chiefs of Staff (JCS), consisting of the U.S. members of the CCS, had emerged as the highest authority in the U.S. military hierarchy (though never formally chartered as such), and responsible directly to the President. Like the CCS, the JCS in time developed a machinery of planning and working committees, the most important of which were the Joint Staff Planners, the Joint Strategic Survey Committee, and the Joint Logistics Committee. No executive machinery was created at either the CCS or JCS level. The CCS ordinarily named either the British Chiefs or the U.S. Joint Chiefs to act as its executive agent, and these, in turn, employed the established machinery of the service departments.

In the spring of 1942 Britain and the United States agreed on a worldwide division of strategic responsibility. The U.S. Joint Chiefs of Staff were to be primarily responsible for the war in the Pacific, and the British Chiefs for the Middle East-Indian Ocean region, while the European-Mediterranean-Atlantic area would be a combined responsibility of both staffs. China was designated a separate theater commanded by its chief of state, Chiang Kai-shek, though within the United States' sphere of responsibility. In the Pacific, the Joint Chiefs established two main theaters, the Southwest Pacific Area (SWPA) and the Pacific Ocean Areas (POA), the former under General MacArthur, the latter under Admiral Chester W. Nimitz. POA was further subdivided into North, Central, and South Pacific areas, the first two directly controlled by Nimitz, the third by his deputy, Admiral William F. Halsey, Jr. (*See Map 42.*) Later in 1942, the U.S. air and service troops operating in China, India, and northern Burma were organized as U.S. Army Forces, China-Burma-India, under Lt. Gen. Joseph W. Stilwell. On various other far-flung lines of communications U.S. Army forces, mostly air and service troops during 1942, were organized under similar theater commands. In June Maj. Gen. Dwight D. Eisenhower arrived in England to take command of the newly established European Theater of Operations, and after the landings in North Africa late in the year a new U.S. theater was organized in that region.

The British and the Americans had decided at the ARCADIA Conference that Allied forces in each overseas theater would operate, as far as possible, under a single commander, and this principle was subsequently applied in most theaters. Within theaters subordinate unified commands were created, in some cases for Allied ground, naval, or air forces, and most frequently for task forces formed to carry out a specific operation or campaign. The authority of Allied theater commanders over national forces was always restricted with respect to areas and missions, and, as a last resort, senior national commanders in each theater could appeal to their own governments against specific orders or policies of the theater commander. In practice, this right of appeal was rarely invoked.

In essence, unified command at the Allied level gave the commander control of certain specific forces for operational purposes, rather than jurisdiction over a given geographical area. Administration of national forces and the allocation of resources were usually handled through separate national channels. In certain cases, inter-Allied boards or committees, responsible to the Allied theater commander, controlled the common use of critical resources (such as petroleum products) or facilities (such as railways and shipping) within a theater. Administration of U.S. forces overseas also generally followed separate Army and Navy channels, except in the Pacific where, from 1943 on, supply, transportation, and certain other services were jointly administered to a limited degree.

Even before Pearl Harbor, Army leaders had realized that the peacetime organization of the War Department General Staff, dating back to 1921, was an inadequate instrument for directing a major war effort. Originally a small co-ordinating and planning body, the General Staff, and especially its War Plans and Supply Divisions, rapidly expanded during the emergency period into a large operating organization, increasingly immersed in the details of supervision to the detriment of its planning and policy-making functions. The Chief of Staff, to whom some sixty-one officers and agencies had direct access, carried an especially heavy burden.

Three additional features of the organization demanded remedy. One was the continued subordination of the Army Air Forces to General Staff supervision, which conflicted with the Air Forces' drive for autonomy. Another was the anomalous position of General Headquarters (GHQ), whose role as command post for the field forces and responsibilities in the fields of training and logistics clashed with the authority of the General Staff at many points. Finally, the division of supply responsibilities between the Supply Division (G–4) and the Office of the Under Secretary of War—with requirements and distribution assigned to the former and procurement to the latter—was breaking down under the pressure of mobilization.

Spurred by the Pearl Harbor disaster, which seemed to accentuate the need for better staff co-ordination in Washington, General Marshall on March 9, 1942, put into effect a sweeping reorganization of the War Department. Under the new plan, which underwent little change during the war years, the General Staff, except for the War Plans and Intelligence Divisions, was drastically whittled down and limited in function to broad planning and policy guidance. An expanded War Plans Division, soon renamed Operations Division (OPD), became General Marshall's command post and, in effect, a superior general staff for the direction of overseas operations. The Army Air Forces, though in some respects on a lower level of administrative authority than before, had virtually complete control of the development of its special weapon—the airplane. Administering its own personnel and training, it organized and supported the combat air forces to be employed in theaters of operations and came also to exercise considerable influence over both strategic and operational planning.

In the reorganization of March 9 two new commands were created, the Army Ground Forces (AGF) and the Services of Supply, later renamed the Army Service Forces (ASF). The former, headed by Lt. Gen. Lesley J. McNair, took over the training mission of GHQ, now abolished, and absorbed the ground combat arms. To the ASF, commanded by Lt. Gen. Brehon B. Somervell, were subordinated the supply (renamed technical) and administrative services, the nine corps areas, and most of the Army posts and installations throughout the United States, including the ports of embarkation through which troops and supplies flowed to the forces overseas. In supply matters, Somervell now reported to two masters, the Chief of Staff for requirements and distribution and the Under Secretary of War, Mr. Robert P. Patterson, for procurement. His subordination to the latter was, in reality, only nominal since most of Patterson's organization was transferred bodily to Somervell's headquarters. Except for equipment peculiar to the Army Air Forces, the ASF thus became the Army's central agency for supply in the United States. It drew up the Army's "shopping list" of requirements, the Army Supply Program; through the seven technical services (Quartermaster, Ordnance, Signal, Chemical, Engineer, Medical, and Transportation) it procured most of the Army's supplies and equipment; it distributed these materials to the Army at home and abroad, as well as to

Allies under lend-lease; it operated the Army's fleet of transports; and it trained specialists and service units to perform various specialized jobs. General Somervell himself became General Marshall's principal logistical adviser.

All this looked to the future. In the first few weeks after Pearl Harbor, while the Navy was salvaging what it could from the wreckage at Pearl Harbor and striving to combat German submarines in the western Atlantic, the War Department made desperate efforts to bolster the defenses of Hawaii, the Philippines, the Panama Canal, Alaska, and the U.S. west coast. By the end of December, the danger of an attack on the Hawaii-Alaska-Panama triangle seemed to have waned, and the emphasis shifted to measures to stave off further disasters in the Far East. The British and Americans decided at ARCADIA that the Allies would attempt to hold the Japanese north and east of the line of the Malay Peninsula and the Netherlands Indies and to re-establish communications with the Philippines to the north. To co-ordinate operations in this vast theater, the Allied leaders created the ABDA (American-British-Dutch-Australian) Command, including the Netherlands Indies, Malaya, Burma, and the Philippines. British Lt. Gen. Sir Archibald P. Wavell was placed in over-all command. Through India from the west and Australia from the east, the Allies hoped in a short time to build up a shield of air power stout enough to blunt the Japanese threat.

For a time it seemed as though nothing could stop the Japanese juggernaut. In less than three weeks after Pearl Harbor, the isolated American outposts of Wake and Guam fell to the invaders, the British garrison of Hong Kong was overwhelmed, and powerful land, sea, and air forces were converging on Malaya and the Netherlands Indies. Picked, jungle-trained troops drove down the Malay Peninsula toward the great fortress of Singapore, infiltrating and out-flanking successsive British positions. Two of the most formidable warships in the British Navy, the battleship *Prince of Wales* and the battle cruiser *Repulse*, were sunk by Japanese torpedo planes off the east coast of Malaya, a loss that destroyed the Allies' last hope of effectively opposing Japan's naval power in the Far East. Attacked from the land side, Singapore and its British force of over 80,000 troops surrendered on February 15, 1942. Meanwhile the Japanese had invaded the Netherlands Indies from the north, west, and east. In a series of actions during January and February, the weak Dutch and Australian naval forces, joined by the U.S. Asiatic Fleet withdrawing from the Philippines, were destroyed piecemeal, only four American destroyers escaping south to Australia. On March 9 the last Allied ground and air forces in the Netherlands Indies, almost 100,000 men (mostly Indonesian troops) surrendered to the invaders. In Burma, the day before, the British had been forced under heavy bombing to evacuate Rangoon and retreat northward. Before the end of April the Japanese had completed the ocupation of Burma, driving the British westward into India and the bulk of U.S. Lt. Gen. Joseph W. Stilwell's Chinese forces back into China; General Stilwell and the remnants of other Chinese units retreated to India. In the process the Japanese had won possession of a huge section of the Burma Road, the only viable route between China and India. Henceforth and until late in the war communication between China and its allies was to be limited to an air ferry from India over the "hump" of the Himalayan Mountains. During the late spring strong Japanese naval forces reached the coastal cities of India and even attacked Britain's naval base on Ceylon.

By May 1942 the Japanese had thus gained control of Burma, Malaya, Thailand, French Indochina, and the Malay Archipelago, while farther to the east they had won strong lodgments on the islands of New Guinea and New Britain and in the Solomons, flanking the approaches to Australia and New Zealand from the United States. This immense empire had been won at remarkably little cost through an effective combination of superior air and sea power and only a handful of well-trained ground divisions. The Japanese had seized and held the initiative while keeping their opponents off balance. They had concentrated their strength for the capture of key objectives such as airfields and road junctions and for the destruction of major enemy forces while diverting only minimum forces on secondary missions, thus giving an impression of overwhelming numerical strength. They had frequently gained the advantage of surprise and had baffled their enemies by their speed and skill in maneuver. The whole whirlwind campaign, in short, had provided Japan's enemies with a capsule course of instruction in the principles of war.

Fall of the Philippines

Only in the Philippines, almost on Japan's southern doorstep, was the timetable of conquest delayed. When the Japanese struck, the defending forces in the islands numbered more than 130,000, including the Philippine Army which, though mobilized to a strength of ten divisions, was ill trained and ill equipped. Of the U.S. Army contingent of 31,000, more than a third consisted of the Philippine Scouts, most of whom were part of the Regular Army Philippine Division, the core of the mobile defense forces. The Far East Air Force, before the Japanese attack, had a total of 277 aircraft of all types, mostly obsolescent but including 35 new heavy bombers. Admiral Thomas C. Hart's Asiatic Fleet, based on the Philippines, consisted of 3 cruisers, 13 old destroyers,

6 gunboats, 6 motor torpedo boats, 32 patrol bombers, and 29 submarines. A regiment of marines, withdrawn from Shanghai, also joined the defending forces late in November 1941. Before the end of December, however, American air and naval power in the Philippines had virtually ceased to exist. The handful of bombers surviving the early attacks had been evacuated to Australia, and the bulk of the Asiatic Fleet, its base facilities in ruins, had withdrawn southward to help in the defense of the Netherlands Indies.

The main Japanese invasion of the Philippines, following preliminary landings, began on December 22, 1941. While numerically inferior to the defenders, the invading force of two divisions with supporting units was well trained and equipped and enjoyed complete mastery of the air and on the sea. The attack centered on Luzon, the northernmost and largest island of the archipelago, where all but a small fraction of the defending forces were concentrated. The main landings were made on the beaches of Lingayen Gulf, in the northwest, and Lamon Bay in the southeast. General MacArthur's plan was to meet and destroy the invaders on the beaches, but his troops were unable to prevent the enemy from gaining secure lodgments. On December 23 MacArthur ordered a general withdrawal into the mountainous Bataan Peninsula, across Manila Bay from the capital city. Manila itself was occupied by the Japanese without resistance. The retreat into Bataan was a complex operation, involving converging movements over difficult terrain into a cramped assembly area from which only two roads led into the peninsula itself. Under constant enemy attack, the maneuver was executed with consummate skill and at considerable cost to the attackers. Yet American and Filipino losses were heavy, and the unavoidable abandonment of large stocks of supplies foredoomed the defenders of Bataan to ultimate defeat in the siege that followed. An ominous portent was the cutting of food rations by half on the last day of the retreat.

By January 7, 1942, General MacArthur's forces held well-prepared positions across the upper part of the Bataan Peninsula. Their presence there, and on Corregidor and its satellite island fortresses guarding the entrance to Manila Bay, denied the enemy the use of the bay throughout the siege. In the first major enemy offensive, launched early in January, the "battling bastards of Bataan" at first gave ground but thereafter handled the Japanese so roughly that attacks ceased altogether from mid-February until April, while the enemy reorganized and heavily reinforced. The defenders were, however, too weak to seize the initiative themselves.

General MacArthur, meanwhile, was ordered by the President to leave his post and go to Australia in order to take command of Allied operations against the Japanese in the Southwest Pacific. In mid-March he and a small party made

GENERAL WAINWRIGHT BROADCASTING TO AMERICAN FORCES

their way through the Japanese lines by motor torpedo boat to Mindanao, and from there were flown to Australia. Command of the forces in the Philippines devolved upon Lt. Gen. Jonathan M. Wainwright.

By April the troops on Bataan were subsisting on about fifteen ounces of food daily, less than a quarter of the peacetime ration. Their diet, consisting mostly of rice supplemented by carabao, mule, monkey, or lizard meat, was gravely deficient in vitamins and provided less than 1,000 calories a day, barely enough to sustain life. Weakened by hunger and poor diet, thousands succumbed to malaria, dengue, scurvy, beriberi, and amoebic dysentery, made impossible to control by the shortage of medical supplies, especially quinine. Desperate efforts were made to send food, medicine, ammunition, and other supplies through the Japanese blockade to the beleaguered forces. But during the early weeks, before the enemy cordon had tightened, it proved impossible, despite promises of lavish pay and bonuses, to muster the necessary ships and crews. Even so, sizable stocks were accumulated in the southern islands, but only about 1,000 tons of rations ever reached Manila Bay. Shipments in converted destroyers from the United States were too late and too few, and only insignificant quantities could be brought in by submarine and aircraft.

At the beginning of April the Japanese, behind a pulverizing artillery barrage, attacked again. The American lines crumpled, and in a few days the defending forces virtually disintegrated. On April 9 Maj. Gen. Edward P. King, Jr., commanding the forces on Bataan, surrendered. For almost another month the garrison on Corregidor and the other islands, swelled by refugees from Bataan, held out under air bombardment and almost continuous plunging fire from heavy artillery massed on adjacent shores and heights—one of the most intense artillery bombardments, for so small a target, of the entire war. On the night of May 5, after a final terrific 5-day barrage, Japanese assault troops won a foothold on Corregidor, and the following night, when it became apparent that further resistance was useless, General Wainwright surrendered unconditionally. Under his orders, which the Japanese forced him to broadcast, other American commanders in the Philippines capitulated one by one. By early June, except for scattered guerrilla detachments in the hills, all organized resistance in the islands had ceased.

Deploying American Military Strength

After more than a year and a half of rearming, the United States in December 1941 was still in no position to carry the war to its enemies. On December 7 the Army numbered some 1,644,000 men (including about 120,000 officers), organized into 4 armies, 37 divisions (30 infantry, 5 armored, 2 cavalry), and over 40 combat air groups. Three of the divisions were overseas (2 in Hawaii, 1 in the Philippines), with other garrison forces totaling less than 200,000. By spreading equipment and ammunition thin, the War Department might have put a substantial force into the field to repel an attack on the continental United States; 17 of the divisions at home were rated as technically ready for combat. But these divisions lacked the supporting units and the training necessary to weld them into corps and armies. More serious still, they were inadequately equipped with many weapons that recent operations in Europe had shown to be indispensable—for example, tank and antitank guns, antiaircraft artillery, radios, and radar—and some of these shortages were aggravated by lack of auxiliary equipment like fire control mechanisms.

Above all, ammunition of all kinds was so scarce that the War Department was unwilling to commit more than one division and a single antiaircraft regiment for service in any theater where combat operations seemed imminent. Only one division-size task force, in fact, was sent to the far Pacific before April 1942. Against air attacks, too, the country's defenses were meager. Along the Pacific coast the Army had only 45 modern fighter planes ready to fly, and only twelve

3-inch antiaircraft guns to defend the whole Los Angeles area. On the east coast there were only 54 Army fighter planes ready for action. While the coastal air forces, primarily training commands, could be reinforced by aircraft from the interior of the country, the total number of modern fighter aircraft available was less than 1,000. Fortunately, there was no real threat of an invasion in force, and the rapidly expanding output of munitions from American factories promised to remedy one of these weaknesses within a few months. Furthermore, temporary diversions of lend-lease equipment, especially aircraft, helped to bolster the overall defense posture within the first few weeks after Pearl Harbor. The Army hoped by April to have as many as thirteen divisions equipped and supplied with ammunition for combat.

To deploy these forces overseas was another matter. Although the U.S. merchant marine ranked second only to Great Britain's and the country possessed an immense shipbuilding capacity, the process of chartering, assembling, and preparing shipping for the movement of troops and military cargo took time. Time was also needed to schedule and organize convoys, and, owing to the desperate shortage of escort vessels, troop movements had to be widely spaced. Convoying and evasive routing, in themselves, greatly reduced the effective capacity of shipping. Moreover, vast distances separated U.S. ports from the areas threatened by Japan, and to these areas went the bulk of the forces deployed overseas during the months immediately following Pearl Harbor. Through March 1942, as a result, the outflow of troops to overseas bases averaged only about 50,000 per month, as compared with upwards of 250,000 during 1944, when shipping was fully mobilized and plentiful and the sea lanes were secure.

There seemed a real danger early in 1942, however, that German U-boats might succeed in reducing transatlantic deployment to a trickle—not so much by attacking troop transports, most of which could outrun their attackers, as by sinking the slow cargo ships on which the forces overseas depended for support. Soon after Germany's declaration of war, the U-boats struck at the virtually unprotected shipping lanes in the western Atlantic, and subsequently extended their attacks to the Gulf of Mexico and Caribbean areas and the mouth of the St. Lawrence. During the spring of 1942 tankers and freighters were torpedoed in plain view of vacationers on east coast beaches, and coastal cities dimmed or extinguished their lights in order that ships might not provide silhouetted targets for the U-boats. The Navy lacked the means to cope with the peril. In late December 1941 it had only twenty assorted surface vessels and about a hundred aircraft to protect the whole North Atlantic coastal frontier. During the winter and spring these were supplemented by another hundred

Army planes of longer range, several armed British trawlers, and as many improvised craft as could be pressed into service.

But the toll of ship sinkings increased. In March 788,000 deadweight tons of Allied and neutral dry cargo shipping were lost, in June 936,000 tons. Tanker losses reached an all-time peak of 375,000 tons in March, leading to complete suspension of coastal tanker movements and to gasoline rationing in the seaboard states. During the first six months of 1942 losses of Allied shipping were almost as heavy as during the whole of 1941 and exceeded new construction by almost 2.8 million deadweight tons. Although the United States was able by May to balance its own current losses by building new ships, Britain and other Allied countries continued until the following August to lose more than they could build, and another year passed before new construction offset cumulative losses.

Slowly and with many setbacks a system of countermeasures was developed. Convoying of coastal shipping, with ships sailing only by day, began in the spring of 1942. North-South traffic between U.S. and Caribbean and South American ports was also convoyed, on schedules interlocked with those of the transatlantic convoys. The latter, during 1942, were protected in the western half of the Atlantic by the U.S. and Canadian Navies, in the eastern half by the British. Troops were transported across the Atlantic either without escort in large, speedy liners like the *Queen Elizabeth* and the *Queen Mary*—which between them carried almost a quarter of all U.S. troops sent to Europe—or in heavily escorted convoys. Throughout the war, not a single loaded troop transport was sunk on the United Kingdom run. The slow merchant ships were convoyed in large groups according to speed.

But with responsibility for U.S. antisubmarine operations divided between the Navy and Army Air Forces, effective co-operation was hampered by sharp disagreement over organization and methods, and available resources throughout 1942 were inadequate. The U-boats, meanwhile, were operating with deadly effect and in growing numbers. Late in the year they began to hunt in packs, resupplied at sea by large cargo submarines ("milch cows"). The Allied convoys to Murmansk and other northern Soviet ports suffered especially heavy losses on their long passage around the top of the Scandinavian peninsula. In November shipping losses from all causes soared above 1.1 million deadweight tons—the peak, as it turned out, for the entire war, but few at the time dared so to predict.

In the Pacific, fortunately, the principal barriers to deployment of U.S. forces were distance and lack of prepared bases, not enemy submarines. Japan's fleet of undersea craft made little effort to prey on the Allied sea lanes and probably, over the vast reaches of the Pacific, could not have inflicted serious damage in any case. The chief goal of American deployment to the Pacific during most of 1942, following the initial reinforcement of Hawaii and the Panama Canal, was to build up a base in Australia and secure the chain of islands leading to it. Australia was a vast, thinly populated, and, except in its southeastern portion, largely undeveloped island continent, 7,000 miles and almost a month's sail from the U.S. west coast. It had provided a haven for some 4,000 American troops who, on December 7, had been at sea, bound for the Philippines, and in January a task force of division size (POPPY Force) was hastily assembled and dispatched to New Caledonia to guard its eastern approaches. During the first few weeks the main effort of the small American forces went into sending relief supplies to the Philippines and aircraft and troops to Java to stem the Japanese invasion. Beginning in March, as the futility of these efforts became evident, and coincident with the arrival of General MacArthur to assume command of all Allied forces in the Southwest Pacific, the construction of base facilities and the build-up of balanced air and ground forces got under way in earnest.

This build-up had as its first object the defense of Australia itself, for at the end of January the Japanese had occupied Rabaul on New Britain Island, thus posing an immediate threat to Port Moresby, the weakly held Australian base in southeastern New Guinea. In February President Roosevelt pledged American help in countering this threat, and in March and April two infantry divisions (the 41st and 32d) left the United States for the Southwest Pacific. At the same time, construction of air and refueling bases was being rushed to completion in the South Pacific islands that formed steppingstones along the ocean routes to Australia and New Zealand. After the western anchor of this chain, New Caledonia, was secured by the POPPY Force, Army and Marine garrisons and reinforcements were sent to various other islands along the line, culminating with the arrival of the 37th Division in the Fiji Islands in June.

These moves came none too soon for, during the spring, the Japanese, after occupying Rabaul, pushed into the southern Solomons, within easy striking distance of the American bases on Espíritu Santo and New Caledonia. They also occupied the northeastern coast of New Guinea, just across the narrow Papuan peninsula from Port Moresby, which the Americans and Australians were developing into a major advanced base in preparation for an eventual offensive northward. The stage was thus set for a major test of strength in the Pacific—American forces spread thinly along an immense arc from Hawaii to Australia, with outposts far to the north in Alaska; the Japanese securely in possession of the vast areas north and west of the arc and, with the advantage of interior lines, prepared to strike in force at any point. The first test came in May, when the Japanese made an attempt from the sea to take Port Moresby. This was successfully countered in the great carrier battle of the Coral Sea. Thereupon the Japanese struck eastward, hoping to destroy the U.S. Pacific Fleet and to seize Midway—a bid for naval supremacy in the Pacific. A diversionary attack on Dutch Harbor, the most forward U.S. base in Alaska, caused considerable damage, and the Japanese were able to occupy the islands of Kiska and Attu in the foggy Aleutian chain. But the main Japanese forces, far to the south, were crushingly defeated, with especially heavy losses in carriers and aircraft. The Battle of Midway in June 1942 was one of the truly decisive engagements of the war. By seriously weakening Japan's mobile striking forces, Midway left the Japanese virtually helpless to prevent the consolidation of American positions and the eventual development of over-whelming military supremacy throughout the Pacific. Only two months later, in fact, American forces took the first step on the long "road back" by landing on Guadalcanal in the southern Solomons.

Although the RAINBOW 5 plan was put into effect immediately after Pearl Harbor, the desperate situation in the Pacific and Far East and the shortage of shipping and escorts ruled out most of the scheduled Atlantic, Caribbean, and South American deployments. In January reinforcements were sent to Iceland and a token force to Northern Ireland, and by June two full divisions (the 34th Infantry and the 1st Armored) had reached Ireland, while the remainder of the 5th Infantry had arrived in Iceland, completing the relief of the U.S. Marine brigade and most of the British garrison. No more divisions sailed eastward until August. Meanwhile, garrisons in the Atlantic and Caribbean were being built up to war strength. But plans to occupy the Azores, Canaries, and Cape Verdes, and to capture Dakar on the west African coast went by the board, primarily for lack of shipping. Also abandoned after lengthy discussion was a project (GYMNAST) proposed by Prime Minister Churchill at the ARCADIA Conference for an Anglo-American occupation of French North Africa.

Thus, despite the reaffirmation of the "Germany first" strategy at ARCADIA, the great bulk of American forces sent overseas during the first half of 1942 went to the theaters of war against Japan. Of the eight Army divisions that left the country before August, five went to the Pacific. Including two more already in Hawaii, and a Marine division at sea, bound for New Zealand (eventually for the landings on Guadalcanal in August), eight divisions were deployed against Japan in July 1942. Of the approximately 520,000 Army troops in overseas bases, 60 percent were in the Pacific (including Alaska) and the newly established China-Burma-India theater; the remainder were almost all in Caribbean and western Atlantic garrisons. Of 2,200 Army aircraft overseas, about 1,300 were in the Pacific (including Alaska) and Far East, 900 in the western Atlantic and Latin America. Not until August did the U.S. Army Air Forces in the British Isles attain sufficient strength to fly a single independent bombing mission over northern France.

Planning for a Cross-Channel Invasion

The Army's leaders and planners, schooled in a tradition that emphasized the principles of mass and offensive, had been fretting over the scale of deployment to the Pacific since early in the year. Late in January Brig. Gen. Dwight D. Eisenhower, then a War Department staff officer whom General Marshall had assigned to handle the crisis in the Pacific, noted, "We've got to go to Europe and fight—and we've got to quit wasting resources all over the world." In the joint committees Army planners urged that as soon as the situation could be stabilized in the Southwest Pacific, U.S. forces should begin to concentrate in the British Isles for an offensive against Germany. Secretary Stimson and others were pressing the same views on the President. In the middle of March the Joint Chiefs of Staff approved this course of action, and in April, at the President's order, General Marshall and Harry Hopkins, the President's personal representative, went to London to seek British approval.

Logistical considerations heavily favored both the general strategy of concentration against Germany and the specific plan of invading northwestern Europe from a base in the British Isles. Because the target area was close to the main sources of British and American power, two to three times as many forces could be hurled against northwestern Europe, with a given amount of shipping, as could be supported in operations against Japan. Britain itself was a highly industrialized country, fully mobilized after two and a half years of war, and well shielded by air and naval power—a ready-made base for a land invasion and air attacks on Germany's vitals. While invasion forces were assembling, moreover, they would serve to garrison the British Isles. Finally, an attack across the English Channel would use the only short water crossing to the Continent from a base already available and would thrust directly at the heart of Fortress Europe by the main historic invasion routes.

Even so, the plan was a desperate gamble. If northwestern Europe offered the Allies a position of strength, the Germans, too, would be strong there, close to their own heartland, served by the superb rail and road net of western and central Europe, shielded by submarines based along the entire length of Europe's Atlantic front. The limited range of fighter aircraft based in southern England narrowly restricted the choice of landing areas. Much hinged on the USSR, where for the present the bulk of Germany's land forces were pinned down. If the Soviet Union collapsed, an invasion from the west would be a suicidal venture. The invasion must therefore be launched before the Soviet armies were crushed and, moreover, in sufficient strength to draw substantial German forces away from the Eastern Front in order to avert that very catastrophe.

On the face of it, these two requirements seemed to cancel each other. For Allied planners had little hope that the Russians could stand up under another summer's onslaught, and it was obvious, in view of the scarcity of shipping, that any attack the Western Allies could mount by the coming summer or early fall would be hardly more than a pinprick. The best solution General Marshall's planners could offer to this dilemma was to set the invasion for the spring of 1943 (ROUNDUP), in the hope that until then, through air bombardment of Germany and a continued flow of matériel to the Soviet Union, the Allies could help the Soviet armies to stave off defeat. If these measures should fail, and Soviet resistance seemed about to collapse, then, with whatever forces were on hand, the Allies would have to invade the Continent in 1942 (SLEDGEHAMMER)— and no later than September, before bad weather closed down over the Channel. The same course would be followed in the unlikely event that Germany itself showed signs of serious weakness in 1942.

In London, Mr. Hopkins and General Marshall found the British delighted that the United States was ready to commit itself to a major offensive against Germany in 1943. The British readily agreed that preparations should begin immediately for an invasion the following spring, and they undertook to provide more than half the shipping needed to move about a million American troops and immense quantities of matériel to the United Kingdom. They warned, however, that their first concern at present was to maintain their position in the Middle East, where, late in January, Rommel's revitalized Africa Korps had inflicted a serious reverse on the Eighth Army. Both sides were now feverishly building up for a new offensive. The British also expressed deep misgivings over the proposed emergency cross-Channel operation in the fall. Nevertheless, the British approved the American plan, essentially the War Department's plan, "in principle"—a phrase that was to give much trouble in the coalition war. The immediate relief felt by General Marshall's staff in Washington was reflected by General Eisenhower, then Chief, Operations Division, War Department General Staff, who noted: ". . . at long last, and after months of struggle . . . we are all definitely committed to one concept of fighting! If we can agree on major purposes and objectives, our efforts will begin to fall in line and we won't just be thrashing around in the dark."

But on the American side, too, there were strong reservations. Admiral King did not contest in principle the "Germany first" strategy. But he was determined not to allow preparations for the cross-Channel invasion to jeopardize "vital needs" in the Pacific, by which, as he candidly stated early in May, he meant the ability of U.S. forces "to hold what we have against any attack that the Japanese are capable of launching." Only the President's peremptory order on May 6 that the invasion build-up in Britain must not be slowed down (it had, indeed, scarcely begun) prevented a large-scale diversion of forces and shipping to the Pacific to counter the Japanese offensive that culminated in the great naval battles of the Coral Sea and Midway. The President himself made it clear, on the other hand, that aid to the Soviet Union would have to continue on a mounting scale, whatever the cost to BOLERO (the American build-up in the United Kingdom) in matériel and shipping. And even Army leaders were unwilling to assign shipping for the movement until the scheduled build-up of garrisons in the Western Hemisphere and various other overseas stations had been completed, which, it was estimated, would not be until August at the earliest. Until then British shipping would have to carry the main burden.

Not until June 1942, therefore, did the first shipload of American troops under the new plan set sail for England in the great British luxury liner, *Queen Elizabeth*. Almost simultaneously a new crisis erupted in the Middle East. At the end of May, after a four-month lull, Rommel seized the initiative and swept around the southern flank of the British Eighth Army, which held strong positions in eastern Libya from El Gazala on the coast south to Bir Hacheim. After two weeks of hard fighting, in which the British seemed to be holding their own, Rommel succeeded in taking Bir Hacheim, the southern anchor of the British line. During the next few days British armor, committed piecemeal in an effort to cover a withdrawal to the northeast, was virtually wiped out by skillfully concealed German 88-mm. guns. The Eighth Army once again retreated across the Egyptian frontier, and on June 21 Tobruk, which the British had expected, as in 1941, to hold out behind Axis lines, was captured with its garrison and large stores of trucks, gasoline, and other supplies.

News of this disaster reached Prime Minister Churchill in Washington, where he had gone early in the month to tell the President that the British were unwilling to go through with an emergency cross-Channel landing late in 1942. General Marshall immediately offered to send an armored division to help the hard-pressed British in Egypt, but it was decided, for the present, to limit American aid to emergency shipments of tanks, artillery, and the ground components of three combat air groups. This move required the diversion for many weeks of a substantial amount of U.K. shipping from the North Atlantic on the long voyage around the Cape of Good Hope. But the heaviest impact on the invasion build-up in the United Kingdom resulted from the diversion of British shipping to the Middle East and the retention there of shipping the British had earmarked for the build-up. For the time being, British participation in the BOLERO program virtually ceased.

By the end of August, with only seven months to go before the invasion was to be launched, only about 170,000 American troops were in or on their way to the British Isles, and the shipment of equipment and supplies, particularly for the development of cantonments, airfields, and base facilities, was hopelessly behind schedule. There seemed little likelihood that enough shipping would be available to complete the movement across the Atlantic of a million troops, with the ten to fifteen million tons of cargo that must accompany them, by April 1943 as scheduled. And even if the shipping could have been found, Britain's ports and inland transportation system would have been swamped before the influx reached its peak. Thus, by the late summer of 1942, a spring 1943 ROUNDUP appeared to be a logistical impossibility.

Torch Replaces Sledgehammer-Roundup

By this time, in fact, American military leaders had become discouraged about a cross-Channel invasion in spring of 1943, though not primarily because of the lag in the build-up program. In June the British had decided that SLEDGEHAMMER, for which they had never had any enthusiasm, could not be undertaken except in a situation which offered good prospects of success—that is, if the Germans should seem about to collapse. At the moment, with the German summer offensive just starting to roll toward the Caucasus and the lower Don, such a situation did not appear to be an imminent possibility. The British decision was influenced in part by the alarming lag in deliveries of American landing craft, of which less than two-thirds of the promised quota for the operation was expected to materialize. The British also argued that the confusion and losses attendant upon executing SLEDGEHAMMER—and the cost of supporting the beachhead once it was established—were likely to disrupt preparations for the main invasion the following spring. Since SLEDGEHAMMER, if carried out, would have to be, in the main, a British undertaking, the British veto was decisive. The operation was canceled.

As a substitute, the British proposed a less risky venture—landings in French North Africa—which they were confident could be accomplished in stride, without harm to ROUNDUP. To Stimson, Marshall, King, and Arnold this proposal was anathema. Failure would be a costly, perhaps fatal rebuff to Allied prestige.

Success might be even more dangerous, the Americans feared, for it might lead the Allies step by step into a protracted series of operations around the southern periphery of Europe, operations that could not be decisive and would only postpone the final test of strength with Germany. At the very least, an invasion of North Africa would, the Americans were convinced, rule out a spring 1943 invasion of the Continent. The Army planners preferred the safer alternative of simply reinforcing the British in Egypt.

The British proposal was, nevertheless, politically shrewd, for it was no secret that President Roosevelt had long ago expressed a predilection for this very undertaking. He was determined, besides, that American ground forces go into action somewhere in the European area before the end of 1942. Already half persuaded, he hardly needed Churchill's enthusiastic rhetoric to win him over to the new project. When General Marshall and his colleagues in the Joints Chiefs of Staff suggested, as an alternative, that the United States should immediately go on the defensive in Europe and turn all-out against Japan, Roosevelt brusquely rejected the idea.

In mid-July, Hopkins, Marshall, and King went to London under orders from the President to reach agreement with the British on some operation in 1942. After a vain effort to persuade the British to reconsider an invasion of the Continent in 1942, the Americans reluctantly agreed on July 24 to the North Africa operation, now christened TORCH, to be launched before the end of October. The President, overruling Marshall's suggestion that final decision be postponed until mid-September in order to permit a reappraisal of the Soviet situation, cabled Hopkins that he was "delighted" and that the orders were now "full speed ahead." Into the final agreement, however, Marshall and King wrote their own conviction that the decision on TORCH "in all probability" rulled out invasion of the Continent in 1943 and meant, further, that the Allies had accepted "a defensive, encircling line of action" in the European-Mediterranean war.

End of the Defensive Stage

With the decision for TORCH, the first stage in the search for a strategic plan against Germany came to an end. In retrospect, 1941–42 had been a period of defensive strategy, and a strategy of scarcity. The British and American approaches to war had had their first conflict, and the British had won the first round. That British notions of strategy had tended to prevail was not surprising. British forces had been mobilized earlier and were in the theaters in far greater numbers than American forces. The United States was still mobilizing its manpower and resources. It had taken the better part of the year after Pearl

Harbor for U.S. forces to have an appreciable effect in the theaters. Strategic planning in 1942 had been largely opportunistic, hand to mouth, and limited by critical shortages in shipping and munitions. Troops had been parceled out piecemeal to meet immediate threats and crises. Despite the "Germany first" decision, the total U.S. Army forces deployed in the war against Japan by the end of the year actually exceeded the total U.S. Army forces deployed in the war against Germany. The one scheme to put Allied planning on an orderly, long-range basis and to achieve the concepts of mass and concentration in which General Marshall and his staff had put their faith had failed. By the close of the critical first year after Pearl Harbor, an effective formula for halting the dissipation of forces and matériel in what it regarded as secondary ventures still eluded the Army high command.

GENERAL MARSHALL

CHAPTER 12

World War II: The War Against Germany and Italy

With the invasion of North Africa (Operation TORCH), the U.S. Army in late 1942 began a ground offensive against the European Axis that was to be sustained almost without pause until Italy collapsed and Germany was finally defeated. More than a million Americans were to fight in lands bordering the Mediterranean Sea and close to four million on the European continent, exclusive of Italy, in the largest commitment to battle ever made by the U.S. Army. Alongside these Americans were to march British, Canadian, French, and other Allied troops in history's greatest demonstration of coalition warfare, while on another front massed Soviet armies were to contribute enormously to the victory.

The North African Campaign, November 1942–May 1943

Although the decision to launch Operation TORCH had been made largely because the Allies could not mount a more direct attack against the European Axis early in the war, there were specific and attractive objectives—to gain French-controlled Morocco, Algeria, and Tunisia as a base for enlisting the French empire in the war, to assist the British in the Libyan Desert in destroying Axis forces in North Africa, to open the Mediterranean to Allied shipping, and to provide a steppingstone for subsequent operations.

The Germans and their Italian allies controlled a narrow but strategic strip of the North African littoral between Tunisia and Egypt with impassable desert bounding the strip on the south. (*Map 40*) Numbering some 100,000 men under a battle-tested German leader, Field Marshal Rommel, the German-Italian army in Libya posed a constant threat to Egypt and the Near East as well as to French North Africa and, since the Axis also controlled the northern shores of the Mediterranean, served to deny the Mediterranean to Allied shipping. Only a few convoys seeking to supply British forces on the island of Malta ever ventured into the Mediterranean, and these took heavy losses.

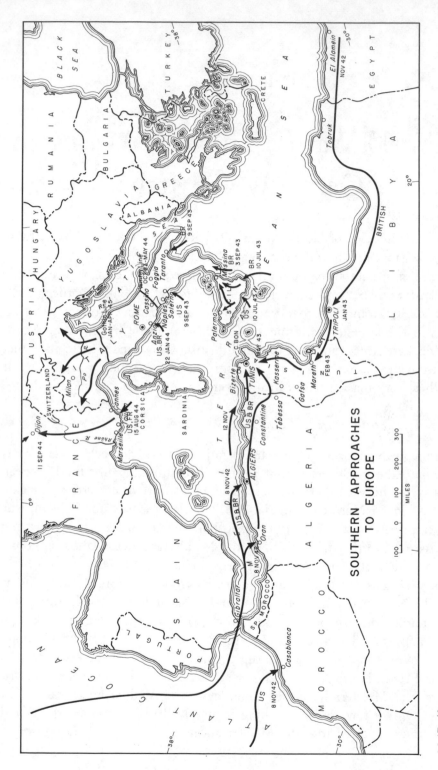

SOUTHERN APPROACHES
TO EUROPE

MAP 40

Moving against French Africa posed for the Allies special problems rooted in the nature of the armistice that had followed French defeat in 1940. Under terms of that armistice, the Germans had left the French empire nominally intact, along with much of the southern half of Metropolitan France, yet in return the French Government was pledged to drop out of the war. Although an underground resistance movement had already begun in France and an Allied-equipped force called the Free French was assembling in the British Isles, that part of the regular French Army and Navy left intact by the armistice was sworn to the service of the Vichy government. This pledge had led already to the anomaly of Frenchman fighting Frenchman and of the British incurring French enmity by destroying part of the fleet of their former ally.

If bloodshed was to be averted in the Allied invasion, French sympathies had to be enlisted in advance, but to reveal the plan was to risk French rejection of it and German occupation of French Africa. Although clandestine negotiations were conducted with a few trusted French leaders, these produced no guarantee that French forces would not resist.

Partly because of this intricate situation, the Allies designated an American, General Eisenhower, to command the invasion in order to capitalize on absence of rancor between French and Americans by giving the invasion an American rather than a British complexion. American troops were to make up the bulk of the assault force, and the Royal Navy was to keep its contribution as inconspicuous as possible.

The operation was to begin in western Egypt, where the British Commander in Chief, Middle East, General Sir Harold R. L. G. Alexander, was to attack with the veteran British Eighth Army under Lt. Gen. Bernard L. Montgomery against Field Marshal Rommel's German-Italian army. Coming ashore in French Africa, General Eisenhower's combined U.S.-British force was to launch a converging attack against Rommel's rear.

In selecting beaches for the invasion, U.S. planners insisted upon a landing on the Atlantic coast of Morocco lest the Germans seal the Strait of Gibraltar and cut off support to forces put ashore on the Mediterranean coast. Because both troops and shipping were limited, a landing on the Atlantic coast restricted the number and size of landings possible inside the Mediterranean. Although a landing as far east as Tunisia was desirable because of vast overland distances (from the Atlantic coast to Tunis is more than a thousand miles), proximity of Axis aircraft on Sicily and Sardinia made that too perilous.

Making the decision on the side of security, the Allies planned simultaneous landings at three points—in Morocco near the Atlantic port of Casablanca and in Algeria near the ports of Oran and Algiers. Once the success of these landings was assured, a convoy was to put ashore small contingents of British troops to seize ports in eastern Algeria while a ground column headed for Tunisia in a race to get there before the Germans could move in.

Given the assignment to invade North Africa only at the end of July 1942, the U.S. Army faced enormous difficulties in meeting a target date in November of the same year. Troops had had little training in amphibious warfare, landing craft were few and obsolete, and much equipment was inferior to that of the Axis forces. So few U.S. troops were available in England that troops for the landing near Casablanca had to be shipped direct from the United States, one of history's longest sea voyages preceding an amphibious assault.

After soundly defeating an Axis attack, Montgomery's Eighth Army on October 23 auspiciously opened an offensive at El 'Alamein, there to score a victory that was to be a turning point in British fortunes. A little over two weeks later, before daylight on November 8, the U.S. Navy put U.S. Army forces ashore near Casablanca, while the Royal Navy landed other U.S. troops and contingents of British troops near Oran and Algiers. The entire invasion force consisted of over 400 warships, 1,000 planes, and some 107,000 men, including a battalion of paratroopers jumping in the U.S. Army's first airborne attack.

Although the invasion achieved strategic surprise, the French in every case but one fought back at the beaches. Dissidence among various French factions limited the effectiveness of some of the opposition, but any resistance at all raised the specter of delay that might enable the Germans to beat the Allies into Tunisia. Three days passed before the French agreed to cease fire and take up arms on the Allied side.

French support at last assured, the Royal Navy put British troops ashore close to the Tunisian border while an Allied column began the long overland trek. The British troops were too few to do more than secure two small Algerian ports, the ground column too late. Over the narrow body of water between Sicily and North Africa the Germans poured planes, men, and tanks. Except for barren mountains in the interior, Tunisia was for the moment out of Allied reach.

The Tunisia Campaign

Recoiling from the defeat at El 'Alamein, Rommel's German-Italian army in January 1943 occupied old French fortifications near the southern border of Tunisia, the Mareth Line, there to face Montgomery's Eighth Army, while more than 100,000 enemy troops under General Juergen von Arnim faced westward against General Eisenhower's Allied force. Although the Italian high command in Italy exercised loose control, the Axis nations failed to establish a unified command over these two forces.

The Allied plan to defeat Rommel by converging attacks having been foiled, General Eisenhower had no choice but to dig in to defend in the Tunisian mountains until he could accumulate enough strength to attack in conjunction with a renewed strike by Montgomery against the Mareth Line. Before this could be accomplished, Rommel on February 14 sent strong armored forces through the passes in central Tunisia against the U.S. II Corps, commanded by Maj. Gen. Lloyd R. Fredendall. Rommel planned to push through the Kasserine Pass, then turn northwestward by way of an Allied supply base at Tébessa to reach the coast and trap the Allied units.

In a series of sharp armored actions, Rommel quickly penetrated thinly held American positions and broke through the Kasserine Pass. Although success appeared within his grasp, lack of unified command interfered. Planning an attack of his own, General von Arnim refused to release an armored division needed to continue Rommel's thrust. Concerned that Rommel lacked the strength for a deep envelopment by way of Tébessa, the Italian high command directed a turn northward, a much shallower envelopment.

The turn played into Allied hands, for the British already had established a blocking position astride the only road leading northward. At the height of a clash between Rommel's tanks and the British, four battalions of American artillery arrived after a forced march from Oran. On February 22 these guns and a small band of British tanks brought the Germans to a halt. Warned by intelligence reports that the British Eighth Army was about to attack the Mareth Line, Rommel hurriedly pulled back to his starting point.

The Axis offensive defeated, the U.S. II Corps, commanded now by Maj. Gen. George S. Patton, Jr., launched a diversionary attack on March 17 toward the rear of the Mareth Line, while Montgomery's Eighth Army a few days later struck the line in force. By the end of the first week of April, the two forces had joined.

With all their forces now linked under the tactical command of General Alexander, the Allies opened a broad offensive that within a month captured the ports of Bizerte and Tunis and compressed all Axis troops into a small bridgehead covering the Cape Bon peninsula at the northeastern tip of Tunisia. The last of some 275,000 Germans and Italians surrendered on May 10.

Although the original Allied strategy had been upset by the delay imposed by French resistance and the swift German build-up in Tunisia, Allied troops achieved victory in six months, which in view of their limited numbers and long lines of communications, was impressive. A few days later the first unopposed British convoy since 1940 reached beleaguered Malta.

American troops in their first test against German arms had made many mistakes. Training, equipment, and leadership had failed in many instances to meet the requirements of the battlefield, but the lessons were clear and pointed to nothing that time might not correct. More imporant was the experience gained, both in battle and in logistical support. Important too was the fact that the Allied campaign had brought a French army back into the war. Most important of all, the Allies at last had gained the initiative.

The Sicily Campaign, July–August 1943

Where the Allies were to go after North Africa had already been decided in January 1943 at the Casablanca Conference. As with the decision to invade North Africa, the next step—invading Sicily (Operation HUSKY)—followed from recognition that the Allies still were unready for a direct thrust across the English Channel. Utilizing troops already available in North Africa, they could make the Mediterranean safer for Allied shipping by occupying Sicily, perhaps going on after that to invade Italy and knock the junior Axis partner out of the war.

As planning proceeded for the new operation, General Eisenhower (promoted now to four-star rank) remained as supreme commander, while General Alexander, heading the 15th Army Group, served as ground commander. Alexander controlled Montgomery's Eighth Army and a newly created Seventh U.S. Army under Patton (now a lieutenant general).

How to invade the Vermont-size, three-cornered island posed a special problem. The goal was Messina, the gateway to the narrow body of water between Sicily and Italy, the enemy's escape route to the Italian mainland. Yet the Strait of Messina was so narrow and well fortified that Allied commanders believed the only solution was to land elsewhere and march on Messina by way of shallow coastal shelves on either side of towering Mount Etna.

Applying the principle of mass, Alexander directed that all landings be made in the southeastern corner of the island, British on the east coast, Americans on the southwest. Behind British beaches a brigade of glider troops was to capture a critical bridge, while a regiment of U.S. paratroopers took high ground behind American beaches. After seizing minor ports and close-in airfields, Patton's Seventh Army was to block to the northwest against Axis reserves while Montgomery mounted a main effort up the east coast.

Because Sicily was an obvious objective after North Africa, complete strategic surprise was hardly possible, but bad weather helped the Allies achieve tactical surprise. As a huge armada bearing some 160,000 men steamed across the Mediterranean, a mistral—a form of unpredictable gale common to the Mediterranean—sprang up, so churning the sea that General Eisenhower was for a time tempted to order delay. While the heavy surf swamped some landing craft and made all landings difficult, it put the beach defenders off their guard. Before daylight on July 10, both British and Americans were ashore in sizable numbers.

As presaged in North Africa, poor performance by Italian units left to German reserves the task of repelling the invasion. Although preattack bombardment by Allied planes and confusion caused by a scattered jump of U.S. paratroopers delayed German reaction, a panzer division mounted a sharp counterattack against American beaches before the first day was out. It came dangerously close to pushing some American units into the sea before naval gunfire and a few U.S. tanks and artillery pieces that had got ashore drove off the German tanks.

To speed reinforcement, the Allies on two successive nights flew in American and British paratroopers. In both instances, antiaircraft gunners on ships standing offshore and others on land mistook the planes for enemy aircraft and opened fire. Losses were so severe that for a time some Allied commanders questioned the wisdom of employing this new method of warfare.

The Germans meanwhile formed a solid block in front of the British along the east coast, prompting General Patton to urge expanding the role of his Seventh Army. First cutting the island in two with a drive by the II Corps, commanded now by Maj. Gen. Omar N. Bradley, Patton sent a provisional corps pushing rapidly through faltering Italian opposition to the port of Palermo and the northwestern tip of the island. This accomplished within fourteen days after coming ashore, Patton turned to aid the British by attacking toward Messina along a narrow northern coastal shelf.

As both Allied armies in early August readied a final assault to gain Messina, the Germans began to withdraw to the mainland. Despite Allied command of sea and air, they managed to evacuate all their forces, some 40,000 troops. When on August 17, thirty days after the invasion, U.S. patrols pushed into Messina, the Germans had incurred some 10,000 casualties, the Italians probably as many as 100,000, mostly prisoners of war. Allied losses were 22,000.

The American force that fought in Sicily was far more sophisticated than that which had gone into battle in North Africa. New landing craft, some capable of bearing tanks, had made getting ashore much quicker and surer, and new amphibious trucks called DUKW's eased the problem of supply over the beaches. Gone was the Grant tank with its side-mounted gun, lacking wide traverse; in its place was the Sherman with 360-degree power-operated traverse for a turret-mounted 75-mm. piece. Commanders were alert to avoid a mistake often made in North Africa of parceling out divisions in small increments, and the men were sure of their weapons and their own ability. Some problems of co-ordination with tactical air remained, but these soon would be worked out.

The Surrender of Italy

Even as the Allies had been preparing to invade Sicily, the Italian people and their government had become increasingly disenchanted with the war. Under the impact of the loss of North Africa, the invasion of Sicily, and a first bombing of Rome, the Italian king forced Mussolini to resign as head of the government.

Anxious to find a way out of the war, a new Italian government made contact with the Allies through diplomatic channels, leading to direct talks with General Eisenhower's representatives. The Italians, it soon developed, were in a quandary—they wanted to pull out of the war, yet they were virtual prisoners of German forces in Italy that Hitler, sensing Italian defection, strongly reinforced. Although plans were drawn for airborne landings to secure Rome coincident with announcement of Italian surrender, these were canceled in the face of Italian vacillation and inability to guarantee strong assistance in fighting the Germans. The Italian government nevertheless agreed to surrender, a fact General Eisenhower announced on the eve of the principal Allied landing on the mainland.

The Italian Campaign, September 1943–May 1945

Since the Allied governments had decided to pursue after Sicily whatever course offered the best chance of knocking Italy from the war, invading the mainland logically followed. This plan also presented an opportunity to tie down German forces and prevent their employment either on the Russian front or against the eventual Allied attack across the English Channel. Occupying Italy also would provide airfields close to Germany and the Balkans.

How far up the peninsula of Italy the Allies were to land depended almost entirely on the range of fighter aircraft based on Sicily, for all Allied aircraft carriers were committed to the war in the Pacific. Another consideration was a desire to control the Strait of Messina to shorten sea supply lines.

On September 3 a British force under Montgomery crossed the Strait of Messina and landed on the toe of the Italian boot against surprisingly moderate opposition. Following Eisenhower's announcement of Italian surrender, a British fleet steamed brazenly into the harbor of Taranto in the arch of the Italian boot to put a British division ashore on the docks, while the Fifth U.S. Army under Lt. Gen. Mark W. Clark staged an assault landing on beaches near Salerno, twenty-five miles southeast of Naples.

Reacting in strength against the Salerno invasion, the Germans two days after the landing mounted a vigorous counterattack that threatened to split the beachhead and force abandonment of part of it. For four days, the issue was in doubt. Quick reinforcement of the ground troops (including a regiment of paratroopers jumping into the beachhead), gallant fighting, liberal air support, and unstinting naval gunfire at last repulsed the German attack. On September 15 the Germans began to withdraw, and the next day patrols of the British Eighth Army arrived from the south to link the two Allied forces. Two weeks later American troops took Naples, thereby gaining an excellent port, while the British seized valuable airfields around Foggia on the other side of the peninsula.

Although the Germans seriously considered abandoning southern Italy to pull back to a line in the Northern Apennines, the local commander, Field Marshal Albert Kesselring, insisted that he could hold for a considerable time on successive lines south of Rome. This proved to be an accurate assessment. The Allied advance was destined to proceed slowly, partly because of the difficulty of offensive warfare in rugged mountainous terrain and partly because the Allies limited their commitment to the campaign, not only in troops but also in shipping and the landing craft that were necessary if the enemy's strong defensive positions were to be broken by other than frontal attack.

Because the build-up for a cross-Channel attack—the main effort against Germany—was beginning in earnest, the Allies could spare few additional troops or shipping to pursue the war in Italy. Through the fall and winter of 1943–44, the armies would have to do the job in Italy with what was at hand, a total of eighteen Allied divisions.

A renewed offensive in October 1943 broke a strong German delaying position at the Volturno River, twenty miles north of Naples, and carried as far as a so-called Winter Line, an imposing position anchored on towering peaks around the town of Cassino. Casting about for a way to break this line, General Eisenhower obtained permission to retain temporarily from the build-up in Britain enough shipping and landing craft to make an amphibious end run. General Clark was to use a corps of his Fifth U.S. Army to land on beaches near Anzio, some thirty miles south of Rome and sixty miles behind the Winter

Line. By threatening or cutting German lines of communications to the Winter Line, the troops at Anzio were to facilitate Allied advance through the line and up the valley of the Liri River, the most obvious route to Rome.

Provided support by a French corps equipped with American arms, General Clark pulled out the U.S. VI Corps under Maj. Gen. John P. Lucas to make the envelopment. While the VI Corps—which included a British division—sailed toward Anzio, the Fifth Army launched a massive attack aimed at gaining access to the Liri valley. Although the VI Corps landed unopposed at Anzio on January 22, 1944, the attack on the Winter Line gained little.

Rushing reserves to Anzio, Field Marshal Kesselring quickly erected a firm perimeter about the Allied beachhead and successfully resisted every attempt at breakout. On February 16 Kesselring launched a determined attack to eliminate the beachhead that only a magnificent defense by U.S. and British infantry supported by artillery, tanks, planes, and naval gunfire at last thwarted.

Through the rest of the winter and early spring, the Fifth and Eighth Armies regrouped and built their combined strength to twenty-five divisions, mainly with the addition of French and British Commonwealth troops. General Eisenhower, meanwhile, had relinquished command in the Mediterranean early in January to go to Britain in preparation for the coming invasion of France. He was succeeded by a Britisher, Field Marshal Sir Henry M. Wilson.

On May 11 the Fifth and Eighth Armies launched a new carefully synchronized attack to break the Winter Line. Passing through almost trackless mountains, French troops under General Clark's command scored a penetration that unhinged the German position. As the Germans began to fall back toward Rome, the VI Corps attacked from the Anzio beachhead but failed to make sufficient progress to cut the enemy's routes of withdrawal. On June 4, 1944, U.S. troops entered Rome.

With D-day in Normandy only two days off, the focus of the Allied war against Germany shifted to France, and with the shift came a gradual diminution of Allied strength in Italy. Allied forces nevertheless continued to pursue the principle of the offensive. Reaching a new German position in the Northern Apennines, the Gothic Line, they started in August a three-month campaign that achieved penetrations, but they were unable to break out of the mountains. This period also saw a change in command as General Clark became commander of the Allied army group and Lt. Gen. Lucian K. Truscott assumed command of the Fifth Army.

In the spring of 1945 the Fifth and Eighth Armies penetrated a final German defensive line to enter the fertile plains of the Po River valley. On May 2, the Germans in Italy surrendered, the first formal capitulation of the war.

A German Trench on the Gothic Line, *overlooking a circling road.*

Less generally acclaimed than other phases of World War II, the campaign in Italy nevertheless had a vital part in the overall conduct of the war. At the crucial time of the Normandy landings, Allied troops in Italy were tying down twenty-six German divisions that well might have upset the balance in France. As a result of this campaign, the Allies obtained airfields useful for strategic bombardment of Germany and the Balkans, and conquest of the peninsula further guaranteed the safety of Allied shipping in the Mediterranean.

Cross-Channel Attack

Even as the Allied ground campaign was proceeding on the shores of the Mediterranean, three other campaigns were under way from the British Isles—the campaign of the U.S. Navy and the Royal Navy to defeat the German submarine, a U.S.-British strategic bombing offensive against Germany, and a third, intricately tied in with the other two, a logistical marathon to assemble the men and tools necessary for a direct assault against the foe.

Most critical of all was the antisubmarine campaign, for without success in that, the two others could progress only feebly at best. The turning point in that campaign came in April 1943, when the full effect of all the various devices used against the U-boat began to be apparent. Despite German introduction of an acoustical torpedo that homed on the noise of an escort's propellers, and later of the *schnorkel*, a steel tube extending above water by means of which the U-boat could charge its batteries without surfacing, Allied shipping losses continued to decline. In the last two years of the war the submarines would sink only one-seventh of the shipping they did in the earlier years.

In the second campaign, the combined bomber offensive that U.S. and British chiefs at Casablanca had directed, the demands of the war in the Pacific and the Mediterranean slowed American participation. Not until the summer of 1943 were sufficient U.S. bombers available in Britain to make a substantial contribution, and not until February 1944 were U.S. airmen at last able to match the big thousand-plane raids of the British.

While the Royal Air Force struck by night, bombers of the U.S. Army Air Forces hit by day, both directing much of their attention to the German aircraft industry in an effort to cripple the German air arm before the invasion. Although the raids imposed delays on German production, the most telling effect was the loss of German fighter aircraft and trained pilots rising to oppose the Allied bombers. As time for the invasion approached, the German air arm had ceased to represent a real threat to Allied ground operations, and Allied bombers could shift their attention to transportation facilities in France in an effort to restrict the enemy's ability to move reserves against the invasion.

The logistical build-up in the British Isles, meanwhile, had been progressing at an ever-increasing pace, easily the most tremendous single logistical undertaking of all time. The program entailed transporting some 1,600,000 men across the submarine-infested Atlantic before D-day and providing for their shelter, hospitalization, supply, training, and general welfare. Mountains of weapons and equipment, ranging from locomotives and big bombers to dental fillings, also had to be shipped.

Planning for the invasion had begun long before as the British, standing alone, looked to the day when they might return to the Continent. Detailed planning began in 1943 when the Combined Chiefs of Staff appointed a Britisher, Lt. Gen. Frederick E. Morgan, as chief of staff to a supreme commander yet to be named. Under Morgan's direction, British and American officers drew up plans for several contingencies, one of which, Operation OVERLORD, anticipated a large-scale assault against a still powerful German Army. This plan served as the basis for a final plan developed early in 1944 after General Eisenhower, designated as the supreme commander, arrived in Britain and established his command, Supreme Headquarters, Allied Expeditionary Force, or SHAEF.

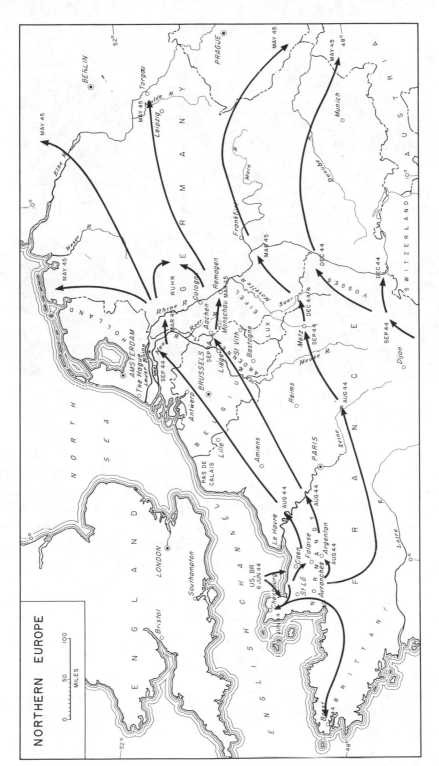

NORTHERN EUROPE

MILES
0   50   100

MAP 41

GENERAL EISENHOWER TALKING TO PARATROOPERS *before their drop behind the Normandy beaches.*

The over-all ground commander for the invasion was the former head of the British Eighth Army, General Montgomery, who also commanded the 21 Army Group, the controlling headquarters for the two Allied armies scheduled to make the invasion. The British Second Army under Lt. Gen. Sir Miles C. Dempsey was to assault on the left; the First U.S. Army under Bradley (promoted now to lieutenant general) on the right.

A requirement that the invasion beaches had to be within easy range of fighter aircraft based in Britain and close to at least one major port sharply limited the choice. The state of German defenses imposed further limitations, leaving only one logical site, the base of the Cotentin peninsula in Normandy, southeast of Cherbourg. (*Map 41*) To facilitate supply until Cherbourg or some other port could be opened, two artificial harbors were to be towed from Britain and emplaced off the invasion beaches.

Despite a weather forecast of high winds and a rough sea, General Eisenhower made a fateful decision to go ahead with the invasion on June 6. During the night over 5,000 ships moved to assigned positions, and at two o'clock, the

U.S. Troops Moving Ashore at Omaha Beach on D-Day

morning of the 6th, the operation for which the world had long and anxiously waited opened. One British and two U.S. airborne divisions (the 82d and 101st) dropped behind the beaches to secure routes of egress for the seaborne forces. Following preliminary aerial and naval bombardment, the first waves of infantry and tanks began to touch down at 6:30, just after sunrise. A heavy surf made the landings difficult but, as in Sicily, put the defenders off their guard.

The assault went well on British beaches, where one Canadian and two British divisions landed, and also at UTAH, westernmost of the U.S. beaches, where the 4th Division came ashore. The story was different at OMAHA Beach; there an elite German division occupying high bluffs laced with pillboxes put the landings in jeopardy. Allied intelligence had detected the presence of the enemy division too late to alter the landing plan. Only through improvisation and personal courage were the men of two regiments of the 1st Division and one of the 29th at last able to work their way up the bluffs and move slowly inland. Some 50,000 U.S. troops nevertheless made their way ashore on the two beaches before the day was out. American casualties were approximately 6,500, British and Canadian, 4,000—in both cases lighter than expected.

The German command was slow to react to the invasion, having been misled not only by the weather but also by an Allied deception plan which continued to lead the Germans to believe that this was only a diversionary assault, that the main landings were to come later on the Pas de Calais. Only in one instance, against the British who were solidly ashore, did the Germans mount a sizable counterattack on D-day.

Build-up and Breakout

While Allied aircraft and French resistance fighters impeded the movement of German reserves, the Allies quickly built up their strength and linked the beachheads. U.S. troops then moved against Cherbourg, taking the port, after bitter fighting, three weeks following the invasion. Other Allied forces had in the meantime been deepening the beachhead between Caen and the road center of St. Lô, so that by the end of June the most forward positions were twenty miles from the sea, and the Germans still had been able to mount no major counterattack.

Commanded by Field Marshal Gerd von Rundstedt, the Germans nevertheless defended tenaciously in terrain ideally suited to the defense. This was hedgerow country, where through the centuries French farmers had erected high banks of earth around every small field to fence livestock and protect crops from coastal winds. These banks were thick with the roots of shrubs and trees, and in many places sunken roads screened by a canopy of tree branches ran between two hedgerows. Tunneling into the hedgerows and using the sunken roads for lines of communication, the Germans turned each field into a small fortress.

For all the slow advance and lack of ports (a gale on June 19 demolished one of the artificial harbors and damaged the other), the Allied build-up was swift. By the end of June close to a million men had come ashore, along with some 586,000 tons of supplies and 177,000 vehicles. General Bradley's First Army included four corps with 2 armored and 11 infantry divisions. British strength was about the same.

Seeking to end the battle of the hedgerows, the British attempted to break into more open country near Caen, only to be thwarted by concentrations of German armor. General Bradley then tried a breakout on the right near St. Lô. Behind an intensive aerial bombardment that utilized both tactical aircraft and heavy bombers, the First Army attacked on July 25. By the second day American troops had opened a big breach in German positions, whereupon armored divisions drove rapidly southward twenty-five miles to Avranches at the base of the Cotentin peninsula. While the First Army turned southeastward, the

Third U.S. Army under General Patton entered the line to swing through Avranches into Brittany in quest of ports.

The arrival of the Third Army signaled a major change in command. General Bradley moved up to command the 12th Army Group, composed of the First and Third Armies, while his former deputy, Lt. Gen. Courtney H. Hodges, assumed command of the First Army. Montgomery's 21 Army Group consisted of the British Second Army and a newcomer to the front, the First Canadian Army under Lt. Gen. Henry D. G. Crerar. General Montgomery continued to function as overall ground commander, an arrangement that was to prevail for another five weeks until General Eisenhower moved his headquarters to the Continent and assumed direct command of the armies in the field.

In terms of the preinvasion plan, General Eisenhower intended establishing a solid lodgment area in France extending as far east as the Seine River to provide room for air and supply bases. Having built up strength in this area, he planned then to advance into Germany on a broad front. Under Montgomery's 21 Army Group, he would concentrate his greatest resources north of the Ardennes region of Belgium along the most direct route to the Ruhr industrial region, Germany's largest complex of mines and industry. Bradley's 12th Army Group, meanwhile, was to make a subsidiary thrust south of the Ardennes to seize the Saar industrial region along the Franco-German frontier. A third force invading southern France in August was to provide protection on Bradley's right.

The First Army's breakout from the hedgerows changed that plan, for it opened the German armies in France to crushing defeat. When the Germans counterattacked toward Avranches to try to cut off leading columns of the First and Third Armies, other men of the First Army held firm, setting up an opportunity for exploiting the principle of maneuver to the fullest. While the First Canadian Army attacked toward Falaise, General Bradley directed mobile columns of both the First and Third Armies on a wide encircling maneuver in the direction of Argentan, not far from Falaise. This caught the enemy's counterattacking force in a giant pocket. Although a 15-mile gap between Falaise and Argentan was closed only after many of the Germans escaped, more than 60,000 were killed or captured in the pocket. Great masses of German guns, tanks, and equipment fell into Allied hands.

While the First Army finished the business at Argentan, Patton's Third Army dashed off again toward the Seine River, with two objects: eliminating the Seine as a likely new line of German defense and making a second, wider envelopment to trap those German troops that had escaped from the first pocket. Both Patton accomplished. In the two pockets the enemy lost large segments of two field armies.

Invasion of Southern France

Even as General Eisenhower's armies were scoring a great victory in Normandy, the Allies on August 15 staged another invasion, this one in southern France (Operation DRAGOON) to provide a supplementary line of communications through the French Mediterranean ports and to prevent the Germans in the south from moving against the main Allied armies in the north. Lack of landing craft had precluded launching this invasion at the same time as OVERLORD.

Under control of the Seventh U.S. Army, commanded now by Lt. Gen. Alexander M. Patch, three U.S. divisions, plus an airborne task force and French commandos, began landing just after dawn. Defending Germans were spread too thin to provide much more than token resistance, and by the end of the first day the Seventh Army had 86,000 men and 12,000 vehicles ashore. The next day French troops staged a second landing and moved swiftly to seize the ports of Toulon and Marseille.

Faced with entrapment by the spectacular Allied advances in the north, the Germans in southern France began on August 17 to withdraw. U.S. and French columns followed closely and on September 11 established contact with Patton's Third Army. Under the 6th Army Group, commanded by Lt. Gen. Jacob L. Devers, the Seventh Army and French forces organized as the 1st French Army passed to General Eisenhower's command.

Pursuit to the Frontier

As Allied columns were breaking loose all over France, men and women of the French resistance movement began to battle the Germans in the streets of the capital. Although General Eisenhower had intended to bypass Paris, hoping to avoid heavy fighting in the city and to postpone the necessity of feeding the civilian population, he felt impelled to send help lest the uprising be defeated. On August 25 a column including U.S. and French troops entered the city.

With surviving German forces falling back in defeat toward the German frontier, General Eisenhower abandoned the original plan of holding at the Seine while he opened the Brittany ports and established a sound logistical base. Determined to take advantage of the enemy's defeat, he reinforced Montgomery's 21 Army Group by sending the First U.S. Army close alongside the British, thus providing enough strength in the northern thrust to assure quick capture of ports along the English Channel, particularly the great Belgian port of Antwerp. Because the front was fast moving away from Brittany, the Channel ports were essential.

Ports posed a special problem, for with the stormy weather of fall and winter approaching, the Allies could not much longer depend upon supply over the invasion beaches, and Cherbourg had only a limited capacity. Even though Brittany now was far behind the advancing front, General Eisenhower still felt a need for the port of Brest. He put those troops of the Third Army that had driven into the peninsula under a new headquarters, the Ninth U.S. Army commanded by Lt. Gen. William H. Simpson, and set them to the task. When Brest fell two weeks later, the port was a shambles. The port problem nevertheless appeared to be solved when on September 4 British troops took Antwerp, its wharves and docks intact; but the success proved to be illusory. Antwerp is on an estuary sixty miles from the sea, and German troops clung to the banks, denying access to Allied shipping.

The port situation was symptomatic of multitudinous problems that had begun to beset the entire Allied logistical apparatus (organized much like Pershing's Services of Supply, but called the Communications Zone). The armies were going so far and so fast that the supply services were unable to keep pace. Although enough supplies were available in Normandy, the problem was to get them to forward positions that sometimes were more than 500 miles beyond the depots. Despite extraordinary measures such as establishing a one-way truck route called the Red Ball Express, supplies of such essential commodities as gasoline and ammunition began to run short. This was the penalty the Allied armies would have to pay for the decision to make no pause at the Seine.

The logistical crisis sparked a difference over strategy between General Eisenhower and General Montgomery. In view of the logistical difficulties, Montgomery insisted that General Patton's Third Army should halt in order that all transportation resources might be concentrated behind his troops and the First Army. This allocation, he believed, would enable him to make a quick strike deep into Germany and impel German surrender.

Acting on the advice of logistical experts on his staff, General Eisenhower refused. Such a drive could succeed, his staff advised, only if all Allied armies had closed up to the Rhine River and if Antwerp were open to Allied shipping. The only choice, General Eisenhower believed, was to keep pushing all along the line while supplies held out, ideally to go so far as to gain bridgeheads over the Rhine.

There were obstacles other than supply standing in the way of that goal. Some were natural, like the Moselle and Meuse Rivers, the Vosges Mountains in Alsace, the wooded hills of the Ardennes, and a dense Huertgen Forest facing the First Army near Aachen. Others were man made, old French forts around Metz and the French Maginot Line in northeastern France, as well as dense fortifications all along the German border—the Siegfried Line, or, as the Germans called it, the West Wall. By mid-September the First Army had penetrated the West Wall at several points but lacked the means to exploit the breaks.

Although General Eisenhower assigned first priority to clearing the seaward approaches to Antwerp, he sanctioned a Montgomery proposal to use Allied airborne troops in a last bold stroke to capitalize on German disorganization before logistics should force a halt. While the British Second Army launched an attack called Operation GARDEN, airborne troops of a recently organized First Allied Airborne Army (Lt. Gen. Lewis H. Brereton) were to land in Operation MARKET astride three major water obstacles in the Netherlands—the Maas, Waal, and Lower Rhine Rivers. Crossing these rivers on bridges to be secured by the airborne troops, the Second Army was to drive all the way to the IJssel Meer (Zuider Zee), cutting off Germans farther west and putting the British in a position to outflank the West Wall and drive into Germany along a relatively open north German plain.

Employing one British and two U.S. airborne divisions, the airborne attack began on September 17. On the first day alone approximately 20,000 paratroopers and glider troops landed in the largest airborne attack of the war. Although the drops were spectacularly successful and achieved complete surprise, the chance presence of two panzer divisions near the drop zones enabled the Germans to react swiftly. Resistance to the ground attack also was greater than expected, delaying quick link-up with the airheads. The combined operation gained a salient some fifty miles deep into German-held territory but fell short of the ambitious objectives, including a bridgehead across the Lower Rhine.

At this point, Montgomery (promoted now to field marshal) concentrated on opening Antwerp to Allied shipping, but so determined was German resistance and so difficult the conditions of mud and flood in the low-lying countryside that it was well into November before the job was finished. The first Allied ship dropped anchor in Antwerp only on November 28.

As a result of a cutback in offensive operations and extraordinary efforts of the supply services, the logistical situation had been gradually improving. In early November resources were sufficient to enable the U.S. armies to launch a big offensive aimed at reaching the Rhine; but, despite the largest air attack in direct support of ground troops to be made during the war (Operation QUEEN), it turned out to be a slow, arduous fight through the natural and artificial obstacles along the frontier. Heavy rain and severe cold added to the difficulties. By mid-December the First and Ninth Armies had reached the Roer River east of Aachen, twenty-three miles inside Germany, and the Third Army had come up to the West Wall along the Saar River northeast of Metz, but only the Seventh Army and the 1st French Army in Alsace had touched any part of the Rhine.

Having taken advantage of the pause imposed by Allied logistical problems to create new divisions and rush replacements to the front, the Germans in the west had made a remarkable recovery from the debacle in France. Just how remarkable was soon to be forcefully demonstrated in what had heretofore been a quiet sector held by the First Army's right wing.

The Ardennes Counteroffensive

As early as the preceding August, Adolf Hitler had been contemplating a counteroffensive to regain the initiative in the west and compel the Allies to settle for a negotiated peace. Over the protests of his generals, who thought the plan too ambitious, he ordered an attack by twenty-five divisions, carefully conserved and secretly assembled, to hit thinly manned U.S. positions in the Ardennes region of Belgium and Luxembourg, cross the Meuse River, and push on northwestward to Antwerp. In taking Antwerp, Hitler expected to cut off the British 21 Army Group and the First and Ninth U.S. Armies.

Under cover of inclement winter weather, Hitler concentrated his forces in the forests of the Eifel region, opposite the Ardennes. Before daylight on December 16, the Germans attacked along a 60-mile front, taking the VIII Corps and the south wing of the V Corps by surprise. In most places, German gains were rapid, for the American divisions were either inexperienced or seriously depleted from earlier fighting, and all were stretched thin.

The Germans nevertheless encountered difficulties from the first. Cut off and surrounded, small U.S. units continued to fight. At the northern shoulder of the penetration, divisions of the V Corps refused to budge from the vicinity of Monschau, thereby denying critical roads to the enemy and limiting the width of the penetration. At St. Vith American troops held out for six days to block a vital road center. To Bastogne to the southwest, where an armored detachment served as a blocking force, General Eisenhower rushed an airborne division which never relinquished that communications center even though

First Army Men Setting Up a 57–mm. Antitank Gun

surrounded. Here Brig. Gen. Anthony C. McAuliffe delivered a terse one-word reply to a German demand for surrender: "Nuts!"

Denied important roads and hampered by air attacks as the weather cleared, the Germans fell a few miles short of even their first objective, the Meuse River. The result after more than a month of hard fighting that cost the Americans 75,000 casualties and the Germans close to 100,000 was nothing but a big bulge in the lines, from which the battle drew its popular name.

Faced with a shortage of infantry replacements during the enemy's counteroffensive General Eisenhower offered Negro soldiers in service units an opportunity to volunteer for duty with the infantry. More than 4,500 responded, many taking reductions in grade in order to meet specified requirements. The 6th Army Group formed these men into provisional companies, while the 12th Army Group employed them as an additional platoon in existing rifle companies. The excellent record established by these volunteers, particularly those serving as platoons, presaged major postwar changes in the traditional approach to employing Negro troops.

Although the counteroffensive had given the Allied command some anxious moments, the gallant stands by isolated units had provided time for the First and Ninth Armies to shift troops against the northern flank of the penetration and for the Third Army to hit the penetration from the south and drive through to beleaguered Bastogne. A rapid shift and change in direction of attack by the Third Army was one of the more noteworthy instances during the war of successful employment of the principle of maneuver.

By the end of January 1945, U.S. units had retaken all lost ground and had thwarted a lesser German attack against the 6th Army Group in Alsace. The Germans having expended irreplaceable reserves, the end of the war in Europe was in sight.

The Russian Campaigns

Much of the hope for an early end to the war rested with tremendous successes of the Soviet armies in the east. Having stopped the invading Germans at the gates of Moscow in late 1941 and at Stalingrad in late 1942, the Russians had made great offensive strides westward in both 1943 and 1944. Only a few days after D-day in Normandy the Red Army had launched a massive offensive which by mid-September had reached East Prussia and the gates of the Polish capital of Warsaw. In January 1945, as U.S. troops eliminated the bulge in the Ardennes, the Red Army started a new drive that was to carry to the Oder River, only forty miles from Berlin.

Far greater masses of troops were employed in the east than in the west over vast distances and a much wider front. The Germans had to maintain more than two million combat troops on the Eastern Front as compared with less than a million on the Western Front. Yet the Soviet contribution was less disproportionate than would appear at first glance, for the war in the east was a one-front ground war, whereas the Allies in the west were fighting on two ground fronts and conducting major campaigns in the air and at sea, as well as making a large commitment in the war against Japan. At the same time, the United States was contributing enormously to the war in Russia through lend-lease—almost $11 billion in materials, including over 400,000 jeeps and trucks, 12,000 armored vehicles (including 7,000 tanks, enough to equip some 20-odd U.S. armored divisions), 14,000 aircraft, and 1.75 million tons of food.

The Final Offensive

Soon after the opening of the Soviet January offensive, the Western Allies began a new drive to reach and cross the Rhine, the last barrier to the industrial heart of Germany. Exhausted by the overambitious effort in the Ardennes and forced to shift divisions to oppose the Russians, the Germans had little chance of holding west of the Rhine. Although Field Marshal von Rundstedt wanted to conserve his remaining strength for a defense of the river, Hitler would authorize no withdrawal. Making a strong stand at the Roer River and at places where the West Wall remained intact, the Germans imposed some delay but paid dearly in the process, losing 250,000 troops that could have been used to better advantage on the Rhine.

Falling back behind the river, the Germans had made careful plans to destroy all bridges, but something went amiss at the Ludendorff railroad bridge in the First Army's sector at Remagen. On March 7 a task force of the 9th Armored Division found the bridge damaged but passable. Displaying initiative and courage, a company of infantry dashed across. Higher commanders acted promptly to reinforce the foothold.

To the south, a division of the Third Army on March 22 made a surprise crossing of the Rhine in assault boats. Beginning late the next day the 21 Army Group and the Ninth U.S. Army staged a full-dress crossing of the lower reaches of the river, complete with an airborne attack rivaling in its dimensions Operation MARKET. The Third Army then made two more assault crossings, and during the last few days of March both the Seventh Army and the 1st French Army of the 6th Army Group crossed farther upstream. Having expended most of their resources west of the river, the Germans were powerless to defeat any Allied crossing attempt.

As the month of April opened, Allied armies fanned out from the Rhine all along the line with massive columns of armor and motorized infantry. Encircling the Ruhr, the First and Ninth Armies took 325,000 prisoners, totally destroying an entire German army group. Although the Germans managed to rally determined resistance at isolated points, a cohesive defensive line ceased to exist.

Since the Russians were within forty miles of Berlin and apparently would reach the German capital first, General Eisenhower put the main weight of the continuing drive behind U.S. armies moving through central Germany to eliminate a remaining pocket of German industry and to link with the Russians. The 21 Army Group meanwhile sealed off the Netherlands and headed toward the base of the Jutland peninsula, while the 6th Army Group turned southeast-ward to obviate any effort by the Nazis to make a last-ditch stand in the Alps of southern Germany and Austria.

By mid-April Allied armies in the north and center were building up along the Elbe and Mulde Rivers, an agreed line of contact with the Red Army approaching from the east. First contact came on April 25 near the town of Torgau, followed by wholesale German surrenders all along the front and in Italy.

With Berlin in Soviet hands, Hitler a suicide, and almost every corner of Germany overrun, emissaries of the German Government surrendered on May 7 at General Eisenhower's headquarters in Reims, France. The next day, May 8, was V–E Day, the official date of the end of the war in Europe.

The Situation on V–E Day

As V–E Day came, Allied forces in Western Europe consisted of 4½ million men, including 9 armies (5 of them American—one of which, the Fifteenth, saw action only at the last), 23 corps, 91 divisions (61 of them American), 6 tactical air commands (4 American), and 2 strategic air forces (1 American). The Allies had 28,000 combat aircraft, of which 14,845 were American, and they had brought into Western Europe more than 970,000 vehicles and 18 million tons of supplies. At the same time they were achieving final victory in Italy with 18 divisions (7 of them American).

The German armed forces and the nation were prostrate, beaten to a degree never before seen in modern times. Hardly any organized units of the German Army remained except in Norway, Czechoslovakia, and the Balkans, and these would soon capitulate. What remained of the air arm was too demoralized even for a final suicidal effort, and the residue of the German Navy lay helpless in captured northern ports. Through five years of war, the German armed forces had lost over 3 million men killed, 263,000 of them in the west, since D-day. The United States lost 135,576 dead in Western Europe, while Britain, Canada, France, and other Allies incurred after D-day approximately 60,000 military deaths.

Unlike in World War I, when the United States had come late on the scene and provided only those forces to swing the balance of power to the Allied side, the American contribution to the reconquest of Western Europe had been predominant, not just in manpower but as a true arsenal of democracy. American factories produced for the British almost three times more lend-lease materials than for the Russians, including 185,000 vehicles, 12,000 tanks, and enough planes to equip four tactical air forces, and for the French, all weapons and equipment for 8 divisions and 1 tactical air force, plus partial equipment for 3 more divisions.

Although strategic air power had failed to prove the decisive instrument many had expected, it was a major factor in the Allied victory, as was the role of Allied navies, for without control of the sea lanes, there could have been no build-up in Britain and no amphibious assaults. It was nonetheless true that the application of the power of ground armies finally broke the German ability and will to resist.

While the Germans had developed a flying bomb and later a supersonic missile, the weapons with which both sides fought the war were in the main much improved versions of those that had been present in World War I—the motor vehicle, the airplane, the machine gun, indirect fire artillery, the tank. The difference lay in such accouterments as excellent radio communications and in a new sophistication, particularly in terms of mobility, that provided the means for rapid exploitation that both sides in World War I had lacked.

From North Africa to the Elbe, U.S. Army generalship proved remarkably effective. Such field commanders as Bradley, Devers, Clark, Hodges, Patton, Simpson, Patch, and numerous corps and division commanders would stand beside the best that had ever served the nation. Having helped develop Army doctrine during the years between the two great wars, these same men put the theories to battlefield test with enormous success. Some indication of the magnitude of the responsibilities they carried is apparent from the fact that late in the war General Bradley as commander of the 12th Army Group had under his command four field armies, 12 corps, and 48 divisions, more than 1,300,000 men, the largest exclusively American field command in U.S. history.

These commanders throughout displayed a steady devotion to the principles of war. Despite sometimes seemingly insurmountable obstacles of weather, terrain, and enemy concentration, they were consistently able to achieve the mass, mobility, and firepower to avoid a stalemate, maintaining the principles of the objective and the offensive and exploiting the principle of maneuver to the fullest. On many occasions they achieved surprise, most notably in the amphibious assaults and at the Rhine. They were themselves taken by surprise twice, in central Tunisia and in the Ardennes, yet in both cases they recovered quickly. Economy of force was particularly evident in Italy, and simplicity was nowhere better demonstrated than in the Normandy landings, despite a complexity inherent in the size and diversity of the invasion forces. From the first, unity of command was present in every campaign, not just at the tactical level but also in the combined staff system that afforded the U.S. and Britain a unity of command and purpose never approached on the Axis side.

CHAPTER 13

World War II: The War Against Japan

In World War II, for the first time, the United States had to fight a war on two fronts. Though the central strategic principle governing allocation of resources to the two fronts provided for concentrating first on the defeat of the European Axis, on the American side this principle was liberally interpreted, permitting conduct of an offensive war against Japan as well as against Germany in the years 1943–45. The U.S. Fleet, expanding after its initial setback at Pearl Harbor much as the Army had, provided the main sinews for an offensive strategy in the Pacific, although the Army devoted at least one-third of its resources to the Pacific war, even at the height of war in Europe. In sum, the United States proved capable, once its resources were fully mobilized, of successfully waging offensives on two fronts simultaneously—a development the Japanese had not anticipated when they launched their attack on Pearl Harbor.

Japan's Strategy

Japan entered World War II with limited aims and with the intention of fighting a limited war. Its principal objectives were to secure the resources of Southeast Asia and much of China and to establish a "Greater East Asia Co-Prosperity Sphere" under Japanese hegemony. In 1895 and in 1905 Japan had gained important objectives without completely defeating China or Russia and in 1941 Japan sought to achieve its hegemony over East Asia in similar fashion. The operational strategy the Japanese adopted to start war, however, doomed their hopes of limiting the conflict. Japan believed it necessary to destroy or neutralize American striking power in the Pacific—the U.S. Pacific Fleet at Pearl Harbor and the U.S. Far East Air Force in the Philippines—before moving southward and eastward to occupy Malaya, the Netherlands Indies, the Philippines, Wake Island, Guam, the Gilbert Islands, Thailand, and Burma. Once in control of these areas, the Japanese intended to establish a defensive perimeter stretching from the Kurile Islands south through Wake, the Marianas, the Carolines, and the Marshalls and Gilberts to Rabaul on New Britain. From

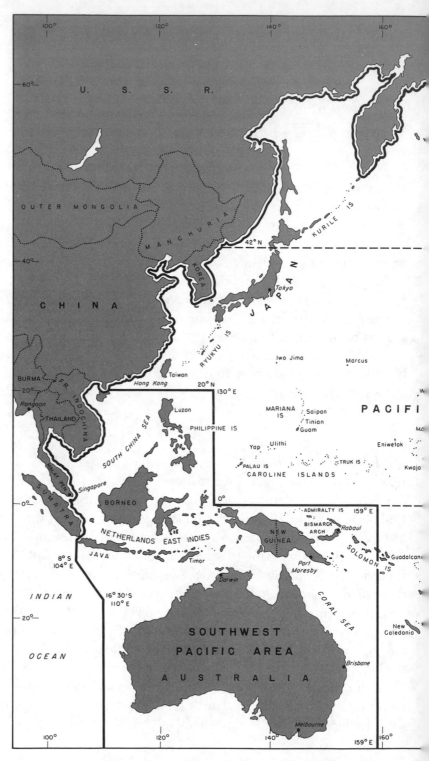

MAP 42

160°　　　　140°　　　　　120°

A L A S K A

CANADA

—60°

ska

TIAN ISLANDS

TH PACIFIC AREA

UNITED

STATES

42° N

—40°

San Francisco

H A W A I I A N　　I S L A N D S

Midway

Oahu

Pearl Harbor

—20°

O C E A N　　　　A R E A S

NTRAL PACIFIC AREA

0°

Canton

SOUTH PACIFIC AREA

SAMOA IS

FIJI IS

THE PACIFIC AREAS

I AUGUST 1942

0　　　500　　　1000
STATUTE MILES ON THE EQUATOR

W
AND

180°　　　　160°

Rabaul the perimeter would extend westward to northwestern New Guinea and would encompass the Indies, Malaya, Thailand, and Burma. Japan thought that the Allies would wear themselves out in fruitless frontal assaults against the perimeter and would ultimately settle for a negotiated peace that would leave it in possession of most of its conquests. (*Map 42*)

The Japanese were remarkably successful in the execution of their offensive plan and by early 1942 had reached their intended perimeter. But they miscalculated the effect of their surprise attack at Pearl Harbor which unified a divided people and aroused the United States to wage a total, not a limited, war. As a result Japan lost, in the long run, any chance of conducting the war on its own terms. The Allies, responding to their defeats, sought no negotiated peace, but immediately began to seek means to strike back. In February and March 1942 small carrier task forces of the Pacific Fleet hit the Marshalls, Wake, and Marcus, and bombers from Australia began to harass the Japanese base at Rabaul. In April Army bombers, flying off a naval carrier, delivered a hit-and-run raid on Tokyo. Meanwhile, the United States began to develop and fortify a line of communications across the southern Pacific to Australia and to strengthen the defenses of the "down-under" continent itself. These new bases, along with Alaska, Hawaii, and India, also strengthened during the period, could become the launching points for counteroffensives. And once the Allies became strong enough to threaten the Japanese defensive perimeter from several directions the Japanese would lose the advantage of interior lines, and with it the strategic initiative, for Japan did not have and could not produce the means to defend and hold at all points.

Perceiving their danger, the Japanese in a second phase offensive tried to sever the Allied lines of communications to Australia and to expand their perimeter in the Pacific. In the spring of 1942 they pushed southeast from Rabaul to Guadalcanal and Tulagi in the Solomons, and seized Attu and Kiska in the Aleutians. But they failed in their main effort to take Midway Island, northwest of Hawaii, and in the naval battles of the Coral Sea and Midway in May and June they lost the bulk of their best naval pilots and planes. Midway was the turning point, for it redressed the naval balance in the Pacific and gave the Allies the strategic initiative. The Japanese, with the mobility of their carrier striking forces curtailed, abandoned plans to cut the Allied South Pacific life line and turned instead to strengthening their defensive perimeter, planning to wage a protracted war of attrition in the hope of securing a negotiated peace.

Guadalcanal and Papua: The First Offensives

After Midway the U.S. Joint Chiefs, responsible for direction of the war in the Pacific, almost naturally turned to the elimination of the threat to their line of communications in the south as the objective of their first offensive. In so doing, they gave to American strategy in the Pacific a twist unanticipated in prewar planning, which had always presupposed that the main offensive in any war against Japan would be made directly across the Central Pacific from Hawaii toward the Philippines. The Joint Chiefs on July 2 directed Allied forces in the South and Southwest Pacific Areas to begin a series of operations aimed at the ultimate reduction of the Japanese stronghold at Rabaul on New Britain Island, thus establishing Allied control of the Bismarck Archipelago.

The campaign would consist of three stages or tasks. In Task One, forces of the South Pacific Area (under Vice Adm. Robert L. Ghormley until November 1942 and thereafter under Admiral William F. Halsey) would seize base sites in the southern Solomons. In Task Two, South Pacific forces would advance up the ladder of the Solomons while Southwest Pacific forces (under General MacArthur) would move up the north coast of New Guinea as far as Lae and Salamaua. In Task Three, the forces of the two theaters would converge on Rabaul and clear the rest of the Bismarck Archipelago. Task One was to be conducted under the general supervision of Admiral Chester W. Nimitz, whose vast Pacific Ocean Areas command included the North, Central, and South Pacific Areas as subtheaters. Tasks Two and Three would be executed under the strategic direction of General MacArthur. The Joint Chiefs of Staff, reserving to themselves final control of the assignment of tasks, allocation of resources, and timing of operations, would provide, in effect, unified command over Nimitz and MacArthur.

The offensive began on August 7, 1942, when the 1st Marine Division landed on Guadalcanal and nearby islands in the southern Solomons. The Japanese, taking full advantage of interior lines from their bases at Rabaul and Truk, reacted vigorously. Six times from August to the end of November they challenged American naval superiority in the South Pacific in a series of sharp surface engagements. Air battles were almost daily occurrences for a month or more after the landings, and the Japanese sent in strong ground reinforcements, gambling and ultimately losing substantial air and naval resources in the effort to hold Guadalcanal. The Americans had to reinforce heavily, deploying naval power, planes, soldiers, and marines in the battle at the expense of other theaters. Before the island was secured in November, another Marine

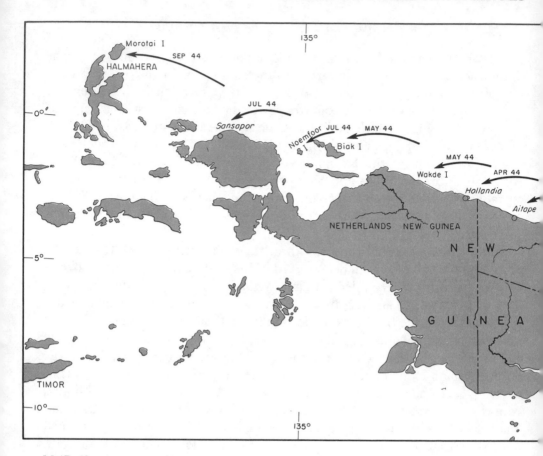

MAP 43

division (the 2d), two Army divisions (25th and American), and one separate regiment, to mention only the major ground combat elements, had been thrown into the battle. The last act came in February 1943, when the 43d Division moved into the Russell Islands, thirty-five miles northwest of Guadalcanal. On Guadalcanal and in the Russells, American forces then began to construct major air and logistical bases for further advances.

A Japanese overland drive toward Port Moresby in New Guinea had meanwhile forced General MacArthur to begin an offensive of his own—the Papua Campaign. (*Map 43*) During the late summer the Japanese had pushed across the towering Owen Stanley Mountains toward Port Moresby from the Buna-Gona area on New Guinea's northeastern coast, and by mid-September were only twenty miles from their objective. Australian ground forces drove the

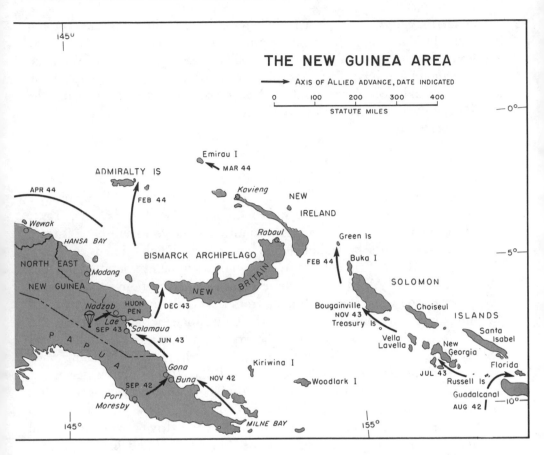

Japanese back to the north coast, where they strongly entrenched themselves around Buna and Gona. It took 2 Australian divisions, 1 U.S. Army division (32d), and another U.S. Army regiment almost four months of bitter fighting to dislodge the Japanese. Casualties were high, but as at Guadalcanal the Allied forces learned much about jungle fighting, the importance of air power, and the need for thorough logistical preparation. They also discovered that the Japanese soldier, though a skillful, stubborn, and fanatic foe, could be defeated. The myth of Japanese invincibility was forever laid to rest in the jungles of Guadalcanal and Papua.

After Papua and Guadalcanal the tempo of operations in the South and Southwest Pacific Areas slowed while General MacArthur and Admiral Halsey gathered resources and prepared bases for the next phase. The Japanese, in turn, undertook to reinforce their main bases in New Guinea and the northern Solomons. In March 1943 they attempted to send a large convoy to Lae in New Guinea but, in the Battle of the Bismarck Sea, lost some 3,500 troops and much valuable shipping, principally to Army land-based aircraft. During the following months Rabaul-based planes, reinforced by carrier planes flown in from the Carolines, sought unsuccessfully to knock out American air power in the southern Solomons.

Search for a Strategy

Meanwhile, in the spring and summer of 1943, a strategy for the defeat of Japan began to take shape within Allied councils. The major Allied objective was control of the South China Sea and a foothold on the coast of China, so as to sever Japanese lines of communications southward and to establish bases from which Japan could first be subjected to intensive aerial bombardment and naval blockade and then, if necessary, invaded. The first plans for attaining this objective envisioned Allied drives from several different directions—by American forces across the Pacific along two lines, from the South and Southwest toward the Philippines and from Hawaii across the Central Pacific; and by British and Chinese forces along two other lines, the first a land line through Burma and China and the second a sea line from India via the Netherlands Indies, Singapore, and the Strait of Malacca into the South China Sea. Within the framework of this tentative long-range plan, the U.S. Joint Chiefs fitted their existing plans for completion of the campaign against Rabaul, and a subsequent advance to the Philippines, and developed a plan for the second drive across the Central Pacific. They also, in 1942 and 1943, pressed the Chinese and British to get a drive under way in Burma to reopen the supply line to China in phase with their Pacific advances, offering extensive air and logistical support.

The North Pacific line running from Alaska through the Kuriles to the northernmost Japanese island of Hokkaido also beckoned in early 1943 as a possible additional avenue of approach to Japan. The Joint Chiefs decided, however, that although the Japanese perimeter should be pushed back in this area, the foggy, cold North Pacific with its rock-bound and craggy islands was not a profitable area in which to undertake a major offensive. In May 1943 the U.S. 7th Division went ashore on Attu and, after three weeks of costly fighting through icy muck and over wind-swept ridges in a cold, almost constant fog, destroyed the Japanese garrison. In August a combined American-Canadian expedition landed on Kiska, some distance away, only to find that the Japanese had evacuated the island three weeks earlier. With the Japanese perimeter pushed back to the Kuriles the Allied advance stopped, and further operations were limited to nuisance air raids against these Japanese-held islands. Ground forces used in the attacks on Attu and Kiska were redeployed to the Central Pacific, and some of the defensive forces deployed in Alaska were also freed for employment elsewhere.

Prospects of an advance through China to the coast faded rapidly in 1943. At the Casablanca Conference in January the Combined Chiefs agreed on an ambitious operation, called ANAKIM, to be launched in the fall of 1943 to retake Burma and reopen the supply line to China. ANAKIM was to include a British amphibious assault on Rangoon and an offensive into central Burma, plus an American-sponsored Chinese offensive in the north involving convergence of forces operating from China and India. ANAKIM proved too ambitious; even limited offensives in Southeast Asia were postponed time and again for lack of adequate resources. By late 1943 the Americans had concluded that their Pacific forces would reach the China coast before either British or Chinese forces could come in through the back door. At the SEXTANT Conference late in 1943 the Combined Chiefs agreed that the main effort against Japan should be concentrated in the Pacific along two lines of advance, with operations in the North Pacific, China, and Southeast Asia to be assigned subsidiary roles.

In this strategy the two lines of advance in the Pacific—the one across the Central Pacific via the Gilberts, Marshalls, Marianas, Carolines, and Palaus toward the Philippines or Formosa (Taiwan) and the other in the Southwest Pacific via the north coast of New Guinea to the Vogelkop and thence to the southern Philippines—were viewed as mutually supporting. (*Map 44*) Although the Joint Chiefs several times indicated a measure of preference for the Central Pacific as the area of main effort, they never established any real priority between the two lines, seeking instead to retain a flexibility that would permit striking blows along either line as opportunity offered. The Central Pacific route promised to force a naval showdown with the Japanese and, once the Marianas were secured, to provide bases from which the U.S. Army Air Forces' new B–29 bombers could strike the Japanese home islands. The Southwest Pacific route was shorter, if existing bases were taken into consideration, and offered more opportunity to employ land-based air power to full advantage. The target area for both drives, in the strategy approved at SEXTANT, was to be the Luzon-Formosa-China coast area. Within this area the natural goal of the Southwest Pacific drive was the Philippines, but that of the Central Pacific drive could be either the Philippines or Formosa. As the drives along the two lines got under way in earnest in 1944, the choice between the two became the central strategic issue.

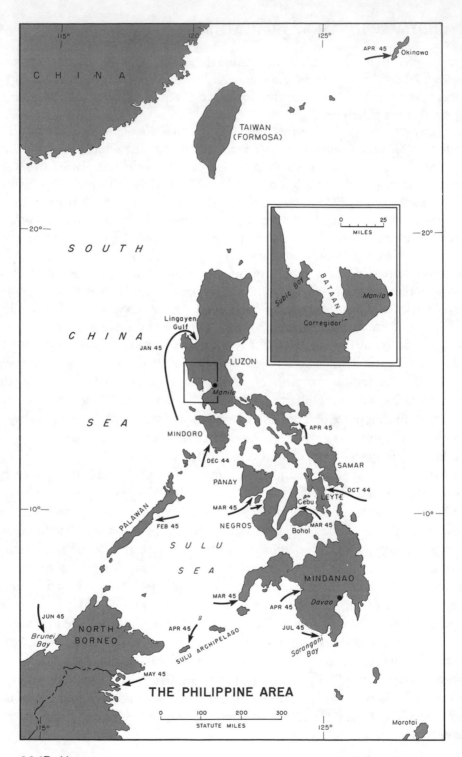

THE PHILIPPINE AREA

MAP 44

Cartwheel: The Encirclement of Rabaul

In June 1943 MacArthur and Halsey resumed their offensive to reduce the Japanese stronghold at Rabaul—a prerequisite to further advances along the Southwest Pacific axis toward the Philippines. The plan for the campaign provided for a carefully phased series of operations in each theater, each designed to secure a strategic position where air cover could be provided for further advances. The first of the series started in late June when MacArthur landed American troops on the Woodlark and Kiriwina Islands off eastern New Guinea and at Nassau Bay on the New Guinea coast, and Halsey's forces made their first landings on the New Georgia group in the Central Solomons. From these beginnings the operations proceeded up the ladder of the Solomons, along the coast of New Guinea, and across the straits to New Britain Island generally as scheduled, despite strong Japanese reaction.

In the Solomons by early August Army forces under Halsey had secured New Georgia with its important Munda airfield, but the campaign was not completed until October when U.S. and New Zealand troops occupied Vella Lavella, between New Georgia and Bougainville. At the end of October, New Zealanders and U.S. marines landed on Treasury and Choiseul Islands to secure bases for the assault on Bougainville; that assault got under way on November 1 when marines landed, followed soon after by the Army's 37th Division. In each phase of the Solomons campaign, the Japanese sought unsuccessfully to contest Allied air and naval supremacy, to land reinforcements, and to launch strong counterattacks against Allied beachheads, losing in the effort both planes and combat ships they could ill afford to spare. Air and naval losses suffered in the Solomons crippled the Japanese Fleet for months to come and helped to pave the way for the successful Central Pacific drive that got under way in November. With the repulse of the Japanese counterattack on Bougainville, by the end of November security of the American beachhead on that island was assured, permitting the development of a major American air base. With the taking of Bougainville, the main part of the South Pacific Area's task in Operation CARTWHEEL was completed.

MacArthur's forces meanwhile continued their offensives, with Australian troops carrying most of the burden in New Guinea. In early September the U.S. Army's 503d Parachute Regiment, in the first airborne operation of the Pacific war, seized an airfield at Nadzab, inland from Lae and Salamaua. Australian troops cleared Lae and Salamaua by mid-September and, flown into Nadzab, moved on to the Huon peninsula. Elements of the U.S. 32d Division landed at the western end of the peninsula in January 1944 in an attempt to trap a large Japanese force, but by the time Australian and American units had sealed the western exits to the peninsula most of the Japanese had escaped northwest to Hansa Bay and Wewak.

In the meantime, MacArthur and Halsey had assembled the forces to launch a final offensive toward Rabaul, but the Joint Chiefs decided that the actual seizure of that objective would be too costly in terms of men, equipment, and time. They preferred to encircle Rabaul, neutralize it by air bombardment, and push on to seize an offensive base farther west, in the Admiralty Islands. A new series of operations toward these ends started in MacArthur's theater on December 15, 1943, when U.S. Army units landed on the south coast of western New Britain, and on the 26th, the 1st Marine Division landed on the north coast. In mid-February 1944 New Zealand troops of the South Pacific Area secured an air base site on Green Island, north of Rabaul, and on the last day of the month MacArthur began landing the 1st Cavalry Division (an infantry unit retaining its former designation) on the Admiralties, closing the western and northwestern approaches to Rabaul. Marines under Halsey seized a final air base site on Emirau, north of Rabaul, on March 20, while Marine and Army units under MacArthur secured additional positions in western and central New Britain from March to May 1944. The major Japanese base at Rabaul, with its 100,000-man garrison, was as effectively out of the war as if it had been destroyed. In the process of encircling Rabaul, the Allies had also left to wither on the vine another important Japanese base at Kavieng on New Ireland, north of Rabaul.

In the last phase of the campaign against Rabaul, a pattern developed that came to characterize much of the war in the Pacific. The Allies would mount no frontal attacks against strongly entrenched Japanese forces if they could avoid it; they would not advance island by island across a vast ocean studded with myriad atolls and island groups. Rather, they would advance in great bounds, limited only by the range of land-based air cover or the availability of carrier-based air support. The Allies would deceive and surprise the Japanese; they would bypass major strongpoints and leave them reduced to strategic and tactical impotence.

The Central Pacific Drive Begins

The necessity for relying primarily on support of land-based aircraft curtailed the length of the jumps in the South and Southwest Pacific in 1943. The Navy's limited supply of aircraft carriers could not be employed to best advantage in the narrow waters around New Guinea and the Solomons. By mid-1943, however, new larger and faster carriers of the *Essex* class (27,000 tons) and lighter carriers of the *Independence* class (11,000 tons) were joining the Pacific

Fleet. Around these new carriers Admiral Nimitz built naval task forces tailored in each case to the particular operation at hand. The task forces consisted of a mix of carriers, destroyers, cruisers, battleships, submarines, minesweepers, and support craft. In the broad expanses of the Central Pacific, these air carrier task forces could provide both air and naval support for far longer leaps forward, while the entire Pacific Fleet stood ready to confront the main Japanese Fleet at any time it chose to give battle.

The Central Pacific drive got under way on November 20, 1943, when Nimitz sent Army and Marine forces to the Gilbert Islands to seize bases from which to support subsequent jumps into the Marshalls. Troops and supplies for the Gilberts loaded at Hawaii on newly developed assault shipping and sailed more than 2,000 miles to be set ashore by specially designed landing craft and amphibian vehicles. Makin, the Army objective, fell to the 27th Division after four days of hard fighting. Tarawa, where the 2d Marine Division went ashore, proved a bloody affair that provided a stiff test for American amphibious doctrine, techniques, and equipment. Naval gunfire vessels and carrier-based aircraft provided support during and after the assault.

The advance to the Gilberts disclosed that U.S. forces had not entirely mastered certain aspects of amphibious warfare, especially naval gunfire support, co-ordination of air support, and ship-to-shore communications. But valuable lessons were learned that, added to the earlier experiences of the South and Southwest Pacific Areas, established a pattern of island warfare which represented one of the major tactical developments of the war. First, air and naval forces isolated an objective and softened its defenses; simultaneously, joint forces would attack or feint toward other islands to deceive the Japanese. The approach of convoys carrying the ground assault forces to the main objective signaled the opening of final, intensive air and naval bombardment of the landing beaches. Whenever practicable, small forces occupied neighboring islands as sites for land-based artillery. Under cover of all these supporting fires, the landing forces moved from ship to shore in echelons, or waves, rocket-firing landing craft in the lead and amphibian tanks and tractors following to carry the assault troops directly onto the beaches and inland. Finally came landing craft with more infantry and with tanks, artillery, and supporting troops. Supplies followed rapidly as the assault forces secured and expanded the beachhead. Amphibious techniques were refined and modified to some extent after the Gilberts, but the lessons learned there made it unnecessary to effect any radical changes in amphibious doctrine throughout the rest of the war.

The Japanese did not react strongly to the loss of the Gilberts, and at the end of January 1944 Nimitz' Army and Marine forces moved into the eastern and central Marshalls to seize Majuro and Kwajalein. The strength employed in this operation proved so preponderant and Japanese defenses so weak that Nimitz was able to accelerate his next advance by two and a half months, and on February 17 landed Marine and Army units on Eniwetok Atoll in the western Marshalls. Concurrently, he conducted a long-awaited carrier strike against Truk in the central Carolines, considered Japan's key bastion in the Central Pacific. The raid revealed that the Japanese had virtually abandoned Truk as a naval base, and the capture of the atoll, set for June, no longer appeared necessary. Nimitz then drew up plans to invade the Marianas in mid-June and move on to the western Carolines and Palaus in mid-September, again accelerating the pace of the advance.

Acceleration of the Pacific Drive

General MacArthur had also pushed forward the Southwest Pacific Area's timetable. Having landed in the Admiralties a month ahead of his original schedule, he proposed to cancel operations against Hansa Bay and Wewak on the northeast coast of New Guinea in favor of a jump to Hollandia and Aitape, on the north-central coast, in April, two months earlier than previously planned. He would then continue northwestward along the coast in a campaign entailing the steady extension of land-based air cover by the seizure of successive air base sites until he reached the Vogelkop, at the eastern end of New Guinea, and then proceed to Mindanao, southernmost of the Philippine Islands.

The Joint Chiefs, quickly seizing the fruits of their strategy of opportunism, on March 12, 1944, rearranged the schedule of major Pacific operations. They provided for the assault by MacArthur's forces on Hollandia and Aitape in April with the support of a carrier task force from the Pacific Fleet, to be followed by Nimitz's move into the Marianas in June and into the Palaus in September. While Nimitz was employing the major units of the Pacific Fleet in these ventures, MacArthur was to continue his advance along the New Guinea coast with the forces at his disposal. In November, he was again to have the support of main units of the Pacific Fleet in an assault on Mindanao. Refusing yet to make a positive choice of what was to follow, the Joint Chiefs directed MacArthur to plan for the invasion of Luzon and Nimitz to plan for the invasion of Formosa early in 1945.

The March 12 directive served as a blueprint for an accelerated drive in the Pacific in the spring and summer of 1944. On April 22 Army forces under MacArthur landed at Hollandia and Aitape. At neither place was the issue ever in doubt, although during July the Japanese who had been bypassed at Wewak launched an abortive counterattack against Aitape. Protected by land-based aircraft from Hollandia, MacArthur's Army units next jumped 125 miles northwest on May 17 to seize another air base site at Wakde Island, landing first on the New Guinea mainland opposite the chief objective. A ground campaign of about a month and a half ensued against a Japanese division on the mainland, but, without waiting for the outcome of the fight, other Army troops carried the advance northwestward on May 27 another 180 miles to Biak Island.

As this point the wisdom of conducting twin drives across the Pacific emerged. The Japanese Navy was preparing for a showdown battle it expected to develop off the Marianas in June. MacArthur's move to Biak put land-based planes in position to keep under surveillance and to harry the Japanese Fleet, which was assembling in Philippine waters before moving into the Central Pacific. Reckoning an American-controlled Biak an unacceptable threat to their flank, the Japanese risked major elements of their fleet to send strong reinforcements to Biak in an attempt to drive MacArthur's forces off the island. They also deployed to bases within range of Biak about half their land-based air strength from the Marianas, Carolines, and Palaus—planes upon which their fleet depended for support during the forthcoming battle off the Marianas.

After two partially successful attempts to reinforce Biak, the Japanese assembled for a third try enough naval strength to overwhelm local American naval units; but just as the formidable force was moving toward Biak the Japanese learned the U.S. Pacific Fleet was off the Marianas. They hastily assembled their naval forces and sailed northwestward for the engagement known as the Battle of the Philippine Sea. Having lost their chance to surprise the U.S. Navy, handicapped by belated deployment, and deprived of anticipated land-based air support, the Japanese suffered another shattering naval defeat. This defeat, which assured the success of the invasions of both Biak and the Marianas, illustrates well the interdependence of operations in the two Pacific areas. It also again demonstrated that the U.S. Pacific Fleet's carrier task forces were the decisive element in the Pacific war.

Army and Marine divisions under Nimitz landed on Saipan in the Marianas on June 15, 1944, to begin a bloody three-week battle for control of the island. Next, on July 21, Army and Marine units invaded Guam, 100 miles south of Saipan, and three days later marines moved on to Tinian Island. An important turning point of the Pacific war, the American seizure of the Marianas brought the Japanese home islands within reach of the U.S. Army Air Forces' B-29 bombers, which in late November began to fly missions against the Japanese homeland.

At Biak Japanese resistance delayed capture of the best airfield sites until late June. On July 2, MacArthur's Army forces moved on to Noemfoor Island, ninety miles to the west, in a combined parachute-amphibious operation designed to broaden the base of the Southwest Pacific's air deployment. On July 30 the 6th Division continued on to the northwestern tip of New Guinea to secure another air base, and on September 15 MacArthur landed the reinforced 31st Division on Morotai Island, between New Guinea and Mindanao in the Philippines. On the same day Nimitz sent the 1st Marine Division ashore on Peleliu in the southern Palaus, and on the 17th the 81st Division from Nimitz' command landed on Angaur, just south of Peleliu. A regimental combat team of the 81st Division secured Ulithi Atoll, midway between Peleliu and the Marianas, without opposition on September 23.

With these landings the approach to the Philippines was virtually completed. The occupation of Morotai proved easy, and the island provided airfields for the support of advances into the Philippines and Indies. The Pacific Fleet employed Ulithi as a forward anchorage. Hard fighting dragged on in the Palaus through November, but as the result of another acceleration in the pace of Pacific operations these islands never played the role originally planned for them.

In twin drives, illustrative of the principles of maneuver, objective, economy of force, surprise, and mass, the Allied forces of the Pacific had arrived in mid-September 1944 at the threshold of their strategic objective, the Luzon-Formosa-China coast triangle. In seven months MacArthur's forces had moved forward nearly 1,500 miles from the Admiralties to Morotai; in ten months Nimitz' forces had advanced over 4,500 miles from Hawaii to the Palaus. The time had now arrived when a final choice had to be made of the main objective in the target area.

The Decision To Invade Luzon

During the summer of 1944, as the battles raged along both lines of advance, the strategic debate over the choice of Luzon versus Formosa also waxed hot. General MacArthur argued fervently that the proper course was to move through the Philippines to Luzon, cutting the Japanese lines of communications southward, establishing a base for bombardment and invasion of Japan, and fulfilling a solemn national obligation to liberate the Philippine people. Admiral Ernest J. King, Chief of Naval Operations, just as adamantly insisted that the war could be shortened by directing the Pacific advance from the Marianas and Palaus toward Formosa, the China coast, and Japan proper, seizing only the essential positions in the southern and central Philippines necessary to render air support for these advances. The arguments for Formosa were cogent enough. Its strategic position made it a better island steppingstone to the China coast or the Japanese home islands, a position from which Japanese communications to the south could be cut more effectively than from Luzon, and a closer-in position from which to conduct strategic bombardment. But it also could prove to be a more difficult position to take, and Nimitz did not have in his theater sufficient Army supporting and service troops, without reinforcement, to sustain a land campaign on the island. It might be difficult, too, to mount an invasion of Formosa as long as the Japanese could, from strong positions on Luzon, interfere with the Allied line of communications. Another consideration involved the real value of a foothold on the China coast. By the early fall of 1944, air base sites in east China from which the Allies had hoped to support Pacific operations and bomb Japan appeared irretrievably lost, and the Marianas already provided bases for the B–29's almost as close to Tokyo as Formosa. The need to seize and develop a port on the China coast thus lost much of its urgency, and the argument that Formosa was the best steppingstone to China became less compelling. Then, too, a successful invasion of either Luzon or Formosa required some concentration of forces from the two theaters. It was far easier to shift highly mobile naval resources in Nimitz' theater to the Philippines than it was to redeploy Army troops from the Southwest Pacific to support Nimitz' invasion of Formosa and the jump to the China coast with which he hoped to follow it.

At the time of the Morotai and Palaus landings, MacArthur's plans for invasion of the Philippines called for a preliminary assault in southern Mindanao on November 15, 1944, to secure air bases for the support of a larger attack at Leyte, in the east-central Philippines, on December 20. He would follow this with a large-scale assault on Lingayen Gulf in February 1945. Nimitz meanwhile planned to mount an invasion of Yap in the Carolines in October 1944 and then would prepare to launch his attack on Formosa as soon afterward as the elements of the Pacific Fleet required for operations in the southern and central Philippines could be returned. Obviously, there had to be a choice between Luzon and Formosa, for the Pacific Fleet would be required to support either operation.

The course of events went far to dictate the final choice. In mid-September Admiral Halsey's carrier task forces providing strategic support for the Morotai and Palaus operations struck the central and southern Philippines. Halsey found Japanese air strength unexpectedly weak and uncovered few signs of significant ground or naval activity. On the basis of Halsey's reports, MacArthur and Nimitz proposed to the Joint Chiefs a move directly to Leyte in October, bypassing Mindanao. Nimitz agreed to divert to the Leyte invasion the 3-division corps then mounting out of Hawaii for the assault against Yap. The Joint Chiefs quickly approved the new plan, and the decision to invade Leyte two months ahead of schedule gave MacArthur's arguments to move onto Luzon almost irresistible force. MacArthur now reported that he could undertake the invasion of Luzon in December 1944, whereas all the planners' estimates indicated that resources for an invasion of Formosa—particularly service troops and shipping— could not be readied before February 1945 at the earliest. Nimitz proposed to shift the Central Pacific attack northward against Iwo Jima in the Bonins in January 1945 and then against Okinawa and other islands in the Ryukyus early in March. On October 3, Admiral King bowing to the inevitable, accepted the new plans and the Joint Chiefs issued directives to MacArthur for the invasion of Luzon on December 20 and to Nimitz for the invasion of Iwo Jima and Okinawa early in 1945.

Pacific strategy had been cast into almost its final mold. In the end, the China coast objective disappeared entirely from planning boards. Final plans for the defeat of Japan envisaged gradual tightening of the ring by blockade and bombardment from the Marianas, Philippines, and Ryukyus with an invasion of the home islands to be mounted from these bases.

The Philippines Campaign

The main assault at Leyte took place on October 20, 1944, as four Army divisions landed abreast in the largest amphibious operation yet conducted in the Pacific. Vice Adm. Thomas C. Kinkaid, MacArthur's naval commander, controlled the amphibious phases, including naval gunfire support and close air support by planes based on escort carriers. Ground forces were under Lt. Gen. Walter Krueger, commanding the U.S. Sixth Army; land-based air forces of the Southwest Pacific Area in general support were commanded by Lt. Gen. George C. Kenney. MacArthur himself exercised unified command over the air, ground, and naval commanders. The fast carrier task forces of the Pacific Fleet, providing strategic support, operated under the control of Admiral Halsey, who reported to Nimitz, not MacArthur. There was no provision for unified naval command, and Halsey's orders were such that he could make his principal mission the destruction of the Japanese Fleet rather than the support of MacArthur's entry into the Philippines.

The Japanese had originally planned to make their stand in the Philippines on Luzon, but the invasion of Leyte moved them to reconsider, since they now decided that the entire Philippine Archipelago would be strategically lost if the

UNLOADING SUPPLIES ON A LEYTE BEACH

U.S. Army secured a foothold in the central islands. They therefore began sending ground reinforcements to Leyte; increased their land-based air strength in the Philippines in the hope of destroying Allied shipping in Leyte Gulf and maintaining local air superiority; and dispatched their remaining naval strength to Leyte Gulf to destroy Kinkaid's invasion fleet and to block Allied access to the Philippines. The ensuing air-naval Battle of Leyte Gulf was the most critical moment of the campaign, and proved one of the most decisive actions of the Pacific war.

Admiral Halsey, without consulting MacArthur or Kinkaid, pulled the bulk of his carrier forces northward to intercept part of the Japanese Fleet, leaving Leyte Gulf open to other Japanese Fleet units. Gallant, desperate action by Kinkaid's old battleships and escort carrier planes turned back the Japanese in the gulf, assuring the safety of the landing forces. It had been a close thing, clearly demonstrating the dangers of divided command. In the end, however, the combined operations of Kinkaid's and Halsey's forces virtually eliminated the Japanese Navy as a factor in the Pacific war.

With the Leyte beaches secure, U.S. Army units proceeded to destroy the Japanese ground forces. Miserable weather bogged down the pace of operations, made supply difficult, delayed airfield construction, curtailed air support, and permitted the Japanese to continue to ship reinforcements to the island. The reinforcement program came to a sudden halt early in December when the 77th Division executed an amphibious envelopment on Leyte's west coast,

GENERAL MACARTHUR AND MEMBERS OF HIS STAFF *wading ashore at Leyte.*

and by late December the Sixth Army had secured the most important sections of the island, those required for air and logistical bases. Japanese troops in the mountains of northwestern Leyte continued organized resistance well into the spring of 1945, occupying the energies of large portions of Lt. Gen. Robert L. Eichelberger's newly formed Eighth Army.

While the fight on Leyte continued, MacArthur's forces moved on to Luzon only slightly behind schedule. The first step of the Luzon Campaign was the seizure of an air base in southwestern Mindoro, 150 miles south of Manila, on December 15, 1944, two Army regiments accomplishing the task with ease. The invasion of Luzon itself started on January 9, 1945, when four Army divisions landed along the shores of Lingayen Gulf. Command arrangements were similar to those at Leyte, and again fast carrier task forces under Halsey operated in general support and not under MacArthur's control. Within three days five Army divisions, a separate regimental combat team, two artillery groups, an armored group, and supporting service units were ashore and had begun a drive down the Central Plains of Luzon toward Manila. The Japanese were incapable of naval intervention at Lingayen Gulf, and their most significant reaction was to throw a number of kamikaze (suicide plane) attacks against Kinkaid's naval forces for four days.

General Tomoyuki Yamashita, commanding Japanese forces in the Philippines, did not intend to defend the Central Plains—Manila Bay region, the strategic prize of Luzon. Knowing he would receive no reinforcements and believing the issue in the Philippines had been decided at Leyte, he sought only to pin down major elements of MacArthur's forces in the hope of delaying Allied progress toward Japan. For this purpose he moved the bulk of his troops into mountain strongholds, where they could conduct a protracted, bloody defensive campaign. But Japanese naval forces on Luzon, only nominally under Yamashita, decided to ignore this concept in favor of defending Manila and Manila Bay. Thus, when U.S. Army units reached Manila on February 3, it took them a month of bitter building-to-building fighting to root out the Japanese. Meanwhile, operations to clear Manila Bay had begun with a minor amphibious landing at the southern tip of Bataan on February 15. The next day a combined parachute-amphibious assault, involving two Army regiments, initiated a battle to clear Corregidor Island. Other forces cleared additional islands in Manila Bay and secured the south shore. By mid-March the bay was open for Allied shipping, but an immense salvage and repair job was necessary before the Allies could fully exploit Manila's excellent port facilities.

The reinforced 38th Division had landed meanwhile near Subic Bay and had cut across the base of Bataan peninsula to prevent the Japanese from holing up on Bataan as had MacArthur's forces three years earlier. The 11th Airborne Division undertook both amphibious and parachute landings in southern Luzon to start clearing that region, and the 158th Regimental Combat Team made an amphibious assault in southeastern Luzon to secure the Bicol peninsula. Turning against the Japanese mountain strongholds, MacArthur continued to pour reinforcements onto Luzon, and the land campaign there ultimately evolved into the largest of the Pacific war. MacArthur committed to Luzon ten divisions, two regiments of another division, and three separate regimental combat teams. Guerrillas also played a large role. One guerrilla unit came to substitute for a regularly constituted division, and other guerrilla forces of battalion and regimental size supplemented the efforts of the Army units. Moreover, the loyal and willing Filipino population immeasurably eased the problems of supply, construction, and civil administration.

Except for a strong pocket in the mountains of north central Luzon, organized Japanese resistance ended by late June 1945. The rugged terrain in the north, along with rainy weather, prevented Krueger's Sixth Army from applying its full strength to the reduction of this pocket. Eichelberger's Eighth Army took over responsibility for operations on Luzon at the end of June and continued the pressure against Yamashita's force in the last-stand area, but they held out there until the end of the war.

While Sixth Army was destroying Japanese forces on Luzon, Eighth Army ultimately employed five divisions, portions of a sixth division, a separate

U.S. Paratroopers Dropping on Corregidor

regimental combat team, and strong guerrilla units in its campaign to reconquer the southern Philippines. This effort began when a regimental combat
team of the 41st Division landed on Palawan Island on February 28, 1945. Here
engineers built an air base from which to help cut Japan's line of communications to the south and to support later advances in the southern Philippines and
the Indies. On March 10, another regimental combat team of the 41st, later
reinforced, landed near Zamboanga in southwestern Mindanao, and soon thereafter Army units began moving southwest toward Borneo along the Sulu
Archipelago. In rapid succession Eighth Army units then landed on Panay,
Cebu, northwestern Negros, Bohol, central Mindanao, southeastern Negros,
northern Mindanao, and finally at Sarangani Bay in southern Mindanao, once
intended as the first point of re-entry into the Philippines. At some locales
bitter fighting raged for a time, but the issue was never in doubt and organized
Japanese resistance in the southern Philippines had largely collapsed by the
end of May. Mopping up continued to the end of the war, with reorganized
and re-equipped guerrilla forces bearing much of the burden.

The last offensives in the Southwest Pacific Area started on May 1 when
an Australian brigade went ashore on Tarakan Island, Borneo. Carried to the
beaches by landing craft manned by U.S. Army engineers, the Australians had
air support from fields on Morotai and in the southern Philippines. On June 10

an Australian division landed at Brunei Bay, Borneo, and another Australian division went ashore at Balikpapan on July 1 in what proved to be the final amphibious assault of the war.

Iwo Jima and Okinawa

Since slow-base development at Leyte had forced MacArthur to delay the Luzon invasion from December to January, Nimitz in turn had to postpone his target dates for the Iwo Jima and Okinawa operations, primarily because the bulk of the naval resources in the Pacific—fast carrier task forces, escort carrier groups, assault shipping, naval gunfire support vessels, and amphibious assault craft—had to be shifted between the two theaters for major operations. The alteration of schedules again illustrated the interdependence of the Southwest and Central Pacific Areas.

The Iwo Jima assault finally took place on February 19, 1945, with the 4th and 5th Marine Divisions, supported by minor Army elements, making the landings. The 3d Marine Division reinforced the assault, and an Army regiment ultimately took over as island garrison. The marines had to overcome fanatic resistance from firmly entrenched Japanese, who held what was probably the strongest defensive system American forces encountered during the Pacific war, and it took a month of bloody fighting to secure the island. In early March a few crippled B–29's made emergency landings on Iwo; by the end of the month an airfield was fully operational for fighter planes. Later, engineers constructed a heavy bomber field and another fighter base on the island.

The invasion of the Ryukyus began on March 26 when the 77th Division landed on the Kerama Islands, fifteen miles west of Okinawa, to secure a forward naval base, a task traditionally assigned to marines. On April 1 the 7th and 96th Divisions and the 2d and 6th Marine Divisions executed the assault on the main objective, Okinawa. Two more Army divisions and a Marine infantry regiment later reinforced it. Another amphibious assault took place on April 16, when the 77th Division seized Ie Shima, four miles west of Okinawa, and the final landing in the Ryukyus came on June 26, when a small force of marines went ashore on Kume Island, fifty miles west of Okinawa. Ground forces at Okinawa were first under the U.S. Tenth Army, Lt. Gen. Simon B. Buckner commanding. When General Buckner was killed on June 18, Marine Lt. Gen. Roy S. Geiger took over until General Joseph W. Stilwell assumed command on the 23d.

The Japanese made no attempt to defend the Okinawa beaches, but instead fell back to prepared cave and tunnel defenses on inland hills. Bitterly defending every inch of ground, the Japanese continued organized resistance until late June. Meanwhile, Japanese suicide planes had inflicted extensive damage on Nimitz' naval forces, sinking about 25 ships and damaging nearly 165 more in an unsuccessful attempt to drive Allied naval power from the western Pacific. Skillful small unit tactics, combined with great concentrations of naval, air, and artillery bombardment, turned the tide of the ground battle on Okinawa itself. Especially noteworthy was the close support that naval gunfire vessels provided the ground forces and the close air support furnished by Army, Navy, and Marine aircraft.

Capture of Okinawa and other positions in the Ryukyus gave the Allies both air and naval bases within easy striking distance of Japan. By early May fighter planes from Okinawa had begun flights over Japan, and as rapidly as fields became available bombers, including units from the Southwest Pacific Area, came forward to mount attacks in preparation for the invasion of the home islands. The forward anchorages in the Ryukyus permitted the Pacific Fleet to keep in almost continuous action against Japanese targets. The Ryukyus campaign had brought Allied forces in the Pacific to Japan's doorstep.

The American Effort in China, Burma, and India

While American forces in the Pacific, under the unified direction of the U.S. Joint Chiefs of Staff, made spectacular advances, the Allied effort in Southeast Asia bogged down in a mire of conflicting national purposes. The hopes Americans held, in the early stages of the war, that Chinese manpower and bases would play a vitally important role in the defeat of Japan were doomed to disappointment. Americans sought to achieve great aims on the Asiatic mainland at small cost, looking to the British in India and the Chinese, with their vast reservoirs of manpower, to carry the main burden of ground conflict. Neither proved capable of exerting the effort the Americans expected of them.

Early in 1942 the United States had sent General Stilwell to the Far East to command American forces in China, Burma, and India and to serve as Chief of Staff and principal adviser to Chiang Kai-shek, the leader of Nationalist China and Allied commander of the China theater. Stilwell's stated mission was "to assist in improving the efficiency of the Chinese Army." The Japanese conquest of Burma, cutting the last overland supply route to China, frustrated Stilwell's designs, for it left a long and difficult airlift from Assam to Kunming over the high peaks of the Himalayas as the only remaining avenue for the flow of supplies. The Americans assumed responsibility for the airlift, but its development was slow, hampered by a scarcity of transport planes, airfields, and trained pilots. Not until late in 1943 did it reach a monthly capacity of 10,000 tons, and in the intervening months few supplies flowed into China. The economy of the country continually tottered on the brink of collapse, and the Chinese Army, although it was a massive force on paper, remained ill organized, ill equipped, poorly led, and generally incapable of offensive action.

Stilwell thought that the only solution was to retake Burma and reopen the land supply line to China, and this became the position of the U.S. Joint Chiefs of Staff. To achieve the goal Stilwell undertook the training and equipping of a Chinese force in India that eventually consisted of three divisions, and sought to concentrate a much larger force in Yunnan Province in China and to give it offensive capability. With these two Chinese forces he hoped to form a junction in north Burma, thus re-establishing land communications between China and India. Stilwell's scheme became part of the larger plan, ANAKIM, that had been approved by the Combined Chiefs of Staff at the Casablanca Conference. Neither the British nor the Chinese, however, had any real enthusiasm for ANAKIM, and in retrospect it seems clear that its execution in 1943 was beyond the capabilities of forces in the theater. Moreover, Chiang was quite dilatory in concentrating a force in Yunnan; Maj. Gen. Claire L. Chennault, commanding the small American air force in China, urged that the Hump air line should be used to support an air effort in China, rather than to supply Chinese ground forces. Chennault promised amazing results at small cost, and his proposals attracted President Roosevelt as well as the British and the Chinese. As an upshot, at the TRIDENT Conference in May 1943, the amphibious operation against Rangoon was canceled and a new plan for operations emerged that stressed Chennault's air operations and provided for a lesser ground offensive in central and northern Burma. Under this concept a new road would be built from Ledo in Assam Province, India, to join with the trace of the old Burma Road inside China. The Americans assumed responsibility for building the Ledo Road in the rear of Chinese forces advancing from India into Burma.

Logistical difficulties in India, however, again delayed the opening of any land offensive and kept the airlift well below target figures. Until the supply line north from Calcutta to the British and Chinese fronts could be improved—and this job took well over a year—both air and ground operations against the Japanese in Burma were handicapped. In October 1943 Chinese troops under Stilwell did start to clear northern Burma, and in the spring of 1944 a U.S. Army unit of regimental size, Merrill's Marauders, spearheaded new offensives to secure the trace for the overland road. But Myitkyina, the key point in the Japanese defenses in north Burma, did not fall until August 2 and by that time the effort in Burma had been relegated to a subsidiary role.

After the SEXTANT Conference in late 1943, in fact, the American staff no longer regarded it as probable that the overland route to China could be opened in time to permit Chinese forces to drive to the coast by the time American forces advancing across the Pacific reached there. While the Americans insisted on continuing the effort to open the Ledo Road, they now gave first priority to an air effort in China in support of the Pacific campaigns. The Army Air Forces, in May 1944, started to deploy the first of its B–29 groups to airfields in East China to commence bombing of strategic targets in Korea, Manchuria, and Japan. At the same time, Chennault's Fourteenth Air Force was directed to stockpile supplies for missions in support of Pacific forces as they neared the China coast. Again these projects proved to be more than could be supported over the Hump air line, particularly since transports had also to be used to supply the ground effort of both British and Chinese forces. Then the Japanese reacted strongly to the increased air effort and launched a ground offensive that overran most of the existing fields and proposed air base sites in east China. Both air and ground resources inside China had to be diverted to oppose the Japanese advance. The B–29's were removed to India in January 1945, and two months later were sent to Saipan where the major strategic bombing offensive against Japan was by that time being mounted. In sum, the air effort in China without the protection of an efficient Chinese Army fulfilled few of the goals proclaimed for it.

To meet the crisis in east China, President Roosevelt urged Chiang to place his U.S. supported armies under the command of General Stilwell; Chiang eventually refused and asked for Stilwell's recall, a request the President honored. In September 1944, Maj. Gen. Albert C. Wedemeyer replaced Stilwell as Chief of Staff to Chiang and commander of American forces in the China Theater; a separate theater in India and Burma was created with Lt. Gen. Dan I. Sultan as its commanding general. The command issue was dropped and the American strategy in China became simply one of trying to realize at least something from previous investments without additional commitments.

Ironically enough, it was in this phase, after the Pacific advances had outrun those in Southeast Asia, that objects of the 1942 strategy were realized, in large part because the Japanese, hard-pressed everywhere, were no longer able to support their forces in Burma and China adequately. British and Chinese forces advanced rapidly into Burma in the fall of 1944, and, on January 27, 1945, the junction between Chinese forces advancing from India and Yunnan finally took place, securing the trace of the Ledo Road. To the south, the British completed the conquest of central Burma and entered Rangoon from the north early in May. The land route to China was thus finally secured on all sides, but the Americans had already decided that they would develop the Ledo Road only as a one-way highway, though they did expand the airlift to the point where, in July 1945, it carried 74,000 tons into China.

With increased American supply support, Wedemeyer was able to make more progress in equipping and training the Chinese Army. Under his tutelage the Chinese were able to halt the Japanese advance at Chihchiang in April 1945, and, as the Japanese began to withdraw in order to prepare a citadel defense of their home islands, Wedemeyer and the Chinese laid plans to seize a port on the Chinese coast. The war came to an end, however, before this operation even started and before the training and equipping of a Chinese Army was any-where near completion. Chiang's forces commenced the reoccupation of their homeland still, for the most part, ill equipped, ill organized, and poorly led.

The Japanese Surrender

During the summer of 1945, Allied forces in the Pacific had stepped up the pace of their air and naval attacks against Japan. In June and July carrier-based planes of the U.S. Pacific Fleet and U.S. Army Air Forces planes from the Marianas, Iwo Jima, and Okinawa struck the Japanese home islands contin-uously. During July Pacific Fleet surface units bombarded Japan's east coast, and in the same month a British carrier task force joined in the attack. Planes from the Philippines hit Japanese shipping in the South China Sea and extended their strikes as far as Formosa and targets along the South China coast. American submarines redoubled their efforts to sweep Japanese shipping from the sea and sever the shipping lanes from Japan to the Indies and Southeast Asia. Throughout the war, in fact, submarines had preyed on Japanese merchant and combat vessels, playing a major role in isolating Japan from its conquests and thereby drastically reducing Japan's ability to wage war.

After Germany's surrender in May the United States embarked upon a huge logistical effort to redeploy more than a million troops from Europe, the United States, and other inactive theaters to the Pacific. The aim was to complete the redeployment in time to launch an invasion of Japan on November 1, and the task had to be undertaken in the face of competing shipping demands for demobilization of long-service troops, British redeployment, and civil relief in Europe. By the time the war ended, some 150,000 men had moved directly from Europe to the Pacific, but a larger transfer from the United States across the Pacific had scarcely begun. In the Pacific, MacArthur and Nimitz had been sparing no effort to expand ports and ready bases to receive the expected influx and to mount invasion forces. The two commanders were also completing plans

ATOMIC CLOUD OVER NAGASAKI

for the invasion of Japan. In the last stage of the war, as all forces converged on Japan, the area unified commands were replaced by an arrangement that made MacArthur commander of all Army forces in the Pacific and Nimitz commander of all Navy forces.

By midsummer of 1945 most responsible leaders in Japan realized that the end was near. In June, those favoring peace had come out in the open, and Japan had already dispatched peace feelers through the Soviet Union, a country it feared might also be about to enter the war despite the existence of a non-aggression treaty between the two nations. As early as the Tehran Conference in late 1943 Stalin had promised to enter the war against Japan, and it was agreed at Yalta in February 1945 that the USSR would do so three months after the defeat of Germany. At the Potsdam Conference in July 1945 the Soviet Union reaffirmed its agreement to declare war on Japan. At this conference the United States and Britain, with China joining in, issued the famed Potsdam Declaration calling upon Japan to surrender promptly, and about the same time President Truman decided to employ the newly tested atomic bomb against Japan in the event of continued Japanese resistance.

Despite the changing climate of opinion in Japan, the Japanese did not immediately accept the terms of the Potsdam Declaration. Accordingly, on August 6 a lone American B–29 from the Marianas dropped an atomic bomb on Hiroshima; on the 9th the Soviet Union came into the war and attacked Japanese forces in Manchuria; and on the same day another B–29 dropped a second atomic bomb on Nagasaki. The next day Japan sued for peace, and, with the signing of surrender terms aboard the USS *Missouri* in Tokyo Bay on September 2, the bitter global war came to an end.

Retrospect

In winning the Pacific war the Allies had found it unnecessary to press home their attacks and destroy the Japanese military forces except for the

Japanese Fleet. By the end of the war Japan's Navy had virtually ceased to exist; Japanese industry had been so hammered by air bombardment that Japan's ability to wage war was seriously reduced; and U.S. submarine and air actions had cut off sources of raw material. At the time of the surrender Japan still had 2,000,000 men under arms in the homeland and was capable of conducting a tenacious ground defense; about 3,000 Japanese aircraft were also operational. Nevertheless, the Japanese could hardly have continued the war for more than a few months. On the other hand, the fact that an invasion was not necessary certainly spared many American lives.

The great arbiter of the Pacific war had been American industrial power, which produced a mighty war machine. Out of this production had come the Pacific Fleet, a potent force that could overcome the vast reaches of the Pacific upon which the Japanese had depended so heavily as a defensive advantage. The decisive combat element of the fleet was the fast carrier task force, which carried the war deep into Japanese territory and supported advances far beyond the range of land-based aircraft. Land-based air power also played a decisive part. When carriers were not available to support offensives, it was land-based aviation that measured the distance of each forward move. Land-based aviation proved important as well in providing close support for ground operations, while aerial supply operations and troop movements contributed greatly to the success of the Allied campaigns.

Both naval and air forces were dependent upon shore bases, and the war in the Pacific demonstrated that even in a predominantly naval-air theater, ground combat forces are an essential part of the offensive team. The Japanese had also been dependent upon far-flung bases, so that much of the Allied effort during the war had gone into the seizure or neutralization of Japan's bases. Thus, the Pacific war was in large measure a war for bases. On the other hand, the U.S. Pacific Fleet, in one of the greatest logistical developments of the war, went far in the direction of carrying its bases with it by organizing fleet trains of support vessels that were capable of maintaining the fleet at sea over extended periods.

Another important facet of the Pacific war was the development and employment of amphibious assault techniques, repeatedly demonstrating the need for unified command. Air, ground, and naval teamwork, supremely important in the struggle against Japan, occasionally broke down, but the success of the Allied campaigns illustrates that all three elements achieved it to a large degree. Strategic air bombardment in the Pacific, designed to cripple Japan's industrial capacity, did not get under way until well along in 1945. The damage inflicted on Japanese cities was enormous, but the effect, as in the case of the bomber offensive against Germany, remains unsettled, though the bombardment finally brought home to the Japanese people that the war was lost. The submarine played a vital role in reducing Japan's capabilities by taking a huge toll of Japanese shipping and by helping to cut Japan off from the resources of Southeast Asia.

In the final analysis Japan lost because the country did not have the means to fight a total war against the combination of industrial, air, naval, and human resources represented by the United States and its Allies. Admiral Isoroku Yamamoto, commander of the Japanese Fleet at the outbreak of the war, put his finger on the fatal weakness of the Japanese concept of the war, when he stated: "It is not enough that we should take Guam and the Philippines, or even Hawaii and San Francisco. We should have to march into Washington and sign the treaty in the White House." This the Japanese could never do, and because they could not they had to lose the war.

A/C EDWIN S. ULANOFF, *one of the thousands of Aviation Cadets who later served as flying officers with the U.S. Army Air Force (U.S.A.A.F.) in the Second World War.*

CHAPTER 14

The Korean War, 1950–1953

After the USSR installed a Communist government in North Korea in September 1948, that government promoted and supported an insurgency in South Korea in an attempt to bring down the recognized government and gain jurisdiction over the entire Korean peninsula. Not quite two years later, after the insurgency showed signs of failing, the northern government undertook a direct attack, sending the North Korea People's Army south across the 38th parallel before daylight on Sunday, June 25, 1950. The invasion, in a narrow sense, marked the beginning of a civil war between peoples of a divided country. In a larger sense, the cold war between the Great Power blocs had erupted in open hostilities.

The Decision for War

The western bloc, especially the United States, was surprised by the North Korean decision. Although intelligence information of a possible June invasion had reached Washington, the reporting agencies judged an early summer attack unlikely. The North Koreans, they estimated, had not yet exhausted the possibilities of the insurgency and would continue that strategy only.

The North Koreans, however, seem to have taken encouragement from the U.S. policy which left Korea outside the U.S. "defense line" in Asia and from relatively public discussions of the economies placed on U.S. armed forces. They evidently accepted these as reasons to discount American counteraction, or their sponsor, the USSR, may have made that calculation for them. The Soviets also appear to have been certain the United Nations would not intervene, for in protest against Nationalist China's membership in the U.N. Security Council and against the U.N.'s refusal to seat Communist China, the USSR member had boycotted council meetings since January 1950 and did not return in June to veto any council move against North Korea.

Moreover, Kim Il Sung, the North Korean Premier, could be confident that his army, a modest force of 135,000, was superior to that of South Korea. Koreans who had served in Chinese and Soviet World War II armies made up a large part of his force. He had 8 full divisions, each including a regiment of artillery; 2 divisions at half strength; 2 separate regiments; an armored brigade with 120

Soviet T34 medium tanks; and 5 border constabulary brigades. He also had 180 Soviet aircraft, mostly fighters and attack bombers, and a few naval patrol craft.

The Republic of Korea (ROK) Army had just 95,000 men and was far less fit. Raised as a constabulary during occupation, it had not in its later combat training under a U.S. Military Advisor Group progressed much beyond company-level exercises. Of its eight divisions, only four approached full strength. It had no tanks and its artillery totaled eighty-nine 105-mm. howitzers. The ROK Navy matched its North Korean counterpart, but the ROK Air Force had only a few trainers and liaison aircraft. U.S. equipment, war-worn when furnished to South Korean forces, had deteriorated further, and supplies on hand could sustain combat operations no longer than fifteen days. Whereas almost $11 million in matériel assistance had been allocated to South Korea in fiscal year 1950 under the Mutual Defense Assistance Program, Congressional review of the allocation so delayed the measure that only a trickle of supplies had reached the country by June 25, 1950.

The North Koreans quickly crushed South Korean defenses at the 38th parallel. The main North Korean attack force next moved down the west side of the peninsula toward Seoul, the South Korean capital, thirty-five miles below the parallel, and entered the city on June 28. (*Map 45*) Secondary thrusts down the peninsula's center and down the east coast kept pace with the main drive. The South Koreans withdrew in disorder, those troops driven out of Seoul forced to abandon most of their equipment because the bridges over the Han River at the south edge of the city were prematurely demolished. The North Koreans halted after capturing Seoul, but only briefly to regroup before crossing the Han.

In Washington, where a 14-hour time difference made it June 24 when the North Koreans crossed the parallel, the first report of the invasion arrived that night. Early on the 25th, the United States requested a meeting of the U.N. Security Council. The council adopted a resolution that afternoon demanding an immediate cessation of hostilities and a withdrawal of North Korean forces to the 38th parallel.

In independent actions on the night of the 25th, President Truman relayed orders to General of the Army Douglas MacArthur at MacArthur's Far East Command headquarters in Tokyo, Japan, to supply ROK forces with ammunition and equipment, evacuate American dependents from Korea, and survey conditions on the peninsula to determine how best to assist the republic further. The President also ordered the U.S. Seventh Fleet from its current location in Philippine and Ryukyu waters to Japan. On the 26th, in a broad interpretation of a U.N. Security Council request for "every assistance" in supporting the June 25

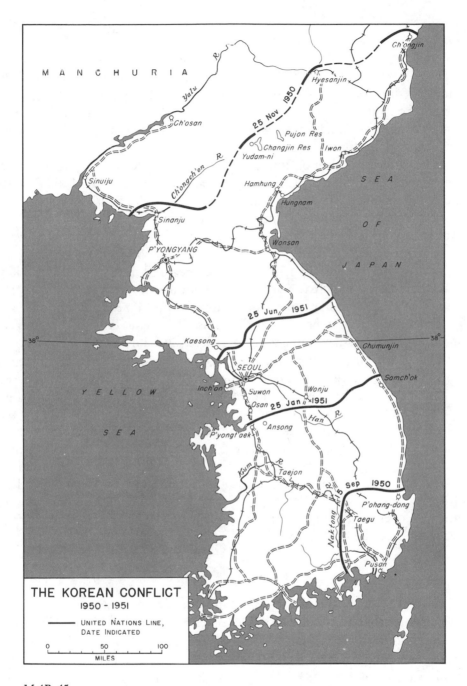

MANCHURIA

Yalu R.

Ch'osan

Sinuiju

Ch'ongch'on R.

Sinanju

P'YONGYANG

25 Nov 1950

Hyesanjin

Ch'ongjin

Pujon Res

Changjin Res
Yudam-ni

Iwon

Hamhung

Hungnam

Wonsan

SEA

OF

JAPAN

25 Jun 1951

38°   38°

Kaesong

Chumunjin

SEOUL

Samch'ok

Inch'on   Suwon

Osan   25 Jan 1951

Wonju

Han R.

YELLOW

P'yongt'aek   Ansong

SEA

Kum R.

Taejon

15 Sep 1950

Naktong R.

P'ohang-dong

Taegu

Pusan

THE KOREAN CONFLICT
1950 - 1951

————— UNITED NATIONS LINE,
DATE INDICATED

0   50   100

MILES

MAP 45

resolution, President Truman authorized General MacArthur to use air and naval strength against North Korean targets below the 38th parallel. The President also redirected the bulk of the Seventh Fleet to Taiwan, where by standing between the Chinese Communists on the mainland and the Nationalists on the island it could discourage either one from attacking the other and thus prevent a widening of hostilities.

When it became clear on June 27 that North Korea would ignore the U.N. demands, the U.N. Security Council, again at the urging of the United States, asked U.N. members to furnish military assistance to help South Korea repel the invasion. President Truman immediately broadened the range of U.S. air and naval operations to include North Korea and authorized the use of U.S. Army troops to protect Pusan, Korea's major port at the southeastern tip of the peninsula. MacArthur meanwhile had flown to Korea and, after witnessing failing ROK Army efforts in defenses south of the Han River, recommended to Washington that a U.S. Army regiment be committed in the Seoul area at once and that this force be built up to two divisions. President Truman's answer on June 30 authorized MacArthur to use all forces available to him.

Thus the United Nations for the first time since its founding reacted to aggression with a decision to use armed force. The United States would accept the largest share of the obligation in Korea but, still deeply tired of war, would do so reluctantly. President Truman later described his decision to enter the war as the hardest of his days in office. But he believed that if South Korea was left to its own defense and fell, no other small nation would have the will to resist aggression, and Communist leaders would be encouraged to override nations closer to U.S. shores. The American people, conditioned by World War II to battle on a grand scale and to complete victory, would experience a deepening frustration over the Korean conflict, brought on in the beginning by embarrassing reversals on the battlefield.

South to the Naktong

Ground forces available to MacArthur included the 1st Cavalry Division and the 7th, 24th, and 25th Infantry Divisions, all under the Eighth U.S. Army in Japan, and the 29th Regimental Combat Team on Okinawa. All the postwar depreciations had affected them. Their maneuverability and firepower were sharply reduced by a shortage of organic units and by a general understrength among existing units. Some weapons, medium tanks in particular, could scarcely be found in the Far East, and ammunition reserves amounted to only a 45-day supply. By any measurement, MacArthur's ground forces were unprepared for battle. His air arm, Far East Air Forces (FEAF), moreover, was organized for air defense, not tactical air support. Most FEAF planes were short-range jet interceptors not meant to be flown at low altitudes in support of ground operations. Some F–51's in storage in Japan and more of these World War II planes in the United States would prove instrumental in meeting close air support needs. Naval Forces, Far East, MacArthur's sea arm, controlled only five combat ships and a skeleton amphibious force, although reinforcement was near in the Seventh Fleet.

When MacArthur received word to commit ground units, the main North Korean force already had crossed the Han River. By July 3, a westward enemy attack had captured a major airfield at Kimpo and the Yellow Sea port of Inch'on. Troops attacking south repaired a bridge so that tanks could cross the Han and moved into the town of Suwon, twenty-five miles below Seoul, on the 4th.

The speed of the North Korean drive coupled with the unreadiness of American forces compelled MacArthur to disregard the principle of mass and commit units piecemeal to trade space for time. Where to open a delaying action was clear, for there were few good roads in the profusion of mountains making up the Korean peninsula, and the best of these below Seoul, running on a gentle diagonal through Suwon, Osan, Taejon, and Taegu to the port of Pusan in the southeast, was the obvious main axis of North Korean advance. At MacArthur's order, two rifle companies, an artillery battery, and a few other supporting units of the 24th Division moved into a defensive position astride the main road near Osan, ten miles below Suwon, by dawn on July 5. MacArthur later referred to this 540-man force, called Task Force Smith, as an "arrogant display of strength." Another kind of arrogance to be found at Osan was a belief that the North Koreans might ". . . turn around and go back when they found out who was fighting."

Coming out of Suwon in a heavy rain, a North Korean division supported by thirty-three tanks reached and with barely a pause attacked the Americans around 8:00 a.m. on the 5th. The North Koreans lost 4 tanks, 42 men killed, and 85 wounded. But the American force lacked antitank mines, the fire of its recoilless rifles and 2.36-inch rocket launchers failed to penetrate the T34 armor, and its artillery quickly expended the little antitank ammunition that did prove effective. The rain canceled air support, communications broke down, and the task force was, under any circumstances, too small to prevent North Korean infantry from flowing around both its flanks. By midafternoon, Task Force Smith was pushed into a disorganized retreat with over 150 casualties and the loss of all equipment save small arms. Another casualty was American morale as word of the defeat reached other units of the 24th Division then moving into delaying positions below Osan.

The next three delaying actions, though fought by larger forces, had similar results. In each case, North Korean armor or infantry assaults against the front of the American position were accompanied by an infantry double envelopment. By July 13, the 24th Division was forced back on Taejon, sixty miles below Osan, where it initially took position along the Kum River above the town. Clumps of South Korean troops by then were strung out west and east of the division to help delay the North Koreans.

Fifty-three U.N. members meanwhile signified support of the Security Council's June 27 action and twenty-nine of these made specific offers of assistance. Ground, air, and naval forces eventually sent to assist South Korea would represent twenty U.N. members and one nonmember nation. The United States, Great Britain, Australia, New Zealand, Canada, Turkey, Greece, France, Belgium, Luxembourg, the Netherlands, Thailand, the Philippines, Colombia and Ethiopa would furnish ground combat troops. India, Sweden, Norway, Denmark, and Italy (the non-United Nations country) would furnish medical units. Air forces would arrive from the United States, Australia, Canada, and the Union of South Africa; naval forces would come from the United States, Great Britain, Australia, Canada, and New Zealand.

The wide response to the council's call pointed out the need for a unified command. Acknowledging the United States as the major contributor, the U.N. Security Council on July 7 asked it to form a command into which all forces would be integrated and to appoint a commander. In the evolving command structure, President Truman became executive agent for the U.N. Security Council. The National Security Council, Department of State, and Joint Chiefs of Staff participated in developing the grand concepts of operations in Korea. In the strictly military channel, the Joint Chiefs issued instructions through the Army member to the unified command in the field, designated the United Nations Command (UNC) and established under General MacArthur.

MacArthur superimposed the headquarters of his new command over that of his existing Far East Command. Air and naval units from other countries joined the Far East Air Forces and Naval Forces, Far East, respectively. MacArthur assigned command of ground troops in Korea to the Eighth Army under Lt. Gen. Walton H. Walker, who established headquarters at Taegu on July 13, assuming command of all American ground troops on the peninsula and, at the request of South Korean President Syngman Rhee, of the ROK Army. When ground forces from other nations reached Korea, they too passed to Walker's command.

U.S. Medium Tank M4A3 *on a South Korean village road.*

Between July 14 and 18, MacArthur moved the 25th and 1st Cavalry Divisions to Korea after cannibalizing the 7th Division to strengthen those two units. By then, the battle for Taejon had opened. New 3.5-inch rocket launchers hurriedly airlifted from the United States proved effective against the T34 tanks, but the 24th Division lost Taejon on July 20 after two North Korean divisions established bridgeheads over the Kum River and encircled the town. In running enemy roadblocks during the final withdrawal from town, Maj. Gen. William F. Dean, the division commander, took a wrong turn and was captured some days later in the mountains to the south. When repatriated some three years later, he would learn that for his exploits at Taejon he was one of 131 servicemen awarded the Medal of Honor during the war (Army 78, Marine Corps 42, Navy 7, and Air Force 4).

While pushing the 24th Division below Taejon, the main North Korean force split, one division moving south to the coast, then turning east along the lower coast line. The remainder of the force continued southeast beyond Taejon toward Taegu. Southward advances by the secondary attack forces in the central and eastern sectors matched the main thrust, all clearly aimed to converge on Pusan. North Korean supply lines grew long in the advance, and less and less tenable under heavy UNC air attacks. FEAF meanwhile achieved air superiority, indeed air supremacy, and UNC warships wiped out North Korean naval

TROOPS KEEPING A LOOKOUT *as phosphorous shells fall on enemy-held territory.*

opposition and clamped a tight blockade on the Korean coast. These achievements and the arrival of the 29th Regimental Combat Team from Okinawa on July 26 notwithstanding, American and South Korean troops steadily gave way. American casualties rose above 6,000 and South Korean losses reached 70,000. By the beginning of August, General Walker's forces held only a small portion of southeastern Korea.

Alarmed by the rapid loss of ground, Walker ordered a stand along a 140-mile line arching from the Korea Strait to the Sea of Japan west and north of Pusan. His U.S. divisions occupied the western arc, basing their position on the Naktong River. South Korean forces, reorganized by American military advisers into two corps headquarters and five divisions, defended the northern segment. A long line and few troops kept positions thin in this "Pusan Perimeter." But replacements and additional units now entering or on the way to Korea would help relieve the problem, and fair interior lines of communications radiating from Pusan allowed Walker to move troops and supplies with facility.

Raising brigades to division status and conscripting large numbers of recruits, many from overrun regions of South Korea, the North Koreans over the next month and a half committed thirteen infantry divisions and an armored division against Walker's perimeter. But the additional strength failed to compensate for the loss of some 58,000 trained men and much armor suffered in the advance to the Naktong. Nor in meeting the connected defenses of the perimeter did enemy commanders recognize the value of massing forces for decisive penetration at one point. They dissipated their strength instead in piecemeal attacks at various points along the Eighth Army line.

Close air support played a large role in the defense of the perimeter. But the Eighth Army's defense really hinged on a shuttling of scarce reserves to block a gap, reinforce a position, or counterattack wherever the threat appeared greatest at a given moment. Timing was the key, and General Walker proved a master of it. His brilliant responses prevented serious enemy penetrations and inflicted telling losses that steadily drew off North Korean offensive power. His own strength meanwhile was on the rise. By mid-September, he had over 500 medium tanks. Replacements arrived in a steady flow and additional units came in: the 5th Regimental Combat Team from Hawaii, the 2d Infantry Division and 1st Provisional Marine Brigade from the United States, and a British infantry brigade from Hong Kong. Thus, as the North Koreans lost irreplaceable men and equipment, UNC forces acquired an offensive capability.

North to the Parallel

Against the gloomy prospect of trading space for time, General MacArthur, at the entry of U.S. forces into Korea, had perceived that the deeper the North Koreans drove, the more vulnerable they would become to an amphibious envelopment. He began work on plans for such a blow almost at the start of hostilities, favoring Inch'on, the Yellow Sea port halfway up the west coast, as the landing site. Just twenty-five miles east lay Seoul where Korea's main roads and rail lines converged. A force landing at Inch'on would have to move inland only a short distance to cut North Korean supply routes, and the recapture of the capital city also could have a helpful psychological impact. Combined with a general northward advance by the Eighth Army, a landing at Inch'on could produce decisive results. Enemy troops retiring before the Eighth Army would be cut off by the amphibious force behind them or be forced to make a slow and difficult withdrawal through the mountains farther east.

Though pressed in meeting Eighth Army troop requirements, MacArthur was able to shape a two-division landing force. He formed the headquarters

THE INCH'ON LANDING

of the X Corps from members of his own staff, naming his chief of staff, Maj. Gen. Edward M. Almond, as corps commander. He rebuilt the 7th Division by giving it high priority on replacements from the United States and by assigning it 8,600 South Korean recruits. The latter measure was part of a larger program, called the Korean Augmentation to the United States Army, in which South Korean troops were placed among almost all American units. At the same time, he acquired from the United States the greater part of the 1st Marine Division, which he planned to fill out with the Marine brigade currently in the Pusan Perimeter. The X Corps, with these two divisions, was to make its landing as a separate force, not as part of the Eighth Army.

MacArthur's superiors and the Navy judged the Inch'on plan dangerous. Naval officers considered the extreme Yellow Sea tides, which range as much as thirty feet, and narrow channel approaches to Inch'on as big risks to shipping. Marine officers saw danger in landing in the middle of a built-up area and in having to scale high sea walls to get ashore. The Joint Chiefs of Staff anticipated serious consequences if Inch'on were strongly defended since MacArthur would be committing his last major reserves at a time when no more General Reserve units in the United States were available for shipment to the

Far East. Four National Guard divisions had been federalized on September 1, but none of these was yet ready for combat duty; and, while the draft and call-ups of members of the Organized Reserve Corps were substantially increasing the size of the Army, they offered MacArthur no prospect of immediate reinforcement. But MacArthur was willing to accept the risks.

In light of the uncertainties MacArthur's decision was a remarkable gamble, but if results are what count his action was one of exemplary boldness. The X Corps swept into Inch'on on September 15 against light resistance and, though opposition stiffened, steadily pushed inland over the next two weeks. One arm struck south and seized Suwon while the remainder of the corps cleared Kimpo Airfield, crossed the Han, and fought through Seoul. MacArthur, with dramatic ceremony, returned the capital city to President Rhee on September 29.

General Walker meanwhile attacked out of the Pusan Perimeter on September 16. His forces gained slowly at first; but on September 23, after the portent of Almond's envelopment and Walker's frontal attack became clear, the North Korean forces broke. The Eighth Army, by then organized as four corps, two U.S. and two ROK, rolled forward in pursuit, linking with the X Corps on September 26. About 30,000 North Korean troops escaped above the 38th parallel through the eastern mountains. Several thousand more bypassed in the pursuit hid in the mountains of South Korea to fight as guerrillas. But by the end of September the North Korea People's Army ceased to exist as an organized force anywhere in the southern republic.

North to the Yalu

President Truman, to this point, frequently had described the American-led effort in Korea as a "police action," a euphemism for war that produced both criticism and amusement. But the President's term was an honest reach for perspective. Determined to halt the aggression, he was equally determined to limit hostilities to the peninsula and to avoid taking steps that would prompt Soviet or Chinese participation. By western estimates, Europe with its highly developed industrial resources, not Asia, held the high place on the Communist schedule of expansion; hence, the North Atlantic Treaty Organization (NATO) alliance needed the deterrent strength that otherwise would be drawn off by a heavier involvement in the Far East.

On this and other bases, a case could be made for halting MacArthur's forces at the 38th parallel. In re-establishing the old border, the UNC had met the U.N. call for assistance in repelling the attack on South Korea. In an early statement, Secretary of State Acheson had said the United Nations was intervening ". . . solely for the purpose of restoring the Republic of Korea to its status prior to the invasion from the north." A halt, furthermore, would be consistent with the U.S. policy of containment.

There was, on the other hand, substantial military reason to carry the war into North Korea. Failure to destroy the 30,000 North Korean troops who had escaped above the parallel and an estimated 30,000 more in northern training camps, all told the equivalent of six divisions, could leave South Korea in little better position than before the start of hostilities. Complete military victory, by all appearances within easy grasp, also would achieve the longstanding U.S. and U.N. objective of reunifying Korea. Against these incentives had to be balanced warnings of sorts against a UNC entry into North Korea from both Communist China and the USSR in August and September. But these were counted as attempts to discourage the UNC, not as genuine threats to enter the war, and on September 27 President Truman authorized MacArthur to send his forces north, provided that by the scheduled time there had been no major Chinese or Soviet entry into North Korea and no announcement of intended entry. As a further safeguard, MacArthur was to use only Korean forces in extreme northern territory abutting the Yalu River boundary with Manchuria and that in the far northeast along the Tumen River boundary with the USSR. Ten days later, the U.N. General Assembly voted for the restoration of peace and security throughout Korea, thereby giving tacit approval to the UNC's entry into North Korea.

On the east coast, Walker's ROK I Corps crossed the parallel on October 1 and rushed far north to capture Wonsan, North Korea's major seaport, on the 10th. The ROK II Corps at nearly the same time opened an advance through central North Korea; and on October 9, after the United Nations sanctioned crossing the parallel, Walker's U.S. I Corps moved north in the west. Against slight resistance, the U.S. I Corps cleared P'yongyang, the North Korean capital city, on October 19 and in five days advanced to the Ch'ongch'on River within fifty miles of the Manchurian border. The ROK II Corps veered northwest to come alongside. To the east, past the unoccupied spine of the axial Taebaek Mountains, the ROK I Corps by October 24 moved above Wonsan, entering Iwon on the coast and approaching the huge Changjin Reservoir in the Taebaeks.

The outlook for the UNC in the last week of October was distinctly optimistic, despite further warnings emanating from Communist China. Convinced by all reports, including one from MacArthur during a personal conference at Wake Island on October 15, that the latest Chinese warnings were more saber-rattling bluffs, President Truman revised his instructions to MacArthur only to the extent that if Chinese forces should appear in Korea MacArthur should continue his advance if he believed his forces had a reasonable chance of success.

In hopes of ending operations before the onset of winter, MacArthur on October 24 ordered his ground commanders to advance to the northern border as rapidly as possible and with all forces available. In the west, the Eighth Army sent several columns toward the Yalu, each free to advance as fast and as far as possible without regard for the progress of the others. The separate X Corps earlier had prepared a second amphibious assault at Wonsan but needed only to walk ashore since the ROK I Corps had captured the landing area. General Almond, adding the ROK I Corps to his command upon landing, proceeded to clear northeastern Korea, sending columns up the coast and through the mountains toward the Yalu and the Changjin Reservoir. In the United States, a leading newspaper expressed the prevailing optimism with the editorial comment that "Except for unexpected developments . . . we can now be easy in our minds as to the military outcome."

UNC forces moved steadily along both coasts, and one interior ROK regiment in the Eighth Army zone sent reconnaissance troops to the Yalu at the town of Ch'osan on October 26. But almost everywhere else the UNC columns encountered stout resistance and, on October 25, discovered they were being opposed by Chinese. "Unexpected developments" had occurred.

In the X Corps zone, Chinese stopped a ROK column on the mountain road leading to the Changjin Reservoir. American marines relieved the South Koreans and by November 6 pushed through the resistance within a few miles of the reservoir, whereupon the Chinese broke contact. In the Eighth Army zone, the first Chinese soldier was discovered among captives taken on October 25 by South Koreans near Unsan northwest of the Ch'ongch'on River. In the next eight days, Chinese forces dispersed the ROK regiment whose troops had reached the Yalu, severely punished a regiment of the 1st Cavalry Division when it came forward near Unsan, and forced the ROK II Corps into retreat on the Eighth Army right. As General Walker fell back to regroup along the Ch'ongch'on, Chinese forces continued to attack until November 6, then, as in the X Corps sector, abruptly broke contact.

At first it appeared that individual Chinese soldiers, possibly volunteers, had reinforced the North Koreans. By November 6, three divisions (10,000 men each) were believed to be in the Eighth Army sector and two divisions in the X Corps area. The estimate rose higher by November 24, but not to a point denying UNC forces a numerical superiority nor to a figure indicating full-scale Chinese intervention.

Some apprehension over a massive Chinese intervention grew out of knowledge that a huge Chinese force was assembled in Manchuria. The interrogation of captives, however, did not convince the UNC that there had been a large Chinese commitment; neither did aerial observation of the Yalu and the ground below the river; and the voluntary withdrawal from contact on 6 November seemed no logical part of a full Chinese effort. General MacArthur felt that the auspicious time for intervention in force had long passed; the Chinese would hardly enter when North Korean forces were ineffective rather than earlier when only a little help might have enabled the North Koreans to conquer all of South Korea. He appeared convinced, furthermore, that the United States would respond with all power available to a massive intervention and that this certainty would deter Chinese leaders who could not help but be aware of it. In an early November report to Washington, he acknowledged the possibility of full intervention, but pointed out that ". . . there are many fundamental logical reasons against it and sufficient evidence has not yet come to hand to warrant its immediate acceptance." His reports by the last week of the month indicated no change of mind.

Intelligence evaluations from other sources were similar. As of November 24, the general view in Washington was that ". . . the Chinese objective was to obtain U.N. withdrawal by intimidation and diplomatic means, but in case of failure of these means there would be increasing intervention. Available evidence was not considered conclusive as to whether the Chinese Communists were committed to a full-scale offensive effort." In the theater, the general belief was that future Chinese operations would be defensive only, that the Chinese units in Korea were not strong enough to block a UNC advance, and that UNC airpower could prevent any substantial Chinese reinforcement from crossing the Yalu. UNC forces hence resumed their offensive. There was, in any event MacArthur said, no other way to obtain ". . . an accurate measure of enemy strength. . . ."

In northeastern Korea, the X Corps, now strengthened by the arrival of the 3d Infantry Division from the United States, resumed its advance on November 11. In the west, General Walker waited until the 24th to move the Eighth Army forward from the Ch'ongch'on while he strengthened his attack force and improved his logistical support. Both commands made gains. Part of the U.S. 7th Division, in the X Corps zone, actually reached the Yalu at the town of Hyesanjin. But during the night of November 25 strong Chinese attacks hit the Eighth Army's center and right; on the 27th the attacks engulfed the leftmost forces of the X Corps at the Changjin Reservoir; and by the 28th UNC positions began to crumble.

U.S. Troops Entering Hyesanjin

MacArthur now had a measure of Chinese strength. Around 200,000 Chinese of the XIII Army Group stood opposite the Eighth Army. With unexcelled march and bivouac discipline, this group, with eighteen divisions plus artillery and cavalry units, had entered Korea undetected during the last half of October. The IX Army Group with twelve divisions next entered Korea, moving into the area north of the Changjin Reservoir opposite the X Corps. Hence, by November 24 more than 300,000 Chinese combat troops were in Korea.

"We face an entirely new war," MacArthur notified Washington on November 28. On the following day he instructed General Walker to make whatever withdrawals were necessary to escape being enveloped by Chinese pushing hard and deep through the Eighth Army's eastern sector, and ordered the X Corps to pull into a beachhead around the east coast port of Hungnam, north of Wonsan.

The New War

In the Eighth Army's withdrawal from the Ch'ongch'on, a strong road-block set below the town of Kunu-ri by Chinese attempting to envelop Walker's forces from the east caught and severely punished the U.S. 2d Division, last away from the river. Thereafter, at each reported approach of enemy forces, General Walker ordered another withdrawal before any solid contact could be made. He abandoned P'yongyang on December 5, leaving 8,000 to 10,000 tons of supplies and equipment broken up or burning inside the city. By December 15, he was completely out of contact with the Chinese and was back at the 38th parallel where he began to develop a coast-to-coast defense line.

In the X Corps' withdrawal to Hungnam, the center and rightmost units experienced little difficulty. But the 1st Marine Division and two battalions of the 7th Division retiring from the Changjin Reservoir encountered Chinese positions overlooking the mountain road leading to the sea. After General Almond sent Army troops inland to help open the road, the Marine-Army force completed its move to the coast on December 11. General MacArthur briefly visualized the X Corps beachhead at Hungnam as a "geographic threat" that could deter Chinese to the west from deepening their advance. Later, with prompting from the Joint Chiefs, he ordered the X Corps to withdraw by sea and proceed to Pusan, where it would become part of the Eighth Army. Almond started the evacuation on the 11th, contracting his Hungnam perimeter as he loaded troops and matériel aboard ships in the harbor. With little interference from enemy forces, he completed the evacuation and set sail for Pusan on Christmas Eve.

On the day before, General Walker was killed in a motor vehicle accident while traveling north from Seoul toward the front. Lt. Gen. Matthew B. Ridgway hurriedly flew from Washington to assume command of the Eighth Army. After conferring in Tokyo with MacArthur, who instructed General Ridgway to hold a position as far north as possible but in any case to maintain the Eighth Army intact, the new army commander reached Korea on the 26th.

Ridgway himself wanted at least to hold the Eighth Army in its position along the 38th parallel and if possible to attack. But his initial inspection of the front raised serious doubts. The Eighth Army, he learned, was clearly a dispirited command, a result of the hard Chinese attacks and the successive withdrawals of the past month. He also discovered much of the defense line to be thin and weak. The Chinese XIII Army Group meanwhile appeared to be massing in the west for a push on Seoul, and twelve reconstituted North Korean divisions seemed to be concentrating for an attack in the central region. From all evidence available, the New Year holiday seemed a logical date on which to expect the enemy's opening assault.

Holding the current line, Ridgway judged, rested both on the early commitment of reserves and on restoring the Eighth Army's confidence. The latter, he believed, depended mainly on improving leadership throughout the command. But it was not his intention to start "lopping off heads." Before he would relieve any commander, he wanted personally to see the man in action, to know that the relief would not adversely affect the unit involved, and indeed to be sure he had a better commander available. For the time being, he intended to correct deficiencies in leadership by working "on and through" the incumbent corps and division commanders.

To strengthen the line, he committed the 2d Division to the central sector where positions were weakest, even though that unit had not fully recovered from losses in the Kunu-ri roadblock, and pressed General Almond to quicken the preparation of the X Corps whose forces needed refurbishing before moving to the front. Realizing that time probably was against him, he also ordered his western units to organize a bridgehead above Seoul, one deep enough to protect the Han River bridges, from which to cover a withdrawal below the city should an enemy offensive compel a general retirement.

Enemy forces opened attacks on New Year's Eve, directing their major effort toward Seoul. When the offensive gained momentum, Ridgway ordered his western forces back to the Seoul bridgehead and pulled the rest of the Eighth Army to positions roughly on line to the east. After strong Chinese units assaulted the bridgehead, he withdrew to a line forty miles below Seoul. In the west, the last troops pulled out of Seoul on January 4, 1951, demolishing the Han bridges on the way out, as Chinese entered the city from the north.

Only light Chinese forces pushed south of the city and enemy attacks in the west diminished. In central and eastern Korea, North Korean forces pushed an attack until mid-January. When pressure finally ended all along the front, reconnaissance patrols ordered north by Ridgway to maintain contact encountered only light screening forces, and intelligence sources reported that most enemy units had withdrawn to refit. It became clear to Ridgway that a primitive logistical system permitted enemy forces to undertake offensive operations for no more than a week or two before they had to pause for replacements and new supplies, a pattern he exploited when he assigned his troops their next objective. Land gains, he pointed out, would have only incidental importance. Primarily, Eighth Army forces were to inflict maximum casualties on the enemy with minimum casualties to themselves. "To do this," Ridgway instructed, "we must wage a war of maneuver—slashing at the enemy when he withdraws and fighting delaying actions when he attacks."

Whereas Ridgway was now certain his forces could achieve that objective, General MacArthur was far less optimistic. Earlier, in acknowledging the Chinese intervention, he had notified Washington that the Chinese could drive the UNC out of Korea unless he received major reinforcement. At the time, however, there was still only a slim reserve of combat units in the United States. Four more National Guard divisions were being brought into federal service to build up the General Reserve, but not with commitment in Korea in mind. The main concern in Washington was the possibility that the Chinese entry into Korea was only one part of a USSR move toward global war, a concern great enough to lead President Truman to declare a state of national emergency on December 16. Washington officials, in any event, considered Korea no place to become involved in a major war. For all of these reasons, the Joint Chiefs of Staff notified MacArthur that a major build-up of UNC forces was out of the question. MacArthur was to stay in Korea if he could, but should the Chinese drive UNC forces back on Pusan, the Joint Chiefs would order a withdrawal to Japan.

Contrary to the reasoning in Washington, MacArthur meanwhile proposed four retaliatory measures against the Chinese: blockade the China coast, destroy China's war industries through naval and air attacks, reinforce the troops in Korea with Chinese Nationalist forces, and allow diversionary operations by Nationalist troops against the China mainland. These proposals for escalation received serious study in Washington but were eventually discarded in favor of sustaining the policy of confining the fighting to Korea.

Interchanges between Washington and Tokyo next centered on the timing of a withdrawal from Korea. MacArthur believed Washington should establish all the criteria of an evacuation, whereas Washington wanted MacArthur first to provide the military guidelines on timing. The whole issue was finally settled after General J. Lawton Collins, Army Chief of Staff, visited Korea, saw that the Eighth Army was improving under Ridgway's leadership, and became as confident as Ridgway that the Chinese would be unable to drive the Eighth Army off the peninsula. "As of now," General Collins announced on January 15, "we are going to stay and fight."

Ten days later, Ridgway opened a cautious offensive, beginning with attacks in the west and gradually widening them to the east. The Eighth Army advanced slowly and methodically, ridge by ridge, phase line by phase line, wiping out each pocket of resistance before moving farther north. Enemy forces fought back vigorously and in February struck back in the central region. During that counterattack, the 23d Regiment of the 2d Division successfully defended the town of Chipyong-ni against a much larger Chinese force, a victory that to Ridgway symbolized the Eighth Army's complete recovery of its fighting spirit. After defeating the enemy's February effort, the Eighth Army again advanced steadily, recaptured Seoul by mid-March, and by the first day of spring stood just below the 38th parallel.

Intelligence agencies meanwhile uncovered evidence of rear area offensive preparations by the enemy. In an attempt to spoil those preparations, Ridgway opened an attack on April 5 toward an objective line, designated Kansas, roughly ten miles above the 38th parallel. After the Eighth Army reached Line Kansas, he sent a force toward an enemy supply area just above Kansas in the west-central zone known as the Iron Triangle. Evidence of an imminent enemy offensive continued to mount as these troops advanced. As a precaution, Ridgway on April 12 published a plan for orderly delaying actions to be fought when and if the enemy attacked, an act, events proved, that was one of his last as commander of the Eighth Army.

Plans being written in Washington in March, had they been carried out, well might have kept the Eighth Army from moving above the 38th parallel toward Line Kansas. For as a gradual development since the Chinese intervention, the United States and other members of the UNC coalition by that time were willing, as they had not been the past autumn, to accept the clearance of enemy troops from South Korea as a suitable final result of their effort. On March 20, the Joint Chiefs notified MacArthur that a Presidential announcement was being drafted which would indicate a willingness to negotiate with the Chinese and North Koreans to make "satisfactory arrangements for concluding the fighting," and which would be issued "before any advance with major forces north of 38th Parallel." Before the President's announcement could be made, however, MacArthur issued his own offer to enemy commanders to discuss an end to the fighting, but it was an offer that placed the UNC in the role of victor and which indeed sounded like an ultimatum. "The enemy . . . must by now be painfully aware," MacArthur said in part, "that a decision of the United Nations to depart from its tolerant effort to contain the war to the area of Korea, through an expansion of our military operations to its coastal areas and interior bases, would doom Red China to the risk of imminent military collapse." President Truman considered the statement at cross-purposes with the one he was to have issued and so canceled his own. Hoping the enemy might sue for an armistice if kept under pressure, he permitted the question of crossing the 38th parallel to be settled on the basis of tactical considerations. Thus it became Ridgway's decision; and the parallel would not again assume political significance.

President Truman had in mind, after the March episode, to relieve MacArthur but had yet to make a final decision when the next incident occurred. On April 5, Joseph W. Martin, Republican leader in the House of Representatives, rose and read MacArthur's response to a request for comment on an address Martin had made suggesting the use of Nationalist Chinese forces to open a second front. In that response, MacArthur said he believed in "meeting force with maximum counterforce," and that the use of Nationalist Chinese forces fitted that belief. Convinced, also, that ". . . if we lose this war to Communism in Asia the fall of Europe is inevitable, win it and Europe most probably would avoid war . . . ," he added that there could be " . . . no substitute for victory . . ." in Korea.

President Truman could not accept MacArthur's open disagreement with and challenge of national policy. There were also grounds for a charge of insubordination, since MacArthur had not cleared his March 24 statement or his response to Representative Martin with Washington, contrary to a Presidential directive issued in December requiring prior clearance of all releases touching on national policy. Concluding that MacArthur was ". . . unable to give his wholehearted support to the policies of the United States government and of the United Nations in matters pertaining to his official duties," President Truman recalled MacArthur on April 11 and named General Ridgway as successor. MacArthur returned to the United States to receive the plaudits of a nation shocked by the relief of one of its greatest military heroes. Before the Congress and the public he defended his own views against those of the Truman Administration. The controversy stirred up was to endure for many months, but in the end the nation accepted the fact that, whatever the merit of MacArthur's arguments, the President as Commander in Chief had a right to relieve him.

Before transferring from Korea to Tokyo, General Ridgway on April 14 turned over the Eighth Army to Lt. Gen. James A. Van Fleet. Eight days later twenty-one Chinese and nine North Korean divisions launched strong attacks in western Korea and lighter attacks in the east, with the major effort aimed at Seoul. General Van Fleet withdrew through successive delaying positions to previously established defenses a few miles north of Seoul where he finally contained the enemy advance. When enemy forces withdrew to refurbish, Van Fleet laid plans for a return to Line Kansas but then postponed the countermove when his intelligence sources indicated he had stopped only the first effort of the enemy offensive.

Enemy forces renewed their attack after darkness on May 15. Whereas Van Fleet had expected the major assault again to be directed against Seoul, enemy forces this time drove hardest in the east central region. Adjusting units to place more troops in the path of the enemy advance and laying down tremendous amounts of artillery fire, Van Fleet halted the attack by May 20 after the enemy had penetrated thirty miles. Determined to prevent the enemy from assembling strength for another attack, he immediately ordered the Eighth Army forward. The Chinese and North Koreans, disorganized after their own attacks, resisted only where their supply installations were threatened. Elsewhere, the Eighth Army advanced with almost surprising ease and by May 31 was just short of Line Kansas. The next day Van Fleet sent part of his force toward Line Wyoming whose seizure would give him control of the lower portion of the Iron Triangle. The Eighth Army occupied both Line Kansas and the Wyoming bulge by mid-June.

Since the Kansas-Wyoming line traced ground suitable for a strong defense, it was the decision in Washington to hold that line and wait for a bid for armistice negotiations from the Chinese and North Koreans, to whom it should be clear by this time that their committed forces lacked the ability to conquer South Korea. In line with this decision, Van Fleet began to fortify his positions. Enemy forces meanwhile used the respite from attack to recoup heavy losses and to develop defenses opposite the Eighth Army. The fighting lapsed into patrolling and small local clashes.

The Static War

On June 23, 1951, Jacob Malik, the USSR delegate to the United Nations, announced in New York during a broadcast of the U.N. radio program, "The Price of Peace," that the USSR believed the war in Korea could be settled. "Discussions," he said, "should be started between the belligerents for a cease-fire and an armistice. . . ." When Communist China endorsed Malik's proposal over Peiping radio, President Truman authorized General Ridgway to arrange armistice talks with his enemy counterpart. Through an exchange of radio messages both sides agreed to open negotiations on July 10 at the town of Kaesong, in territory which was then no-man's-land in the west but which would become a neutral area.

At the first armistice conference the two delegations agreed that hostilities would continue until an armistice agreement was signed. Except for brief, violent episodes, however, action along the front would never regain the momentum of the first year. By July 26, the two armistice delegations fixed the points to be settled in order to achieve an armistice. But then the enemy delegates began to delay negotiations, to gain time, it seemed, in which to strengthen their military forces, and thus also to strengthen their bargaining position. In any case, the enemy delegation continued to delay and finally broke off negotiations on August 22.

General Van Fleet, at that juncture, opened limited-objective attacks. In east-central Korea, he sent forces toward terrain objectives five to seven miles above Line Kansas—among them places named the Punchbowl, Bloody Ridge, and

Heartbreak Ridge—to drive enemy forces from positions that favored an attack on Line Kansas. These objectives were won by the last week of October. In the west, Van Fleet's forces struck northwest on a forty-mile front to secure a new line three to four miles beyond the Wyoming line in order to protect important supply roads that lay only a short distance behind the existing western front. The new line was reached by October 12.

These successes may have had an influence on the enemy, who agreed to return to the armistice conference table. Negotiations resumed on October 25, this time at Panmunjom, a tiny settlement seven miles southeast of Kaesong. Hope for an early armistice grew on November 27 when the two delegations agreed that a line of demarcation during an armistice would be the existing line of contact provided an armistice agreement was reached within thirty days. Hence, while both sides awaited the outcome of negotiations, fighting during the remainder of 1951 tapered off to patrol clashes, raids, and small battles for possession of outposts in no-man's-land. The first tactical use of helicopters by U.S. forces occurred about this time when almost a thousand marines were lifted to a front-line position and a like number returned to the rear.

Discord over several issues, including the exchange of prisoners of war, prevented an armistice agreement within the stipulated thirty days. The prisoner of war quarrel heightened in January 1952 after UNC delegates proposed to give captives a choice in repatriation proceedings, maintaining that those prisoners who did not wish to return to their homelands could be simply "set at liberty" according to the Geneva Conventions of 1949. The enemy representatives protested vigorously. While argument continued, both sides tacitly extended the November 27 provisions for a line of demarcation. This had the effect of holding battle action to the pattern of the thirty-day waiting period.

By May 1952 the two delegations were completely deadlocked on the repatriation issue. On the 7th of that month inmates of UNC Prison Camp No. 1 on Koje-do, an island off the southern coast, on orders smuggled to them from North Korea managed to entice the U.S. camp commander to a compound gate, drag him inside, and keep him captive. The strategy, which became clear in subsequent prisoner demands, was to trade the U.S. officer's life and release for UNC admissions of inhumane treatment of captives, including alleged cruelties during previous screenings of prisoners in which a large number of prisoners refused repatriation. The obvious objective was to discredit the voluntary repatriation stand taken by the UNC delegation at Panmunjom.

Although a new camp commander obtained his predecessor's release, in the process he signed a damaging statement including an admission that ". . . there have been instances of bloodshed where many prisoners of war have been killed and wounded by U.N. Forces." There was no change in the UNC stand on repatriation but the statement was widely exploited by the Communists at Panmunjom and elsewhere for its propaganda value.

Amid the Koje-do trouble, General Ridgway received transfer orders placing him in command of NATO forces in Europe. General Mark W. Clark became the new commander in the Far East, with one less responsibility than Mac-Arthur and Ridgway had carried. On April 28 a peace treaty with Japan had gone into effect, restoring Japan's sovereignty and thus ending the occupation. Faced immediately with the Koje-do affair, General Clark had the impression of walking ". . . into something that felt remarkably like a swinging door. . . ." He immediately repudiated the prison camp commander's statement. Moving swiftly, he placed Brig. Gen. Haydon L. Boatner in charge of the camp with instructions to move the prisoners into smaller, more manageable compounds and to institute other measures that would eliminate the likelihood of another uprising. General Boatner completed the task on June 10.

While argument over repatriation went on at Panmunjom, action at the front continued as a series of artillery duels, patrols, ambushes, raids, and bitter contests for outpost positions. But for all the furious and costly small-scale battles that took place, the lines remained substantially unchanged at the end of 1952. The armistice conference meanwhile went into an indefinite recess in October with the repatriation issue still unresolved.

In November, the American people elected a Republican President, Dwight D. Eisenhower. An issue in the campaign had been the war in Korea, over which there was a growing popular discontent, in particular with the lack of progress toward an armistice. In a campaign pledge to "go to Korea," Eisenhower implied that if elected he would attempt to end the war quickly. Consequently, when the President-elect in early December fulfilled his promise to visit Korea, there was indeed some expectation of a dramatic change in the conduct of the war. General Clark went so far as to prepare detailed estimates of measures necessary to obtain a military victory. But it quickly became clear that Eisenhower, like President Truman, preferred to seek an honorable armistice. As he would write later, however, the President-elect did decide to let Communist authorities know that if satisfactory progress toward an armistice was not forthcoming, ". . . we intended to move decisively without inhibition in our use of weapons, and would no longer be responsible for confining hostilities to the Korean peninsula." Immediately after taking office, President Eisenhower made sure this word reached Moscow, Peiping, and P'yongyang.

In the hope of prompting a resumption of armistice negotiations, General Clark in February 1953 proposed to his enemy counterpart that the two sides exchange sick and wounded prisoners. But there was no response and no break in the deadlock at Panmunjom by spring. At the front, where in February Lt. Gen. Maxwell D. Taylor had replaced General Van Fleet as the Eighth Army commander, the battle action continued in the mold of the previous year. The break finally came near the end of March, about three weeks after the death of Josef Stalin, when enemy armistice delegates not only replied favorably to General Clark's proposal that sick and wounded captives be exchanged but also suggested that this exchange perhaps could ". . . lead to the smooth settlement of the entire question of prisoners of war." With that, the armistice conference resumed in April. An exchange of sick and wounded prisoners was carried out that same month; and before the middle of June, the prisoner repatriation problem was settled through agreement that each side would have an opportunity to persuade those captives refusing return to their homelands to change their minds.

The pace of battle quickened in May when Chinese forces launched regimental attacks against outposts guarding approaches to the Eighth Army's main line in the west. A large battle flared on June 10 when three Chinese divisions penetrated two miles through a South Korean position in central Korea before being contained. That engagement could have been the last of the war since the terms of an armistice by then were all but complete. But on June 18 ROK President Rhee, who from the beginning had objected to any armistice that left Korea divided, ordered the release of North Korean prisoners who had refused repatriation. Within a few days most of these North Korean captives "broke out" of prison camp and disappeared among a co-operative South Korean populace. Since the captives had been guarded by South Korean troops, UNC officials disclaimed responsibility for the break, but the enemy armistice delegates denounced the action as a serious breach of faith. It took more than a month to repair the damage done by Rhee's order.

Enemy forces used this delay to wrest more ground from UNC control, attacking on July 13 and driving a wedge eight miles deep in the Eighth Army's central sector. General Taylor deployed units to contain the shoulders and point of the wedge, then counterattacked. But he halted his attack force on July 20 short of the original line since by that date the armistice delegations had come to a new accord and needed only to work out a few small details. Taylor's order to halt ended the last major battle of the war.

After a week of dealing with administrative matters, each chief delegate signed the military armistice agreement at Panmunjom at 10:00 a.m. on July 27. General Clark and the enemy commanders later affixed their signatures at their respective headquarters. As stipulated in the agreement, all fighting stopped twelve hours after the first signing, at 10:00 p.m., July 27, 1953. When the final casualty report for the thirty-seven months of fighting was prepared, total UNC casualties reached over 550,000, including almost 95,000 dead. U.S. losses numbered 142,091, of whom 33,629 were killed, 103,284 wounded, and 5,178 missing or captured. U.S. Army casualties alone totaled 27,704 dead, 77,596 wounded, and 4,658 missing or captured. The bulk of these casualties occurred during the first year of the fighting. The estimate of enemy casualties, including prisoners, exceeded 1,500,000, of which 900,000, almost two-thirds, were Chinese.

The Aftermath

By the terms of the armistice, the line of demarcation between North and South Korea closely approximated the front line as it existed at the final hour. (*Map 46*) Slanting as the line did from a point on the west coast fifteen miles below the 38th parallel northeastward to an east coast anchor forty miles above the parallel, the demarcation represented a relatively small adjustment of the

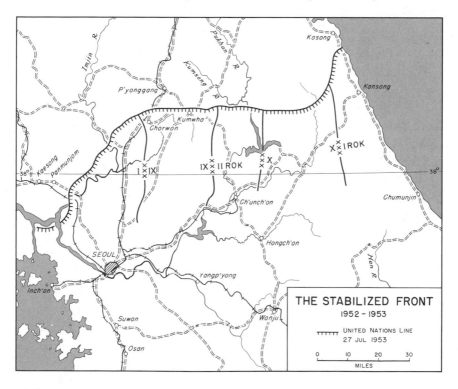

MAP 46

prewar division. Within three days of the signing of the armistice, each opposing force withdrew two kilometers from this line to establish a demilitarized zone that was not to be trespassed.

The armistice provisions forbade either force to bring additional troops or new weapons into Korea, although replacement one for one and in kind was permissible. To oversee the enforcement of all armistice terms and to negotiate settlements of any violations of them, a Military Armistice Commission composed of an equal number of officers from each side was established. This body was assisted by a Neutral Nations Supervisory Commission whose members came from Sweden, Switzerland, Czechoslovakia, and Poland. Representatives of those same countries, with India furnishing an umpire and custodial forces, formed a Neutral Nations Repatriation Commission to handle the disposition of prisoners refusing repatriation. Finally, a provision of the armistice recommended that the belligerent governments convene a political conference to negotiate a final settlement of the whole Korean question.

By September 6, all prisoners wishing to be repatriated had been exchanged. From the UNC returnees came full details of brutally harsh treatment in enemy prison camps and of an extensive Communist indoctrination program, of "brainwashing" techniques, designed to produce prisoner collaboration. Several hundred U.S. returnees were investigated on charges of collaborating with the enemy, but few were convicted.

The transfer of nonrepatriates to the Neutral Nations Repatriation Commission was undertaken next. In the drawn out and troublesome procedure that followed, few of the prisoners changed their minds as officials from both sides attempted to convince former members of their respective commands that they should return home. Of twenty-three Americans who at first refused repatriation, two decided to return. On February 1, 1954, the Neutral Nations Repatriation Commission dissolved itself after releasing the last of the nonrepatriates as civilians free to decide their own destinations.

The main scene then shifted to Geneva, Switzerland, where the political conference recommended in the armistice agreement convened on April 26. There was a complete impasse from the beginning: the representatives of UNC member nations wanted to reunify Korea through elections supervised by the United Nations; the Communist delegation refused to recognize the U.N.'s authority to deal with the matter. The conference on Korea closed June 15, 1954, with the country still divided and with opposing forces, although their guns remained silent, still facing each other across the demilitarized zone. The prognosis was that this situation would continue for some time to come.

The Geneva impasse leaving Korea divided essentially along the prewar line could scarcely be viewed as merely re-establishing the land's *status quo ante bellum*. For by the end of the war, the ROK Army had grown to a well-organized force of sixteen divisions and was scheduled to raise four more divisions, a force North Korea's resources would be strained to match. Within days of the armistice, moreover, South Korea had a mutual security pact with the United States and a first installment, $200 million, of promised American economic aid.

The war's impact reached far beyond Korea. Despite criticism of the armistice by those who agreed with General MacArthur that there was "no substitute for victory," the UNC had upheld the U.N. principle of suppressing armed aggression. True, the U.N. Security Council had been able to enlist forces under the U.N. banner in June 1950 only in the absence of the USSR veto. Nevertheless, the UNC success strengthened the possibility of keeping or restoring peace through the U.N. machinery.

More far reaching was the war's impact on the two Great Power blocs. The primary result for the western bloc was a decided strengthening of the NATO alliance. Virtually without military power in June 1950, NATO could call on fifty divisions and strong air and naval contingents by 1953, a build-up directly attributable to the increased threat of general war seen in the outbreak of hostilities in Korea. With further reinforcement in the NATO forecast at the end of the Korean War, USSR armed aggression in western Europe became unlikely. For the east, the major result was the emergence of Communist China as a Great Power. A steady improvement in the Chinese army and air force during the war gave China a more powerful military posture at war's end than when it had intervened; and its performance in Korea, despite vast losses, won China respect as a nation to be reckoned with not only in Asian but in world affairs.

Outside these direct impacts of the war, the relative positions of west and east also had been affected during the war years by the development of thermonuclear devices. The United States exploded its first such device in 1952, the USSR in August 1953. The exact consequences of all these changes were incalculable. But it was certain that the cold war would continue and that both power blocs would face new challenges and new responses.

CHAPTER 15

The U.S. Army in Vietnam

In an effort to prevent French Indochina from falling to Communism, the United States in 1950 began to grant military aid to French forces in Southeast Asia, including those in Vietnam. This commitment was at the outset minor, only a fragment of the worldwide Military Assistance Program, but over the years it was destined to grow in size and complexity until it overshadowed other commitments and became a test of American resolve.

In Vietnam the United States acted at first to help the French regain military control in the face of a Communist-dominated nationalist movement. When a climate for true self-determination could be achieved, it was hoped that France would grant the nation independence.

Before the United States was deeply committed, the conflict in Vietnam had lost the complexion of colonial war and emerged as a struggle for survival of a small nation in the pattern of what the Communists call wars of national liberation. It was complicated by similar but less well-organized Communist aggression against the neighboring countries of Laos and Cambodia, by an ideological split in the Sino-Soviet Communist bloc, and by a possibility that as a testing ground between Communists and non-Communists it might explode into broader war and bring the world powers into direct conflict.

Role of the United States Through the Geneva Accords

Since the conflict from the start involved primarily ground operations, officers and men of the U.S. Army made up the bulk of the U.S. military forces committed. Only a few Americans were involved at first, constituting the Military Assistance Advisory Group, Indochina, subsequently redesignated Military Assistance Advisory Group, Vietnam. The task was limited initially to administering financial and military aid to the French and those Vietnamese forces loyal to the French-sponsored government of the emperor, Bao Dai.

This situation prevailed for almost four years as the French continued a long-term effort to wrest control of the countryside from Communist forces known as the Viet Minh under the veteran Communist leader, Ho Chi Minh. The Viet Minh early had proclaimed a separate government professing jurisdiction over the entire country, a self-styled Democratic Republic of Vietnam. Provided extensive military assistance from China, including advisers and technicians, the Communists had established control over most of the northern and central provinces, leaving to the French and the Bao Dai government little more than the principal cities and a few provinces near the city of Saigon in the south.

Unwilling to grant the Vietnamese full independence, the French were never able to rally widespread support from the populace. Beset by opposition in France to a colonial war and lacking the military forces to meet Communist insurrections in all of Indochina, the French in 1954 agreed to an international conference to be convened at Geneva to negotiate a settlement.

The discussion at Geneva involved nine nations, including the United States, France, Great Britain, the Soviet Union, and Communist China, representatives of Laos and Cambodia, and separate delegates from the Democratic Republic of Vietnam (Ho Chi Minh) and the State of Vietnam (Bao Dai). The conference produced what became known as the Geneva Accords, a signed cease-fire agreement and an unsigned Final Declaration, with separate documents covering Laos and Cambodia. For Vietnam, the Geneva Accords directed a military disengagement based on a temporary demarcation line across the narrow waist of the country at the 17th parallel. (*Map 47*) The territory north of the line was to be administered by the Viet Minh, that south of the line by the French. Military forces were to regroup on either side of a demilitarized zone ten kilometers wide, while civilians were to be free to choose between the two zones. No increase in foreign military aid was to be made. To reunite the country, Vietnam-wide elections were to be held two years later.

The Vietnamese government in the south, objecting—as did Ho Chi Minh's government—to any division of the country and convinced that free elections were impossible in the north, refused to accept these two provisions as binding. The United States in turn declined to endorse the decisions but agreed to abide by them and to forego use of force to disturb them so long as others did the same. In regard to elections, the United States noted its long commitment to achieving unity in divided countries through elections supervised by the United Nations.

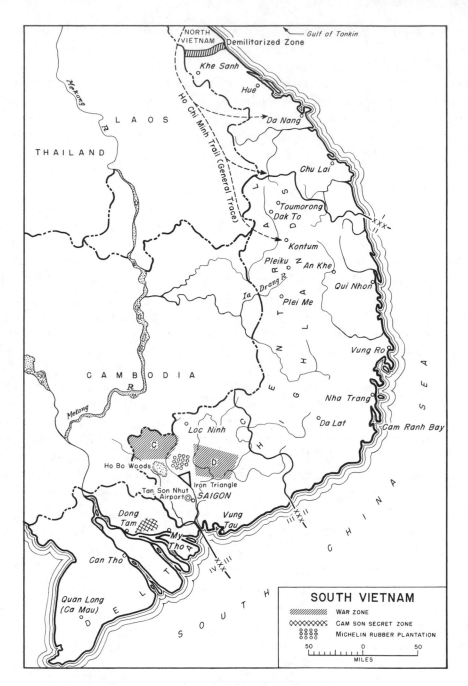

MAP 47

Early Growth of the Insurgency

As an armistice settled over what became, unintentionally but actually, two Vietnams—North and South—over 800,000 North Vietnamese moved to the south. Approximately 100,000 South Vietnamese moved north, most of them active Viet Minh insurgents, while Ho Chi Minh called on a political cadre of the Viet Minh to remain in the south in preparation for what he expected would be a sure Communist victory in the elections. The Viet Minh also retained control of their base areas, the secret zones they had established in the south.

The United States, meanwhile, acted to create a bulwark against further Communist expansion in Southeast Asia by preserving the southern half of Vietnam outside the Communist sphere. Approximately 400 American advisers, already present in Saigon at the time of the Geneva Accords, remained to assist the South Vietnamese government. Through them the United States worked to improve a South Vietnamese Army of some 200,000 men that had fought with the French and to provide extensive economic aid to the government, which with promise at last of full independence had gained a strong premier in Ngo Dinh Diem. Convinced that a large majority of Vietnamese desired a free nation outside the bonds of totalitarian Communism and that by the example of successful resistance to Communism in Vietnam other free Asian peoples would be encouraged to resist, the United States under four successive presidents—Eisenhower, Kennedy, Johnson, and Nixon—worked to make the institutions of a free society available to that half of the nation to which circumstances afforded access.

Among the first obstacles was the inevitable stigma attached to a government originally sponsored by a colonial power, as well as the problem of convincing a people exploited by foreigners through much of their history that the United States had no colonial designs. In a country where a majority of the people were Buddhists, resentment was strong against heavy representation in the government of a Catholic minority, many of whom were refugees from North Vietnam. Two relatively small but powerful religious sects, the Cao Dai and the Hoa Hao, exerted strong political pressures even after the South Vietnamese Army succeeded in establishing authority over autonomous military forces the sects had long maintained. In the sparsely populated plateaus and mountains of the interior—the Central Highlands—tribal groups known as the Montagnards continued a long resistance to governmental authority. The basically agrarian South Vietnamese economy, lacking the industry and minerals of the north, was near chaos. Long under Viet Minh control, much of the countryside was devoid of government services; and corruption that had flourished under colonial rule was rampant. The emperor, Bao Dai, was of no assistance, having deserted his country to reside abroad.

Ruling autocratically, Premier Diem managed to bring a measure of order to the country, and the economy improved. Late in 1955 he conducted a national referendum in which the people chose between him and the absent emperor. Winning the referendum handily, he proclaimed a republic with himself as president. He outmaneuvered dissident Army officers seeking to seize power, defeated a strong band of Saigon gangsters, the Binh Xuyen, resettled refugees from the north, and made a start on a program of land reform.

Early in 1956, shortly before the time designated by the Geneva Accords for general elections, the French pulled the last of their forces out of Vietnam. President Diem then reiterated South Vietnamese objections to Vietnam-wide elections, again declaring that free expression was impossible in the north under a totalitarian regime. The United States backed this position with the notice that "there must first be conditions which preclude intimidation or coercion of the electorate."

Since the Viet Minh anticipated some support in the south and were sure of their controlled electorate in the more populous north, they had allowed the Communist insurgency in the south to lie quiescent while they awaited triumph in the elections. They were preoccupied for the moment in any case with asserting their authority in the north, crushing a popular revolt, and conducting a reign of terror to bring agricultural lands under state control. When the elections failed to come off, it took time for the Viet Minh to reactivate the insurgency, since the organization they had left behind in the south had to be rebuilt and strengthened.

Called by the South Vietnamese the Viet Cong, a contraction meaning Vietnamese Communist, the insurgents in the south gradually increased their numbers through a campaign of propaganda and coercion. At the same time the North Vietnamese government made the decision to bring down the South Vietnamese government by aggression, and in 1958 began to infiltrate political cadres and military reinforcements from the north. Terrorism, assassination, sabotage, abduction, and attacks on civil guard and local defense units mounted. In late 1960 North Vietnam sponsored a National Front for the Liberation of South Vietnam, designed to attract other nationalists in addition to Communists, a device practiced by the Viet Minh in earlier days with considerable success.

Organized and trained to counter a conventional invasion, the South Vietnamese Army was ill prepared to deal with insurgency, and the limited

numbers of U.S. advisers were hard put to provide the comprehensive assistance needed. The task was complicated when the French in 1955 began to
pull out their forces and started a precipitate transfer of American military
equipment to the South Vietnamese Army. To bring some order to the process,
the United States early in 1956 sent 350 more military men to form the
Temporary Equipment Recovery Mission. Aware of the proviso of the
Geneva Accords prohibiting increased foreign military strength, the United
States maintained that these men replaced departing French advisers. Four
years later the International Control Commission, set up to police the Accords,
approved expansion of the Military Assistance Advisory Group, Vietnam,
to 685 spaces, thus accommodating most of the 350.

The American advisers were concentrated in Saigon, helping the Vietnamese with high-level planning, training, and logistical organization. Only
in early 1960, as the insurgency continued to increase and it became apparent
that the South Vietnamese Army had to be drastically improved, did President Diem agree to assigning U.S. advisers to field units down to battalion
level. Even then, because of the limited number of advisers, assignments had
to be selective and temporary.

While the Viet Cong insurgency was expanding, President Diem fell
more and more under the influence of members of his family, whom he had
placed in high positions, and the government grew remote from the needs
and desires of the people. Many South Vietnamese were alienated because
Diem continued to rule autocratically, failed to involve the people in government at the local level, moved slowly in land reform, employed arbitrary
policies in military and civil administration, and used oppressive police
methods. Although Diem rationalized his policies as either necessary to defeat
the insurgency or correctable only after national security was achieved, dissatisfaction with his rule spread.

Limited Increase in U.S. Commitment

During 1961 the Viet Cong campaign of murder and abduction continued to increase, directed not only at local officials but often at their families
and at the civilian population in general. With such means was awe of the
Viet Cong induced, and a belief spread that the government was incapable
of protecting the people. Supported at this point by aid from both China and
the Soviet Union, the Viet Cong by the fall of the year had achieved enough
power to threaten the existence of the Diem regime.

Seriously perturbed by these developments, President Kennedy reviewed in detail the reports and recommendations of a number of special missions sent to study the extent of the crisis. Conscious of the violence already done the Geneva Accords by North Vietnamese infiltration and support of the Viet Cong, he finally decided to increase U.S. support, but to stop short of committing combat troops. With this decision, the U.S. commitment grew in 1962 to more than 11,000 men, two-thirds of them U.S. Army.

In February 1962 the U.S. Military Assistance Command, Vietnam, was established in Saigon with General Paul D. Harkins as commander. This new command, which eventually absorbed the Military Assistance Advisory Group, was a subordinate unified command under the operational control of the Commander in Chief, Pacific, who was in turn responsible to the Secretary of Defense through the Joint Chiefs of Staff. General Harkins also directly commanded the Army component.

During 1962 the increase in U.S. strength more than tripled the number of officers and men directly engaged in the advisory effort, and for the first time made possible the attachment of advisers to most South Vietnamese Army units in the field. Men of the U.S. Army Special Forces also were introduced to train Civilian Irregular Defense Groups, formed among the Montagnard tribesmen in the highlands and other South Vietnamese in remote border regions.

The Communist threat to the highlands had been growing fast in conjunction with a Communist movement, supported by the North Vietnamese, in neighboring Laos. In establishing loose control over large portions of Laos, the Communists had firmly secured a wide strip along the South Vietnamese frontier through which they built trails and roads leading from North Vietnam around the flank of the demilitarized zone into South Vietnam. Known collectively as the Ho Chi Minh Trail, these supply routes contained logistical bases and relay stations adequate for a sustained war effort by large forces.

Manning fortified outposts and patrolling extensively, the Civilian Irregular Defense Groups with their Special Forces advisers sought to disrupt a steady infiltration of North Vietnamese from Laos into South Vietnam and to prevent a Communist takeover in the highlands. Even though interested world powers achieved a semblance of peace in Laos with another Geneva conference in mid-1962, the Communists retained possession of the border zone and continued their build-up. Some 60,000 South Vietnamese, trained during 1962 and 1963 by the U.S. Army Special Forces, nevertheless held their positions in the highlands and elsewhere along the frontier.

The role of the advisers throughout Vietnam was difficult and challenging. These were men charged with developing leadership among a people whose colonial rulers had for long years discouraged leadership. These were men who had to adapt swiftly to social, political, and economic conditions foreign to their experience; to communicate their ideas and military acumen to Vietnamese counterparts separated from them by a substantial language and cultural barrier; and to entrust their own welfare and safety to foreign troops often unproven and sometimes infiltrated by an enemy almost impossible to detect. All their goals they had to achieve in an advisory rather than a command role.

When U.S. strength increased in 1962, most of the American effort went into a new task of operational support for South Vietnam armed forces, with special attention to mobility, communications, intelligence, and logistics. Easily the most dramatic and portentous development was the introduction of the helicopter to provide Vietnamese Army units, heretofore mainly road-bound and thus highly vulnerable to ambush, a new mobility.

The first helicopter to fly in large numbers in South Vietnam was the CH–21, the Shawnee, followed in 1963 by the faster and more versatile UH–1, the Huey. The helicopter became the symbol of a new kind of war, a checkerboard campaign in which units might be picked up and set down swiftly almost anywhere from the highland plateaus and jungle-canopied mountains to the densely populated rice-growing regions of the coast and the Mekong Delta. An original assignment of one helicopter company to each of four Vietnam Army corps gradually grew to one per division. As the enemy reacted by bringing in more antiaircraft guns, armed versions of the Huey were added.

By the spring of 1963 South Vietnam had made considerable progress in the military struggle, but the political situation had worsened. Continuing governmental repression, coercion, favoritism, and corruption alienated more and more of the people. The ambassador and other U.S. representatives pressed for reforms, but to little avail. After the government's serious mishandling of a nationwide demonstration by Buddhists in mid-1963, the United States withheld subsidies for imports and for the Vietnam Army Special Forces, which President Diem had used to attack Buddhist pagodas.

On 1 November 1963, a military junta of senior South Vietnamese officers staged a *coup d'etat* in which the president and his brother Nhu were killed. There followed a year and a half of political instability, uncertainty, and disintegration of government control that the Viet Cong exploited to the fullest. Despite a gradual American build-up to approximately 23,000 men (not quite two-thirds Army) that afforded additional operational support

ARMED HELICOPTERS BOMBARDING THE ENEMY IN THE CENTRAL HIGHLANDS

and provided many more advisory teams for provinces and districts, the Viet Cong increased their strength to approximately one hundred thousand, of which about one-third were "main force" troops (first-line combat soldiers organized in battalions and regiments). The added strength included infiltrated North Vietnamese Army regulars.

In much of South Vietnam the Viet Cong were sufficiently in control to levy taxes in rural regions, and even though government troops might control many areas in daylight, it was generally accepted in much of the countryside that "the night belongs to the Viet Cong." A government program to relocate people in supposedly secure "strategic hamlets" all but collapsed. For the first time Viet Cong units launched numerous daylight attacks, and South Vietnamese casualties increased sharply. Although U.S. troops continued to serve only in advisory and support roles, U.S. losses also rose: 42 U.S. Army troops were killed, for example, in 1963; in 1964, 118 died.

Communist attacks against U.S. facilities were also mounting. In August 1964 North Vietnamese patrol boats engaged U.S. destroyers in the Gulf of Tonkin. In retaliation, President Johnson ordered air strikes by U.S. Navy planes against North Vietnamese patrol boats, their bases, and supporting facilities in North Vietnam. The Congress at this point passed a resolution authorizing the President to take necessary measures to repel attack against U.S. forces and to prevent further aggression in Southeast Asia.

Growing U.S. Commitment

Beginning early in 1965, the Viet Cong, reinforced by North Vietnamese Army units, opened a series of savage assaults. Under attacks that destroyed on an average the equivalent of a battalion a week, the South Vietnamese Army began to crumble. Leadership failed. Desertions increased. In the delta and Central Highlands the Communists demonstrated their strength by seizing and temporarily holding some district capitals. A Communist push from the highlands to the sea to cut South Vietnam in half and isolate Saigon appeared in the offing. The morale of the people dropped sharply, and some observers gave the nation no more than six months to live.

Having reaffirmed U.S. commitment to South Vietnam upon taking office after the death of President Kennedy, President Johnson viewed the situation with grave concern. When in February 1965, the Viet Cong attacked a U.S. compound and helicopter base in the Central Highlands, killing eight Americans, the President ordered retaliatory air strikes against selected military targets in North Vietnam. He also directed that dependents of U.S. military and government personnel be evacuated from South Vietnam, sent to the country a Hawk air defense battalion, and authorized U.S. Air Force jets to assist South Vietnamese Army units in emergencies. Amid continuing terrorism against U.S. installations, including the explosion of a bomb at the U.S. Embassy in Saigon, and mounting evidence of North Vietnamese support of the Viet Cong, the President ordered sustained bombing of military targets in North Vietnam in hope of bolstering South Vietnamese morale, reducing North Vietnamese infiltration into the south, and making North Vietnam pay a higher price for its aggression.

To guard American installations, the President ordered the first U.S. ground troops to Vietnam, two U.S. Marine Corps battalions that arrived in March at Da Nang, the country's second largest city. A U.S. Army military police battalion arrived two weeks later at Saigon. In early April the President ordered two more Marine battalions and an air squadron to Da Nang and authorized the marines to expand their operations beyond their defensive perimeters. This marked the start of a short-lived "enclave strategy," under which U.S. troops were to secure selected areas, free Vietnamese troops for other operations, and demonstrate American resolve.

In May the 173d Airborne Brigade arrived to provide security for an air base at Bien Hoa, north of Saigon. The next month U.S. B–52 strategic bombers launched the first of what came to be continuing raids against entrenched enemy bases in remote regions of South Vietnam. The B–52's were based on Guam and later in Thailand. Under new authority granted by President Johnson to use ground troops when necessary to strengthen the South Vietnam Army, the 173d Airborne Brigade late in June conducted the first U.S. ground offensive of the war, a brief incursion with Vietnam Army units into War Zone D, an enemy sanctuary close to the Bien Hoa air base.

Since the situation continued to deteriorate, President Johnson concluded that only by commitment of large numbers of U.S. combat troops could Communist takeover of the Republic of Vietnam be prevented. Responding to a request by the South Vietnamese government, the President in mid-July ordered two more U.S. Army brigades to Vietnam, the vanguard of some 180,000 troops that were to reach the country by the end of the year.

As the U.S. build-up began, from the chaos in Saigon a government at last emerged that was to provide a measure of stability unseen since Diem's overthrow. It was a military government with an Army general, Nguyen Van Thieu, as chief of state, and an Air Force marshal, Nguyen Cao Ky, as premier, but one that gave promise of an eventual return to representative rule.

Logistical Build-Up

The U.S. combat troops arriving in South Vietnam at first occupied and secured key positions and existing U.S. installations and began preparing a logistical base for whatever additional troops might be needed later. Creating a logistical base was particularly difficult but essential in a country where the only major port, Saigon, was already clogged with shipping, where the enemy continually made roads unusable, and where the only major railroad had ceased to function. Ports, warehouses, cantonments, airfields, maintenance facilities, communications—all had to be built where there was at the beginning almost nothing.

The logistics system expanded swiftly until at the end of 1967 the Army was supporting more than 1.3 million men, including South Vietnamese armed forces, troops of other free world nations, and a number of U.S. civilian agencies. An average of 850,000 short tons of supplies arrived each month. Troops consumed 10 million field rations each month, expended 80,000 tons of ammunition, and used 80 million gallons of petroleum products. Manning a highly sophisticated military machine, the individual American soldier in Vietnam received about 96 pounds of supply support per day, more than twice the amount per man in the Pacific theaters of World War II.

The engineer construction program in particular provided tangible and dramatic evidence of the extent of the logistical effort. The United States built completely new ports or vastly expanded existing facilities at Cam Ranh Bay, Qui Nhon, Nha Trang, Vung Tau, Da Nang, and Saigon, thereby making possible discharge and ready supply to all portions of the country in which U.S. Army units operated. Engineers paved 4 million square yards for airfields and heliports, providing the country with these facilities in a density seldom found elsewhere in the world. They constructed 20 million square feet of covered and open storage facilities, and half a million cubic feet of refrigerated storage, the latter immensely important in a country with a year-round tropical climate. At Dong Tam in the Mekong Delta, millions of cubic yards of sand were dredged from the bottom of an arm of the Mekong River to create a 600-acre island base amidst the rice paddies.

Maintenance in the presence of heat, humidity, and monsoon rains posed an ever-present problem. It was solved at first by improvisation, long hours of extra maintenance work, adaptation of the Red Ball Express concept of World War II to speed critical items from the United States by air, and sending general support maintenance units forward to assist direct support units. In the end new inspection methods and new techniques of maintenance management, including use of complex electronic computers housed in air-conditioned buildings, enabled a return to more normal maintenance procedures.

Never before had an army been served by more comprehensive and effective medical support than was the U.S. Army in Vietnam. A casualty was seldom more than half an hour by air from a hospital, and the mortality rate among wounded receiving hospital attention was cut to less than 1 percent, lowest in the history of warfare. The old bane of tropical climates, malaria and intestinal diseases, nevertheless continued to plague the Army, despite modern advances in preventive medicine. Medical assistance to the Vietnamese, who were woefully short of doctors, nurses, and hospitals, was freely administered.

The organization for logistical support embraced five principal commands, four of them to handle specialized support for aviation, engineers (primarily construction), Hawk missiles, and hospitals, and the fifth, the 1st Logistical Command, to provide all other support. The last operated on an area basis keyed to four corps tactical zones established early by the South Vietnamese Army. Operating in the chain of command of the United States Army, Pacific, the Army in Vietnam obtained additional logistical support from U.S. bases in Japan and Okinawa.

Early U.S. Operations

As the immense logistical effort grew, the increase of U.S. combat troops proceeded apace and U.S. forces were soon engaged in conflict with the Viet Cong and with regular units of the North Vietnamese Army. The latter began to appear early in 1965 in regimental and later divisional formations.

The strategy adopted by the U.S. commander, General William C. Westmoreland, who had succeeded General Harkins in the summer of 1964, was holding action combined with spoiling attacks to keep the enemy off balance and gain the time needed to build base camps and logistical facilities. This accomplished, U.S. units with assistance from the South Vietnamese Army were to engage in search and destroy operations designed to find and eliminate Communist main force units and their base areas rather than to seize and hold territory permanently. These operations were to provide a shield behind which other South Vietnamese Army and U.S. forces could operate against the local guerrillas in support of a rural pacification program, designed to bring security and government control to the countryside. The South Vietnamese Army also was responsible for defending government centers, including the cities and the provincial and district capitals.

It was early agreed that U.S. support in the I Corps Tactical Zone, composed of the fire northernmost provinces, was to be primarily a Marine Corps responsibility; the U.S. Army was to operate mainly in the II and III Corps zones, which embraced the Central Highlands, adjacent coastal regions, and the area around Saigon. South Vietnamese Army troops were to retain primary responsibility for the delta region of the IV Corps Tactical Zone. The U.S. Air Force was to provide tactical air support and airlift while continuing the B–52 bomber campaign and, along with U.S. Navy carrier-based planes, the strategic bombardment of North Vietnam. Air operations against North Vietnam and naval patrols of the U.S. Seventh Fleet were under the direct control of the Commander in Chief, Pacific, rather than the U.S. Military Assistance Command, Vietnam.

U.S. resources still were meager when in late summer of 1965 the enemy build-up in the Central Highlands began to reach alarming proportions, apparently presaging the long-expected attempt to push through to the sea and cut South Vietnam in two. With only three U.S. Army brigades available at the time, General Westmoreland nevertheless thought it better to risk a setback at the start than to allow the concentration in the highlands to go unchecked. Leaving two brigades to protect Saigon, he sent a third to An Khe, midway between Qui Nhon on the coast and Pleiku, deep in the highlands, to stake out and secure a site for a base camp for the 1st Cavalry Division (Airmobile), scheduled to arrive in September. When the division reached Qui Nhon, its combat troops flew to An Khe in their helicopters within hours.

The airmobile concept faced a battlefield trial a few weeks after the arrival of the 1st Cavalry Division. South Vietnamese reinforcements had broken the siege of a Special Forces camp at Plei Me near the entrance to the Ia Drang valley southwest of Pleiku, but intelligence revealed that three North Vietnamese regiments were regrouping in the vicinity for renewed attack. General Westmoreland ordered the cavalry division into the fight to find and destroy the enemy regiments.

ARMY OF THE REPUBLIC OF VIETNAM TROOPS LANDING IN A FIELD

The operation lasted for over a month. The enemy stood and fought in densely wooded mountainous country close to the Cambodian border, using every tactic at his disposal: ambush, attack and counterattack, night infiltration, "hugging" (sticking in close to U.S. troops to forestall air and artillery strikes), and human wave assaults. In the end, American troops killed more than 1,300 North Vietnamese and sent the survivors fleeing to safe havens across the border. The 1st Cavalry Division lost 300 men killed.

Although it had proved impossible to encircle and destroy the entire enemy force—something that was to frustrate many a U.S. unit in the years to come—what became known as the Ia Drang valley campaign thwarted the enemy's build-up in the highlands, proved the validity of the airmobile concept under conditions existing in Vietnam, and confirmed the ability of U.S. troops to defeat the enemy even in inhospitable jungle terrain. The

Communists relied on surprise, mobility, and mass, but these they could achieve only by carefully planned movements that took weeks to execute, whereas an entire brigade of the airmobile division could move into battle hours after an alert.

As foreshadowed by earlier South Vietnamese Army operations with U.S. helicopter support, the airmobile concept had opened a new chapter in the history of land warfare, the helicopter introducing for the first time a flexible third dimension to the battlefield. In the continuing U.S. build-up, the Army placed heavy emphasis on providing enough helicopter companies to assure airmobile support for all infantry units. The helicopter companies were to provide transportation not only for long distance moves, but also for maneuvers during an engagement over short or long distances, superior firepower either from gunships or from artillery lifted by helicopter, superior logistical, medical, and intelligence support, and flexible control through aerial command posts.

The Nature of the War

Within three years, U.S. military strength gradually built up in South Vietnam from less than 25,000 to almost 500,000. U.S. Army forces grew to include two corps headquarters, seven divisions, two separate infantry brigades, an airborne brigade, and an armored cavalry regiment. U.S. Marine forces increased to two divisions and a separate regiment.

Regular South Vietnam Army forces meanwhile rose to over 340,000 men, and the militia—called Regional and Popular Forces—to 300,000. The Republic of Korea furnished 48,000 men, including two divisions and a marine brigade; Thailand, a division; Australia, a brigade; the Philippines and New Zealand, smaller units. Some form of nonmilitary aid was provided by thirty-five other nations. The total support rendered South Vietnam by nations other than the United States was greater than that given South Korea under the United Nations flag.

Despite nearly 180,000 Communists reported killed during these three years and almost 70,000 captured, the Communists still managed to build their strength to 240,000, including main force units, local guerrillas, and supporting troops. This feat they accomplished by stepping up recruitment in the south and by sharply increasing the numbers of North Vietnamese regulars. As their casualties rose, Viet Cong main force units often were kept up to strength only by incorporating North Vietnamese replacements.

While not foreign to American experience, the nature of the war in Vietnam was by any standards unusual. It was a war without clearly defined front lines. The enemy could be anywhere and everywhere and often indistinguishable from the native population. Without the usual standards for measuring success or failure, substitutes had to be devised—how many Communists killed by "body count," how many hamlets and villages "pacified," how many miles of essential highways open to travel. These provided some but no certain indication of progress.

It was a war with no shot fired at Fort Sumter, no sinking of the *Maine,* no Zimmermann telegram, no Pearl Harbor, no massed armies crossing the 38th parallel to afford a clear call for American involvement. Toward this war some Americans developed a new form of isolationism. Some feared becoming mired in war on the Asian mainland, others accepted the Communist-promoted view that an aggressive North Vietnam was in reality a "Little Belgium," much sinned against by American power; and still others wearied of a struggle that appeared to afford no quick or decisive end.

It was the first war that Americans viewed in their homes on television; and in base camps in Vietnam U.S. troops also had television. Many men flew to war by commercial aircraft. U.S. civilians of the State Department, the U.S. Information Agency, the Central Intelligence Agency, and the Agency for International Development were involved close alongside the soldiers. There was no censorship of the soldier's mail nor any involuntary censorship of the American press. The Army contracted some of its construction work with U.S. civilian firms. The American commander, General Westmoreland, had no command authority over the South Vietnamese Army and most allied troops. In an effort to keep the war from spreading, neither American nor allied troops pursued the enemy into Cambodia and Laos or beyond the demilitarized zone between South and North Vietnam, even though the enemy maintained bases there and brought supplies through the Cambodian port of Sihanoukville and over the Ho Chi Minh Trail complex through Laos. In hope of promoting negotiations, the U.S. proclaimed intermittent halts in the bombing of North Vietnam. Both sides declared truces at Vietnamese holiday periods.

How the U.S. Army fought the war was also unusual. All U.S. divisions and separate brigades had fortified base camps. From these they might operate in neighboring districts on security and pacification missions. At other times, leaving a security and housekeeping cadre behind, they might shift far afield to construct a temporary base camp and forward fire support bases from which artillery could support far-ranging search and destroy operations. On many of these missions, particularly in the thick jungles of the highlands, companies

ARMORED PERSONNEL CARRIER

and battalions were far from any road or trail and wholly dependent upon the helicopter for resupply and evacuation. If fire support bases came under attack, artillerymen often had to employ their pieces in point-blank fire. Long-range patrols on which small groups of men might be away for several days were common. Ambush and counterambush were familiar tactics on both sides.

In a war fought with modern weapons in populated areas, property destruction and civilian casualties, which occur in any armed conflict, were inevitable. The enemy used terrorism and murder as instruments to coerce the people; the most notable instance was the massacre of nearly 3,000 civilians during a temporary occupation of the old imperial capital of Hue in 1968. Despite strong emphasis by the U.S. command on avoiding civilian losses, U.S. units in a few instances experienced serious lapses of discipline, as at the village of My Lai in 1968 when a large number of civilians were killed.

The helicopter and radio communications were the two essential ingredients in U.S. conduct of the war. There were, too, sophisticated weapons and items of equipment—troop and cargo-carrying C–123's, C–130's, and CV–2's, the light, automatic M16 rifle; the recoilless rifle; a one-shot antitank rocket; the claymore mine that was activated electrically and spewed hundreds of dartlike projectiles; "beehive" artillery projectiles, and armored personnel carriers modified to serve as fighting vehicles, some of them equipped with flame throwers; the Patton (M48A3) tank. There were also chemical defoliants and Rome plows, the latter bulldozers equipped with a special blade capable of demolishing all but the giants of the forest, used, as were defoliants, to deny the enemy and his base camps the concealment of the jungle. The troops also employed a powerful grenade-launcher firing a 40-mm. projectile; highly complex electronic sensors; HueyCobra helicopter gunships; and the Sheridan armored reconnaissance vehicle, equipped with a 152-mm. gun. In sharp contrast to the sophistication of other items, barbed wire and the sandbag were used as extensively as in World War I.

The enemy also had excellent weapons, mainly Chinese Communist copies of Soviet models. In the automatic AK47 rifle he had an individual weapon respected by both sides. He had an ample supply of mortars and heavy rockets, but other than along the demilitarized zone he employed almost no artillery and, except in defense against U.S. air strikes on North Vietnam, no aircraft. He also had recoilless rifles and a Chinese version of the claymore mine, and he was a master of the booby trap, which included explosives and sharpened bamboo spikes called punji stakes. In the antiaircraft defense of North Vietnam, he employed Soviet-supplied surface-to-air missiles.

The ability and morale of the American soldier were remarkable. Better educated than the soldier of earlier generations, both in civilian schooling and military training, he was conscious of the excellent medical, logistical, and fire support available to him. Although individual fights might be as fierce and as harrowing as any ever fought in any war, there were sometimes long intervals between engagements, and, except along the demilitarized zone, the constant nagging dread of enemy shelling was less pronounced than in earlier wars. Then too the knowledge that his tour would end in a year was a strong morale factor. Fully integrated with white troops, Negro soldiers proved their worth and, in retrospect, revealed the illogic of earlier segregation practices, however reflective of the nation's social system. Only late in the war, as the United States began to withdraw from Vietnam, did serious morale problems arise, a not unusual development when the combat role of an army decreases.

The Communist soldier, too, was accomplished; he had infinite patience and stamina, and he could subsist for long periods on a diet that to a westerner would have been debilitating. Although thousands defected to the South Vietnamese side under a government-sponsored *Chieu Hoi* (open arms, or amnesty) program, continued recruitment or impressment and North Vietnamese reinforcement made up for these as well as for the enemy's other losses.

The Military Campaign

After the U.S. victory in the Ia Drang valley, General Westmoreland for the remainder of 1965 and well into 1966 proceeded with his plan to keep the enemy off balance while building base camps and logistical resources. This plan involved search and destroy operations to protect the logistical bases under construction along the coast and the base camps for incoming U.S. units in the provinces near Saigon. It also involved another campaign to disperse an enemy build-up in the highlands. By midyear of 1966 progress was such that the enemy had become reluctant to mass for large-scale attack and Ho Chi Minh had proclaimed a strategy of protracted war, thus tacitly admitting that a quick military victory had eluded him.

U.S. forces at this point entered a new phase of operations, a prolonged offensive aimed at finding and annihilating the enemy's main force units and invading and destroying his long-established base areas, or secret zones. South Vietnamese Army units turned more of their attention to making the countryside secure in support of the pacification program.

In the II Corps zone, largest but least populous of the four tactical zones, U.S. operations had two basic objectives. One was to eradicate main force units from the rice-rich flatlands along the coast, denying the enemy this source of food and, by a sustained presence, providing a shield for pacification. The other was to maintain mobile forces in the sparsely populated Central Highlands that, by shifting here and there as the enemy was found, could prevent him from establishing control over the region as a base for operations against the northern provinces and the coastal plain. The troops in the highlands also afforded a reserve force to thwart the enemy's strikes against the Special Forces camps and other outposts along the frontier, from which the South Vietnamese harassed North Vietnamese infiltration routes into the country.

In early summer of 1966, sizable enemy units were again returning to the highlands and there were indications that another attack was forming to hit the Special Forces camp at Plei Me. When contingents of the 25th Infantry Division, 1st Cavalry Division, and 101st Airborne Division met the enemy, he stood and fought, oftentimes from sturdy bunkers located on advantageous hilltops. Only after fighting that lasted through much of August did the enemy finally withdraw across the border, leaving behind over a thousand dead.

As additional U.S. forces arrived in Vietnam, the 4th Infantry Division constructed a base camp in the Central Highlands near Pleiku and built a road deep into the western highlands to within a few miles of the Laotian frontier. The Communists reacted with sharp attacks, primarily against the 4th Division's fire support bases, in which they lost approximately 700 killed; but in general the enemy avoided prolonged fighting and fell back behind the border whenever he was seriously threatened.

With the 4th Division present in the highlands, the 1st Cavalry Division and a brigade of the 101st Airborne Division were free to concentrate on sustained operations in the coastal provinces. By late fall of 1966 they had broken the enemy's hold on this agriculturally rich region. One operation of the 1st Cavalry Division in conjunction with Korean and South Vietnamese units ended in a classic encirclement maneuver in which more than 2,000 Communists were killed. Shattered remnants of a North Vietnamese divison fled into mountains to the northwest.

In the provinces near Saigon, the III Corps zone, American strength had increased to the point where operations could be conducted in an effort to drive the enemy away from the environs of Saigon into his secret zones, then destroy them. The first began in January 1966, when the 1st Infantry Division struck to eliminate a Viet Cong regional headquarters in the Ho Bo Woods, about 25 miles northwest of Saigon and close to an enemy stronghold known as the Iron Triangle. As was so often to be the case, the enemy escaped, in this instance through an elaborate underground tunnel system. Beginning in February, the 1st Division and contingents of the 25th invaded the enemy's War Zone C, 75 miles northwest of Saigon along the Cambodian border, and War Zone D, 40 miles north of the capital. Fighting was sporadic as the Viet Cong fled across the frontier, but U.S. troops found and destroyed large underground supply caches and training installations.

Possibly because of these sweeps or in an effort to open up infiltration routes, the enemy massed a division in the vicinity of a Special Forces camp at Loc Ninh, close along the Cambodian border, seventy-five miles north of Saigon. In a series of engagements involving thrusts and counterthrusts over a period of two months, the 1st Division killed close to a thousand of the Viet Cong and drove the rest across the Cambodian border.

In the fall of 1966, a sweep into a big rubber plantation in War Zone C by the 196th Infantry Brigade provoked a counterthrust by a Viet Cong division. Elements of three U.S. divisions, the 173d Airborne Brigade, and the 11th Armored Cavalry Regiment were quickly committed in the first U.S. operation of the war to be controlled directly by a corps headquarters. Yet despite the large numbers of troops engaged, the fighting was, as it had been everywhere, at the squad and platoon level. Over a thousand of the elusive enemy eventually were killed, but the Viet Cong's ability to fade away when confronted with American strength and firepower made campaigning here and elsewhere tedious and often exasperating.

As 1966 drew to an end, the fact that the enemy could not be found in large numbers in the II and III Corps zones was frustrating but at the same time proof that U.S. and South Vietnamese Army units had dealt the Communists telling blows. Early in 1967 the North Vietnamese began a build-up of several divisions in and just south of the demilitarized zone, apparently in an effort to draw U.S. strength from the south. Along with the build-up, heavy artillery fire was directed against U.S. Marine Corps positions.

The Pacification Program

Since U.S. and South Vietnamese Army forces were limited and thus unable to be everywhere at once, the North Vietnamese could readily achieve a build-up in the north. Like the periodic massing against outposts, the build-up pulled U.S. forces away from conducting search and destroy operations and from securing villages. Keeping American forces away from the villages adversely affected pacification, a program that had to succeed if the insurgency ever was to be suppressed.

PARAPET CONCEALING GUN EMPLACEMENTS AT SPECIAL FORCES CAMP

Communist political cadres composed of an estimated 40,000 men, backed by regular and local units, secretly controlled vast numbers of communities outside the cities by means ranging from propaganda and cajolery to intimidation and murder. This Viet Cong shadow government exacted taxes, drafted young men for its military ranks, and bent the population to its ends. Its grip had to be broken in order to deprive the guerrillas of sustenance and base support.

The history of pacification was often a history of frustration and failure. Because of inadequate resources, lack of peasant support, and political problems, several programs under President Diem had failed. After Diem, a new program oriented more toward economic assistance also foundered in the face of political instability, growing insecurity in the countryside, and the defeats the Viet Cong had inflicted on the South Vietnamese Army.

At the beginning of 1966 a new program called Revolutionary Development seemed promising. At the core of the program were teams of fifty-nine specially trained South Vietnamese. Moving into a hamlet, a team worked to identify and eliminate the secret political cadre of Viet Cong, remove corrupt South Vietnamese officials from office, organize democratic institutions, and create a hamlet defense force. These objectives accomplished, the team moved on to the next hamlet, leaving the first to the South Vietnamese government agencies to develop programs in education, health, land reform, and financial credit. Supplementing these teams, U.S. civilian agencies worked at various levels in information, agriculture, and public health programs.

A Typical Viet Cong Tunnel System

Organizational responsibility for the support of pacification shifted in early 1966 from several competing U.S. government agencies to the Deputy U.S. Ambassador. The civilian programs were further unified later in the year under a U.S. Embassy Office of Civil Operations, which had a military counterpart in the Revolutionary Development Support Directorate of the Military Assistance Command, Vietnam. In search of further co-ordination, President Johnson in May 1967 gave full responsibility for pacification support to the Military Assistance Command, fusing the Office of Civil Operations and the Revolutionary Development Support Directorate in a unique civil-military amalgam known as CORDS, an acronym for its components. A civilian with the rank of ambassador was assigned to head the program.

Through CORDS the U.S. Army's role in pacification went far beyond civic action. Army officers or their civilian colleagues gave pacification advice and support to the Vietnamese on a wide range of subjects, including local security and village elections. The purpose of the new pacification program was sustained local security with unprecedented attention given to improving and augmenting the Vietnamese militia. CORDS also initiated a program, later known as PHOENIX, to eliminate the secret Viet Cong political organization in South Vietnam. Although CORDS pursued an aggressive policy and U.S. forces often provided such assistance as digging wells, building schools, and furnishing medical aid, pacification focused on getting the Vietnamese themselves to do the job. In the long run the success or failure of pacification would depend upon the ability of the South Vietnamese government to protect the people and enlist their support.

The Thieu-Ky government moved closer to the people in the fall of 1966 by calling an election for a constituent assembly. Despite disruptive efforts of the Viet Cong, the electorate turned out in impressive numbers. Hamlet and village elections and then national assembly and presidential elections, the last for a four-year term, followed the next year. One of several candidates, Thieu failed to gain a majority of the vote, but he achieved a clear plurality to provide his government with at least a measure of popular support.

The Military Campaign in 1967

In response to the North Vietnamese build-up along the demilitarized zone in early 1967, General Westmoreland sent the first major U.S. Army units into the southern portion of the I Corps zone, thereby freeing U.S. Marine Corps units to move farther north. Among the Army units eventually committed were the 11th, 196th, and 198th Infantry Brigades, which subsequently constituted a new division, the 23d (Americal), the parenthetical designation dating back to a division that had been organized during World War II on New Caledonia.

In the Central Highlands, alert intelligence and quick U.S. action thwarted enemy attempts during the summer of 1967 to converge against the Special Forces camps. At the same time in the provinces near Saigon, the campaign continued against the Viet Cong base areas.

Early in the year, in an operation called CEDAR FALLS, U.S. and South Vietnamese Army forces in the equivalent of more than two divisions sealed off the Iron Triangle and systematically swept that tangle of woods, caves, and bunkers north of Saigon; but the enemy returned to his hideouts once U.S.

and South Vietnamese troops had departed. After a second sweep a few weeks later, U.S. engineers leveled much of the area with Rome plows.

In late February, many of these same units, including the 173d Airborne Brigade, which made the only U.S. combat parachute jump of the war, participated in Operation JUNCTION CITY, a large offensive employing four South Vietnamese and twenty-two U.S. combat battalions. While some units formed a giant horseshoe cordon around War Zone C, cavalry and mechanized forces swept up the open end of the horseshoe. Because of the proximity of the Cambodian border, many of the enemy escaped, but over a period of three months, more than 2,700 were killed. Vast numbers of fortifications, headquarters complexes, and other installations were destroyed, and intelligence documents, equipment, and tons of supplies were either captured or destroyed.

The ratio of enemy to U.S. troops killed was in most cases disproportionately high for the enemy. In U.S. search and destroy operations, a ratio of 10 Viet Cong to 1 American was common, and in enemy assaults against prepared U.S. positions, the ratio was higher. In one two-day assault against a fire support base in War Zone C, for example, 609 Viet Cong died as against 10 Americans.

With completion early in 1967 of the Dong Tam base among the rice paddies of the Mekong Delta, a brigade of the 9th Infantry Division initiated the first U.S. operations in the IV Corps zone, a region crisscrossed by canals and rivers. Employing barracks ships, U.S. Navy armored troop carriers and fire support boats, and artillery mounted on barges, this brigade extended fighting to the delta and its inland waterways. One of the first operations was against a heretofore sacrosanct base called the Cam Son Secret Zone. By the end of the year, the Mobile Riverine Force had killed approximately 1,500 Viet Cong.

For all the success of U.S. and South Vietnamese Army operations and the large numbers of Viet Cong and North Vietnamese killed, there were indications in the fall of 1967 of another enemy build-up, particularly in areas close to Communist havens in Laos and Cambodia. In late October the Viet Cong struck again at the Special Forces camp at Loc Ninh, but intensive air and artillery support and quick arrival of American and South Vietnamese reinforcements saved the camp. The enemy nevertheless continued to give battle. He finally left the field ten days later after losing 800 dead and killing 50 men from U.S. and South Vietnamese Army units. Success was in no small part attributable to a preponderance of U.S. firepower—30,000 rounds of artillery fire, 450 close support air sorties, and 8 bombardments by B–52's.

At the same time, the Communists again increased their strength in the Central Highlands, concentrating some 12,000 men around a Special Forces camp at Dak To, in the northern part of Kontum Province where the borders of Laos, Cambodia, and South Vietnam meet. As the enemy probed, U.S. and South Vietnamese reinforcements brought a total commitment to the defense of sixteen battalions. After repulsing a Communist assault, American and South Vietnamese units moved out from their fire support bases to dislodge an enemy apparently determined to hold in surrounding hills. In the ensuing fight, the Communists lost 1,400 dead in the largest and most costly fight in the highlands since the Ia Drang valley campaign two years before.

The enemy resurgence there and at Loc Ninh and another heavy concentration in the vicinity of a Marine base at Khe Sanh, in the northwestern corner of the country, were disturbing to U.S. commanders. There was also disquieting evidence that the enemy was planning an offensive to begin with the lunar new year holiday (*Tet*) in early 1968, but there was no clue to its magnitude.

The Tet Offensive—1968

As the date for the offensive neared, the Communists shifted supplies to concealed sites close to the towns and cities, while with the help of sympathizers among the population, soldiers in civilian dress mingled with the holiday crowds to infiltrate the densely populated areas. The offensive appears to have had two objectives: to foster antigovernment uprisings among the South Vietnamese population and to further antiwar sentiment in the United States. Some captured enemy documents indicated that the Communists intended the offensive to lead to total victory.

The assaults began in the northern and central provinces before daylight on 30 January and in the Saigon and Mekong Delta regions that night. Some 84,000 Viet Cong and North Vietnamese attacked 36 of 43 provincial capitals, 5 of 6 autonomous cities, 34 of 242 district capitals, and at least 50 hamlets. Never before had the enemy mounted such a concentrated effort.

The Communists penetrated in strength into ten cities, including Saigon and Hue; but even though many South Vietnamese troops were away from their posts on leave, the South Vietnamese police, militia, and soldiers repulsed the attacks in four cities in a matter of hours. Fighting lasted for up to three days in four others, while in Saigon and Hue the battle was protracted.

The attack in Saigon began with a sapper assault against the U.S. Embassy. Other assaults were directed against the Presidential Palace, the compound of the Vietnamese Joint General Staff, and nearby Tan Son Nhut air base, but the only successes were brief incursions into the compound and into the fringes of Tan Son Nhut. Considerable fighting remained, nevertheless, before American and South Vietnamese troops cleared all the enemy from some sections of Saigon.

In Hue, a low fog facilitated infiltration of 8 enemy battalions, which gained control of most of the city, including the ancient Citadel, a walled enclave encompassing historic buildings of the imperial court. Involving at times 3 U.S. Marine Corps, 3 U.S. Army, and 11 South Vietnamese battalions, the fight to recapture Hue lasted for almost a month.

Apparently in co-ordination with the offensive, heavy fighting occurred in two remote regions: around the Special Forces camp at Dak To in the Central Highlands and around the U.S. Marine Corps base at Khe Sanh. Detected while on the move, a North Vietnamese division near Dak To was systematically battered by U.S. Air Force planes, the 4th Infantry Division, and a South Vietnamese regiment, while at Khe Sanh a prolonged battle developed between U.S. marines and at least two North Vietnamese divisions. Against every enemy effort to dislodge them the marines and a battalion of South Vietnamese Rangers held fast, while artillery, including 16 U.S. Army 175-mm. pieces, and air power, including B–52 bombers in a close support role, inflicted heavy casualties. As the North Vietnamese began to fade away in the face of such awesome firepower, a Marine regiment and contingents of the 1st Cavalry Division in early April re-established ground contact with Khe Sanh. With the arrival of more U.S. Army troops to reinforce the marines in the northern provinces—including the 101st Airborne Division, converted to an airmobile unit; a mechanized brigade; and a new headquarters, the XXIV Corps—Khe Sanh was abandoned in favor of mobile defensive tactics.

As in other instances in recent military history—such as the German offensive at Chemin des Dames in 1918 and in the Ardennes in 1944 and the Chinese Communist intervention in Korea in 1950—the sudden enemy offensive, following close upon optimistic reports from the field, shocked the American public and spurred demands by many for a pull-out from Vietnam. The *Tet* offensive thus was an apparent psychological victory for the enemy. Yet it was at the same time a military defeat. It failed to engender either an uprising or appreciable support among the South Vietnamese. Indeed, the determination of both South Vietnamese units and the populace appeared to increase. In the *Tet* offensive, the Communists lost 6,000 captured and 32,000 killed as against U.S. and South Vietnamese losses of just over 2,000 each. Three times during the next six months the enemy tried to mount new offensives, but in most cases these degenerated into sporadic mortar and rocket attacks. By coming into the open, the enemy had exposed himself to massive American firepower and in the first nine months of 1968 lost 137,000 men killed.

The heavy losses may have had something to do with the Communists' agreement in May to open negotiations aimed at ending the war, although their acceptance ostensibly came as a result of a decision by President Johnson at the end of March to halt the bombing of North Vietnam north of the 19th parallel. Early hopes that the discussions, held in Paris, might lead to peace were soon dispelled. Although the President tried to spur the negotiations by halting all bombing of North Vietnam in November, the talks remained largely sterile.

The *Tet* offensive appeared at first to have dealt a severe setback to the pacification program. It was true that many local defense units and Revolutionary Development teams had abandoned the countryside to take refuge in the cities, but the enemy had incurred too many losses to take advantage of it before the South Vietnamese forces returned. In the fall of 1968, the South Vietnamese government with major U.S. support launched an Accelerated Pacification Campaign that brought new vitality to pacification. Local militia advised by special teams of U.S. Army combat veterans strengthened security. Government influence expanded into widespread areas of the countryside previously dominated by the Viet Cong to such an extent that two years later at least some measure of government control was evident in all but a few remote regions.

Invasions of Cambodia and Laos

Following the enemy's 1968 offensive, the level of combat through much of the country dropped perceptibly. General Creighton W. Abrams, who succeeded General Westmoreland in mid-1968 as the head of the Military Assistance Command, Vietnam, was able to scale down the size of the forces he sent into the field searching for the foe. General Abrams was also able to afford the forces for a sustained campaign in the A Shau valley, a rugged stretch of mountainous country along the Laotian border that heretofore had been almost the sole province of the enemy.

The enemy's heavy losses strengthened the prospect of South Vietnam's assuming the entire combat role and eventually the support and logistical assignments as well. That the South Vietnamese armed and paramilitary forces had increased to a million men further encouraged the possibility. A concerted effort to supply all South Vietnamese units, including paramilitary forces, with modern weapons and equipment began. Called "Vietnamization," the program was to allow American units to begin a phased withdrawal from the country. President Nixon on 8 June 1969 announced the first of a series of withdrawals.

With the emergence in Cambodia of an anti-Communist government replacing an ostensibly neutral regime, President Nixon relaxed the restriction on moving against the enemy bases inside Cambodia. On 29 April 1970 South Vietnamese Army troops entered the "Parrot's Beak" section of Cambodia, which extends into South Vietnamese territory to within thirty miles of Saigon. Three days later American and South Vietnamese troops entered the "Fish Hook," another promontory farther north. Other South Vietnamese troops subsequently moved up the Mekong River corridor in the direction of the Cambodian capital of Phnom Penh, while the Cambodian Army denied Communist use of the port of Sihanoukville. All together, 31,000 U.S. troops and 43,000 South Vietnamese entered Cambodia. President Nixon limited the depth of the penetration by American troops to twenty-one miles and specified that all U.S. forces would be out of Cambodia within sixty days. The last withdrew on 29 June.

Although many of the Communist troops fled from their Cambodia bases, the enemy still lost more than 11,000 killed. American losses were 337 killed. The important result was the denial of Sihanoukville to the enemy and elimination of the sanctuaries, the impact of which was soon manifest in a further reduction in enemy activity in the III and IV Corps zones.

The only route for supplies and reinforcement left to the North Vietnamese was the Ho Chi Minh Trail, already subject to air attacks. On 8 February 1971 the vanguard of 21,000 South Vietnamese troops entered Laos to disrupt the trail complex. Temporarily reactivating the base at Khe Sanh, the U.S. furnished air, artillery, and logistical support, although no U.S. ground combat units operated in Laos. The North Vietnamese fought with determination, inflicting sharp losses on four of twelve South Vietnamese battalions, but in turn taking severe losses themselves. The heaviest concentration of anti-aircraft fire yet encountered destroyed eighty-nine American helicopters. Near the end of March, the South Vietnamese withdrew. Despite the fierce fighting, an encouraging aspect of both the Cambodian and Laotian operations was the improved performance and morale of the South Vietnamese Army.

Toward the end of the seventh year of large-scale U.S. involvement in Vietnam, almost all major U.S. Army combat units had returned to the United States, and American troop strength in Vietnam was down below 200,000 with indications of continuing withdrawals. It had been one of the nation's costliest wars: more than 45,000 men were killed in combat (30,200 of them soldiers) and almost 10,000 died from other causes. Approximately 150,000 were wounded seriously enough to require hospital care, of whom two-thirds were soldiers.

Enemy losses were impossible to determine with certainty, but the North Vietnamese at one point admitted the loss of over half a million men.

In Vietnam, the United States Army fought a war of contrasts. On the one hand, the war was more sophisticated than any in history, introducing not only complex weapons and equipment but also, with the helicopter, a third dimension that the airborne attacks of World War II and Korea had only foreshadowed. On the other hand, there was a return to the primitive, often pitting man against man in a conflict and an environment where wile and stamina might determine who would prevail. In a way it was two wars, a military campaign involving a compendium of all the Army had learned from the Revolution through Korea and at the same time a vast civic action project, using the men and tools of war in the task of winning the confidence and support of a people. For the United States Vietnam was a limited war in the classic sense of the American Revolution, the War of 1812, the Indian wars, the wars with Mexico and Spain, and Korea. In the same way that history cannot prophesy, only illuminate, this war of contrasts produced no clear pattern for the warfare of the future.